THE MEN WHO MADE THE CONSTITUTION

Lives of the Delegates to the Constitutional Convention

John R. Vile

THE SCARECROW PRESS, INC.
Lanham • Toronto • Plymouth, UK
2013

Published by Scarecrow Press, Inc.
A wholly owned subsidary of The Rowman & Littlefield Publishing Group, Inc.
4501 Forbes Boulevard, Suite 200, Lanham, Maryland 20706
www.rowman.com

10 Thornbury Road, Plymouth PL6 7PP, United Kingdom

British Library Cataloguing in Publication Information Available

Library of Congress Cataloging-in-Publication Data

Vile, John R.
  The men who made the Constitution : lives of the delegates to the Constitutional
Convention / John R. Vile.
        pages cm
  Includes bibliographical references and index.
  ISBN 978-0-8108-8864-7 (cloth : alkaline paper) — ISBN 978-0-8108-8865-4
(ebook)
  1. United States Constitution—Signers—Biography. 2. United States Constitutional
Convention (1787). 3. United States—Politics and government—1783–1789.
4. Constitutional history—United States. 5. Constitutional conventions—United
States—History—18th century. 6. +Founding Fathers of the United States—
Biography. I. Title.
  E302.5.V55 2013
  973.3092'2—dc23   2013014081

∞™ The paper used in this publication meets the minimum requirements of
American National Standard for Information Sciences—Permanence of Paper
for Printed Library Materials, ANSI/NISO Z39.48-1992.

Printed in the United States of America.

To my mother, Joanna Virginia Vile; to the memory of my father, Ralph Vile; and to the memory of my parents-in-law, C. D. and Frances Christensen. Thanks for all the trips to historical sites!

Contents

Introduction

I often joke that it was not until my daughters got married and began taking vacations with their husbands that my wife and I realized that other families vacationed at the beach! As I think back on our most meaningful vacations other than trips to visit family, both when I was a child and when my wife and I took our own children on vacation, I realize that most were to historical sites. In part because I grew up in Virginia, I especially remember visits to Mt. Vernon, Monticello, Jamestown, Yorktown, Williamsburg, and to museums, monuments, and historic sites in Washington, D.C.

My wife had similar experiences when she was growing up in New Jersey, so it was not surprising that we met at the College of William and Mary in Williamsburg, or that during the summers when I went to graduate school at "Mr. Jefferson's University" and she began her career teaching elementary school, we both ended up working at James Monroe's house outside of Charlottesville, Virginia. We took our honeymoon on the Outer Banks of North Carolina, but even on this romantic occasion, it did not seem odd to stop by Williamsburg on the way and spend as much time visiting the historic sites in New Bern or going to the campus of Duke University than spending time at the beach. Our mutual interest in history has been one of the loves that we continue to share. One sign of my wife's enduring devotion was her willingness both to visit a president's house and to spend the evening of our twenty-fifth wedding anniversary in a university library as I gathered information for a book on presidential victory and concession speeches!

Such interests have led me to write and edit numerous books on the Founding Fathers, the U.S. Constitution, and related issues. I am particularly proud of my two-volume, alphabetically arranged reference work, *The Constitutional Convention of 1787: A Comprehensive Encyclopedia of America's Founding*, published in 2005. The two volumes are so capacious that at least one reviewer erroneously assumed that I must have been the editor, rather than the author, of the volumes. More recently, I have authored a more accessible narrative entitled *The Writing and Ratification of the U.S. Constitution: Practical Virtue in Action*, which allowed me to revisit the proceedings. While writing that book I came to have even greater appreciation not only of the Constitution that the delegates produced, but also of the delegates themselves. This book is thus designed to highlight their role.

EVENTS LEADING TO THE U.S. REVOLUTION

Readers who are chiefly seeking a blow-by-blow account of the Constitutional Convention and its ratification should consult my earlier book or other narratives for a more detailed understanding of these proceedings, but this is certainly a propitious place to detail some of the central events in this chronicle. Spread up and down the east coast of North America, the residents of the 13 colonies that provided the foundation for the United States of America only gradually came to see themselves, not simply as citizens of a particular colony, but as members of a nation in their opposition to perceived oppression by their English overlords. Believing that they had brought their rights as Englishmen with them to the North American continent, the colonists were particularly insistent that the British legislature, or Parliament, was not—as it claimed—legally all-powerful, or sovereign. Under the principle of "no taxation without representation" that the colonists traced back to the Magna Carta of 1215, they asserted that Parliament could not tax colonists, who did not send representatives to that body and were therefore unrepresented in its councils. Although the colonists initially retained their loyalty to the English king, immigrant Thomas Paine published an influential essay titled *Common Sense* in January, 1776, in which he questioned the doctrine of hereditary succession by which monarchs ascended to office and argued that continuing association with the British king would involve the colonies in continuing oppression and unnecessary wars.

The colonists had met together to protest British taxes and other grievances in the Stamp Act Congress of 1765 and later in the First and Second Continental Congresses that began in 1774 and 1775. The latter Congress issued the Declaration of Independence in July of 1776, which fifty-six members of Congress signed. Chiefly authored by Thomas Jefferson, and extensively revised by the Congress, this document asserted the colonists' right to separate from Great Britain and govern themselves, and it articulated a laundry list of colonial grievances against the English king and Parliament. Appealing to wider philosophical principles, the colonists proclaimed that "all men are created equal"; that they were entitled to the rights to "life, liberty, and the pursuit of happiness"; and that they had the right to overthrow and replace a government that was not securing such rights. In time, they did this by successfully winning the Revolutionary War.

EVENTS LEADING UP TO THE CONSTITUTIONAL CONVENTION

During this conflict, in 1777 the Continental Congress drafted a document, initially authored by John Dickinson, known as the Articles of Confederation, which was ratified by the last state (Maryland) in 1781. With each of the former colonies seeking to protect its own prerogatives, Article II of the Articles specifically vested primary sovereignty in the states. The weak central government centered on a unicameral (one house or chamber) congress, in which states were represented by two to seven delegates with one-year terms that were renewable up to three years, but in which each state cast a single vote. The Articles did not create an independent executive or national judiciary. The Articles required the consent of nine of the thirteen states on most key matters and required unanimous state consent for constitutional amendments, many of which were proposed but none of which ever succeeded in being unanimously ratified.

States too tended to vest undue power in their legislative branches, which often wrote and adopted their own constitutions without seeking popular endorsement. Most governors had very short terms and overly limited powers. State legislatures frequently adopted legislation that reflected short-term popular passions over more permanent public interests. Judges were often under the control of the legislatures.

Although the government under the Articles succeeded in winning the war for independence, the aftermath was not promising. The national government depended on requisitions of the states for taxes and troops; these often went unheeded and had no way to act directly on individual citizens. Congress lacked the power to regulate interstate and foreign commerce, and the nation suffered as Britain withdrew earlier trading privileges. As states coined their own money and taxed one another, the advantages of a continental market dissipated. The nation had to borrow money from foreign governments that it had difficulty repaying and was unable to enforce treaties that it had signed with them.

After an historic March 1785 meeting between delegates from Maryland and Virginia at George Washington's home at Mt. Vernon to deal with mutual matters of navigation and commerce, delegates issued a call for a wider convention to be held at Annapolis, Maryland in September, 1786. It was called to deal more generally with commercial concerns throughout the colonies. Although delegates from only five states attended the meeting, they sought to snatch victory from defeat by calling for a convention of all the states to deal with the wider problems of the Union.

States initially reacted tepidly, but new impetus was given to this meeting by a taxpayers' revolt known as Shays's Rebellion in Massachusetts and by other popular movements that seemed to threaten the security of the states and in the face of which Congress seemed largely impotent. In time, Congress adopted a resolution that helped persuade all of the states except for Rhode Island to send delegates to the convention that began meeting at the State House (Independence Hall) in Philadelphia in May 1787. This convention continued until September 17, when 39 of the 42 delegates that remained of the original 55 delegates signed the document.

DELIBERATIONS AT THE U.S. CONSTITUTIONAL CONVENTION

Selecting a Chair, Adopting Rules, and Taking Notes

One of the delegates' first acts was to elect George Washington, the stalwart "father" of the nation and the Revolutionary War hero who had demonstrated a firm indisposition to seize power, to preside over the proceedings. His very presence inspired confidence and lent an austere solemnity to the proceedings. As under the Articles, each state delegation had a single vote. In a desire to promote deliberation, the delegates agreed to debate in secret, did not record votes under individual names, and permitted the convention to retake votes.

In a development that has been of immeasurable help to historians and political scientists, James Madison, who had been disappointed at the paucity of information about the formation of prior governments, appointed himself as the unofficial secretary, seated himself in front of Washington's chair, and kept extensive notes of the debates. These, along with notes and letters from other delegates, have been painstakingly collected by historian Max Farrand, whose four-volume *Records of the Federal Convention of 1787* (and a supplement by James H. Hutson published in 1987) will be the most frequently cited in this book (after the first citation to Farrand within each entry, the specific reference will have a volume and page number separated by a colon in Arabic numbers). Although they are far from word-for-word transcripts, these records provide a fairly comprehensive view of the convention's day-to-day proceedings that illumine nearly every controversy.

The Virginia Plan and the Committee of the Whole

Seizing the initiative, the Virginia delegates, who represented the largest state, presented a plan (thus usually designated the Virginia Plan) that dominated the first two weeks of deliberation. Although Virginia's winsome Governor Edmund Randolph introduced and initially spoke on its behalf, it largely appears to be the brainchild of the physically diminutive but scholarly James Madison. In the months leading up to the convention, he had been examining, and writing essays on, what he believed to be the weaknesses of earlier democratic confederations in general and the Articles of Confederation in particular. Whereas most delegates probably assembled with the intention of *revising* the Articles of Confederation, he called for starting a whole new government from scratch in which the national government would not only be strengthened but in which large states like Virginia (the most populous among the original thirteen) would have increased representation and power.

In contrast to the Articles of Confederation, the Virginia Plan proposed a bicameral legislature in which states would be represented according to population in both chambers and under which Congress could exercise power in "all cases to which the separate States are incompetent, or in which the harmony of the United States may be interrupted by the exercise of individual Legislation" (Farrand 1966, 1:21). The plan further proposed three independent branches of government—legislative, executive, and judicial. The plan proposed vesting Congress with a veto of state legislation and a national Council of Revision with the power to invalidate acts of congressional legislation.

Using a familiar parliamentary procedure for legislative bodies, the Constitution initially met as a Committee of the Whole, presided over by Nathaniel Gorham of Massachusetts, to discuss this proposal that the delegates refined in early debates. These debates proceeded fairly smoothly during the first two weeks, but the proponents of the Virginia Plan arguably underestimated the opposition that their plan had generated.

The New Jersey Plan

As this committee was summarizing the result of its early deliberations, William Paterson of New Jersey received permission to introduce an alternate plan that he and other delegates, largely from less-populated states, had formulated. Although the plan affirmed the agenda-setting power of the Virginia Plan by incorporating a number of innovations introduced by that plan, including the division of the national authority into three branches, Paterson favored continuing a unicameral legislature under which states would be equally represented. While the Committee of the Whole had called for a unitary executive, the New Jersey Plan proposed that it be plural. Whereas the Virginia Plan had proposed vesting the appointment of judges in Congress, New Jersey favored vesting this power in the executive branch.

The New Jersey Plan prompted the introduction of at least one other plan by Alexander Hamilton. In a long speech that was widely lauded and long remembered but seems to have had little immediate influence, Hamilton called for a far stronger national government than either the Virginia or New Jersey Plans that had preceded it, but Madison followed with a long, and apparently persuasive, speech on behalf of the Virginia Plan. Although the delegates ultimately voted to continue discussion of the Committee of the Whole's version of the revised Virginia Plan, the introduction of rival plans indicated that the delegates were far from united on the details of the Virginia Plan or on its proposal to apportion both houses of the proposed Congress on the basis of population.

Further Debates and Compromises

The conflict between more-populous and less-populous states over representation in Congress remained the chief Gordian knot for the delegates to resolve. Further fissures developed between northern and southern delegates over whether slaves should be represented in the formula for congressional representation, and between those who favored increased national powers and those who feared that the proposed national government would destroy the independence of its constituent states. Other issues included the respective terms of members of each of the three branches of government, what their qualifications should be, and what the relationship should be between the proposed two houses of Congress. On this and other issues, the convention often established committees, typically consisting of a representative from each state delegation that was present, to hammer out palatable compromises that were then discussed by the convention as a whole.

The most important compromise, variously designated the Great Compromise or the Connecticut Compromise (in light of that state's delegates influence on it), was adopted in mid-July. It provided that states would be represented according to population in one house, as the Virginia Plan had proposed, and equally in the second, as the New Jersey Plan had proposed. This compromise was so important that the delegates voted to make the provision for equal representation in the Senate un-amendable, without their own consent.

Other compromises provided for presidential selection and senatorial confirmation of ambassadors, judges, and heads of executive departments. Delegates from South Carolina and Georgia were able to get fellow delegates to agree to count slaves as three-fifths of a person for purposes of representation in the House of Representatives, to permit continuation of the slave trade for another twenty years, and to require the return of fugitive slaves from free to slave states. Building in part on the formula for state representation under the Connecticut Compromise, delegates devised a complex electoral college to select the president, who now became more independent of Congress.

On August 6, a Committee of Detail compiled convention resolutions, and a long list of congressional powers, into a coherent document. This provided the basis for further discussion and compromise that lasted into the next month. These deliberations were, in turn, further refined by a Committee of Style and Arrangement, on which Gouverneur Morris of Pennsylvania played a leading part, including formulating the now familiar words "We the People" that introduce the document.

Signing the Constitution

Despite hopes for unanimity and a persuasive speech by Benjamin Franklin arguing that the document was as good as could be expected from a collective body, three of the remaining forty-two delegates refused to sign the document on September 17. Bypassing the provision for amendment under the Articles of Confederation that required unanimous consent of the state legislature, the delegates provided that the new Constitution would go into effect among ratifying states after conventions among nine or more of them approved the document (although had Virginia and/or two or three of the most populous states failed to ratify, it is doubtful that the Constitution could have succeeded). Ratification by conventions was designed to ground the Constitution in popular sovereignty and make the Constitution superior to ordinary acts of legislation that had not received such approval.

RATIFICATION OF THE U.S. CONSTITUTION

The debates over the ratification of the Constitution continued for more than a year. Indeed, North Carolina and Rhode Island did not ratify the Constitution until it went into effect among the other ratifying states. Those who supported the Constitution were known as Federalists and could point to problems under the Articles of Confederation that almost everyone acknowledged. Although Antifederalist opponents acknowledged some deficiencies in the existing system of government, they expressed numerous reservations about the new document, many centering on their fears that the power of the national government created by the new Constitution would be too great and would obliterate the states.

Proponents and opponents of the Constitution published numerous essays during the time that the document was being debated. The most famous essays in support of the Constitution were written by Alexander Hamilton, James Madison, and John Jay as *The Federalist* under the pen name of Publius, a Roman statesman. In one of the most famous of these essays (Federalist No. 10), James Madison touted the advantages of a representative, or republican, government spread out over a large land area in tempering the vices and injustices of factions. In Federalist No. 51, Madison further praised the advantages of separation of powers, while in Federalist No. 78, Hamilton explained how the federal courts would help enforce the new document.

The objection to the Constitution that resonated most closely with popular sentiment was that the document lacked a bill of rights, specifically protecting individual liberties. Although leading Federalists initially claimed that such a bill was unnecessary, some Federalists (most notably James Madison, who had received letters from his friend Thomas Jefferson favoring the delineation of such rights) eventually saw the wisdom of accepting such a bill rather than taking the chance that states might convene a second convention that would enact structural changes that could undo the work of the first. Federalists refused to allow states to ratify the Constitution conditionally, but Madison promised to work for a bill of rights once the new union went into effect. After the new Constitution was ratified in 1789, James Madison collected proposed amendments from state ratifying conventions and ultimately succeeded in introducing twelve amendments in the first Congress, ten of which the states ratified in 1791.

BRIEF OUTLINE OF THE CONSTITUTION

The Constitution that the convention proposed and that the states ratified was divided into a preamble, stating the purposes of the document, and seven divisions, known as the Articles. These articles outlined governmental structures, powers, and limits. The first three articles embodied the principles of separation of powers and checks and balances by outlining the structures and powers of the legislative, executive, and judicial branches of the national government.

The first and most extensive of these articles delineated the organization and enumerated the powers of, and some limits on, the legislative branch. It consisted of a House of Representatives whose members were selected by popular vote and in which states were represented according to population (counting slaves as three-fifths of a person), and a Senate in which each state had two members selected by state legislatures—later changed by the Seventeenth Amendment, to popular vote. Members of the House served for two years and those of the Senate for six. Legislation required the approval of both houses.

Article II outlined the power of the president, who was selected by an elaborate electoral college mechanism that was largely independent of Congress, to serve for four-year renewable terms. The Article designated the president as commander-in-chief of the armed forces, vested the president with power to enforce the laws, and entrusted the executive with power to negotiate treaties and appoint key officials, subject to Senate confirmation. The president had power to veto acts of congressional legislation, subject to an override of two-thirds majorities in both houses.

Article III indicated that a single Supreme Court would head the federal judicial system. All members of the judiciary would serve "during good behavior." The language of this article, which vested jurisdiction over numerous issues in the federal courts, was capacious enough that such courts were later able to claim the power (affirmed in debates by some, albeit not all, of the convention delegates and now known as judicial review) to review and void legislation that they considered to be unconstitutional.

The English had a unitary government, with colonies (later transformed into a Commonwealth), but no permanent states. The government under the Articles is what contemporary political scientists call a confederal government, in which states dominated. The new government combined elements of both systems by creating what is today known as a federal government. Such a government more evenly divided power between a central government and state authorities, each with their own constitution and each with power to operate directly on individual citizens. Article IV accordingly dealt with relations among the states and between them and the central government, which guaranteed certain privileges and immunities to citizens throughout the nation.

Article V outlined an amending clause that permitted two-thirds of the states to propose amendments, or petition Congress to call a convention to propose amendments. These would go into effect when ratified by three-fourths of the states. An entrenchment clause protected the Great Compromise by prohibiting states from being deprived of their equal representation in the Senate without their consent. Article VI proclaimed the supremacy of federal laws, and Article VII bypassed the amending process under the Articles of Confederation by providing for ratification of the Constitution by special conventions called within the states.

The first ten amendments were ratified shortly thereafter and dealt almost solely with the protection of individual rights rather than with the proposed structural changes in the new government that some Antifederalists had favored. Prominent provisions include the protections for freedom of religion, speech, and press in the First Amendment; the "right to bear arms" delineated in the Second Amendment; the protections against "unreasonable searches and seizures" in the Fourth Amendment; the protections in the Fifth and Sixth Amendments for individuals who are accused of, or on trial for crimes, and especially the provision for "due process of law" in the Fifth Amendment; and the prohibition of "cruel and unusual punishment" in the Eighth Amendment. The Ninth and Tenth Amendments somewhat more ambiguously refer to rights retained by the states and by the people.

Originally adopted to limit the national government, the Supreme Court has subsequently incorporated most provisions of the Bill of Rights into the due process clause of the Fourteenth Amendment, which was adopted in 1868, three years after the U.S. Civil War, and three years after the Thirteenth Amendment ended chattel slavery. This means that these provisions of the Bill of Rights now equally limit both state and national governments.

Subsequent amendments have sought to protect discrimination in voting on the basis of race, gender, or age above eighteen.

For sake of parallelism, in detailing positions that delegates took at the Constitutional Convention, this book generally proceeds not according to when they made them but according to the constitutional outline. Thus, for delegates who participated extensively, there will be separate sections on their positions regarding the legislative, executive, and judicial branches, followed by provisions that are found in subsequent constitutional articles. Similarly, each essay describes each delegate prior to the convention as well as his life after its adjournment.

THE CONSTITUTION AS A COLLECTIVE PRODUCT

It is common to identify James Madison as the "father" of the Constitution. Were the designation completely accurate (and Madison, who emphasized the collective nature of the deliberations, denied that it was), then the lives of the rest of the Founders would hardly be of significant consequence. While affirmation can be important, the biographies of one group of yes-men would be of little more importance than that of another.

In truth, however, the fifty-five men who attended the Constitutional Convention of 1787 as delegates were far more than this. As noted by David Brian Robertson, all the delegates, including Madison, who came to the convention with a master plan quickly learned that they would have to concede some points to gain others. Although Thomas Jefferson, who was serving during the convention as an ambassador to France, once referred to the delegates as "an assembly of demi-gods," it seems far more accurate to say that the group contained many of the leading men of the one-time thirteen colonies, with several—James Madison, James Wilson, Gouverneur Morris, Roger Sherman, George Mason, Nathaniel Gorham, and Hugh Williamson (the list is not exhaustive)—being especially important, others doing fairly yeoman service, and still others participating negligibly.

Even those who did not speak out publicly at the convention, however, had a vote within their state delegations and undoubtedly served as sounding boards for the more loquacious among them. In a description that I have borrowed for the subtitle of this book, on the day after the delegates returned to their deliberations after celebrating Independence Day, Gouverneur Morris (a once and future New Yorker who was representing Pennsylvania at the convention) observed that he came to the convention "as a Representative of America" (Farrand 1:529). Indeed, "he flattered himself [that] he came here in some degree as a Representative of the whole human race; for the whole human race will be affected by the proceedings of this Convention" (1:529). As a nationalist, Morris stressed the need to represent America; other delegates may have considered themselves to be primary representatives of the states who had selected them. In both cases, delegates realized that they were not simply drawing up a form of government for themselves but also for their friends, neighbors, and fellow countrymen.

At a time when women, African Americans, and individuals without property have the right to vote, it is difficult to accept Morris's claim to be a representative American at face value. All the delegates to the convention were white males, and many of them owned slaves. Delegates were far richer and far better educated than most of those whom they represented (at least 30 had attended college), and most had extensive records of public service, often including military experience and even experience in drafting state constitutions. One of the remarkable aspects of the convention, which may well continue to validate the delegates' decision to establish a federal system that retained the states, is that the delegates were not mere "theoretical" politicians who were engaging in government for the first time but were experienced veterans, many of whom had already been able to see variants of democracy play out within their own states. In the context of their own time, they were probably as representative a body as any could be, and, it is important to remember, their own work did not become law of the land until it was ratified by conventions within each of the states. Diverse state and regional interests were certainly ably represented at the Constitutional Convention, as were those who favored variants of republicanism, liberalism, and even the British system. As I have argued in my own narrative of the convention, the delegates' work at the convention was an example of "practical virtue in action."

Delegates ranged in age from 26 to 81 and averaged just over 43. Almost all were married. Many delegates (a sign of their cosmopolitanism) were married to women from other states; their family sizes, which ranged from no children to fifteen, were somewhat smaller than that of the general population. They were members of a variety of churches with Episcopalians, Presbyterians, and Congregationalists being the most dominant and with some thought to be Deists. Thirty-four of the delegates were attorneys, but more than half were also farmers or planters; others were merchants and doctors. Delegates varied significantly in their attendance patterns, but about thirty delegates attended on an average day.

Geographic Divisions

Geographically, the delegates represented three fairly distinct regions. Eastern (what we would call northeastern) states were especially involved with merchant trade and with fisheries. Congregational churches, many with Puritan origins, tended to predominate in this region. In the middle states, where climate was more temperate, grain was probably the most abundant product. Largely because of the influence of William Penn, this region had a history of religious tolerance. Southern states were closely associated with tobacco, cotton, and slavery and with the Anglican Church. Although all thirteen states hugged the Atlantic Coast, they were on the periphery of a vast continent, which opened up tremendous possibilities both for immigration and trade but also difficulties in maintaining communication and mutual feelings of nationhood with the frontier. In notes that he made for a speech that formulated a good argument for federalism, Pennsylvania's Jared Ingersoll observed that:

> The Fisheries & Manufacturers of New-England, the Flour Lumber Flaxseed & Ginseng of New York New Jersey Pennsylvania & Delaware The Tobacco of Maryland & Virginia the Pitch Tar, Rice & Indigo & Cotton of North Carolina South Carolina & Georgia, can never be regulated by the same Law nor the same Legislature, nor is this diversity by any means confined to Articles of Commerce, at the Eastward Slavery is not acknowledged, with us it exists in a certain qualified manner, at the Southward to its full extent. (Hutson 1987, 103)

A State-by-State Survey of the Delegates from the Eastern (Northern) States

Delegates voted at the convention by states, and signed the document by delegations from north to south. Although each state had a single vote, the size of the delegations varied. States shared many problems, but each state had its own unique history and interests.

The northernmost delegates hailed from New Hampshire (Vermont had not yet been admitted into the Union), whose residents fell into three distinct sections corresponding to the state's watersheds. The state faced funding problems, and former state president Nicholas Gilman (who financed the trip) and fellow merchant John Langdon did not arrive until after the Great Compromise. Gilman was not recorded as making a single comment, but both he and Langdon, who participated more actively, stayed to sign the final document.

Massachusetts, which had been a hub of revolutionary activities and which had adopted a visionary constitution in 1780, supplied four delegates. Elbridge Gerry, a merchant who was suspicious of centralized power, would be one of the three delegates who remained at the convention on September 17 but refused to sign. Nathaniel Gorham, another merchant who had distinguished himself in service in Congress, would serve in the opening days as president of the Committee of the Whole. Attorneys Rufus King and Caleb Strong rounded out the delegation. King would play a particularly active role on committees at the convention.

In 1787, Connecticut was still governed by a variant of the Fundamental Orders of Connecticut, which preceded other state constitutions. Scholars generally agree that Connecticut's delegation was one of the strongest, a reputation reflected in the frequency with which the Great Compromise is also dubbed the Connecticut Compromise. A one-time cobbler named Roger Sherman, who was then serving as a judge, was probably the shrewdest and most influential, but the delegation also included Dr. William Samuel Johnson, the newly installed president of King's College (today's Columbia University), and Oliver Ellsworth, all of whom would sign the Constitution. Ellsworth would later serve as the primary author of the Judiciary Act of 1789.

Survey of Delegates from the Middle States

New York, originally settled by the Dutch but later taken over by the British, was the northernmost of the middle states, and its constitution served in part as a source for mechanisms that would find their way into the new government. Apart from Rhode Island, New York may have been the most underrepresented at the convention. Robert Yates and John Lansing Jr., the former a distinguished judge and the latter the mayor of Albany, were talented enough, but they had little sympathy for the direction the convention was taking in strengthening the national government. They had largely been appointed to block the actions of fellow delegate Alexander Hamilton, a gifted lawyer, the brilliant former aide-de-camp to George Washington, and the nation's future secretary of the treasury, who impressed the convention with his oratory, appears to have had little influence on the deliberations, but served on the final Committee of Style and Arrangement and went on to be one of the Constitution's most effective spokesmen. After the departure of Yates and Lansing left him unable to cast a vote on behalf of the state at the convention, he himself left for an extended period, and was the only one of the delegation who returned in the final days to sign the document.

New Jersey, which was politically divided between the east with closer ties to New York, and the west with closer ties to Pennsylvania, had been originally settled by immigrants from Sweden and Holland. The state sent a total of five delegates, the best known probably William Paterson (after whom the New Jersey Plan is sometimes named) who had attended the Annapolis Convention, and William Livingston who was serving at the time as state governor. David Brearley, Jonathan Dayton, and William Churchill Houston rounded out the delegation. Brearley, who had been chief justice of his state, served on two committees at the convention. Dayton, a future lawyer who was filling in for his father, was somewhat intimidated due to his age (at 26, he was the Convention's youngest member), and Houston, a lawyer who had been born in South Carolina, left the convention very early because of tuberculosis.

Founded by the Quaker William Penn, Pennsylvania had the advantage of hosting the convention, and it sent eight delegates, all of whom resided in or near the city. The most prominent, Benjamin Franklin, had served during the Revolutionary War as an American ambassador to France and was a Renaissance man known not only throughout the states, but throughout the world. Although his health was an obstacle to full participation, he often stepped forward with sage advice and a mediating spirit, and his very presence lent credibility to the meeting. A gifted writer who had pulled himself up by his own bootstraps, he remained one of the convention's most articulate spokesmen for the common man. Gouverneur Morris was a tour de force in his own right and is recorded as giving the greatest number of speeches at the convention and as providing the final style to the emerging document as a member of the Committee of Style and Arrangement. James Wilson, a future Supreme Court justice, was one of the convention's most influential delegates and was especially associated with the development of a strong presidency. Robert Morris, the wealthy businessman who had helped finance the American Revolution, hosted George Washington and said virtually nothing at the convention, but may have been a force behind the scenes. George Clymer, Thomas Fitzsimons, Jared Ingersoll, and

Thomas Mifflin rounded out the delegation and said little. Ingersoll was an attorney, and the others were merchants.

Delaware, which like Pennsylvania had been founded by William Penn, was one of the smallest states. Its most influential delegate was undoubtedly John Dickinson. The only delegate to sign the Constitution by proxy, he had previously established himself as the independent-minded "Penman of the Revolution" and the primary author of the Articles of Confederation. Gunning Bedford Jr. would earn a reputation as a hothead for intemperate, but arguably effective, remarks he made during debates over state representation in Congress. Jacob Broom is perhaps most notable for being the only signer of the Constitution for whom no portrait has been located. George Read, who had been born in Maryland, created a family political dynasty in Delaware.

Maryland had been established by Cecilius Calvert (Lord Baltimore), partly as a haven for Roman Catholics. A relatively small state, it was arguably underrepresented by its five delegates. Luther Martin, a brilliant attorney with a deserved reputation for overimbibing, gave one of the longest speeches at the convention but carried little weight and left the proceedings to oppose adoption of the Constitution, in the government of which he would later serve. Daniel Carroll is best known for being one of two Roman Catholics who attended and for his connection to his brother, who had signed the Declaration of Independence. John Francis Mercer, an attorney who had studied under Thomas Jefferson, attended for less than two weeks. Daniel of St. Thomas Jenifer, a planter and merchant, and Dr. James McHenry, who would lend his name to one of the most famous forts in American history, rounded out the delegation.

Survey of Delegates from the Southern States

Virginia (which then included today's Kentucky and West Virginia) was the largest and most populous state. Its delegation ranks in influence with that of Connecticut and Pennsylvania. Like Franklin, George Washington did more by attending than many other delegates could do by talking. Unanimously chosen as the president of the convention, his presence lent a quiet dignity to the proceedings and gave the nation confidence that it was acting in the public interest. James Madison Jr. was one of the convention's intellectual powerhouses who spent months preparing for the meeting, and was the primary force behind the writing of the Virginia Plan, which the state's handsome governor Edmund Randolph introduced. Although he ultimately refused to sign the document, George Mason, a prominent planter who had largely authored the Virginia Declaration of Rights, contributed significantly to convention debates and provided some of the impetus for the later introduction of a bill of rights. George Wythe, the first law professor in America, had barely enough time to chair the Rules Committee before heading home to Williamsburg to care for his dying wife. John Blair, a lawyer and judge, and James McClurg, a medical doctor, were definitely in the shadow of their more illustrious colleagues.

North Carolina (which included today's Tennessee) sent five delegates, but Dr. Hugh Williamson, perhaps the closest to a Renaissance man of anyone other than Franklin at the convention, clearly dominated. William Blount would gain fame later as one of the founders of Tennessee, which was then the westernmost part of the state, and a reputation that he shared with Williamson for speculation in western lands. North Carolina's other delegates were William Richardson Davie, an immigrant from England who would help found the University of North Carolina; Alexander Martin, a merchant and attorney whose primary participation appears to have been attending and seconding a few motions; and Richard Dobbs Spaight, a Revolutionary War veteran who supported the expansion of national powers.

South Carolina, which was politically divided between the eastern "low country" and the western "backcountry," was ably represented by Pierce Butler, cousins General Charles Cotesworth Pinckney and Charles Pinckney, and John Rutledge. Butler, the only member of the delegation without formal legal training, nonetheless participated ably in convention debates. Charles Cotesworth Pinckney, who had distinguished himself by his patriotism in the Revolutionary War, was also an active participant in debates and later helped found the University of South Carolina. Charles Pinckney, soon dubbed "Constitution Charlie," did little to correct the impression that he, rather than New Jersey's Jonathan Brearly, was the youngest convention delegate and does not, as he later claimed, appear to have been the architect of a grand plan that anticipated most of the compromises that the convention would adopt. Rutledge, who had experience in all three branches of government, was an active debater who served on several committees at the convention, including the influential Committee of Detail. The South Carolina delegates worked with delegates from Georgia not only to guarantee that slaves would be counted as three-fifths of a person for ascertaining state representation in the House of Representatives, but also in assuring that the Congress could not restrict the slave trade for another 20 years. To the chagrin of successors who would suffer under what they considered to be oppressive tariffs, they did not succeed in requiring two-thirds majorities of Congress to adopt navigation acts.

Georgia had been established in 1732 by James Oglethorpe. In 1787, it was the southernmost state. Its delegates were Abraham Baldwin, William Few, William Houstoun, and William Pierce. Baldwin, a lawyer with political experience who had once lived in Connecticut, may have provided ties to this powerful and conciliatory delegation. Few, a self-taught lawyer, gave no speeches, and Houstoun, an English-trained attorney, left early. Pierce, a merchant and Revolutionary War veteran, made the greatest literary contribution through his sketches of fellow delegates, which continue to be engaging and were the first of many such treatments of the signers or delegates (including this book).

RANKING THE DELEGATES

It is common to rank presidents and Supreme Court justices, and many readers will undoubtedly be interested in knowing which delegates to the convention were most important and influential. To some degree the importance of delegates will be reflected by the length of the essays that describe them, but this length is influenced not simply by their service at the convention but (as in the case of Alexander Hamilton) by what is known about their public and private lives outside the convention as well. In my previous encyclopedia of the Constitutional Convention, I included an essay on the individual rankings of delegates by a variety of scholars (Vile 2005, 1:219–22), showing in part how assessments have changed as scholars have gained further information about the proceedings. As I indicated there, the most thorough assessment of delegates that has been published to date is by historian Clinton Rossiter in *1787: The Grand Convention* (1987). In this book he divided the delegates into eight categories, which might prove useful to readers of this book who are hoping to gain some sense of which delegates were the most important. Rossiter's categories (roughly from best to worst), which lack scientific precision but reflect his own nuanced assessments of a variety of factors, are as follows: the Principals, the Influentials, the Very Usefuls, the Usefuls, the Visibles, the Ciphers, the Dropouts and Walkouts, and the Inexplicable Disappointments.

The individuals that Rossiter identified as "the Principals" includes James Madison, James Wilson, George Washington, and Gouverneur Morris. He further identified John Rutledge, Benjamin Franklin, Roger Sherman, Charles Pinckney, Rufus King, Charles Cotesworth Pinckney, Oliver Ellsworth, Nathaniel Gorham, George Mason, Edmund Randolph, and Elbridge Gerry as "the Influentials." His list of "the Very Usefuls" included John Dickinson, Hugh Williamson, William Samuel Johnson, George Read, Pierce Butler, William Paterson, and Luther Martin. Under "the Usefuls," he included David Brearly, William Livingston, Richard Dobbs Spaight, Gunning Bedford Jr., Abraham Baldwin, Daniel Carroll, John Langdon, and William R. Davie.

Rossiter identified John Blair, Daniel of St. Thomas Jenifer, William Few, Jacob Broom, Caleb Strong, William Houstoun, George Clymer, Jonathan Dayton, James McHenry, and James McClurg, as "the Visibles." Rossiter referred to Richard Bassett, Thomas Mifflin, William Blount, Jared Ingersoll, Thomas Fitzsimons, Nicholas Gilman, and Alexander Martin as "the Ciphers," and William Churchill Houston, William Pierce, George Wythe, John Francis Mercer, Robert Yates, and John Lansing Jr. as "the Dropouts and Walkouts." Finally, rounding out his categories, he described Robert Morris and Alexander Hamilton as "the Inexplicable Disappointments" (Rossiter 1987, 247–53).

ORIGINS AND PREDECESSORS OF THIS BOOK

In this volume, I have corrected (yes, I found a few mistakes!), updated, and expanded the essays on convention delegates that I wrote for my earlier encyclopedia of the Constitutional Convention. I have consulted and added references to additional sources, especially those that have been published since my encyclopedia. As befits a book that focuses solely on the delegates, I have aimed for greater consistency among entries compared to the previous volume with respect to their content, including more information on families, on post-convention arguments and activities, and on death dates and burial sites. In an attempt to continue to set this book apart from most of its counterparts, however, I have drawn from my wide knowledge of the Constitutional Convention and its proceedings to retain the emphasis of the earlier encyclopedia entries on what motions the delegates made and seconded, on what they actually said, and on the committees on which they served at the convention.

My encyclopedia was primarily designed as a reference work. While this book will serve a similar function, my intent is to make this material accessible not only for those who desire quick reference about the lives and contributions of the delegates, but for those who would like to further understand the origins of the Constitution by gaining a view of the delegates as a group. In this respect, I hope that it will be a worthy, and equally readable, complement to the recent narrative that I wrote about the Constitutional Convention.

In addition to the ever-multiplying biographies of George Washington, James Madison, Benjamin Franklin, Alexander Hamilton, Gouverneur Morris, and other delegates who wielded disproportionate influence at the convention (and many of whom had fairly adventurous lives apart from the convention), there are, of course, a number of works that, like this book, deal with the lives of one or another group of Founders. My general impression—consistent with the manner in which anniversaries and celebrations of the Declaration of Independence usually receive greater coverage than those of the Constitution—is that there are somewhat more books on the fifty-six men who signed the Declaration of Independence (there is at least one book on their wives entitled *The Wives of the Signers* and a more recent book on *Women of the Constitution*) than there are on those who attended the Constitutional Convention or signed the Constitution. Being a signer of one or the other document appears to have been a fairly early guarantee of fame in the early American republic, and those like Benjamin Franklin, Robert Morris, and Roger Sherman who signed both are justly celebrated. While others were introducing and debating resolutions, William Pierce, a delegate to the Constitutional Convention from Georgia, was already busy writing word portraits of himself and of his fellow delegates.

I have profited immensely from the works of predecessors, including those who have compiled such collective portraits. The earliest compilation of biographies (other than those of William Pierce of Georgia) that I have found of those who attended the Constitutional Convention is entitled "Biographies of the Members of the Federal Convention" and is found on pages 135 to 238 in the first of two massive volumes edited by Hampton L. Carson, the Secretary of the Constitutional Centennial Commission, titled *History of the Celebration of the One Hundredth Anniversary of the Promulgation of the Constitution of the United States*. (Sanderson, Wain, and Gilpin, 1823–1826, published a multivolume book on the lives of the signers of the Declaration of Independence in connection with the 50-year commemorations of this event.) I have attempted both to provide some continuity to Carson's book, and to include a visual component to the biographical sketches by including copies of the beautiful sepia engravings of the delegates that he included in his original volume.

In addition to general biographical reference works, I have found M. E. Bradford's *Founding Fathers*, which is now in a second edition; David C. Whitney's *Founders of Freedom in America: Lives of the Men Who Signed the Constitution of the United States and So Helped to Establish the United States of America;* and Dorothy Horton McGee's *Framers of the Constitution* to be especially useful. Robert Wright Jr. and Morris J. MacGregor Jr.'s *Soldier-Statesmen of the Constitution* presents solid portraits of those with military experience who attended the convention. More recently, Denise Kiernan and Joseph D'Agnese have complemented an early book, *Signing Their Lives Away: The Fame and Misfortune of the Men Who Signed the Declaration of Independence,* with a second excellent volume curiously (and, I think, somewhat inaccurately since I believe that by further securing liberty under law, those who signed the Constitution actually enhanced rights rather than diminished them) titled *Signing Their Rights Away: The Fame and Misfortune of the Men Who Signed the United States Constitution.* Joseph C. Morton has also presented solid treatments of the delegates in his *Shapers of the Great Debate at the Constitutional Convention of 1787: A Biographical Dictionary.* Charles W. Meister does not aim for the same breadth but presents in depth treatments of a baker's dozen of the leading delegates in *The Founding Fathers.* Similarly, Gary L. Gregg II and Mark David Hall include biographies of five of the delegates among ten that they identify as *America's Forgotten Founders.* Confining herself to spouses of those who actually signed the Constitution, Janice McKenney's *Women of the Constitution* is the first volume that specifically focuses on their wives.

THE BOOK'S ORGANIZATION

As the title of Kiernan and D'Agnese's second volume suggests, there are probably more books that focus on the thirty-nine signers of the Constitution than there are that focus on all fifty-five men who attended the Constitutional Convention. Moreover, the most common way to study delegates has been to examine them on a state-by-state basis. Some treatments also focus on labels and quirks that will make it easier for readers to remember the delegates.

I have broken with all three traditions in this book. While I understand the desire to glorify those who took the ultimate plunge to risk their reputations by signing the document, some of the signers were relative nonentities compared to those who did not sign, and I do not think we can adequately understand the Constitution without including the substantial contributions to debates that were made by those who participated but did not sign. Prime examples would be Virginia's George Mason and Edmund Randolph, and Elbridge Gerry of Massachusetts; all three engaged vigorously in debates at the convention but all three refused to sign, in part because of the lack of a bill of rights. Luther Martin is an example of a delegate who left the convention and did not sign, but whose publication of his view of its proceedings influenced the ratification debates and whose portrait will enliven almost any book. Had there been no opposition to the proposals and compromises at the convention, the document would have been radically different, and the Bill of Rights would probably never have been adopted. Moreover, it often takes far more courage to resist the crowd than to go with it. It seems almost contrary to the principles of the First Amendment to suggest that only those who end up on the winning wide are worthy of attention. While it is a truism that the winners typically write history, there is no reason that accounts cannot include both winners and losers; indeed, the adoption of the Bill of Rights would suggest that the "losers" helped us all become "winners," and that the "winners" continue to owe them a debt.

The decision to treat the 55 delegates who attended the convention alphabetically rather than by states was more difficult. The 55 delegates from 12 states (Rhode Island did not send representatives) who attended the Constitutional Convention did not vote individually but by state. Anyone who has ever watched a national nominating convention knows that when they get their turn at the microphone, the heads of the delegation from one great state will herald their leaders and their state's accomplishments, only to be followed by others who claim to be from even greater and more heralded states as they cast their votes for their party's nominees. Moreover, almost all fifty states cast their votes in the electoral college that selects the president collectively rather than as individuals.

The practice of voting by states shows the continuing vitality of federalism, but neither the U.S. House of Representatives nor the U.S. Senate follows this practice—delegates to the convention specifically voted to allow "per capita" voting in the Senate rather than risking frequent tie votes that might have stymied Senate action. While there are thus precedents for my own approach, my decision to follow alphabetical order is totally practical. I simply find it easier, as I believe readers will, to locate delegates by their last names than by first having to know the states that they represented. In deference to those who would like to read about all the delegates from a particular state in a single setting, a list of delegates by state follows this introduction so that readers can locate entries without knowing the names of the delegates who represented a particular state.

Intended Audience

I have designed this book both as a general reference tool for high school, college and university, and public libraries, as well as a book that individuals can either read from cover to cover or choose essays on Founding Fathers (perhaps those from a home state) that particularly interest them. Although I have designed the book to be accessible to the general public, I have resisted the temptation to describe each delegate by a single adjective that may conceal more than it reveals. Moreover, while those who contributed to the Constitution undoubtedly shared in the misfortunes of others of their generation, I do not think that as a whole they necessarily suffered more than others. Unlike those who signed the earlier Declaration of Independence, most did not, to repeat a metaphor that Benjamin Franklin made at the Second Continental Congress, anticipate either hanging together or hanging as traitors separately from the ends of British nooses. Those who faced subsequent misfortunes were generally reaping the "rewards" of their own financial speculations or personal recklessness (at least two died in duels) rather than suffering as a result of their support for the Constitution.

In addition to this general introduction to the convention, I have included a dictionary of key terms and a quiz that picks out some of the more noteworthy facts about individual delegates, but in seeking to publish the most useful and comprehensive work on the subject, I have attempted to focus less on individual quirks than on what the records of the convention tell us about the arguments and contributions that each delegate made to deliberations in the summer of 1787. As in the larger encyclopedia from which I initially drew these essays, I have focused on the arguments that the delegates made at the convention and that I think are of continuing importance in understanding that document.

The Founders' Continuing Legacy

As a written constitution, the U.S. Constitution is second in longevity only to that of the state of Massachusetts, which was largely written by John Adams and adopted in 1780 through a ratification process not dissimilar to that adopted by the Philadelphia conventioneers. The 225th anniversary of the U.S. Constitution largely went unheralded as I was writing this volume (the nation tends to focus major celebrations on multiples of 50), but the occasion spurred me to continue my work on what I believe to have been one of the most pivotal events, not simply in the history of America, but in the history of the world.

In writing the first essay of *The Federalist*, Alexander Hamilton said that the debates over the ratification of the Constitution would establish "whether societies of men are really capable or not of establishing good government from reflection and choice, or whether they are forever destined to depend for their political constitutions on accident and force." Because I think that both the writing and ratification of the Constitution point to an affirmative answer to this question, I continue to believe that the lives of those who attended the convention that framed it are of enduring relevance to contemporary Americans. Gathering as "representatives of America," the diverse personalities who attended the Constitutional Convention of 1787 left an enduring legacy that we should do our best to understand if we intend, as the Preamble to the Constitution states, to "secure the blessings of liberty to ourselves and our posterity."

SOURCES CITED

Farrand, Max, ed. 1966. *The Records of the Federal Convention.* 4 vols. New Haven, CT: Yale University Press.

Hutson, James H., ed. 1987. *Supplement to Max Farrand's The Records of the Federal Convention of 1787.* New Haven, CT: Yale University Press.

Robertson, David Brian. 2005. "Madison's Opponents and Constitutional Design." *The American Political Science Review* 99 (May): 225–43.

Rossiter, Clinton. 1987. *1787: The Grand Convention.* New York: W.W. Norton & Company.

Vile, John R. 2005. *The Constitutional Convention of 1787: A Comprehensive Encyclopedia of America's Founding.* 2 vols. Santa Barbara, CA: ABC-CLIO.

———. 2012. *The Writing and Ratification of the U.S. Constitution: Practical Virtue in Action.* Lanham, MD: Rowman & Littlefield.

COLLECTIVE BIOGRAPHIES

Bakeless, John, and Katherine Little Bakeless. 1969. *Signers of the Declaration.* Boston: Houghton Mifflin.

Bloom, Sol. 1937. *The Story of the Constitution.* Washington, DC: United States Constitutional Sesquicentennial Commission. See "Portraits and Sketches of the Signers of the Constitution," 54–64.

Bradford, M. E. 1994. *Founding Fathers: Brief Lives of the Framers of the United States Constitution.* Lawrence: University Press of Kansas.

Brown, Richard D. July, 1976. "The Founding Fathers of 1776 and 1787: A Collective View." *The William and Mary Quarterly,* 3rd Ser., 33: 465–80.

Carson, Hampton L. 1889. "Biographies of the Members of the Federal Convention," *History of the Celebration of the One Hundredth Anniversary of the Promulgation of the Constitution of the United States,* edited by Hampton L. Carson, 1:135–237. Philadelphia: J. P. Lippincott Company.

Charleton, James H., et al. 1986. *Framers of the Constitution.* Washington, DC: National Archives and Records Administration.

Fehrenbach, T. R. 1968. *Greatness to Spare: the Heroic Sacrifices of the Men Who Signed the Declaration of Independence.* Princeton, NJ: Van Nostrand.

Ferris, Robert G. 1976. *Signers of the Constitution: Historic Places Commemorating the Signing of the Constitution.* Washington, DC: U.S. Department of the Interior.

"The Founding Fathers: A Brilliant Gathering of Reason and Creativity." 1987. Special issue of *Life* magazine, *The Constitution* (Fall): 51–58.

Fradin, Dennis B., and Michael McCurdy. 2005. *The Founders: The 39 Stories Behind the U.S. Constitution.* New York: Walker. [Note: this and the entry that follows are for children].

———. 2001. *The Signers: The 56 Stories Behind the Declaration of Independence.* New York: Walker.

Goodrich, Charles A. 1856. *Lives of the Signers to the Declaration of Independence.* New York: William Reed & Co.

Green, Harry Clinton, and Mary Wolcott Green. 1997. *Wives of the Signers: The Women Behind the Declaration of Independence.* Aledo, TX: WallBuilder Press.

Gregg, Gary L., II, and Mark David Hall. 2011. *America's Forgotten Founders.* 2nd ed. Wilmington, DE: Intercollegiate Studies Institute.

Judson, L. Carroll. 1970. *The Sages and Heroes of the American Revolution. Including the Signers of the Declaration of Independence. Two Hundred and Forty Three of the Sages and Heroes Are Presented in Due Form and Many Others Are Named Incidentally.* First printing 1851. Port Washington, NY: Kennikat Press.

Kiernan, Denise, and Joseph D'Agnese. 2009. *Signing Their Lives Away: The Fame and Misfortune of the Men Who Signed the Declaration of Independence.* Philadelphia: Quirk Books.

———. 2011. *Signing Their Rights Away: The Fame and Misfortune of the Men Who Signed the United States Constitution.* Philadelphia: Quirk Books.

Losing, Benson J. 1995. *Lives of the Signers of the Declaration of Independence.* Aledo, TX: WallBuilder Press. Reprint of 1848 edition.

Mason, Ed. 1975. *Signers of the Constitution.* Builders of a Nation Series, Book 2. Columbus, OH: The Dispatch Printing Company.

McGee, Dorothy Horton. 1968. *Framers of the Constitution.* New York: Dodd, Mead & Company.

McKenney, Janice E. 2012. *Women of the Constitution: Wives of the Signers.* Lanham, MD: Scarecrow Press.

Meister, Charles W. 2012. *The Founding Fathers.* Jefferson, NC: McFarland.

Mitchell, Memory F. 1964. *North Carolina's Signers: Brief Sketches of the Men Who Signed the Declaration of Independence and the Constitution.* Raleigh: Division of Archives and History, North Carolina Department of Cultural Resources.

Morton, Joseph C. 2006. *Shapers of the Great Debate at the Constitutional Convention of 1787: A Biographical Dictionary.* Westport, CT: Greenwood Press.

Pelton, Robert W. 2012. *Men of Destiny: The Signers of Our Declaration of Independence and Our Constitution.* Charleston, SC: Freedom & Liberty Foundation Press.

Quinn, C. Edward. 1986. *Signers of the Constitution of the United States.* New York: Bronx County Historical Society.

Ross, George E. 1963. *Know the 56 Signers of the Declaration of Independence.* Chicago: Rand McNally.

Sanderson, John, Robert Wain, and Henry D. Gilpin. 1823–1827. *Biography of the Signers to the Declaration of Independence.* 9 vols. Philadelphia: R.W. Pomeroy.

Whitney, David C. 1974. *Founders of Freedom in America: Lives of the Men Who Signed the Constitution of the United States and So Helped to Establish the United States of America.* Chicago: J. G. Ferguson Publishing.

Wright, Robert K., Jr., and Morris J. MacGregor. 1987. *Soldier-Statesmen of the Constitution.* Washington, DC: Center of Military History, U.S. Army.

Delegates by State

Connecticut

Delaware

Georgia

Maryland

Massachusetts

New Hampshire

New Jersey

Delegates to the Constitutional Convention of 1787

ABRAHAM BALDWIN (1754–1807)
GEORGIA

Abraham Baldwin was born on November 22, 1754 in Connecticut, the third of five children of Michael and Lucy Dudley Baldwin. His father was a blacksmith; a brother by his father's second marriage to Theodora Wolcott, Henry Baldwin, later served on the U.S. Supreme Court. Abraham entered Yale at an early age to study theology and stayed to tutor and study law. He served with Joel Barlow, an American republican writer of some distinction, as a chaplain for Connecticut troops during the Revolutionary War. Barlow married Baldwin's sister, while Baldwin remained a lifelong bachelor.

Baldwin was admitted to the Georgia bar shortly after moving to Savannah in 1784. Within three months he was elected to the state legislature, where he helped create Franklin College. The college developed into the University of Georgia where Baldwin served as president from 1786 to 1801, a time that included the period before the university actually offered classes. He also served from 1786 to the end of his life as a delegate from Georgia to the Continental Congress, to the Annapolis Convention, to the U.S. House of Representatives, and to the U.S. Senate. Baldwin did not speak extensively at the convention, but he served on four committees and his ties to Connecticut appear to have proven useful in forging compromises related both to representation in Congress and to slave importation.

At the Convention

Baldwin was seated at the Constitutional Convention on June 11. His first recorded comments came on June 29 in reaction to a speech in which Oliver Ellsworth of Connecticut had proposed granting small states equal representation in the Senate. By contrast, Baldwin thought that the Senate should represent property. At this time Baldwin also indicated that "He concurred with those who thought it wd. be impossible for the Genl. Legislature to extend its cares to the local matters of the States" (Farrand 1966, 1:470), a likely indication of his opposition to the proposed congressional negative of state laws.

On July 2, faced with a five-to-five vote over congressional representation, Baldwin split his vote with William Houstoun (Baldwin voting, contrary to early expressions of opinion, for the small states and Houstoun for the large ones) so as to prevent either from winning. This resulted in a five-to-five-to-one vote that led to eventual compromise (1:510). Maryland's Luther Martin accused him of having done so not from conviction, but from the fear that the delegates from the small states would otherwise leave and dissolve the convention. Others have credited Baldwin for this conciliatory and statesman-like action (see Saye 1988, 85). After such an accommodating gesture, it is not surprising that fellow delegates appointed him to the Committee of Eleven that proposed the Great Compromise between the large states and the small states regarding congressional representation.

On August 13 the convention was discussing qualifications for members of the U.S. House of Representatives. Some delegates thought it would be unfair to immigrants to require that, as a condition of election, they be citizens longer than required under the Articles of Confederation. Baldwin said he could see no difference between this qualification and the twenty-five-year minimum age requirement (2:272).

Although he had not lived very long in Georgia, Baldwin defended continuation of the slave trade, a position that appeared to coincide with his advocacy of states' rights. When the convention was discussing the limitation of slave importation, Baldwin expressed the view that the delegates should distinguish between "national" and "local" matters. He also voiced concerns typical for someone from the southernmost state, which put him at some odds with other southerners (like those from Virginia) as well as with northerners:

> Georgia was decided on this point. That State has always hitherto supposed a Gen[eral] Governm[en]t to be the pursuit of the central States who wished to have a vortex for every thing—that her distance would preclude her from equal advantage—& that she could not prudently purchase it by yielding national powers. From this it might be understood in what light she would view an attempt to abridge one of her favorite prerogatives. If left to herself, she may probably put a stop to the evil. (2:372)

Although referring to the slave trade as an "evil" that Georgia might one day eliminate, Baldwin immediately questioned whether Georgia would in fact be inclined ever to end it. Thus, he offered as "one ground for this conjecture" the belief of a sect, presumably Hindus (see Bradford 1994, 205) "who carried their ethics beyond the mere equality of men, extending their humanity to the claims of the whole animal creation" (2:372). If the people of Georgia were not altogether certain whether African Americans were equal, it hardly seemed likely that they would ever believe that the rest of the animal kingdom were so. In a foreshadowing of the increasing racism that would dominate the South in the period leading up to the Civil War (1861–1865), Baldwin was rather shockingly comparing claims for equality for African Americans to claims for the equality between men and beasts!

On August 18, Baldwin served on the Committee on State Debts and Militia. Four days later he was appointed to the Committee on Slave Trade and Navigation, and on August 31, delegates appointed him to the Committee on Postponed Matters. Perhaps in part because of his service on the Committee on Slave Trade and Navigation, Baldwin altered a resolution on August 25 to provide that slave imports would be taxed according to the "common impost on articles not enumerated" (2:416).

On September 3 Baldwin argued that the example of state eligibility to other offices was inapplicable to Congress. He reasoned that the state legislatures were "so numerous that an exclusion of their member would not leave proper men for offices. The case would be otherwise in the General Government" (2:491). Baldwin's observation on September 14, indicating that the incompatibility clause would not apply to offices created by the Constitution itself, does not seem to have been followed up with any action on the part of the convention delegates (2:613–14).

During a discussion of the electoral college for choosing the president on the following day, Baldwin indicated that he was warming to the plan. He observed that "the increasing intercourse among the people of the States" would diffuse knowledge about national characters and thus make it less and less likely that the Senate would have to resolve such matters (2:501).

Life after the Convention

Baldwin signed the Constitution on September 17 and returned to his duties in the Congress under the Articles of Confederation, where he was part of a five-man committee responsible for putting the new Constitution into operation. He also served in the first Congress under the new Constitution, on the committee that helped draw up the Bill of Rights. Baldwin supported James Madison and gravitated toward the Democratic-Republican Party, and was selected to the U.S. Senate in 1799. When he died on March 4, 1807, he was serving as president pro tempore of that body. Joel Barlow observed that Baldwin "lived without reproach, and has probably died without an enemy" (quoted in Johnson 1987, 139). Baldwin had a full state funeral in Washington and was buried in Rock Creek Cemetery, about five miles from the Capitol.

Baldwin is probably best remembered for his role in founding the University of Georgia as the capstone institution of learning in that state. Although Baldwin wrote legislation that would have provided for a minister (the denomination went unspecified) to inculcate morality in Georgia primary schools in communities with 30 or more families (see Whitescarver 1993, 460–61), significantly, the University of Georgia was to be a state-supported, secular institution. A provision forbidding the exclusion of anyone "on account of his, her or their speculative sentiments in religion" later became the basis by which women were admitted to the institution (Johnson 1987, 143).

Further Reading

Bradford, M. E. 1994. *Founding Fathers: Brief Lives of the Framers of the United States Constitution.* Lawrence: University Press of Kansas.

Coulter, E. Merton. 1987. *Abraham Baldwin: Patriot, Educator, and Founding Father.* Arlington, VA: Vandamere Press.

Farrand, Max., ed. 1966. *The Records of the Federal Convention of 1787.* 4 vols. New Haven, CT: Yale University Press.

Folden, April D. 1999. "Baldwin, Abraham." In *American National Biography*, edited by John A. Garraty and Mark C. Carnes, 2:43–44. New York: Oxford University Press.

Johnson, Eldon L. 1987. "The 'Other Jeffersons' and the State University Idea." *Journal of Higher Education* 58 (March–April): 127–50.

Saye, Albert B. 1988. "Georgia: Security through Union." In *The Constitution and the States: The Role of the Original Thirteen in the Framing and Adoption of the Federal Constitution*, edited by Patrick T. Conley and John P. Kaminski. Madison, WI: Madison House.

Whitescarver, Keith. 1993. "Creating Citizens for the Republic: Education in Georgia, 1776–1810." *Journal of the Early Republic* 13 (Winter): 455–79.

Richard Bassett (1745–1815)
Delaware

Richard Bassett was born on April 2, 1745 in Cecil County, Maryland, the son of a tavern-keeper. After his father abandoned the family, his uncle, Peter Lawson, adopted him. A lawyer, Lawson trained Bassett in that profession and left him a huge Maryland estate, known as Bohemia Manor. Bassett developed his law practice in Delaware, where he commanded a militia unit and was elected to the state legislature. Bassett was described as "heavy-built" (Pattison 1900, 19). He married Ann (Nancy) Ennals (1752–1784), by whom he had two surviving daughters; after her death, he married Betsy Garnett (1760–1819) in 1795. He also took James Bayard under his wing. Bayard married one of Bassett's daughters and joined Bassett in the high ranks of Delaware politics.

Bassett founded something of a Delaware political dynasty. He would become a U.S. senator from Delaware, as would Bayard, two of Bassett's grandsons, one of his great-grandsons, and one of his great-great-grandsons. Bassett was one of the more evangelically minded delegates at the Constitutional Convention. He was a friend of Francis Asbury, the first U.S. Methodist bishop, served for a time as a Methodist lay minister, and helped construct a Methodist church in Dover. He allowed his property to be used for huge religious camp meetings. In the late nineteenth century, a Methodist church in Philadelphia led by Dr. Charles W. Buoy chose Bassett as one of four men that it honored by carving their busts on Corinthian columns—the other three were Bishop Thomas Coke of England, Bishop Francis Asbury of

America, and Captain Thomas Webb, a Revolutionary War hero who represented the positive effects of Methodism in the army (Pattison 1900, 3–4).

Bassett served as a delegate to Maryland's constitutional convention, as a member of the state legislature, as a member of the Maryland Council of Safety, and as a delegate to the Annapolis Convention before being selected for the U.S. Constitutional Convention. In 1787, Bassett freed his slaves and introduced legislation in his state making it easier for others to do so.

At the Convention

Bassett began attending the Constitutional Convention as a representative from Delaware on May 25, and he signed the Constitution on September 17. Although he attended almost every session, he was not recorded as making a single speech or motion. Records indicate that he voted on June 8 to oppose the proposed congressional veto of state laws, but they are otherwise silent as to Bassett's positions.

He did not serve on any committees at the convention. His political experience, both before and after the convention, suggests that he was a man of great ability. It is unclear whether he was largely silent because his state was small, because he was intimidated by the reputations of other delegates, because he was preoccupied with other matters, or because he was in general agreement with the direction that the convention took, but it seems a shame that he did not participate further.

Life after the Convention

In the U.S. Senate, Bassett helped draft the Judiciary Act of 1789, voted to move the nation's capital to the District of Columbia, and favored vesting the president with power to remove non-judicial officials that he had appointed. He left his service in the Senate in 1793 to become chief justice of the Delaware Court of Common Pleas. After then serving as Delaware's governor, and as a presidential elector for John Adams, Adams appointed Bassett as a federal appellate judge, a position later abolished by the incoming Democratic-Republicans. Bassett was the only such judge to author a public protest in which he referred to the Constitution as "that great and irrepealable *law of the people*" (Bassett 2010, 5). Bassett went on to outline a case for judicial review (the ability of courts to declare laws to be unconstitutional) that is quite similar to the arguments that Chief Justice John Marshall would articulate in his famous decision the next year in *Marbury v. Madison*. Bassett noted that "it is the right, and indeed, the highest duty of the judges, if convinced that a law of congress is opposed to the law of the people, as enacted in the constitution, to pronounce it, for that reason, a nullity and void" (Bassett 2010, 34). Bassett died on August 15, 1815 and was buried in the Wilmington and Brandywine Cemetery.

Further Reading

Bassett, Richard. 2010. *The Protest of the Hon. Richard Bassett*. Belmont, CA: Gale. Reprint of 1802 original.

Monroe, John A. 1945. "The Philadelawareans: A Study in the Relations between Philadelphia and Delaware in the Late Eighteenth Century." *Pennsylvania Magazine of History and Biography* 69 (April): 128–49.

Pattison, Robert E. 1900. "The Life and Character of Richard Bassett." *Papers of the Historical Society of Delaware* 29: 3–19.

Saladino, Gaspare J. 1999. "Bassett, Richard." In *American National Biography*, edited by John A. Garraty and Mark C. Carnes, 2: 43–44. New York: Oxford University Press.

Whitney, David. 1974. *Founders of Freedom in America: Lives of the Men Who Signed the Constitution of the United States and So Helped to Establish the United States of America*. Chicago: J. G. Ferguson Publishing Company.

GUNNING BEDFORD JR. (1747–1812)
DELAWARE

Gunning Bedford Jr. was born in 1747 to the family of a Philadelphia architect who had served in the French and Indian War. Bedford attended the Philadelphia Academy and College of New Jersey (today's Princeton) and roomed with James Madison. After graduation he studied law under Joseph Reed, moved to Delaware, and joined the bar. He married Jane (Jenny) Ballareau Parker (1746–1831) in late 1772 or early 1773. Bedford served as Delaware's attorney general from 1784 to 1789 and was a delegate to the Continental Congress, where his attendance was sporadic. Delaware chose Bedford as a delegate to the Annapolis Convention, but he did not attend. Biographical information about Bedford can be confusing because he had an older cousin by the same name (generally, however, designated as Jr.) who was also active in governmental affairs, serving as a state governor and, like his cousin, as a representative from Delaware to the Continental Congress. Bedford has been described as "a handsome man, and a very fluent and agreeable speaker" ("Notice" 1870, 510). He was known for wearing knee britches, buckled shoes, and a queue with powdered hair (McKenney 2013, 9).

At the Convention

Bedford began attending the convention on May 28. He believed that the situation of the Union called for vesting increased powers in Congress. He is best known, however, for his passionate, arguably intemperate, defense of the small states and their equal representation in Congress and for suggesting that such states might seek foreign alliances if they were not treated fairly by the large states.

Congress

During discussion of the presidential veto, Bedford must have shocked some of his fellow delegates on June 4 when he said that he was opposed "to every check on the Legislative, including the Council of Revision first proposed" (Farrand 1966, 1:100). He continued:

> It would be sufficient to mark out in the Constitution the boundaries to the Legislative Authority, which would give all the requisite security to the rights of the other departments. (1:100–1)

He did observe that the fact that the Congress was divided into two houses would itself provide some security (1:101).

On July 17, Bedford supported a resolution that would have allowed Congress "to legislate in all cases for the general interests of the Union, and also in those to which the States are separately incompetent" (1:26). Virginia's Edmund Randolph almost immediately objected that this power would be so broad that it would enable Congress to meddle in the police powers of the states, but Bedford argued that his resolution was not in fact very different from the one already under discussion (2:27).

On September 14, Bedford opposed a constitutional provision that would have expressed concern over the presence of standing armies in time of peace. He presumably agreed with Pennsylvania's Gouverneur Morris in believing that this would set "a dishonorable mark of distinction on the military class of Citizens" (2:617).

Presidency

Bedford was less firmly disposed to a strong presidency than to a strong Congress. When, on June 1, the delegates were discussing a seven-year term for the president, Bedford expressed strong opposition. He believed that this would be too long for someone who was discovered not to have the necessary abilities or for someone who once had them but lost them while in office, presumably because of physical or mental infirmity. He observed that impeachment would not be a solution since it "would reach misfeasance only, not incapacity" (1:69). His own solution was to propose a three-year term, with presidents being ineligible after three terms (1:69). The following day, Bedford seconded a motion by fellow delegate John Dickinson that would make the president removable by Congress at the request of a majority of the state legislatures (1:85).

Judiciary

Bedford, who later served as a federal judge, favored selection of judges by the Senate rather than by the president. He feared that presidents would use such a power to curry favor with the larger states by appointing their citizens. Consistent with concerns expressed below, Bedford further indicated that "The responsibility of the Executive so much talked of was chimerical. He could not be punished for mistakes" (2:43).

Federalism

Although Bedford had expressed willingness to give broad powers to Congress, he did not think that this power should include a negative over state laws. On June 8, Bedford raised the possibility that this power could be used to injure the small states. He figured that, under the Virginia Plan then being discussed, Delaware would have about one-ninetieth of the power in Congress whereas Pennsylvania and Virginia would together have almost one-third of the power (1:167; also see Hutson 1987b, 61–62). He said that these ratios demonstrated "the impossibility of adopting such a system as that on the table, or any other founded on a change in the principle of representation" (1:167). Having addressed the issue of fairness, Bedford went on to raise practical questions:

> How can it be thought that the proposed negative can be exercised? Are the laws of the States to be suspended in the most urgent cases until they can be sent seven or eight hundred miles, and undergo the deliberations of a body who may be incapable of Judging of them? Is the National Legislature too to sit continually in order to revise the laws of the States? (1:168)

Bedford expanded on his views in a speech on June 30, which, although criticized by fellow delegates as one of the most inflammatory at the convention, may have only verbalized what other delegates were thinking. At a time when what is today described as a federal government had not yet been invented, Bedford began by incorrectly prophesying that "there was no middle way between a perfect consolidation and a mere confederacy of the States. The first is out of the question, and in the latter they must continue if not perfectly, yet equally sovereign" (1:490). Bedford did not believe that states could be separated from their interests, and he cut through what he considered to be the pretensions of states present to higher ideals. Identifying Georgia, South Carolina, North Carolina, Virginia, Maryland, Pennsylvania, and Massachusetts (most of which had supported the Virginia Plan), Bedford argued that each had pursued either its present interest, or its expectation of future interests based on population growth. He further argued that Great Britain had not embodied equal representation, and it would be unwise to hold the United States to a higher standard. Interestingly, Robert Yates's notes, which contain a fuller account of this speech than Madison's, quote Bedford as saying, "*I do not, gentlemen, trust you.* If you possess the power, the abuse of it could not be checked; and what then would prevent you from exercising it to our destruction?" (1:500).

Arguing that "We must like Solon [an ancient Greek lawgiver] make such a Governt. as the people will approve," Bedford did not think the smaller states would submit to "the proposed degradation of them" (1:491). It was not that the people of the small states were unwilling to accept an increase in congressional powers but simply that they were unwilling to part with their own equality. Responding to delegates who had argued that this might be "the last moment for a fair trial in favor of a good Governmt," he said "The Large States dare not dissolve the confederation" (1:492). He continued with language that would stir apprehension in his fellow delegates: "If they do the small ones will find some foreign ally of more honor and good faith, who will take them by the hand and do them justice" (1:492).

Almost as soon as he spoken the words, he said that they were not intended "to intimidate or alarm" (1:492). When Rufus King of Massachusetts objected to the "intemperance" of Bedford's remarks, Bedford attributed them to "passion" and indicated that he would not personally "court relief from a foreign power" (1:493).

Bedford was still trying to defend his remarks on July 5. This time he attributed his remarks to "the habits of his profession in which warmth was natural & sometimes necessary" (1:531). He argued that he had not been recommending that the small states seek outside intervention but only pointing to the fact that "no man can foresee to what extremities the small States may be driven by oppression" (1:531). Pointing to discussion of the executive veto, Bedford argued that it was just as important that the states be protected as that the president should be. Agreeing that the situation called for something to be done, Bedford said:

> It will be better that a defective plan should be adopted, than that none should be recommended. He saw no reason why defects might not be supplied by meetings 10, 15, or 20 years hence. (1:532)

Bedford, who served on the 11-man committee appointed on July 2 that formulated the Connecticut Compromise, apparently agreed to it, but as late as September 15, he was still trying to get an increase in the number of representatives allocated to his state and to Rhode Island (2:624). Bedford was among the delegates who signed the Constitution on September 17.

Life after the Convention

Bedford returned to Delaware after signing the Constitution to urge its ratification. He served as a presidential elector for George Washington in 1789 and 1793. Washington subsequently appointed him as the first U.S. district judge for Delaware, a capacity in which he served from 1789 until his death in 1812 in Wilmington where he was buried at the First Presbyterian Church; he was later reinterred on the ground of the Delaware Masonic Home in 1921. Prominent in the Masons, Bedford was president of the Wilmington Academy Board of Trustees and a member of the Delaware Society for Promoting the Abolition of Slavery. A monument placed over his grave by his daughter Henrietta in 1858 states, "His form was goodly, his temper amiable, his manners winning, and his discharge of private duties exemplary" ("Notice," 511). Lombardy Hall in Wilmington, Delaware, the home that Bedford purchased in 1785, was declared a National Historic Landmark in 1975 but remains in private hands.

Further Reading

Farrand, Max, ed. *The Records of the Federal Convention of 1787.* 4 vols. New Haven, CT: Yale University Press.

Green, Charles E. 1976. "Bedford Was Delaware's Strong Voice at the Constitutional Convention." *The Northern Light: A Window for Freemasonry* 7 (April): 14–15.

Hutson, James H. ed. 1987. *Supplement to Max Farrand's The Records of the Federal Convention of 1787.* New Haven, CT: Yale University Press.

McKenney, Janice E. 2013. *Women of the Constitution: Wives of the Signers.* Lanham, MD: Scarecrow Press.

"Notice of Gunning Bedford," 1870. In William Thompson Read, *Life and Correspondence of George Read.* Philadelphia: J. B. Lippincott & Co.

Whitney, David C. 1974. *Founders of Freedom in America: Lives of the Men Who Signed the Constitution of the United States and So Helped To Establish The United States of America.* Chicago: J. G. Ferguson Publishing Company.

JOHN BLAIR JR. (1732–1800)
VIRGINIA

Although Virginia had sent seven delegates to the Constitutional Convention, two returned home before the convention ended and two refused to sign, leaving only three state delegates who did so. Of these three, only James Madison spoke extensively at the convention. By contrast, George Washington was recorded as delivering only two speeches, and John Blair Jr. is not recorded as having spoken once. Given Blair's previous political experience, it appears as though he might have had something substantial to say, especially regarding the organization of the judicial branch of the national government.

Born in Williamsburg, Virginia in 1732 to a wealthy family, Blair's father, after whom he was named, was a merchant who also participated in Virginia politics. He had served as interim governor and in other positions that his son would later occupy. Not coincidentally, he also owned the Raleigh Tavern in Williamsburg, a gathering place for many of the early revolutionaries.

Blair attended the College of William and Mary before studying law at the Middle Temple of London and returning to Virginia with a new wife, Jean Blair (1736–1792), whom he married in Edinburgh and with whom he fathered two children. In Virginia he developed a profitable law practice. He has been described as "tall, with a generous forehead, blue eyes, red hair, and a gentle disposition" (Holt 1998, 156). He was a delegate from Williamsburg to the Virginia House of Burgesses when it voted for independence, and he served to draw up the new state constitution and draft its Declaration of Rights. In 1778, he was appointed to the General Court of Virginia. After becoming its chief justice, he became a judge of the state's high court of chancery and of its court of appeals, where he participated in the ruling for *The Commonwealth of Virginia v. Caton et. al.* (1782), asserting the court's right to strike down legislation that it considered to be unconstitutional. From his position on the judiciary, Blair was selected to serve at the Constitutional Convention.

At the Convention

About all is known about Blair's contributions to the Constitution is that he signed the document and spoke in its favor at the Virginia state ratifying convention. Madison's notes on the votes of various Virginia delegates further record that Blair, like Virginia's Governor Edmund Randolph, opposed the establishment of a unitary executive (Farrand 1966, 1:97), favored a congressional veto of state laws (1:168), voted for a series of agreements about the president on July 26 (2:121), opposed the requirement that money bills originate in the House of Representatives (2:280), voted for requiring a two-thirds majority in Congress to enact export taxes rather than banning them altogether (2:363), and opposed reducing the majority in Congress needed to override a presidential veto from three-fourths to two-thirds (2:587). He did not serve on any of the convention's committees.

Life after the Convention

After the convention Blair accompanied George Washington back to Virginia, during which both escaped unharmed when one of the horses pulling their carriage fell through a bridge. As noted above, Blair supported the Constitution as a delegate to the state's ratifying convention, but, again, did not give any speeches on its behalf. Washington appointed Blair as one of the original associate justices of the U.S. Supreme Court. He served in this position from 1789 to 1796. He earned a reputation as "A Safe and Conscientious Judge" (Holt 1998, 155, quoting a book review by Earl Gregg Swem), joining the majority in deciding that a state could be sued without its consent in the case of *Chisholm v. Georgia*, 2 U.S. 419 (1793), which was later overturned by the Eleventh Amendment. He resigned because of ill health. Blair died in the town of his birth in 1800 and is buried outside the Bruton Parish Church in that city. The John Blair House and Kitchen is today a private residence in Colonial Williamsburg.

Further Reading

Cushman, Clare, ed. 1995. *The Supreme Court Justices, Illustrated Biographies, 1789–1995*. Washington, DC: Congressional Quarterly.

Farrand, Max, ed. 1966. *The Records of the Federal Convention of 1787*. 4 vols. New Haven, CT: Yale University Press.

Holt, Wythe. 1998. "John Blair, 'A Safe and Conscientious Judge.'" In *Seriatim: The Supreme Court before John Marshall*, edited by Scott Douglas Gerber, 155–97. New York: New York University Press.

Kiernan, Denise, and Joseph D'Agnese. 2012. *Signing Their Rights Away*. Philadelphia: Quirk Books.

WILLIAM BLOUNT (1749–1800)
NORTH CAROLINA

Although it is common to idolize the Founding Fathers, a book on them observed that William Blount "was more interested in what his country could do for him than in what he could do for his country" (Whitney 1974, 55). Born on March 26, 1749, to a wealthy landholding family in Bertie County, North Carolina, Blount gained an insatiable appetite for more land, wealth, and power. During the Revolutionary War he served as paymaster of Continental troops, married Mary (Mosley) Grainger (1761–1802), with whom he would have six children, and moved into a home named Piney Grove in Martinsborough. Elected in the early 1780s to the North Carolina legislature, and to the Continental Congress, Blount seems not to have taken his legislative responsibilities altogether seriously but often found ways to use his position to press for financial advantages.

At the Convention

Blount was not seated at the Constitutional Convention until June 20, having been delayed by problems with "blind piles," or hemorrhoids, an ailment he referred to as "undoubtedly the most painful teasing Complaint that I have ever experienced" (Hutson 1987, 14). Once at the convention, William Blount is not recorded as participating in a single discussion until it came time to sign the document. Then relying on a somewhat legalistic distinction, he indicated that while he had "declared that he would not sign so as to pledge himself in support of the plan," he was willing to sign, without committing himself, to "attest the fact that the plan was the unanimous act of the States in Convention" (Farrand 1966, 2:646).

Blount's fullest exposition of his thoughts on the convention was contained in a letter of July 19 that probably violated the convention's rule of secrecy. Posted from New York, indicating that Blount had returned to Congress where he was fighting for rights to navigate the Mississippi River, Blount referred to H. W. [Hugh Williamson] as the head of the North Carolina delegation. He reported that North Carolina was following the lead of Virginia, primary leadership of which he attributed to James Madison. Further reporting that the convention had settled on the main outlines of a new system, he reported that, "I must confess not withstanding all I heard in favour of this System I am not in sentiment with my Colleagues for as I have before said I still think we shall ultimately end not many Years just be separate and distinct Governments perfectly independent of each other." Blount further noted that "The little States were much opposed to the Politicks of the larger they insisted that each State ought to have an equal vote as in the present Confederation" (Hutson 1987, 175). Blount returned to the convention on August 7 and signed the document on September 17.

Life after the Convention

Blount supported ratification of the new Constitution in North Carolina where he served as a delegate to the second convention in Fayetteville that ratified the document. George Washington appointed Blount to be governor and superintendent of Indian Affairs for territories south of the Ohio River; he built a house in Knoxville, Tennessee, where he had decided to place the territory's new capital. In this position, he engaged in extensive land speculation and in attempts to take land from the Indians. He eventually turned against the Federalist administration when it failed to support him in this endeavor.

Blount built an impressive house in Knoxville and helped organize the state of Tennessee, which had previously been part of North Carolina. He served as president of the Tennessee constitutional convention in 1796. Afterward elected as one of the state's two U.S. senators, he was the first and only such senator ever to be impeached after he was discovered to have conspired with Aaron Burr to stir up an Indian war against Spain. Although expelled from the Senate, he was not convicted on impeachment charges after a consensus developed that such a mechanism was not designed to apply to members of Congress.

Still popular in the state he had helped to found, Blount resisted appeals to return to the nation's capital for his impeachment trial. He was, indeed, elected speaker of the Tennessee Senate. Blount died of a fever on March 21, 1800 and was buried at the cemetery of Knoxville's First Presbyterian Church. The house where he lived in Knoxville is open to the public. A younger brother, Thomas (1759–1812), served both in the North Carolina legislature and in the U.S. House of Representatives; another brother, John Gray (1752–1833), was an influential merchant and land speculator. William Blount's son, William Grainger Blount (1784–1827), was a Tennessee representative and its secretary of state and a delegate to the U.S. House of Representatives.

Further Reading

Farrand, Max, ed. 1966. *The Records of the Federal Convention of 1787.* 4 vols. New Haven, CT: Yale University Press.

Hutson, James H., ed. 1987. *Supplement to Max Farrand's The Records of the Federal Convention of 1787.* New Haven, CT: Yale University Press.

Masterson, William H. 1954. *William Blount.* Baton Rouge: Louisiana State University Press.

Melton, Buckner F. Jr. 1998. *The First Impeachment: The Constitution's Framers and the Case of Senator William Blount.* Macon, GA: Mercer University Press.

Mitchell, Memory F. 1964. *North Carolina's Signers: Brief Sketches of the Men Who Signed the Declaration of Independence and the Constitution.* Raleigh: Division of Archives and History, North Carolina Department of Cultural Resources.

Morton, Joseph C. 2006. *Shapers of the Great Debate at the Constitutional Convention of 1787: A Biographical Dictionary.* Westport, CT: Greenwood Press.

Whitney, David D. 1974. *Founders of Freedom in America: Lives of The Men Who Signed the Constitution of the United States and So Helped To Establish The United States of America.* Chicago: J. G. Ferguson Publishing Company.

DAVID BREARLY (1754–1790)
NEW JERSEY

Born to a farm family on June 11, in 1745 in Spring Grove, New Jersey, David Brearly (sometimes spelled Brearley) studied law and became an ardent patriot. He married relatively early, and he and his wife Elizabeth Mullen (b. 1741) had four children before her death in 1777. He later had three additional children by Elizabeth (Betsy) Higbee (1751–1832), whom he married in 1783. Brearly served during the Revolutionary War as a captain and a lieutenant colonel before being appointed as chief justice of New Jersey. In this position, he issued a decision in the case of *Holmes v. Walton* (1780), which helped establish the right of his court to strike down unconstitutional legislation. Brearly was a grand master of the Masons in New Jersey and a member of the Society of the Cincinnati (a group of Revolutionary War veterans). In 1782, he served as one of seven commissioners who helped settle a dispute between Pennsylvania and Connecticut over title to the Wyoming Valley in Pennsylvania, and in 1785 he helped compile the prayer book of the U.S. Episcopal Church.

At the Convention

Brearly was the first delegate to be selected to attend the Constitutional Convention. He was present on May 25 for the convention's opening day of business in Philadelphia, and signed the document on September 17. The first record of Brearly's participation in convention debates was on June 9, when he seconded a motion by fellow New Jersey delegate, William Paterson, for a reconsideration of the Virginia Plan's proposal for apportioning suffrage in both houses of Congress according to population. Like Paterson, Brearly clearly supported the desire of the small states for equal representation. In his longest speech at the convention, Brearly observed that this matter had already once been settled in creating the Articles of Confederation and argued that equal representation was essential to the preservation of the small states. He estimated that if representation were to be apportioned according to population, Virginia would have sixteen votes to Georgia's one. He further believed that the states of Virginia, Pennsylvania, and Massachusetts "will carry every thing before them" (Farrand 1966, 1:177). He observed that within his home state of New Jersey, large counties overwhelmed smaller ones when they were combined together.

Admitting that it did not seem fair to give the smallest states equal representation with the largest, Brearly made a radical proposal. He suggested spreading out a U.S. map and "that all the existing boundaries be erased, and that a new partition of the whole be made into 13 equal parts" (1:177). Neither Brearly nor the convention appears to have pursued this idea, which would only have worked, and then only temporarily, if population were spread out equally, and it is probable that Brearly made the suggestion not so much because he favored it but because he hoped thereby to get the attention of the delegates from the larger states. In any event, Brearly continued to focus on a single theme at the convention, namely the necessity of providing small states adequate representation so that they could protect their interests in the new government.

The convention did not resolve the issue of state representation until it adopted the Great Compromise on July 16. In the meantime, Rhode Island, the smallest state, had refused to send delegates, and those from New Hampshire had not arrived. On June 30, Brearly accordingly moved that the president should write to the New Hampshire governor informing him "that the business depending before the convention was of such a nature as to require the immediate attendance of the deputies of that State" (1:481). The Convention rejected the request by a vote of five to two. Madison observed that "it was well understood that the object was to add N. Hamshire to the no. of States opposed to the doctrine of proportional representation, which it was presumed from her relative size she must be adverse to" (1:481).

Brearly is next recorded as speaking on August 24. Consistent with his earlier concerns about the small states, Brearly opposed the idea of electing the president by a "joint" ballot by both houses of Congress (2:402). He undoubtedly feared that, in such joint ballots, the more populous states would swallow up the votes of the smaller states. When the convention voted to accept such a joint ballot, Brearly seconded a motion by New Jersey's Jonathan Dayton to grant each state a single vote (2:403).

Brearly served on two committees at the Constitutional Convention— the 11-man committee to reconsider proportional representation that was created on July 9, and the Committee on Postponed Matters created on August 31. He chaired the latter committee, which proposed on September 1: "The members of each House shall be ineligible to any civil office under the authority of the U.S. during the time for which they shall respectively be elected, and no person holding an office under the U.S. shall be a member of either House during his continuance in office" (2:484).

On September 15, Brearly further seconded a motion introduced by Connecticut's Roger Sherman that would have eliminated the proposed constitutional amending process (2:630). Sherman and Brearly appear to have been reacting, however, to the convention's failure, to that point, to guarantee the provision for equal state suffrage within the Senate against further amendment. Although the motion to strike the amending process failed, it did result in a provision entrenching equal state representation in the Senate against such amendment (2:631).

Life after the Convention

Brearly chaired the New Jersey convention that ratified the Constitution. He also served as a presidential elector for George Washington, who appointed him as a federal district judge of New Jersey. Brearly died at the age of 45 on August 16, in 1790 and was interred at St. Michael's Episcopal Church Cemetery in Trenton.

Further Reading

Farrand, Max, ed. 1966. *The Records of the Federal Convention of 1787*. 4 vols. New Haven, CT: Yale University Press.

Ward, Harry M. 1999. "Brearly, David." *American National Biography* Online. http://www.anb.org/articles/02/02–00041.-article.html. Accessed 6/21/2012.

Whitney, David. 1974. *Founders of Freedom in America: Lives of the Men Who Signed the Constitution of the United States and So Helped to Establish the United States of America*. Chicago: J. G. Ferguson Publishing Company.

JACOB BROOM (1752–1810)
DELAWARE

Born in Wilmington, Delaware in 1752 to a family that had acquired substantial parcels of land (Broom's father had started as a blacksmith), Broom was educated at the Wilmington Academy, after which he became a surveyor. He and his wife Rachel Pierce (1752–1823) had three sons, two of whom were later elected to Congress, and five daughters. Prior to serving at the Constitutional Convention, Broom served as a burgess of the city of Wilmington for almost ten years and as a member of the Delaware legislature for two years. In 1782, Broom and a colleague had drawn up an address to Congress requesting that they consider Wilmington as the nation's permanent capital. The next year Broom composed an address to George Washington when he passed through Wilmington after resigning his commission in the army. Broom had been appointed to, but had not attended, the Annapolis Convention, which issued the call for the Constitutional Convention. A biographer describes Boom's demeanor as "quite, meditative, [and] judicial" (Campbell 1909, 18).

At the Convention

Broom was present for the opening day of the convention on May 25, 1787, but he remained silent during the first month of business. Thereafter, he did not speak extensively. Indeed, he is more noted for seconding the proposals of others than for making his own or giving long speeches. However, he seems to have emerged as an individual willing to invest substantial power in the new government as long as the interests of Delaware and other small states were accommodated.

Congress

On June 26, Broom supported a motion to increase the term of senators from six years to nine. He said that he favored service "during good behavior" but thought that nine years was the most he might realistically request. He observed that this number, like the number six, would allow for one-third of the members to rotate out in each election (Farrand 1966, 1:426).

On July 10, Broom agreed to setting the number of members of the U.S. House of Representatives at 65, with Delaware having a single vote. He did so, however, with the understanding that his state should continue to have equal representation in the Senate (2:570).

On August 14, Broom seconded a motion by Pennsylvania's Gouverneur Morris allowing members of Congress to vacate their seats in order to accept appointments in the army or navy (2:290). On that same day, he supported a motion allowing members of Congress to set their own salaries. He observed, "The State Legislatures had this power, and no complaint had been made of it" (2:291). He also favored a motion by which members of both congressional houses would be paid the same (2:293).

On August 20, Broom seconded a motion by Rufus King of Massachusetts granting the Senate the "sole" power to declare punishments for treason (2:348). Three days later, he seconded a far more important motion by South Carolina's Charles Pinckney that would have granted the power to two-thirds of the members of both houses of Congress to invalidate acts of state legislation that they thought conflicted "with the General interest and harmony of the Union" (2:390). On August 25, however, Broom supported a motion by Pennsylvania's Gouverneur Morris to strike out as unnecessary a provision granting the president the right to correspond with state governors, implying that without such a provision, the president would not have this power (2:419).

Presidency

On July 17, Broom expressed the opinion that a presidential term of seven years was too long. He linked this position to the convention's decision to make the president re-eligible for election. Otherwise, he indicated that he would have supported a longer term (2:33). Indeed, shortly thereafter, he supported a motion by Virginia's James McClurg to allow the president to serve "during good behavior" (2:33). Two days later, Broom seconded a motion providing for selecting the president by state legislatures, allowing states to choose one to three electors depending on their size (2:57). He later moved to postpone a somewhat different allocation of electors proposed by Elbridge Gerry of Massachusetts (2:63–64; see also 2:103).

Continuation of the Convention

On July 16, the day on which the convention agreed to the Connecticut Compromise, after Virginia's Edmund Randolph had suggested an adjournment, New Jersey's William Paterson had suggested that the secrecy rule should be suspended and that the delegates should adjourn and go home to receive instructions from their constituents. Broom was opposed to such a "sine die" adjournment. He thought this would be "fatal" to the convention's work and said that "Something must be done by the convention tho' it should be by a bare majority" (2:19).

Signing the Constitution

Broom is the only one of the signers of the Constitution for whom no portrait has been located. In a 1940 painting, Howard Chandler Christy hides his face behind that of John Dickinson. In the painting by Louis Glanzman, which was made in 1987 and displayed in the room at Independence Hall where visitors gather for orientation prior to going into the court room and the East Room, Broom is accordingly pictured as signing the Document with his back to the viewers.

Life after the Convention

After signing the Constitution, Broom returned to Delaware and devoted himself chiefly to business affairs. He built a number of mills, was Wilmington's first postmaster, served as director of the Delaware Bank, and helped establish the Chesapeake & Delaware Canal. He died in Philadelphia on April 25, 1810, bequeathing some of his considerable wealth to the Female Benevolent Society and to a Wilmington group formed to educate African American children. He is buried in the cemetery of Philadelphia's Christ Church. A son, James Madison Broom, served in Congress from 1804 to 1807, and a grandson, Jacob, ran for president in 1852 as a member of the National American Party.

Further Reading

Campbell, William W. 1909. "Life and Character of Jacob Broom." *Papers of the Historical Society of Delaware*. Vol. 51. Wilmington: The Historical Society of Delaware.

Farrand, Max, ed. 1966. *The Records of the Federal Convention of 1787*. 4 vols. New Haven, CT: Yale University Press.

Kiernan, Denise, and Joseph D'Agnese. 2011. *Signing Their Rights Away: The Fame and Misfortune of the Men Who Signed the United States Constitution*. Philadelphia: Quirk Books.

Whitney, David. 1974. *Founders of Freedom in America: Lives of the Men Who Signed the Constitution of the United States and So Helped to Establish the United States of America*. Chicago: J. G. Ferguson Publishing Company.

Pierce Butler (1744–1822)
South Carolina

Pierce Butler was born to the family of an English baronet in County Carlow, Ireland on July 11, 1744. He came to North America and immigrated to South Carolina to fight against the French and Indians with a commission

as a major in the English army that his family had purchased for him when he was eleven. He sold this commission in 1763 after marrying Mary (Polly) Middleton (1750–1790), the daughter of a wealthy plantation owner, and was soon supporting the patriot cause. He was chosen as a state legislator in 1778 and served there for about a decade, also being appointed the next year as the state's adjutant general. The British burned his house and confiscated many of his slaves, but he evaded capture during the Revolutionary War and spent the last year of the war in North Carolina. Unlike the other delegates from South Carolina, he had no formal legal training.

At the Convention

Butler was present for the first day of convention business on May 25, 1787, having arrived with General Charles Cotesworth Pinckney on a ship the previous day. On May 28 Butler proposed that the convention provide against having its business interrupted by preventing the absence of members and by presenting "licentious publications of their proceedings" (Farrand 1966, 1:13). The convention did not, and probably could not, have adopted the first of these suggestions but it did take secrecy very seriously.

Congress

Representation. On June 6, Butler indicated that he favored apportionment in the House of Representatives on the basis of wealth (a euphemism for slaves) as well as population, and that if his plan were adopted, he was even willing to consider abolishing the state legislatures (1:144). The next day, he was unwilling to give his view on the size of the Senate until he knew "the ratio of representation" (1:151). On June 25, Butler further indicated that it would be better to settle on how representation would be allocated in the Senate before deciding on what powers to give that body (1:407; also see 2:290).

On June 11, Butler joined fellow South Carolinian John Rutledge in proposing that suffrage in the House of Representatives should be apportioned according to states' tax contributions. He argued that "money was power; and that the States ought to have weight in the Govt.—in proportion to their wealth" (1:196).

In time, the issue of House and Senate apportionment was tied in part to whether the Senate would be able to originate money bills. On June 13, Butler indicated that he saw no reason for limiting the origination of money bills to the House of Representatives. At a time when delegates were seeking to justify this limitation on the basis of British practice, Butler observed, "We were always following the British Constitution when the reason of it did not apply." He further observed:

> There was no analogy between the Ho[use] of Lords and the body proposed to be established. If the Senate should be degraded by any such discriminations, the best men would be apt to decline serving in it in favor of the other branch. And it will lead the latter into the practice of tacking other clauses to money bills. (1:233)

On July 5, Butler reiterated his view that the privilege of originating money bills was inconsequential. At this time he also indicated that he thought that states should be represented in the Senate according to their property (1:529). It is not clear that Butler changed his mind on the wisdom of the provision related to the introduction of money bills, but on August 8, he indicated that he favored sticking with the existing compromise (2:224).

When the convention appointed a committee on July 6 to examine a proposal made by an earlier committee to grant states one representative for every 40,000 inhabitants, Butler indicated that he favored such reexamination. He continued to believe that population was an inadequate basis of representation. He cited the "changeableness" of this number as one reason, but he emphasized the role of government in supporting property, contending "that property was the only just measure of representation. This was the great object of Governt: the great cause of war, the great means of carrying it on" (1:542). In this same speech, Butler indicated that he thought it was necessary to provide some "balance" between the existing states and any new western states that might be admitted (1:542). He reiterated his view that property should be factored into representation on July 9 (1:562).

When a second committee appointed to deal with the subject of the size of representation proposed that it should consist of a House of Representatives consisting of 65 members, it initially apportioned five such representatives to Butler's South Carolina. Butler was among those who attempted to get adjustments for their own states, unsuccessfully proposing that his state should be granted six representatives instead (1:568). He may not have been particularly bothered by his loss on this issue, as he later expressed the firm conviction that the movement of population growth in the nation was toward the South and West (1:605).

Although Butler disfavored apportioning Congress on the basis of population, he proposed on July 11 that the Three-fifths Clause should be struck out in favor of a provision that would count blacks equally with whites (1:580). Although such a formula would have obvious benefits for his state, like others Butler viewed counting blacks as a way of providing the representation for wealth that the convention had otherwise rejected (1:580). He thus observed:

> The labour of a slave in S. Carola. was as productive & valuable as that of a freeman in Massts., that as wealth was the great means of defence and utility to the Nation they were equally valuable to it with freemen; and that consequently an equal representation ought to be allowed for them in a Government which was instituted principally for the protection of property, and was itself to be supported by property. (1:581; also see 1:592)

Selection and Pay. On May 31, Butler said that he thought did not think that it would be practical for the people to elect members of the U.S. House of Representatives (1:50); as under the Articles of Confederation, he thought state legislatures were "better calculated to make choice of such (1:58). Along with fellow South Carolinian John Rutledge, Butler proposed that members of the Senate should receive no compensation (1:219), a motion undoubtedly prompted by the hope that the Senate would thereby become a more aristocratic body. When he later served as a U.S. senator, Butler proposed that senators should be paid eight dollars a day (it set that of representatives at six and that of senators at seven), arguing that "a member of the Senate should not only have a handsome income, but should spend it all" (Whitney 1974, 69).

Butler appears to have supported the idea that states should pay members of Congress (1:374, where he seemed to push for a reconsideration after the convention had voted otherwise). He thought this was particularly important in the case of senators, whose longer tenure and residence at the national capital might cause them to "lose sight of their Constituents unless dependent on them for their support" (2:290).

Butler opposed a motion by Pennsylvania's Gouverneur Morris on August 7 that would have limited the right to vote for members of Congress to freeholders. Butler observed that "There is no right of which the people are more jealous than that of suffrage" (2:202). He further associated the imposition of such qualifications with the establishment of aristocracy (2:202).

Eligibility for Other Offices. Butler favored a measure restricting members of Congress from accepting offices during their term or for a year afterwards. He viewed this as a way of preventing "corruption," which he believed had helped ruin the British government (1:376). He thought a motion by Virginia's James Madison limiting this restriction to offices created or augmented during the terms of a member was too weak and could be too easily evaded (1:386). He did not fear the consequences of disablement, believing that "Characters fit for office Wd. never be unknown" (1:389). On June 26, however, Butler favored striking a prohibition on the eligibility of members of the Senate to state offices (1:428).

Qualifications of Members. On August 8, after two delegates had proposed a minimal residency requirement of one year for members of the House of Representatives, Butler joined John Rutledge in proposing that this be raised to three years (2:218). The next day, Butler indicated that he did not favor allowing individuals to serve in Congress unless they had long resided in the country. This argument must have been especially effective coming from someone who was himself an immigrant. He observed that immigrants "bring with them, not only attachments to other Countries; but ideas of Govt. so distinct from ours that in every point of view they are dangerous." He further said that had he been admitted into government shortly after coming to the United States, "his foreign habits opinions & attachments would have rendered him an improper agent in public affairs" (2:236). Again on August 13, Butler indicated that he "was strenuous agst. admitting foreigners into our public Councils" (2:269).

Powers. On May 30, Butler introduced a motion, seconded by Virginia's Edmund Randolph, postponing a resolution that Randolph had introduced and substituting language providing "that a national government ought to be established consisting of a supreme legislative, judiciary and executive" (1:30). The convention adopted this substitute motion, which took it far beyond its charge of revising, correcting, and enlarging the existing Articles of Confederation. Butler indicated that same day that he had been reluctant to grant further powers to a congress constructed like that under the Articles of Confederation, but that "the proposed distribution of the powers into different bodies changed the case, and would induce him to go great lengths" (1:34). Apparently, Butler had previously asked Randolph to show how a strengthened national government was needed to preserve the states (1:41). On June 1, Butler opposed a provision granting Congress the power to invalidate state laws, believing that it would be particularly detrimental to the "distant States" (1:168).

On July 16, Butler questioned a provision that would have granted Congress the power to "legislate in all cases to which the separate States are incompetent." He observed that "the vagueness of the terms rendered it impossible for any precise judgment to be formed" (2:17).

On August 16, Butler seconded a motion by Gouverneur Morris to strike a provision granting Congress power to emit bills of credit (2:309). The next day, he indicated that he thought it preferable to vest war-making powers in the president rather than in the Senate (2:318). If Congress were to be granted the power to declare war, he thought that it should also have the power to make peace (2:319). On September 7, Butler seconded a motion by James Madison that would grant two-thirds of the Senate to enter into a treaty of peace without the president's consent (2:540). Madison's concern, which Butler may or may not have shared, was that presidents, who would gain power during war, might otherwise seek to impede the establishment of peace (2:540). On August 18, Butler indicated that he believed that since the national government had the responsibility of providing for the common defense, it should also have the power to govern all the state militia (2:331).

On August 21, Butler supported a motion by Elbridge Gerry of Massachusetts to apportion taxes prior to the first census according to apportionment in the House of Representatives. Arguing that it was "founded in reason and equity" (2:358), perhaps Butler congratulated himself on the fact that the convention had rejected his earlier proposal to grant his state an extra representative in that body.

Like many other delegates from the Deep South, Butler opposed allowing Congress to tax exports. On August 21, he argued that such a power would be "unjust and alarming to the staple States" (2:360). The next day, he was even more emphatic: "he never would agree to the power of taxing exports" (2:374).

When it was proposed on August 23 that Congress should assume state debts, Butler displayed a passion that would later show itself when this same issue was debated in the first Congress. He indicated that he feared that "it should compel payment as well to the Blood-suckers who had speculated on the distresses of others, as to those who had fought & bled for their country" (2:392). He further indicated that he favored making distinctions between classes of bondholders. On August 25, however, Butler said that he intended "neither to increase nor diminish the security of the Creditors" (2:413).

Butler was willing to give up the requirement for a two-thirds congressional majority to adopt regulations relating to commerce. He viewed this as an important concession. His explanation says much about the way delegates from different sections of the country viewed one another. Butler thus observed that "He considered the interests of these [southern states] and of the Eastern States, to be as different as the interests of Russia and Turkey" (2:451).

Presidency

Butler joined fellow South Carolina delegate Charles Pinckney on June 2 in favoring a single executive. His arguments were practical but effective:

> If one man should be appointed he would be responsible to the whole, and would be impartial to its interests. If three or more should be taken from as many districts, there would be a constant struggle for local advantage. In Military matters this would be particularly mischievous. (1:88–89)

Butler illustrated the problems of a plural executive in military affairs by citing examples from Holland. He qualified his views on June 4, however, by indicating that he would not have favored a single executive if he thought that this executive would be invested with an absolute veto over legislation. Noting that executive power had a tendency to increase, he feared that an absolute negative would allow "a Cataline [a Roman dictator] or a Cromwell [an English dictator]" to arise in the United States (1:100). Butler proposed that the executive should only have the power to suspend legislation for a fixed period (1:103).

On July 19, after rejection of a motion that would have granted presidents a seven-year term, Butler expressed concern that elections might become too frequent. Ever cognizant of his home state, he observed that Georgia and it were "too distant to send electors often" (2:59).

On September 4, Butler indicated that he favored choosing the president through an electoral college rather than by Congress. He feared that "cabal[,] faction & violence would be sure to prevail" if the decision were entrusted to the latter body (2:501). Butler later claimed to have originated the electoral college (See Ulmer 1960, 364), and while this claim may have been exaggerated, he did serve on the Committee on Postponed Matters (as well as on an earlier committee on commercial discrimination) from which this mechanism emerged.

Judiciary

Consistent with his concern for federalism, Butler said that the people would not bear the establishment of lower federal courts and that "the States will revolt at such encroachments" (1:125). His backup argument was perhaps more indicative of Butler's general view of the world. Observing that the delegates should not institute such courts even if they thought them desirable, Butler noted, "We must follow the example of Solon who gave the Athenians not the best Govt. he could devise; but the best they wd. receive" (1:125). On July 18, Butler reiterated his view that the establishment of lower federal tribunals would be unnecessary (1:45).

Federalism

On May 31, Butler expressed his fears "that we were running into an extreme in taking away the powers of the States," and he asked Edmund Randolph to provide further explanation of the Virginia Plan (1:53). On June 5, however, Butler indicated that the term "perpetual," which had been included in the language of the Articles of Confederation, "meant only the constant existence of our Union, and not the particular words which compose the Articles of the union" (1:129). Moreover, on June 6, Butler said that if representation in the House of Representatives were to be apportioned not only by population but also by wealth, he was willing to join Delaware's George Read in proposing to abolish the state legislatures and to institute "one Nation instead of a confedn. of Republics" (1:144). On June 8, Butler expressed strong opposition to the congressional negative of state laws. He feared that this would cut off "all hope of equal justice to the distant States," and he was sure that it would be opposed (1:168).

On August 29, Butler opposed forming new states from existing states without their consent. Otherwise, he indicated that new states should not be formed within states without the consent of such states. He observed that otherwise demagogues would attempt to create new states any time that the people thought that taxes in existing states were unduly pressing on them (2:455). On September 12, Butler seconded a motion by Delaware's John Dickinson designed to secure states against unjust taxes by their neighbors by requiring congressional consent to inspection duties (2:589).

Slavery

As noted above, Butler favored counting slaves equally with free persons in the allocation of seats in the House of Representatives, as giving a measure of representation to wealth in this body as well as to population. The convention rejected this idea in favor of a provision counting blacks as three-fifths of a person. After Pennsylvania's Gouverneur Morris questioned even this representation, Butler went on the defensive, indicating that "The security of the Southn. States want is that their negroes may not be taken from them which some gentlemen within or without doors, have a very good mind to do" (1:605).

On August 28, Butler introduced a motion that would "require fugitive slaves and servants to be delivered up like criminals" (2:443). He withdrew the motion on this occasion with a view toward incorporating the provision in a more appropriate part of the Constitution. He successfully moved to do so the next day when the proposal was placed in what later became Article IV (2:453–54), which deals with state/national relations.

Other Matters

Cognizant of his state's status near the periphery of the Union, Butler was among those who favored the establishment of the nation's capital in a central location (2:128). Significantly, Butler had been influential in moving the capital in his own state from Charleston to Columbia (Whitney 1974, 67).

Ratification

On August 30, Butler indicated that he favored allowing the new Constitution to go into effect when ratified by nine or more states. He thought it would be unreasonable to allow a single state or two to veto such a change (2:469).

S. Sidney Ulmer, a scholar of Butler's role at the convention. observes that his efforts "were negative and defensive in nature" (1960, 369). Ulmer went on to say, "On the question of state power his concern was to maintain it; on the question of executive power his concern was how to control it; on the question of property his concern was how to protect it" (1960, 369).

Life after the Convention

Butler attended a session of his state's legislature and urged its members to call a ratifying convention (Whitney, 69). Butler's letters seemed to reveal mixed feelings about the Constitution. In a letter he wrote to an Englishman, Weedon Butler, on October 8, 1787, he said that "a Copy of the result of Our deliberations . . . is not worth the expence of postage, or I wou'd now enclose it to You" (quoted in Ulmer 1960, 374). However, in a letter he wrote to Elbridge Gerry on March 3, 1788, Butler took a more positive tact:

> The Constitution, with all its imperfections is the only thing at this critical moment that can rescue the states from civil discord and foreign contempt—reflecting naturally our circumstances, on the too little disposition of most of the states to submit to any government. I preferred giving my consent to a trial of the Constitution in question with all its deficiencies, to what appeared to me the inevitable alternative—that there are parts of it I do not like you well know, but still I prefer a trial of it having within itself a power of amendment, to seeing the Gordian knot cut—the Knot of Union in my judgment Will be no more if this Constitution is rejected. (quoted in Ulmer 1960, 374)

Similarly, in another letter to Weedon Butler dated May 5, 1788, Butler observed:

> The Convention saw I think justly, the Critical Situation of the United States. Slighted from abroad and tottering on the brink of Confusion at home; they therefore thought it wise to bring forward such a system as bid fairest for general approbation and adoption so as to be brought soon into operation. (quoted in Sikes 1979, 40)

In another provocative portal into Butler's thinking, he wrote a letter on July 18, 1788 to Weedon Butler indicating that his support for slavery may have come from his belief that southern states would not ratify the Constitution without it rather than because he favored the institution:

> You may natural[l]y ask me why, with these sentiments, do You hold so many in Bondage. I answer You, that I would free every one of them tomorrow if I could do it, that is If the Legislature would permit it. I ardently wish I never had anything to do with such property. I daily beg of them to seek some Master that they think they would be happy with, that I may get done with them; but tho it is an Indulgence not unusual here they will not try for One. Nothing prevents my parting with them but the fear of their not bettering by the Change. (quoted in Sikes 1979, 34)

After supporting the new Constitution in his home states, the legislature chose him as one of its first two senators. Initially leaning to the Federalists, he later gravitated to the Democratic-Republicans. He took a dim view of the adoption of the Bill of Rights and of the creation of lower federal courts under the Judiciary Act of 1789 and resigned from the Senate in 1796. He served for two more years beginning in 1802, during which time he supported the Louisiana Purchase but opposed the change in the electoral college proposed by the Twelfth Amendment, which he feared would limit the influence of the most populous states.

Butler gained considerable wealth from his South Carolina plantations, but he spent the last years of his life in Philadelphia where he served as director of the second Bank of the United States from 1816 to 1819. Butler died in Philadelphia in 1822 and was buried in the city outside Christ Church. A sympathetic chronicler observed that "Butler's aristocratic attitudes were firmly mixed with a genuine attachment to democratic ideals" (Coghlan 1977, 118).

Although he had no sons, Butler persuaded a son-in-law to name a child after him. When this namesake later married the English actress Fanny Kemble and took her to South Carolina, she was so horrified over slavery that she divorced him and published her "Journal of a Residence in America."

Further Reading

Coghlan, Francis. 1977. "Pierce Butler, 1744–1822, First Senator from South Carolina." *The South Carolina Historical Magazine* 78 (April): 104–19.

Farrand, Max, ed. 1966. *The Records of the Federal Convention of 1787*. 4 vols. New Haven, CT: Yale University Press.

Lipscomb, Terry W. I. 2007. *The Letters of Pierce Butler, 1790–1794: Nation-Building and Enterprise in the New American Republic*. Columbia: University of South Carolina Press.

Sikes, Lewright B. 1979. *The Public Life of Pierce Butler, South Carolina Statesman*. Washington, DC: University Press of America.

Ulmer, S. Sidney. 1960. "The Role of Pierce Butler in the Constitutional Convention." *Review of Politics* 72 (January): 361–74.

Whitney, David C., 1974. *Founders of Freedom in America: Lives of the Men Who Signed the Constitution of the United States and So Helped to Establish the United States of America*. Chicago: J. G. Ferguson Publishing Company.

DANIEL CARROLL (1730–1796)
MARYLAND

Daniel Carroll was born on July 22, in 1730 to Daniel and Eleanor Darnall Carroll in Upper Marlboro, Maryland. His father was a wealthy merchant and planter, and the family was Roman Catholic. A younger brother, John Carroll, was eventually selected as both the first Roman Catholic bishop and archbishop of the United States. Initially educated at home, Carroll received a Catholic education at St. Omer's College in French Flanders. Shortly after he returned home, his father died, leaving him in charge of his business and plantations, on which there were many slaves. Carroll married a distant relative, Eleanor Carroll (1732–1763), and received a handsome dowry and became thereby connected to Charles Carroll of Carrolton, another wealthy merchant. The couple had two children, but Eleanor died in 1763, and her widower never remarried.

Carroll was elected to the Maryland Council of State on which he served from 1777 to 1781; thereafter he was elected to the Continental Congress where he signed the Articles of Confederation. He was subsequently elected to the Maryland state senate, where he served for a time as president. He also served on the commission for the Potomac Canal Company.

At the Convention

Carroll received notice in Annapolis of his appointment to the Constitutional Convention on May 24, 1787. He had been appointed in place of a cousin, Charles Carroll, a signer of the Declaration of Independence who had declined his appointment but had shared his ideas for a new government (many of which involved reform of the states rather than of the Articles of Confederation) with his cousin (Crowl 1941). Carroll wrote to a friend the next day saying that the appointment "was neither wished for, [n]or expected by me," and indicating that it would be some time before he would be able to attend. He was in fact not seated until July 9, which means that despite missing much of the opening debates, he still had time to cast his vote on the Connecticut Compromise. He did not, however, express his views on the subject in recorded debates. Although he missed the initial two months of debate, Carroll took positions on many subsequent issues, rarely however giving long speeches.

Congress

Powers. Nine days after arriving at the convention, Carroll indicated that he thought it was essential to allow the national government to suppress rebellion within the states. He noted that the states should want such support, that it was not clear that they had it under the Articles of Confederation, and that the convention should leave no doubt about the matter (Farrand 1966, 2:48).

On July 24, Carroll opposed allowing Congress to enact direct taxes in proportion to representation prior to the first census (2:106). Believing this to be a matter of fundamental fairness, he repeated this opinion on August 20 (2:350).

Carroll's support of a ban on congressional imposition of ex post facto laws (retroactive criminal laws) on August 22 is fascinating. Whereas Connecticut's Oliver Ellsworth had argued that such a prohibition was unnecessary because lawyers knew that such laws were in and of themselves void, Carroll responded that "experience overruled all other calculations" (2:376). Such experience had demonstrated that, whatever lawyers thought, legislatures passed them, and they thereby needed to be prohibited.

Qualifications and Voting. On July 23, Carroll indicated that he did not necessarily oppose per capita (voting by person rather than by state) voting in the Senate, but that he did not think such a decision should be made in haste (2:95)—on a number of occasions throughout the convention, Carroll is on record as asking for postponements of votes (see, for example, 2:300; 2:468; 2:475). Three days later, Carroll opposed a provision that would have barred individuals who had unsettled accounts from running for office (2:125). On August 13, Carroll unsuccessfully attempted to get the citizenship requirement for members of the House of Representatives lowered from seven years to five (2:272).

On August 10, Carroll said that he did not think Congress should have the power to expel members from office without at least a two-thirds vote (2:254), the majority that the convention eventually settled on for this purpose. On this same day, Carroll unsuccessfully supported a motion that would require roll-call votes in the House on the application of one-fifth of the members but would have allowed any member of the Senate to record his dissent at any time (2:255).

Carroll was displeased with the provision of the Connecticut Compromise that provided for the origination of money bills in the House of Representatives. He observed on August 13 that the attempt to decide which bills so qualified has been "a source of continual difficulty & squabble between the two houses" in his home state of Maryland (2:280).

Carroll seconded one of the final motions at the Constitutional Convention, supporting a provision permitting one representative for each state in the House of Representatives for every 30,000 residents, in place of the previous provision of one for every 40,000 (2:644). Significantly, this issue was the only one that prompted George Washington's verbal support in a speech at the convention.

Carroll expressed concern about whether two-thirds of the Congress should be able to overturn a presidential veto. He observed that when this majority had been set, the convention had not agreed that a majority of each house would be sufficient to form a quorum, and he feared that if the two were combined together it might be necessary "to call for greater impediments to improper laws" (2:300). On August 15, however, he favored postponing this matter until it was clear how the executive department was going to operate. The next day, he further suggested that, given the differing interests of the states in regard to duties, it might be wise to see a higher quorum for issues related to the imposition of duties (2:305). He favored a blanket prohibition against taxation of exports (2:308).

Carroll and fellow Marylander Luther Martin subsequently expressed fears that Congress might use its power over trade to favor ports in particular states, and they introduced a constitutional provision designed to prevent this from happening (2:417–18). On August 31, Carroll reiterated that this issue "was a tender point in Maryland" (2:481). However, on September 15, he indicated that he favored allowing states to lay duties for the purpose of "clearing harbours and erecting light-houses" (2:625).

Location of the Capital. On August 11, Carroll expressed his fears that the capital would remain at New York (2:262). This might have been tied to fears that this would give the North improper influence in the new government.

Pay. Carroll opposed a provision that would have allowed state legislatures to pay members of Congress. He feared that this mechanism, in combination with the ability of states to offer offices to members of

Congress as inducements, made "the dependence of both houses on the States Legislatures" complete (2:292). He observed that, if these provisions remained, "The new Govt. in this form was nothing more than a second edition of Congress in two volumes, instead of one, and perhaps with very few amendments" (2:292). Carroll further argued that senators should represent the interest of the American people as a whole and not those of the individual states (2:292).

Presidency

On July 24, Carroll seconded a motion by Pennsylvania's James Wilson favoring selection of the president by legislators chosen by lot to vote immediately (2:105). This mechanism was presumably designed to avoid the likelihood that presidential candidates could corrupt the legislators. Carroll subsequently moved, with Wilson's second, to replace presidential selection by Congress with presidential selection by the people (2:402). When this failed, Carroll seconded a motion by Pennsylvania's Gouverneur Morris that provided for the people of the states the power to appoint electors who would elect the president (2:404).

Federalism

Maryland had withheld its ratification of the Articles of Confederation until states with large land claims had ceded them to the United States. Carroll raised this issue on August 30 in opposing a provision stating that states must give their consent to being divided. Madison recorded Carroll as saying "that it might be proper to provide that nothing in the Constitution should affect the Right of the U.S. to lands ceded by G. Britain in the Treaty of peace, and proposed a commitment to a member from each State" (2:462). Carroll indicated that if this issue were not satisfactorily resolved, some states could never agree to the document (also see 2:465–66). Carroll's willingness to allow Congress to suppress rebellions within states and his view that senators should represent all the people, and not simply those of their states, would indicate, however, that he was largely a nationalist.

Ratification

On August 30, when other delegates were suggesting that nine states might be sufficient to ratify the new Constitution, Carroll said that he did not think it would be possible to dissolve a confederation that had been created by unanimous consent without a similar vote (2:469). He took the same position the next day (2:477). When the convention discussed ratifying the Constitution by convention, Carroll pointed out that his state provided only for one mode of ratification—presumably by state legislative approval (2:475).

Two days before the Constitution was signed, Carroll wanted the convention to prepare an address to the people to accompany the Constitution. He said "The people had been accustomed to such on great occasions, and would expect it on this," but his motion to create a committee to formulate such an address was defeated (2: 623). Carroll nonetheless signed the Constitution.

Life after the Convention

Carroll returned to Maryland to support the new Constitution and wrote essays supporting it under the designation of "A Friend of the Constitution." He stated his position in an essay of October 16, 1787, which is similar to the arguments that Benjamin Franklin had used in the convention to persuade fellow delegates to sign the Constitution:

> It is neither extraordinary nor unexpected, that the Constitution offered to your consideration should meet with opposition . . . I will confess indeed that I am not a blind admirer of this plan of government, and that there are some parts of it, which if my wish had prevailed, would certainly have been altered. But when I reflect how widely men differ in their opinions, and that every man . . . has an equal pretension to assert his own, I am satisfied that anything nearer to perfection could not have been accomplished. If there are errors, it should be remembered, that the seeds of reformation are sown in the work itself, and the concurrence of two-thirds of the Congress may, at any time, introduce alterations and amendments. . . . Regarding it, then, in every point of view with a candid and disinterested mine, I am bold to assert, that it is the best form of government which has ever been offered to the world. (quoted in Geiger 1943, 140–41).

Carroll served as one of Maryland's first members of the U.S. House of Representatives; in this capacity, he contributed to the wording of the First and Tenth Amendments. He is probably best known for his role as one of three commissioners responsible for laying out the new nation's capital at the District of Columbia, a position that put him into conflict with Major Pierre Charles L'Enfant. Carroll died on May 7, in 1796 at Rock Creek, Maryland. He may have been buried at the Holy Trinity Convent in Washington, DC.

Further Reading

Burnett, Edmund C. 1938. "The Catholic Signers of the Constitution." In *The Constitution of the United States: Addresses in Commemoration of the Sesquicentennial of its Signing 17 September 1787*, edited by Herbert Wright, 40–54. Washington, DC: Catholic University of America.

Crowl, Philip A. 1941. "Charles Carroll's Plan of Government." *American Historical Review* 46 (April): 588–95.

Farrand, Max, ed. 1966. *The Records of the Federal Convention of 1787.* 4 vols. New Haven, CT: Yale University Press.

Geiger, Mary Virginia. 1943. *Daniel Carroll: A Framer of the Constitution.* Washington, DC: Catholic University of America.

Standiford, Les. 2008. *Washington Burning: How a Frenchman's Vision for Our Nation's Capital Survived Congress, the Founding Fathers, and the Invading British Army.* New York: Crown Publishing.

Whitney, David. 1974. *Founders of Freedom in America: Lives of the Men Who Signed the Constitution of the United States and So Helped to Establish the United States of America.* Chicago: J. G. Ferguson Publishing Company.

GEORGE CLYMER (1739–1813)
PENNSYLVANIA

George Clymer was born in Philadelphia on March 16, 1739 to the family of a sea captain. After his parents died a year later, a maternal aunt and her husband, a merchant and a leader of the Proprietary Party with a large personal library, raised him and imparted a love for books. Clymer inherited a large sum of money from his uncle, formed a merchant partnership, and also became active in the Proprietary Party. Clymer married Elizabeth Meredith (1743–1815), the daughter of a merchant, in 1765, and her father made him a partner in his firm. The couple had eight children, five of whom survived to adulthood; the family had to hide from the British during the Revolutionary War.

Clymer was one of the delegates to the Continental Congress who signed the Declaration of Independence. After serving in a number of positions that aligned him with the patriots, he again represented Pennsylvania in Congress from 1780–1782 and then served in Pennsylvania's state legislature. With Oliver Evans, Clymer had written a letter to the Continental Congress, "Reflections on the Patent Laws," in which they argued for congressional protection of patents.

Serving simultaneously in the Pennsylvania state legislature and as a delegate to the Constitutional Convention, Clymer apparently devoted most of his attention to his former responsibilities and at the convention was a relatively silent delegate in a state delegation known for its brilliance and for its participation in debates.

At the Convention

Although seated at the Constitutional Convention on May 28, Clymer does not appear to have spoken until August 21. Three days earlier he had been appointed to his first committee at the convention, an 11-man committee on state debts and militia. On August 22, he was appointed to a similar committee on slave trade and navigation, the only other such committee on which he would serve.

On August 21 the convention was discussing whether state or national governments should be permitted to tax exports. Virginia's George Mason had indicated that the South was particularly concerned about the possibility that the other states might tax its tobacco. Clymer responded that other states had their own concerns. Middle states like Pennsylvania had just as much cause to be concerned about their "wheat flour, provisions, &c. and with more reason, as these articles were exposed to a competition in foreign markets not incident to Tobo. rice &c." (Farrand 1966, 2:363). He further observed that these middle states had as much cause to fear a combination of the eastern and southern states as the southern states had to fear from a combination of the eastern and middle ones. Clymer then introduced a motion, rejected by a vote of seven to three, that would have qualified the prohibition of taxes on exports by limiting the prohibition to those taxes enacted "for the purpose of revenue" (2:363).

Clymer became involved in another North/South conflict on August 25 when he concurred with a motion by Connecticut's Roger Sherman not to mention the word slavery in the Constitution. His apparent motivation was to avoid sectional offense (2:415).

Although he had thus attempted to reconcile the North and South, Clymer, who had served in 1777 as a member of a congressionally appointed commission investigating conditions on the frontier, was among those who feared the future development of the American West. On August 28, after Pennsylvania's Gouverneur Morris indicated that the coastal states might use the taxing power to prevent western states' access to the Mississippi River, Clymer indicated that he "thought the encouragement of the Western Country was suicide on the old States" (2:442). He observed, "If the States have such different interests that they can not be left to regulate their own manufactures without encountering the interests of other States, it is a proof that they are not fit to compose one nation" (2:442).

The next day, the convention was discussing whether two-thirds majorities should be required in Congress for regulating matters of commerce. Clymer opposed this provision, again pointing to the diversity of interests within the United States:

> The diversity of commercial interests, of necessity creates difficulties, which ought not to be increased by unnecessary restrictions. The Northern & middle States will be ruined, if not enabled to defend themselves against foreign regulations. (2:450)

On August 31, Clymer supported a motion by Virginia's James Madison to allow the new Constitution to go in effect when ratified by a majority of people in a majority of the states (2:476). Clymer later opposed a proposal by Alexander Hamilton of New York referring the Constitution to Congress for its approval, on the basis that it might "embarrass" that body (2:563). On September 6, Clymer further indicated that he thought an earlier plan whereby the Senate would appoint public officials was too "aristocratic" (2:524).

Life after the Convention

After signing the Constitution, Clymer used his influence in the Pennsylvania legislature to call a convention to ratify the new document, even approving mob action in bringing opponents into the legislature to provide a quorum for action. Although he was not elected to the state ratifying convention, Pennsylvania chose Clymer to represent it in the first House of Representatives. There he supported the fiscal program advocated by Alexander Hamilton and helped secure the temporary establishment of the nation's capital in Philadelphia. Clymer opposed an amendment that would have allowed constituents to "instruct" their representatives, believing that representatives were elected to exercise their better judgment on their constituents' behalf. He later was a tax collector in his state during the volatile period leading to the Whiskey Rebellion, which tested the power of the new national government.

Washington appointed Clymer in 1795 to negotiate a peace treaty with Creek Indians in Georgia. He devoted much of the rest of his life to philanthropy and served as a trustee of the University of Pennsylvania and as president of the Pennsylvania Academy of Fine Arts. Clymer died on January 23, 1813 and was buried in the Friends Burial Ground in Trenton, New Jersey. A house known as Summerseat, in Morrisville, Pennsylvania, which Clymer acquired from Robert Morris in 1806 and where he lived until his death, is today a museum that is open to the public once a week (McKenney 2013, 205).

Further Reading

Farrand, Max, ed. 1966. *The Records of the Federal Convention of 1787*. 4 vols. New Haven, CT: Yale University Press.

Grundfest, Jerry. 1982. *George Clymer: Philadelphia Revolutionary, 1739–1813*. New York: Arno Press.

McKenney, Janice E. 2013. *Women of the Constitution: Wives of the Signers*. Lanham, MD: Scarecrow Press.

Whitney, David. 1974. *Founders of Freedom in America: Lives of the Men Who Signed the Constitution of the United States and So Helped to Establish The United States of America*. Chicago: J. G. Ferguson Publishing Company.

WILLIAM RICHARDSON DAVIE (1756–1820)
NORTH CAROLINA

William Richardson Davie was born in Egremont, Cumberlandshire, England in 1756 to the family of a fabric manufacturer, which migrated to America. There his mother's brother, a Presbyterian minister after whom he had been named, was particularly solicitous of his welfare (some accounts say he adopted Davie). He willed him his library and 150 acres of property. After studying at Queen's Museum (later known as Liberty Hall) in Charlotte, Davie attended the College of New Jersey (today's Princeton), where he graduated with honors.

Davie served in a number of important positions during the Revolutionary War, including captain of a cavalry unit and service as North Carolina's commissary general. Davie was a model soldier to future president Andrew Jackson who served for a time under him. After completing his study of law, Davie became an accomplished lawyer. Voters selected Davie to the state legislature where he served from 1786 to 1798, during which time he helped to found the University of North Carolina. Davie was present on May 25, the opening day of the convention. Archibald Murphey, a contemporary reformer, described Davie as "a tall, elegant man in his person, graceful and commanding in his manners" (quoted in Broadwater, n.d.).

Congress

On June 30, the convention was debating the possibility of granting each state equal representation in the Senate. Perhaps because other delegates were speaking of the conflict between the North and the South, because some were accusing some states (North Carolina does not appear to have been mentioned by name) of failing to fulfill their obligations, or, more likely, because he could not make up his mind, Davie professed to be "embarrassed" (Farrand 1966, 1:487). He indicated that he thought it impractical to allow state legislatures to choose members of the Senate on a proportional basis because this would result in an initial body of at least 90 members (presumably based on the idea that the smallest state would get at least one senator), which would be too large to carry out the Senate's functions. Faced with a choice between proportional representation and equal representation, he would have to support the latter.

Davie did not favor a plan whereby senators would be chosen from larger districts (probably embracing more than one state) because he feared that the larger divisions would prevail over the smaller divisions with which they were paired. He realized that selection by state legislatures might be more likely to result in the representation of "local prejudices & interests," but he thought that such prejudices "would find their way into the national Councils" either way (1:488). However, he feared that if the Senate were considered to be representative of the states, the new government would look like the Articles of Confederation and would not accomplish the objectives the convention was seeking. Thus, Davie groped for a middle way:

> We were partly federal, partly national in our Union. And he did not see why the Govt. might [not] in some respects operate on the States, in others on the people. (1:488)

Perhaps thinking that he was a conciliatory voice on this issue, the convention appointed Davie on July 2 to the committee designed to formulate a mechanism for representation within the Senate; this was the only committee on which Davie served at the convention. He initially may not have been completely satisfied with the Connecticut Compromise. Thus, on July 6, Madison reported that Davie wanted to recommit the issue of congressional representation. Madison believed that Davie favored a plan whereby "wealth or property ought to be represented in the 2d. branch; and numbers in the 1st. branch" (1:542).

Davie further weighed in on the issue of representation on July 12, but at that time his primary concern was how states with slaves should be represented. The summary of his comments appear to indicate considerable passion:

> Mr. Davie, said it was high time now to speak out. He saw that it was meant by some gentlemen to deprive the Southern States of any share of Representation for their blacks. He was sure that N. Carola. would never confederate on any terms that did not rate then at least as 3/5. If the Eastern States meant therefore to exclude them altogether the business was at an end. (1:593)

Davie appears to have had an important role in North Carolina's acceptance of the Great Compromise (Robinson 1957, 186).

Presidency

On June 2, Davie seconded a motion by fellow North Carolina delegate Hugh Williamson providing that the executive should be removable on conviction of impeachment for "mal-practice or neglect of duty" (1:78).

On July 24, Davie supported an eight-year term for the presidency (2:102). Two days later, he seconded a motion by Virginia's George Mason providing that the executive should serve a single seven-year term (2:120).

Life after the Convention

On August 23, Davie wrote to the governor of North Carolina indicating that he had left the convention on the 13th. He observed that the other state delegates had agreed to stay, that "the general principles were already fixed," that he had other business to attend to, and that under the circumstances he felt "at liberty" to return home (3:75).

Davie gave a reasoned defense of the Constitution at the North Carolina ratifying conventions. Speaking in defense of the Connecticut Compromise, Davie there observed that "The protection of the small states against the ambition and influence of the larger members, could only be effected by arming them with an equal power in one branch of the legislature" (3:341). He also observed that the convention had represented a wide variety of interests and that "mutual concessions were necessary to come to any concurrence" (3:341). Davie hoped that the same "spirit of amity, and of that mutual deference and concession which the peculiarity of their political situation rendered indispensable" would also pervade the North Carolina convention (3:342). Davie helped publish the proceedings of the first North Carolina convention, which apparently help set the stage for the state's eventual ratification of the Constitution.

In 1797, Davie became commander of North Carolina's militia, and the next year the state elected him as governor. The following year he served as a commissioner to France. Subsequent disagreements with the Democratic-Republicans over their preference for France over England sent him back to private life, and he retired to his plantation, named Tivoli, near Lancaster, South Carolina.

Davie was involved from the beginning in the founding of the University of North Carolina in 1789. Much as Thomas Jefferson later involved himself with the University of Virginia, Davie is said to have been "intimately involved in every significant aspect of the university's evolution until his trustee term expired in 1807" (Johnson 1987, 135). He helped choose the site at Chapel Hill, raised funds for the university and donated to it, laid out a curriculum that stressed practical knowledge, and helped secure state support. In 1811, the grateful university awarded Davie its first doctor of law degree. Davie's wife Sarah Jones (1762–1802), with whom he had six children, died in 1802, and he did not remarry. He died in 1820 and was buried in the family plot at the Old Waxhaw Presbyterian Church.

Further Reading

Bradford, M. E. 1994. *Founding Fathers: Brief Lives of the Framers of the United States Constitution.* 2nd ed. Lawrence: University Press of Kansas.

Broadwater, Jeff. n.d. "William Richardson Davie." North Carolina History Project. http://www.northcarolinahistory.org/commentary/115/entry. Accessed 7/12/2012.

Farrand, Max, ed. 1966. *The Records of the Federal Convention of 1787.* 4 vols. New Haven, CT: Yale University Press.

Johnson, Eldon L. 1987. "The 'Other Jeffersons' and the State University Idea." *Journal of Higher Education* 58 (March–April): 127–50.

Mitchell, Memory F. 1964. *North Carolina's Signers: Brief Sketches of the Men Who Signed the Declaration of Independence and the Constitution*. Raleigh: Division of Archives and History, North Carolina Department of Cultural Resources.

Robinson, Blackwell P. 1957. *William R. Davie*. Chapel Hill: University of North Carolina Press.

JONATHAN DAYTON (1760–1824)
NEW JERSEY

Jonathan Dayton was born in 1760 in Elizabethtown, New Jersey; his father later commanded a battalion of troops during the Revolutionary War. Dayton, who graduated from the College of New Jersey (today's Princeton) in 1776 at the age of sixteen, had served throughout the Revolutionary War as an officer, being captured for a time by the British and present at the British surrender at Yorktown. Dayton married Susan Williamson (1758–1843) in March, 1779, and they had four children. Elected in 1787 to the New Jersey legislature, his father declined nomination as a representative to the Constitutional Convention in deference to his son, who would eventually earn a law degree.

At the Convention

Dayton, who was then twenty-six, is chiefly known for having been the youngest man to attend the Constitutional Convention. Unlike South Carolina's Charles Pinckney, the next oldest delegate who dissembled about his age in order to make people believe he was the youngest, Dayton spoke relatively rarely at the convention and was quite conscious that he was in the presence of men with far greater experience. Writing in June to fellow delegate David Brearly before Dayton had begun attending the convention, he observed: "I feel about me on this occasion all that diffidence with which the consciousness of my youth and inexperience as well as inability to discharge so important a trust, cannot but impress me" (Hutson 1987, 59).

Because the confirmation of the younger Dayton encountered delay, he was not seated at the convention until June 21 (Farrand 1966, 1:353). The first position about which he is on record is that of senatorial pay. He observed on June 26 that he thought that state payment of senators would be "fatal to their independence" and therefore advocated that they should be paid out of the national treasury (1:428).

Since the New Jersey Plan, advocating equal state representation in Congress, originated from his home state, it is not surprising to find that on June 28, Dayton supported a motion that representation in the first branch of Congress should be the same as it had been under the Articles of Confederation (1:445). On this occasion, he also wanted the vote postponed until Governor William Livingston from his state was able to attend. Objecting to the scare tactics that he thought advocated change (substituting "assertion" for "proof" and "terror" for "argument"), on June 30 Dayton questioned whether the evils to which critics of the Articles of Confederation really stemmed from state equality in Congress. He also formulated one of the convention's most colorful analogies when he indicated that "he considered the system on the table as a novelty, an amphibious monster; and was persuaded that it never would be recd. by the people" (1:490). On July 14, just two days before adoption of the Connecticut Compromise, Dayton indicated that "The smaller States can never give up their equality" (2:5). Like other representatives of the smaller states, he connected such equality to "security for their rights" (2:5).

On August 24, when the convention was still contemplating whether Congress would choose the president, Dayton was on record as opposed to having this decision made by joint ballot. He feared that such a mechanism would effectively grant this power to the House of Representatives and thus sidestep the provision that had been made for the smaller states by granting them equal representation in the Senate (2:402). When the convention initially accepted such a joint ballot, Dayton unsuccessfully moved to provide that each state would have a single vote—an agreement that has subsequently found its way in the mechanism by which the House of Representatives selects among the top three candidates for president in cases where no candidate gains a majority of the votes (2:403).

After adoption of the Connecticut Compromise, delegates from the North and South continued to argue about how slaves should be counted in the formula for representation in the House. After Gouverneur Morris gave one of the convention's most blistering speeches denouncing the institution of slavery and thus arguing that only free persons should be counted in apportioning representation in the U.S. House of Representatives, Dayton, who owned slaves of his own but represented a state where slavery was dying out, seconded his motion. Recognizing that the delegates were unlikely to agree with him, he thought it was important "that his sentiments on the subject might appear whatever might be the fate of the amendment" (2:223).

In assessing the relative strength of the northern and southern states, Dayton indicated on July 10 that he thought the balance was relatively equal. He considered Pennsylvania to be the state in the middle, with six to her north and six to her south (1:567).

On August 18, Dayton opposed providing a specific constitutional limit on the number of troops that could be kept in times of peace. He sagely observed that "preparations for war are generally made in peace, and a standing force of some sort may, for ought we know, become unavoidable" (2:330). This subject evidently interested him since on August 23, he proposed a motion that would grant the national government the power to adopt laws "organizing, arming, disciplining & governing *such part of them as may be employed in the service of the U.S.*" (2:385–86). Under this resolution, other powers related to the militia, including the right to appoint officers, would be reserved to the states. On that same day, Dayton opposed uniform regulations of the militia throughout the country in the belief that needs, in terms of the kinds of troops and weapons, would vary from one area of the country to another (2:386). On September 8, Dayton made another foray into the area of foreign policy by moving along with Pennsylvania's James Wilson to strike the requirement for a two-thirds vote of the Senate to ratify treaties (2:549).

The only committee on which Dayton served at the convention was the 11-man Committee on Commercial Discrimination that was created on August 25. On a related matter, Dayton expressed concern that the provision allowing states to enact fees for inspection duties might be used to allow Pennsylvania to tax New Jersey under the guise of such duties (2:589).

On August 24, Dayton concurred with a motion to strike a rather awkward mechanism, similar to a provision under the Articles, for deciding disputes between the states. He concurred with other delegates in believing that the establishment of a national judiciary would be adequate to deal with such problems (2:401).

On August 30, Dayton opposed a provision that would require an application on the part of state legislatures before the national government could send in protection against domestic violence. In a sentiment with which other delegates must undoubtedly have concurred, he believed that the example of Rhode Island showed "the necessity of giving latitude to the power of the U.S. on this subject" (2:467).

Life after the Convention

Dayton resumed his service in the New Jersey legislature and worked for adoption of the Constitution. He served from 1791 to 1789 as a delegate to the House of Representatives, where he supported Federalist policies and rose to the position of House Speaker. His election to the U.S. Senate subsequently brought him into close association with vice president Aaron Burr. Dayton owned about a quarter of a million acres in Ohio, where the city of Dayton now bears his name. Perhaps in part because of these interests as well as his personal friendship, Dayton appears to have conspired with Burr to join western parts of the United States with Mexico in an empire. Charged, but never tried, for treason, Dayton's political career was effectively ended except for a year of service in the state legislature.

Like George Washington and a number of other founders, Dayton was a member of the Society of the Cincinnati. He died in the town of his birth on October 9, 1824, and was buried in the cemetery of St. John's Episcopal Church. Known for adhering to earlier customs, he was sometimes called "the last of the cocked hats" (Wright and MacGregor 1987, 79). Dayton's Boxwood Hall in Elizabeth, New Jersey, where he lived from 1805 until his death, is now a museum.

Further Reading

Farrand, Max, ed. 1966. *The Records of the Federal Convention of 1787*. 4 vols. New Haven, CT: Yale University Press.

Hutson, James H., ed. 1987. *Supplement to Max Farrand's The Records of the Federal Convention of 1787*. New Haven, CT: Yale University Press.

Whitney, David C. 1974. *Founders of Freedom in America: Lives of the Men Who Signed the Constitution of the United States and So Helped to Establish the United States of America*. Chicago: J. G. Ferguson Publishing Company.

Wright, Robert K., Jr., and Morris J. MacGregor Jr. 1987. *Soldier-Statesmen of the Constitution*. Washington, DC: Center of Military History, U.S. Army.

JOHN DICKINSON (1732–1808)
DELAWARE

Delaware's John Dickinson was an attorney with a long history of service to two different states. Born in Talbot County, Maryland on November 8, 1732 to Samuel Dickinson and Mary Cadwalader Dickinson, wealthy Quaker

planters (his father also served as a judge), Dickinson finished his study of law under a Philadelphia attorney by attending the Middle Temple in London. Dickinson married Mary ("Polly") Norris (1740–1803), the daughter of a wealthy Philadelphian in 1770, and he and his wife had two daughters.

Elected first to the Delaware colonial assembly and then to the assembly in Pennsylvania, Dickinson earned the reputation as the "Penman of the Revolution." His works included the "Declaration of Rights" that the Stamp Act Congress adopted; his "Letters from a Farmer in Pennsylvania to the Inhabitants of the British Colonies," in which he presented the colonial case against the Townshend Acts; and his "Petition to the King" and "Declaration of the Causes and Necessity of Taking Up Arms," both of which the Second Continental Congress adopted. He also authored a patriotic anthem entitled "The Liberty Song."

Although he justified the resort to force against the English, Dickinson was a conservative man who continued to hope for reconciliation, and he did not think the colonists were adequately united or that they could succeed without first securing foreign allies. He and fellow delegate Robert Morris absented themselves from the Second Continental Congress so that the Pennsylvania delegation on which he served could vote for independence, but Dickinson did not personally vote for independence or sign the Declaration of Independence. This prompted Benjamin Rush to deride Dickinson's prudence as "a rascally virtue" and John Adams to comment negatively on what he considered to be Dickinson's "piddling genius" (quoted in Colbourne 1959, 272). Jane Calvert, who puts emphasis on Dickinson's close associations with Quakers, explains that Dickinson's "Letters" were written "from a sense of duty to testify," and that "they were not a call for revolution; they were written to prevent revolution by giving Americans a peaceful and productive outlet for their frustrations with British policy" (2007, 243). A devoted patriot, Dickinson did enlist in the militia, serving first in the capacity of a private and later being appointed a brigadier general.

As a member of the Second Continental Congress, Dickinson wrote the first draft of what became the Articles of Confederation, but Congress modified his draft so as to give greater powers to the states than he had anticipated. Dickinson served from 1781 to 1782 as president of Delaware and from 1782 to 1785 as president of Pennsylvania; during the latter term, he donated property for the establishment of what became Dickinson College. Dickinson chaired the Annapolis Convention that proposed the Constitutional Convention of 1787. Having been a legislator and an executive in two states—one large and another small—Dickinson understood the respective positions of both sets of states in regard to representation and other matters. The state that sent Dickinson to Philadelphia had specifically instructed its delegates not to change the method of representation under the Articles of Confederation.

At the Convention

Dickinson was a tall, frail, and slender man with white hair. When he arrived at the Constitutional Convention on Tuesday, May 29, he came believing that "the confederation is defective" and "that it ought to be amended" (Farrand 1966, 1:42). Although professing to be obliged to Edmund Randolph for introducing the Virginia Plan, Dickinson believed the better way to proceed would be to ask what the legislative, executive, and judicial powers were lacking and "then proceed to the definition of such powers as may be thought adequate to the objects for which it [the government] was instituted" (1:42).

Dickinson prepared a plan of government, but he never presented it to the convention. He did not speak from June 21 through July 25, presumably being sick and/or absent much of this time. On his return to the convention, this absence might well have given him a perspective on intervening developments (including adoption of the Great Compromise) that other members did not have.

Congress

Representation. At the Continental Congress, Dickinson had been an effective advocate for equal state representation. Indeed, Joseph C. Morton believes this may have been Dickinson's "major contribution to constitution making during the revolutionary epoch" (2006, 73). On June 2, however, Dickinson argued that it would be necessary for the large and small states to practice "mutual concession." He indicated that he thought states should have equal representation in at least one house and favored apportioning the other according to state contributions to the national treasury (1:87; also see 1:196). Dickinson later introduced the proviso that each state should have at least one representative in the branch to be apportioned according to tax contributions (2:223).

Similarly, on August 21 Dickinson expressed fears that the number of representatives of the large states should be limited; one reason he offered was that, without such a limitation, "encouragement" might be "given to the importation of slaves" (2:356). Dickinson, who had freed his own slaves in 1777, returned to this theme the next day, saying that it was "inadmissible on every principle of honor & safety that the importation of slaves should be authorized to the States by the Constitution" and urging that Congress be given authority over this issue (2:372). Although he may well have been mistaken, Dickinson did not believe that southern states would refuse to join the new Union simply over this point. When the convention decided to allow states to continue importation of slaves until 1808, Dickinson tried unsuccessfully to leave this power open only to the states that were currently exercising it (2:416).

Dickinson favored drawing one branch "immediately from the people," but proposed that the other might be chosen by state legislatures (1:136). Favoring state legislative choice of senators, Dickinson advocated giving them terms of three, five, or seven years and not making them (as were delegates under the Articles of Confederation) subject to recall (1:136).

Selection and Qualifications of Senators. Dickinson elaborated on state legislative selection of senators on June 7, when he proposed this as a formal motion. He argued both that "the sense of the States would be better collected through their Government; than immediately from the people at large," and that such a mechanism would be more likely to result in a Senate "of the most distinguished characters, distinguished for their rank in life and their weight of property, and bearing as strong a likeness to the British House of Lords as possible" (1:150). In contrast to a number of other delegates who anticipated that the Senate would gain weight if its numbers were relatively limited, Dickinson favored a Senate of 80 members, or even twice that. He feared that "if their number should be small, the popular branch could not be [ba]lanced by them. The legislature of a numerous people ought to be a numerous body" (1:150). Similarly, he argued later in the day that "the Senate ought to be composed of a large number, and that their influence [from family weight & other causes] would be increased thereby" (1:153).

On June 15, the day that William Paterson introduced the New Jersey Plan, Madison observed that Dickinson had upbraided him, accusing his intransigence of having led to the plan:

Mr. Dickinson said to Mr. Madison you see the consequences of pushing things too far. Some of the members from the small States wish for two branches in the General Legislature, and are friends to a good National Government; but we would sooner submit to a foreign power, than submit to be deprived of an equality of suffrage, in both branches of the legislature, and thereby be thrown under the dominion of the large States. (1:242)

On July 26, after George Mason had moved that the convention spec- ify "certain qualifications of landed property & citizenship" for members of Congress (1:121), Dickinson indicated that he opposed specifying such qualifications within the Constitution. He observed that it was impossible to recite all qualifications that might be necessary and that a partial list "would by implication tie up the hands of the Legislature from supplying the omissions" (2:123). Despite what he had earlier said about modeling the Senate on the English House of Lords, he now "doubted the policy of interweaving into a Republican constitution a veneration for wealth." Indeed, he sagely observed that "He had always understood that a venera- tion for poverty & virtue, were the objects of republican encouragement. It seemed improper that any man of merit should be subjected to disabilities in a Republic where merit was understood to form the great title to public trust, honors & rewards" (2:123).

Nonetheless, on August 7, Dickinson indicated that he was willing to limit the vote to "freeholders," even though some states did not at the time have such a requirement:

He considered them as the best guardians of liberty: And the restriction of the right to them as a necessary defence agst. the dangerous influence of those multitudes without property & without principle, with which our Country, like all others, will in time abound. As to the unpopularity of the innovation it was in his opinion chimerical. The great mass of our Citizens is composed at this time of freeholders, and will be pleased with it. (2:202)

Powers. Dickinson was among the delegates who supported the provi- sion limiting the origination of money bills to the House of Representatives. In a frequently cited August 13 speech advocating this limitation, Dickinson argued that the delegates needed to be guided by "experience" rather than by "reason" (2:278). He believed that experience both in Great Britain and in the states confirmed the policy of limiting the origination of such money bills to the lower houses, although he was willing to allow the upper house to make amendments. He further thought that such a provision would help inoculate the document against anticipated criticisms:

> When this plan goes forth, it will be attacked by the popular leaders. Aristocracy will be the watchword; the Shibboleth among its adversaries. Eight States have inserted in their Constitutions the exclusive right of originating money bills in favor of the popular branch of the Legislature. Most of them however allowed the other branch to amend. This he thought would be proper for us to do. (2:278)

Contrary to the convention's eventual decision granting most appointment powers to the president subject to the "advice and consent" of the Senate, Dickinson believed that Congress should make the "great appointments" rather than the president (2:329). He also opposed prohibiting Congress from taxing all exports, although he did not oppose designating "particular articles from the power" (2:361).

Dickinson favored allowing both houses of Congress, and not simply the Senate, to make treaties. He did so despite believing that this would be "unfavorable to the little States" like the one he was representing (2:393). As a way of protecting the small states, Dickinson believed that congressional consent should be required to any inspection duties (2:589).

Presidency

Dickinson offered a plan on June 2 whereby "the Executive be made removeable by the National Legislature on the request of a majority of the Legislatures of individual States" (1:85). He thought that this removal mechanism would be superior to impeachment. Dickinson indicated that although he favored separation of powers into three independent branches, he feared that a single executive was not consistent with a republic; "that a firm Executive could only exist in a limited monarchy" (1:86).

Dickinson opposed the idea of a Council of Revision that would unite the executive with members of the judiciary. He feared that this would undermine executive responsibility and that it "involved an improper mixture of powers" (1:140). However, on September 7, Dickinson indicated that he favored an executive council, which he apparently anticipated would act, much like today's cabinet, in a purely advisory capacity. He observed on this occasion that "It wd. be a singular thing if the measures of the Executive were not to undergo some previous discussion before the President" (2:542).

The plan of government that Dickinson prepared had called for a tripartite executive to be selected by state legislatures. On his return to debates at the convention on July 25, Dickinson indicated that he "had long leaned towards an election by the people which he regarded as the best and purest source" (2:114), but he actually proposed a mediated form of election, not altogether dissimilar to the electoral college that the convention eventually adopted. Dickinson favored having each state nominate its best citizen and then allowing either Congress, or electors appointed by Congress for this purpose, to decide which of these would be president (2:115). On September 5, Dickinson indicated that he thought the entire Congress, and not simply the Senate, should resolve deadlocks in the electoral college when any individual failed to achieve a majority (2:513).

Judiciary

When South Carolina's John Rutledge proposed on June 5 to eliminate the provision for lower federal courts—relying instead on courts within the states—Dickinson indicated that he thought that "if there was to be a National Legislature, there ought to be a national Judiciary, and that the former ought to have authority to institute the latter" (1:125).

Dickinson agreed on August 15 with Maryland's John Mercer in believing that federal courts should not exercise the power, now known as judicial review, to invalidate acts of Congress. However, although "He thought no such power ought to exist," he also indicated that "He was at the same time at a loss what expedient to substitute" (2:299).

When the convention was discussing treason, Dickinson indicated that he thought the term "giving aid & comfort" to the enemy was too vague. He further proposed that the testimony of two witnesses should be required to an overt act (2:346), and not simply to a series of events that might be so interpreted. He also wanted to make it clear that war against any one state was war against the whole (2:349).

On August 27, Dickinson indicated that he wanted to modify judicial service during good behavior so as to specify that the executive could remove judges on the application of Congress (2:428). The convention wisely rejected this proposal, which could have interfered with judicial independence. Dickinson appeared to believe that the division of Congress into two branches made it unlikely that the two "would improperly unite for the purpose of displacing a Judge" (2:429). Dickinson successfully modified what became Article III of the Constitution by introducing the motion granting jurisdiction to federal courts "both as to law & fact" (2:431).

Federalism

On June 2 Dickinson indicated that he "had no idea of abolishing the State Governments as some gentlemen seemed inclined to do. The happiness of this Country . . . required considerable powers to be left in the hands of the States" (1:85). He reiterated this point later in the day, when he observed that one of the remedies for the diseases of republican government was the "division of this country into distinct States" (1:87). He believed that such a division would lead to "stability" (1:86); he seemed to believe that "A House of Nobles," which might also lead to stability, would be impossible in the United States since such nobles "were the growth of ages, and could only arise under a complication of circumstances none of which existed in this Country" (1:87).

Perhaps as much as any delegate, Dickinson believed that the division between state and national governments was a vital part of checks and balances. Arguing on June 7 for retaining the states, Dickinson explained his view at length:

> To attempt to abolish the States altogether, would degrade the Councils of our Country, would be impracticable, would be ruinous. He compared the proposed National System to the Solar System, in which the States were the planets, and ought to be left to move freely in their proper orbits. . . . If the State Governments were excluded from all agency in the national one, and all power drawn from the people at large, the consequences would be that the national Govt. would move in the same direction as the State Govts. now do, and would run into all the same mischiefs. The reform would only unite the 13 small streams into one great current pursuing the same course without any opposition whatever. (1:153)

Despite advocating state legislative selection of senators, Dickinson expressed support on June 8 for the congressional negative on state laws. Arguing that there was greater danger of the states encroaching on the national government rather than the reverse (at least under the system he favored, whereby members of the Senate were to be chosen by state legislatures), he said, "To leave the power doubtful, would be opening another spring of discord, and he was for shutting as many of them as possible" (1:167).

Similarly, on August 30 Dickinson indicated that he believed that Congress should be able to protect states against domestic violence whether the state legislatures requested such aid or not. He was apparently contemplating situations in which such controversies might "proceed from the State Legislature itself, or from disputes between the two branches where such exist" 2:467). The convention agreed to allow either the state legislature or the state executive to apply for such help (2:467).

Dickinson indicated on August 14 that he did not favor leaving members of Congress dependent on state legislatures for their pay. He suggested that Congress might set wages every 12 years. He further observed that "If the Genl. Govt. should be left dependent on the State Legislatures, it would be happy for us if we had never met in this Room" (2:292). Although Dickinson originally thought that the pay for both houses of Congress should be the same, he withdrew his motion after Nathaniel Gorham made an argument as to why senators should receive more (2:293).

Dickinson wanted to preserve a role for the states in regulating militia. He favored a plan on August 18 that would invest the national government with the power to regulate only one-fourth of the militia at a time, hoping that through rotation, the entire militia would ultimately be so disciplined (2:331).

Dickinson observed on August 29 that he had been reading William Blackstone's legal *Commentaries on the Laws of England* and had discovered that a prohibition on states against adopting ex post facto laws would apply only to criminal laws. He accordingly suggested that some provision should be made against state adoption of retroactive civil laws as well (2:449).

Perhaps with an eye to fears that Pennsylvania might seek to swallow Delaware, on August 30 Dickinson introduced the provision in the Constitution that provided that new states could not be formed within existing states or parts of states without their consent and that of Congress (2:465).

Dickinson's Plan

At the time the convention was comparing the Virginia and New Jersey Plans, Dickinson drafted a plan of his own. This plan combined elements of both plans as well as developing some mechanisms that were unique to Dickinson. Perhaps in deference to Alexander Hamilton who offered a plan at about the same time, or perhaps because Dickinson did not succeed in getting approval for a motion that would have introduced this plan, Dickinson never formally introduced his plan at the convention. It nonetheless gives insight into what he and other delegates may have been thinking.

Dickinson's plan was divided into seven parts. The first called for a revision and an amendment of the Articles of Confederation, but the second recognized the need for three distinct branches of government. The third article further called for, as in the Virginia Plan, a bicameral Congress. Article IV provided that members of one branch should be chosen by states, each with one vote, as under the Articles. Members were to be thirty years of age and to serve for seven-year terms; members selected to fill a vacant term would only serve to the end of this term, thus assuring the turnover of one-seventh of its members each year (Hutson 1987, 88).

Article V provided for the selection of the other house by people of the states for terms of three years, again to serve rotating terms. Members of this branch were to be proportioned according to the money that each state contributed to the common treasury, with new states to be treated the same as the original states.

Much as the Committee of Detail would later do, Article VI proceeded to outline new powers for the government. These included powers "to pass Acts for enforcing an Observance of the Laws of Nations and an Obedience to their own Laws"; to levy duties, imposts, and stamps; power to transfer suits from state to national courts; to emit money; to regulate "the Value and Alloy of Coin"; to negate state acts; to judge contests within states that might disturb the public peace; to secure "the Writ of Habeas Corpus and Trial by Jury in proper Cases"; and "for preventing Contests concerning the Authority of the United States and the Authority of individual states" (Hutson 1987, 90).

Article VII contained a modified Supremacy Clause. It provided:

> That all Laws and Resolves of any state in any Manner opposing or contravening the powers now vested or hereby to be vested in the United States or any Act of the United States made by Virtue and in pursuance of such powers or any Treaties made and ratified under the United States shall be utterly null and void (this nearly as in the proposals from New Jersey). (Hutson 1987, 90)

Article VII further outlined the executive branch. Consistent with Dickinson's earlier reservations that a single executive might become a monarchy, Dickinson proposed that two-thirds of the state legislatures should be able to elect an executive of three persons "one of them a Resident of the Eastern States, another of the Middle States and the third of the Southern States" (Hutson 1987, 90). Initially, one would serve for two years, another for four years and a third for seven years, with seven years becoming the eventual norm. The individual elected to the seven-year term, and thereafter the individual with the longest service, would be president. Members of the executive could be removed by Congress "if they judge it proper on Application by a Majority of the Executives of the several states" (Hutson 1987, 91). Members of the executive branch would also be impeachable "for Malconduct or Neglect of Duty" (91). The members of the executive would be jointly responsible for everything they did, unless they recorded their dissents to the same. They would exercise the power of the veto subject to an override by two-thirds of Congress.

Dickinson further specified that the legislature would appoint members of the judiciary, and that "this Judiciary would have Authority to determine in the first Instance in all Cases touching the Rights of Ambassadors and other foreign Ministers" (Hutson 1987, 91). Congress would have power to establish inferior tribunals.

Dickinson then indicated that he favored the Report of the Committee of the Whole "from the 14th Resolution of the Report, inclusive to the End" (Hutson 1987, 91). These provisions respectively provided for: the admission of new states; the continuance of Congress until a new government could be instituted; guaranteeing each state a republican form of government; an amending provision; for state officials to be bound to the new Constitution by oath; and for ratification of the new Constitution by special conventions within the states elected by the people (1:237).

Ratification

The plan that Dickinson prepared but never introduced at the convention indicated that he favored ratification of the Constitution by ratifying conventions. He appeared to reiterate this point on August 30 when he questioned whether the Congress under the Articles of Confederation "could concur in contravening the system under which they acted" (2:469).

Committees

Dickinson served on three committees at the convention. He was appointed on August 18 to the Committee on State Debts and Militia, on August 22 to the Committee on Slave Trade and Navigation, and on August 31 to the Committee on Postponed Matters. This latter committee was responsible for the invention of the electoral college mechanism for choosing the president. Dickinson claimed in a letter of 1802 that his concern for a method of making the president accountable to the people was influential in creating this mechanism, although he attributed its actual writing to James Madison (see Flower 1983, 246–47).

Life after the Convention

Exhausted by ill health, Dickinson left Philadelphia before the convention ended. Perhaps with a view to the criticism he had received for not signing the Declaration of Independence, Dickinson designated fellow delegate George Read to sign his name. Dickinson wrote some essays for the *Delaware Gazette* under the name "Fabias" in support of the new Constitution (for analysis, see Ahern 1998). In an essay he published on April 17, 1788, Dickinson likened the powers that individual states had surrendered to those that human beings give up when they entered society. He further observed that: "If as some persons seem to think, *a bill of rights* is the *best security* of rights, the sovereignties of the several states have *this* best security by the proposed constitution; more than this best security, for they are not barely *declared* to be rights, but are taken into it as *component parts*, for *their* perpetual preservation by *themselves*" (Bailyn 1993, 2:411).

In 1792, Dickinson served as a delegate to the Delaware state constitutional convention, and was elected as its president. He did some further writing, which did not, however, have the same force as his earlier works. He died in Wilmington, Delaware on February 14, 1808 and was interred in the city's Friends Burial Ground. His house, Poplar Hall, in Delaware is owned by the state and is open to the public.

Further Reading

Ahern, Gregory S. 1998. "The Spirit of American Constitutionalism: John Dickinson's *Fabius Letters.*" *Humanitas* 11, no. 2. The Center for Constitutional Studies. http://www.nhinet.org/ccs/ccs-res.htm. Accessed 4/8/2004.

Bailyn, Bernard, ed. 1993. *The Debate on the Constitution: Federalist and Antifederalist Speeches, Articles, and Letters during the Struggle over Ratification.* 2 vols. New York: The Library of America.

Calvert, Jane E. 2007. "Liberty without Tumult: Understanding the Politics of John Dickinson." *Pennsylvania Magazine of History and Biography* 131 (July): 233–62.

———. 2008. *Quaker Constitutionalism and the Political Thought of John Dickinson.* Cambridge: Cambridge University Press.

Colburne, H. Trevor. 1959. "John Dickinson: Historical Revolutionary." *Pennsylvania Magazine of History and Biography* 83 (July): 271–92.

Dickinson, John. 1970. *The Political Writings of John Dickinson, 1764–1776*, edited by Paul Leicester Ford. New York: Da Capo.

Farrand, Max, ed. 1966. *The Records of the Federal Convention of 1787*. 4 vols. New Haven, CT: Yale University Press.

Flower, Milton E. 1983. *John Dickinson: Conservative Revolutionary*. Charlottesville: University Press of Virginia.

Hutson, James H. 1983. "John Dickinson at the Federal Constitutional Convention." *William and Mary Quarterly*, 3rd Ser., 40: 256–82.

Hutson, James H., ed. 1987. *Supplement to Max Farrand's The Records of the Federal Convention of 1787*. New Haven, CT: Yale University Press.

Lubert, Howard L. 2011. "John Dickinson." In *America's Forgotten Founders*, 2nd ed., edited by Gary L. Gregg II and Mark David Hall, 105–16. Wilmington, DE: Intercollegiate Studies Institute.

Morton, Joseph C. 2006. *Shapers of the Great Debate at the Constitutional Convention of 1787: A Biographical Dictionary*. Westport, CT: Greenwood Press.

Murchison, William. 2012. *The Cost of Liberty: The Life of John Dickinson*. Wilmington, DE: Intercollegiate Studies Institute.

Natelson, Robert G. 2003. "The Constitutional Contributions of John Dickinson." *Pennsylvania State Law Review* 108 (Fall): 415–77.

Powell, J. H. 1936. "John Dickinson and the Constitution." *The Pennsylvania Magazine of History and Biography* 60 (January): 1–14.

Richards, Robert H. 1901. "The Life and Character of John Dickinson." *Papers of the Historical Society of Delaware*. Vol. 30.

Webking, Robert H. 1988. *The American Revolution and the Politics of Liberty*. Baton Rouge: Louisiana State University Press.

OLIVER ELLSWORTH (1745–1807)
CONNECTICUT

Born to Captain David Ellsworth and his wife Jemima Leavitt Ellsworth on April 29, 1745 in Windsor, Connecticut, Oliver Ellsworth attended Yale (where he was disciplined for his pranks) before finishing a degree at the College of New Jersey (today's Princeton). There he met William Paterson, who would also attend the Constitutional Convention and with whom he would later serve on the U.S. Supreme Court. After abandoning the study of theology (he remained a devout Calvinist and later coauthored a religious tract entitled *A Summary of Christian Doctrine and Practice*), Ellsworth took up law and was admitted to the Connecticut bar.

In 1772 he married then sixteen-year-old Abigail Wolcott (1755–1818), and they had nine children, of whom seven lived to adulthood. Oliver wrote one of the more amusing letters from the convention in which he confessed to his wife that he had clasped "the hand of a woman who died many hundred years ago" (Hutson 1987, 177). The hand of the other woman in question turned out to be on an arm that had been detached from an Egyptian mummy and that Ellsworth, who had tried to cut it with a knife, described as looking "much like smoked beef kept till it grows hard" (177).

As his legal business began to pick up, Ellsworth also began participating in politics. He was elected as a state representative, served on the Council of Safety, and was elected in 1777 to the Continental Congress where he served on the Committee on International Treaties and on the Committee of Appeals, which has been described as "the first forerunner of the present Supreme Court of the United States" (Brown 1905, 754). He was subsequently appointed to the Connecticut Supreme Court of Errors and to the state's superior court. For this reason, he was often referred to at the Constitutional Convention as "Judge" Ellsworth. He was a tall, thin man, about six feet two inches in height, and was known for being a good orator and for dressing elegantly.

At the Convention

Ellsworth began attending the convention on May 28, and although he was not present for the signing of the document, he participated significantly in its formulation. He worked closely with fellow Connecticut delegate Roger Sherman and is perhaps best known for being one of those delegates who helped effect a compromise between the large states and the small states on representation in Congress and for formulating a description of the new government as "partly national, partly federal" (Farrand 1966, 1:468).

The Great Compromise

The first time that Ellsworth's name appears in relation to convention debates, he is seconding a motion by fellow Connecticut delegate Roger

Sherman recommending that each state have an equal vote in the U.S. Senate (1:201). Significantly, after weeks of exasperating debate over representation in Congress, Ellsworth said on June 29 that "I do not despair but that we shall be so fortunate as to devise and adopt some good plan of government" (1:471).

It was on June 29, after the convention had agreed to allow for proportional state representation in the House of Representatives, that Ellsworth proposed that representation in the Senate should remain like representation under the Articles of Confederation, that is, with each state having an equal vote. Professing that he was not opposed to the motion that had just been adopted, Ellsworth hoped that it might become the basis of a compromise. He further introduced a formulation for describing the new government that James Madison (who strongly opposed it at the time) would later use in Federalist No. 39 to describe and justify the new Constitution:

> We were partly national; partly federal. The proportional representation in the first branch was conformable to the national principle & would secure the large States agst. the small. An equality of voices was conformable to the federal principle and was necessary to secure the Small States agst. the large. He trusted that on this middle ground a compromise would take place. He did not see that it could on any other. (1:468–69)

Ellsworth did not think the small states would accept a plan that did not give them equality in at least one house, and he did not think such equality would undermine the large states. He offered an analysis designed to appeal to both groups of states:

> He could never admit that there was no danger of combinations among the large States. They will like individuals find out and avail themselves of the advantage to be gained by it. It was true the danger would be greater, if they were contiguous and had a more immediate common interest. A defensive combination of the small States was rendered more difficult by their greater number. (1:469)

Ellsworth further argued that states had some obligation to recognize the equality that states enjoyed at the time under the Articles. He urged caution:

> Let a strong Executive, a Judiciary & Legislative power be created; but Let not too much be attempted; by which all may be lost. He was not in general a half-way man, yet he preferred doing half the good we could, rather than

do nothing at all. The other half may be added, when the necessity shall be more fully experienced. (1:469)

When Pennsylvania's James Wilson attacked Ellsworth's proposal as allowing for minority rule, Ellsworth held his ground. Strengthened by the fact that the convention had already provided for majority rule in the House of Representatives, Ellsworth presented equal representation within the Senate as a defensive mechanism: "The power is given to the few to save them from being destroyed by the many" (1:484). Citing the House of Lords in Britain, which a number of delegates had commended, Ellsworth said that equal representation in the Senate would provide for a similar check. He moved from theory to practice, with a homey but effective example: "We are running from one extreme to another. We are razing the foundations of the building. When we need only repair the roof" (1:484). Ellsworth further outlined a case where the three largest states might attempt to favor themselves, and he again cited representation under the Articles as a kind of faith into which the states had mutually entered. He further defended Connecticut's contributions under the Articles of Confederation—he said that Connecticut had fielded more troops during the revolution than had Virginia—indicating that "If she had been delinquent, it had been from inability, and not more so than other States" (1:487).

Later in the day, Ellsworth indicated that it was possible to appreciate both the objects of general union and of an individual's own state. Acknowledging that the general government would provide for national security, he demonstrated even greater attachment to his state:

> I want domestic happiness, as well as general security. A general government will never grant me this, as it cannot know my wants or relieve my distress. My state is only as one out of thirteen. Can they, the general government, gratify my wishes? My happiness depends as much on the existence of my state government, as a new-born infant depends upon its mother for nourishment. (1:502)

The convention appointed Ellsworth to the committee that developed the Great Compromise, but he was apparently unable to attend. Not surprisingly, however, he supported it (1:532). Ellsworth posed two critical questions on July 14, just two days before the convention adopted the Great Compromise. He asked Wilson whether he had ever known a measure to fail in Congress for lack of a majority of states in its favor, and he asked Madison whether the negative by the Senate "could be any more dangerous" than the negative over state laws that Madison had proposed investing in Congress (2:11)? Far later in the convention, Ellsworth stated that he did not believe the privilege of originating money bills in the House of Representatives amounted to much but that "he was willing it should stand" (2:224; also see 2:233).

Congress

Terms. On June 12, Ellsworth joined Roger Sherman in proposing to set terms for members of the U.S. House of Representatives at one year. At least in Sherman's case, however, he appears to have introduced the motion to hasten convention business rather than because he favored it (1:214). The fact that Ellsworth reintroduced this motion on June 21 suggests that he may have felt more strongly on the matter than Sherman (1:361).

On June 16, Ellsworth proposed "that the Legislative power of the U.S. should remain in Congs" (1:255). He apparently hoped that this would be a substitute for William Paterson's motion introducing the New Jersey Plan which had called for revising, correcting, and enlarging the Articles so as "to render the federal Constitution adequate to the exigencies of Government, & the preservation of the Union" (1:242). Along a similar line, on June 20, Ellsworth proposed dropping the word "national" out of the resolution introducing the revised Virginia Plan (1:335). On this occasion, Ellsworth further denied that a breach of one of the Articles would dissolve the whole. He expressed the view that needed changes in the Articles could go forward as amendments, which state legislatures could then ratify.

Pay. On June 22 Ellsworth proposed that members of Congress should be paid out of state treasuries rather than by Congress. He observed that standards of living varied within the states, and he feared that what would be deemed reasonable in one state would be regarded as unreasonable in others, thus undermining confidence in the proposed system (1:371–72). In opposing New York's Alexander Hamilton on this point, Ellsworth argued that "If we are jealous of the State Govts. they will be so of us" (1:374). On June 26, Ellsworth attempted to see that the states would at least maintain control over the salaries of senators. He deftly combined a theoretical with a practical argument by observing:

> If the Senate was meant to strengthen the Govt. it ought to have the confidence of the States. The States will have an interest in keeping up a

representation and will make such provision for supporting the members as will ensure their attendance (1:427).

By August 14, Ellsworth had changed his mind on the subject. He feared that state payment of members of Congress would lead to overdependence on the state legislatures. He proposed that members should be paid an unspecified per diem payment out of the national treasury (2:290). He hoped to tie it to its current exchange value so as to obviate concerns over granting Congress unlimited authority to set its own salary (2:292). He proposed an initial salary of five dollars per day and for every thirty miles (2:293).

Selection of Senators. On June 25, Ellsworth favored allowing state legislatures, rather than electors chosen directly by the people, to choose U.S. senators. He believed that senators would reflect views distinctive to their states, no matter how they were chosen. He thought that legislative selection was more likely to result in getting senators who were wise. He further advanced his view that, given the size of the United States, it would be necessary to preserve the states:

> He urged the necessity of maintaining the existence & agency of the States. Without their co-operation it would be impossible to support a Republican Govt. over so great an extent of County. An army could scarcely render it practicable. . . . If the principles & materials of our Govt. are not adequate to the extent of these single states [Virginia, Massachusetts, and Pennsylvania]; how can it be imagined that they can support a single Govt. throughout the U. States. The only chance of supporting a Genl. Govt. lies in engrafting it on that of the individual States. (2:406–7)

Size of Congress. Ellsworth opposed a motion by James Madison to double the size of the initial House of Representatives from 65 to 130 members. He objected both because of the expense of so many representatives and because he thought such a size would slow congressional business. He further argued "that a large number was less necessary in the Genl. Legislature than in those of the States, as its business would relate to a few great, national Objects only" (1:569). Ellsworth indicated that he favored allowing member of the Senate to vote on a "per capita" basis rather than casting a single vote for each state delegation (2:94).

Three-fifths Provision. Just as he had smoothed the way for a compromise on representation of the large and small states, so too, Ellsworth attempted to reconcile differences between free and slave states. He proposed that the three-fifths formula be used for representation in the House "until some other rule shall more accurately ascertain the wealth of the several States" (1:594). Ellsworth subsequently withdrew this motion in deference to a motion by Virginia's Edmund Randolph that gave greater security to the rule by making it permanent (1:595). Ellsworth thought this same formula could be used for levying poll taxes, although he did not anticipate that any would be needed (2:597). He thought requiring taxes to be apportioned in the interim according to representation in the House of Representatives was an unwise attempt to micromanage the new government (1:602).

When delegates proposed that Congress should be able to tax slave importations, Ellsworth expressed his opposition. Consistent with earlier expressions of deference to state decision making, he believed that the "morality or wisdom of slavery" were state matters that should be left to them. He further believed that what helped states individually would help the whole and that there was no more reason for the proposed government to regulate this matter than there would have been for the government under the Articles of Confederation (2:364).

Although he professed not to believe this was a national matter, there is some indication that Ellsworth reacted negatively to George Mason's speech against slavery, possibly because Ellsworth regarded it as hypocritical. Mason, a slave owner, had argued that "Every master of slaves is born a petty tyrant" (2:370). Ellsworth observed that "As he had never owned a slave" he "could not judge of the effects of slavery on character" (2:371). He suggested that if slavery was as bad as Mason said, however, that the convention should consider not only excluding their future importation but freeing those who were already in the country. He went on to make a poor prophesy, but probably one that other delegates shared at the time:

> Let us not intermeddle. As population increase; poor laborers will be so plenty as to render slaves useless. Slavery in time will not be a speck in our Country. Provision is already made in Connecticut for abolishing it. And the abolition has already taken place in Massachusetts. (2:371)

Finding a silver lining in what was otherwise a fairly dark cloud, Ellsworth further observed that fears of slave insurrections would serve to motivate their masters to good behavior (2:371).

Qualifications. Ellsworth opposed a provision to disqualify individuals with debts from running for Congress. He thought it better to leave "to the wisdom of the Legislature and the virtue of the Citizens, the task of providing agst. such evils" (2:126). He further observed that the reason the British had excluded pensioners from running for office was that they were dependent upon the Crown, and thus increased the influence of the monarch (2:126). Ellsworth later elaborated on his opposition of specifying qualifications within the Constitution. His arguments indicate continuing sensitivity to state differences:

> The different circumstances of different parts of the U.S. and the probable difference between the present and future circumstances of the whole, render it improper to have either *uniform* or *fixed* qualifications. Make them so high as to be useful in the S. States, and they will be inapplicable to the E. States. Suit them to the latter, and they will serve no purpose in the former. In like manner what may be accommodated to the existing State of things among us, may be very inconvenient in some future state of them. (2:249)

Ellsworth thought it would be less dangerous to allow Congress to set qualifications for its own members than for their electors (2:250).

Ellsworth believed that one year of residency within a state should be an adequate time for individuals running for Congress (2:218). Similarly, Ellsworth opposed a motion by Gouverneur Morris to raise the citizenship requirement from four to fourteen years for senators. Ellworth feared that this would discourage "meritorious aliens from emigrating to this Country" (2:235).

Voting. Ellsworth opposed fixing voting qualifications within the Constitution. He observed that voting rights were "a tender point" and that "The people will not readily subscribe to the Natl. Constitution, if it should subject them to be disfranchised" (2:201). This fit nicely with his view of the functions of the states, which he regarded as "the best Judges of the circumstances and temper of their own people" (2:201). He also anticipated practical problems in defining the freehold, especially in commercial areas: "Shall the wealthy merchants and manufacturers, who will bear a full share of the public burdens be not allowed a voice in the imposition of them" (2:202).

Powers. Ellsworth opposed granting Congress power to tax exports (2:307). He later offered three reasons against such taxation. He argued that it would discourage industry, that it would be difficult to apportion such taxes equitably since states had different products, and that it would "engender incurable jealousies" (2:360). He did not think that the provision related to exports would prevent Congress from imposing complete embargoes if such became necessary (2:361).

Ellsworth thought that the convention represented a propitious time "to shut and bar the door against paper money" and that doing so would gain support for the new Constitution (2:309). He argued, "Paper money can in no case be necessary—Give the Government credit, and other resources will offer—The power may do harm, never good" (2:310). Ellsworth introduced the motion granting Congress power "to define and punish piracies and felonies committed on the high seas, counterfeiting the securities and current coin of the U. States, and offences agst. the law of Nations" (2:316).

Ellsworth indicated that that he did not generally think Congress should have the power to intervene in force within states unless requested to do so. However, he was willing to allow the governor to request such aid when the legislature was not in session (2:317).

Ellsworth thought that a distinction should be made between making war and making peace. Specifically, he argued that "It shd. be more easy to get out of war, than into it." His reasoning, however, did not necessarily appear to support this assertion: "War also is a simple and over declaration. peace attended with intricate & secret negociations" (2:319).

Ellsworth thought that Congress should assume state debts to the degree that it could equitably do so (2:327). He later became a strong supporter of Alexander Hamilton's economic plan that was introduced in the first Congress.

Ellsworth opposed a motion by George Mason granting Congress power to regulate the militia as going too far:

> The whole authority over the Militia ought by no means to be taken away from the States whose consequence would pine away to nothing after such a sacrifice of power. He thought the Genl. Authority could not sufficiently pervade the Union for such a purpose, nor could it accommodate itself to the local genius of the people. It must be vain to ask the States to give the Militia out of their hands. (2:331)

He opposed the idea of a select militia as impractical and did not believe the states would agree to it (2:332). He instead favored leaving a provision in the Constitution specifying that states retained the right to train their militia as well as to appoint their officers (2:385), and later introduced a provision "to refer the plan for the Militia to the General Govt. but leave the execution of it to the State Govts." (2:386).

When George Mason proposed granting Congress the power to enact sumptuary legislation, Ellsworth said that it would be sufficient simply to allow Congress "to enforce taxes & debts. As far as the regulation of eating & drinking can be reasonable, it is provided for in the power of taxation" (2:344).

When the convention discussed the issue of treason, Ellsworth spoke out for allowing both the states and the national government to protect their respective sovereignties (2:349). He further proposed that Congress should carry out the first census within three, rather than within six, years (2:350). He did not believe it would be fair to apportion taxes according to the initial number of congressional representatives since he did not believe the initial apportionment would be that accurate (2:358).

Ellsworth opposed a congressional veto of state laws. He believed that it would either require that states submit all such legislation beforehand to Congress or require the general government to appoint state governors (2:391).

Other Matters. Ellsworth was among those who favored fixing the time of congressional meetings in the Constitution. He thought this was a matter about which "the Convention could judge . . . as well as the Legislature" (2:198). He believed that summer would not be a good time since he anticipated that most members of Congress would be tied in some manner to agriculture (2:200). Ellsworth opposed a motion setting one-half of the initial membership of Congress as a quorum on the basis that this number would prove to be inadequate in the future. He favored granting each house the power to compel absent members to attend (2:253). Ellsworth agreed with Roger Sherman in opposing congressional roll call votes since the reasons that members of Congress voted as they did would not be recorded along with their votes (2:255). After the requirement that Congress publish its proceedings was qualified, Ellsworth thought that it would be better to strike it out completely, arguing that the people would assure that Congress published its records (2:260).

Ellsworth saw no problem with requiring that members of Congress be ineligible to accept other offices. He observed both that "merit will be most encouraged, when most impartially rewarded," and that "if rewards are to circulate only within the Legislature, merit out of it will be discouraged" (2:288).

Presidency

Ellsworth attempted to resolve the issue of presidential selection somewhat as he had proposed resolving representation in Congress. When the convention was still contemplating allowing Congress to select the president, he proposed that states should choose electors, having one, two, or three according to whether their populations had up to 200,000 residents, from 200,000 to 300,000 residents, or above 300,000 (2:57). He believed that New Hampshire and Georgia should both be entitled to two electors (2:63). Ellsworth thought that members of Congress should be barred from serving as electors, but he did not think this disability needed to be further extended (2:58).

On July 19 Ellsworth indicated that he thought the president should serve for a six-year term. His central objective was to give the office sufficient firmness. He further observed: "If the Elections are too frequent, the best men will not undertake the service and those of an inferior character will be liable to be corrupted" (2:59).

Even when the convention was contemplating a plan whereby Congress would elect the president, Ellsworth favored allowing the president to be re-eligible for election. He explained:

> The Executive . . . should be reelected if his conduct proved him worthy of it. And he will be more likely to render him[self] worthy of it if he be rewardable with it. The most eminent characters also will be more willing to accept the trust under this condition, than if they foresee a necessary degradation at a fixt period. (2:101)

Somewhat later Ellsworth proposed a plan whereby a sitting president would be chosen by electors appointed by state legislatures rather than by Congress (2:108–9). Ellsworth was concerned, however, that the systems of election being discussed at the convention tilted too much in the direction of the most populous states (2:111).

Ellsworth favored a provision whereby the president could supply vacancies in the U.S. Senate but did not anticipate that the president would need to exercise such a power when the state legislature was in session (2: 231). He did not oppose allowing either state governors or state legislatures to make such appointments, but he did not want to divide the power between them (2:232).

Just as he had supported a Council of Revision (see below), Ellsworth favored establishing a presidential council. He wanted it to consist of the president of the Senate, the chief justice, and the ministers of leading departments. He anticipated that they "should advise but not conclude the President" (2:329).

Ellsworth favored leaving in a provision that would have required a two-thirds majority of Congress to enact navigation acts at a time when some wanted to eliminate the provision and others wanted to make the majority even larger. His motivation was purely practical:

> If we do not agree on this middle & moderate ground he was afraid we should lose two States, with such others as may be disposed to stand aloof, should fly into a variety of shapes & directions, and most probably into several confederations and not without bloodshed. (2:375)

Ellsworth did not favor the prohibition on ex post facto (retroactive criminal) laws, but for fairly lawyerly reasons: he believed they were "void of themselves" and therefore it could not "be necessary to prohibit them" (2:376). Similarly, he thought it unnecessary to grant Congress the power to fulfill the engagements of the Articles of Confederation since it would automatically become the agent of this former body (2:377).

Judiciary

Ellsworth, a Connecticut judge who later served as chief justice of the U.S. Supreme Court, approved of the plan to associate members of the judiciary with the executive in a Council of Revision. He saw several advantages:

> The aid of the Judges will give more wisdom & firmness to the Executive. They will possess a systematic and accurate knowledge of the Laws, which the Executive can not be expected always to possess. The law of Nations also will frequently come into question. Of this the Judge alone will have competent information. (2:74)

In discussing judicial appointments on July 21, Ellsworth indicated that he could support allowing the Senate to nominate judges, subject to a presidential veto, which could be overridden by a two-thirds vote, but that he would prefer a system whereby the Senate had the absolute appointment power. He seemed in part concerned about popular reaction, and in part about a number of practical problems:

> The Executive will be regarded by the people with a jealous eye. Every power for augmenting unnecessarily his influence will be disliked. As he will be stationary it was not to be supposed he could have a better knowledge of characters. He will be more open to caresses & intrigues than the Senate. The right to supersede his nomination will be ideal only. A nomination under such circumstances will be the equivalent to an appointment. (2:81)

Ratification

On June 20, Ellsworth expressed the view that what changes were needed in the Articles could go forward by amendments that states could ratify. He feared that if state conventions were to be used, it would take a number of them. He further observed that "He did not like these conventions. They were better fitted to pull down than to build up Constitutions" (1:335). Ellsworth repeated his support for state legislative ratification on July 23, where he portrayed the idea that constitutions needed to be ratified by conventions as a new idea. He attempted to answer arguments by George Mason that legislatures had no authority to ratify constitutions, and that if they exercised such authority, future legislatures could rescind it. As to the first argument, Ellsworth argued that legislatures had until recently been accepted as competent to ratify constitutions as the very existence of the Articles demonstrated: "The fact is that we exist at present, and we need not enquire how, as a federal Society, united by a charter one article of which is that alterations therein may be made by the Legislative authority of the States" (2:91). Intentionally or perhaps unintentionally sidestepping the second issue, Ellsworth argued that legislative ratification did not need, as some delegates had argued, to be unanimous:

> if such were the urgency & necessity of our situation as to warrant a new compact among a part of the States, founded on the consent of the people; the same pleas would be equally valid in favor of a partial compact, founded on the consent of the Legislatures. (2:91)

Life after the Convention

Ellsworth left the Constitutional Convention on August 25. He appears to have done so in order to attend to his judicial duties rather than, as in the case of some other delegates, because he opposed the direction that the convention had taken. He emerged as a defender of the Constitution during the debates over ratification in his state.

Writing under the pen name, "A Landholder," Ellsworth published an essay on November 19, 1787 in which he observed: "The present question is should we have a constitution or not? We allow it to be a creation of power; but power when necessary for our good is as much to be desired as the food we eat or the air we breathe" (Bailyn 1993, 1:330). Acknowledging that there were objections to the document, he further observed that "The new Constitution is perhaps more cautiously guarded than any other in the world, and at the same time will be able to protect the subject" (*Debate* 1993, 1:330).

Selected as one of Connecticut's first two U.S. senators, Ellsworth gravitated toward the Federalist Party. Ellsworth chaired the Senate Judiciary Committee. In this capacity he was the primary author of the Judiciary Act of 1789 where he put flesh on the bare bones of Article III of the Constitution (the sketchiest of the three distributing articles, allocating powers to the branches of the national government) by creating a three-tier system of federal courts, with circuit and district courts below the Supreme Court. President Washington appointed Ellsworth as the third chief justice of the U.S. Supreme Court in 1796, where Ellsworth often expressed his admiration for the English common law. Ellsworth served in this capacity until 1800 but issued few landmark cases.

President John Adams appointed Ellsworth and two other Americans to France to negotiate over its interference in American shipping. Although the trip resulted in a treaty that Congress ratified, the travel and Ellsworth's prior circuit riding duties as a justice were not good for his health. After a brief sojourn in England, Ellsworth returned to Connecticut and became a member of the Governor's Council and the Connecticut Supreme Court of Errors. He interpreted Jefferson's election in 1801 to the providence of God, who "will turn all the wrath & folly of men to good account" (quoted in Casto 1994, 520). In 1802, when Jefferson was advocating complete separation of church and state, Ellsworth was influential in repelling a plea by Baptists for disestablishment of the church in Connecticut. He observed that "Institutions for the promotion of good morals, are [proper] objects of Legislative provision and support: and among these, in the opinion of the committee, religious institutions are eminently useful and important" (quoted in Casto 1994, 525).

Ellsworth died at his farm in Windsor, Connecticut on November 26, 1807 and was buried in the Palisado Cemetery in the town. He left behind a statement suggesting that he had died a very contented man:

> I have visited several countries and I like my own the best. I have been in all the states of the Union, and Connecticut is the best state. Windsor is the pleasantest town in the state of Connecticut, and I have the pleasantest place in the town of Windsor. I am content, perfectly content, to die on the banks of the Connecticut. (quoted in Toth 2011, 211)

"Elmwood," the Ellsworth homestead (and now a museum) in Windsor, is open to the public from May 18 to October 14.

Further Reading

Bailyn, Bernard, ed. 1993. *The Debate on the Constitution: Federalist and Antifederalist Speeches, Articles, and Letters during the Struggle over Ratification.* 2 vols. New York: The Library of America.

Brown, William Garrott. 1905. "A Continental Congressman: Oliver Ellsworth, 1777–1783." *American Historical Review* 10 (July): 751–81.

Casto, William R. 1994. "Oliver Ellsworth's Calvinism: A Biographical Essay on Religion and Political Psychology in the Early Republic." *Journal of Church and State* 36: 507–26.

———. 1995. *The Supreme Court in the Early Republic: The Chief Justiceships of John Jay and Oliver Ellsworth.* Columbia: University of South Carolina Press.

Cushman, Clare, ed. 1995. *The Supreme Court Justices: Illustrated Biographies, 1789–1995,* 2nd ed. Washington, DC: Congressional Quarterly.

Farrand, Max, ed. 1966. *The Records of the Federal Convention of 1787.* 4 vols. New Haven, CT: Yale University Press.

Hutson, James H., ed. 1987. *Supplement to Max Farrand's The Records of the Federal Convention of 1787.* New Haven, CT: Yale University Press.

Meister, Charles W. 1987. *The Founding Fathers.* Jefferson, NC: McFarland & Company.

Toth, Michael C. 2011. *Founding Federalist: The Life of Oliver Ellsworth.* Wilmington, DE: Intercollegiate Studies Institute.

WILLIAM FEW (1748–1828)
GEORGIA

William Few was born near Baltimore, Maryland on June 18, 1748 to William Few Sr. and Mary Wheeler Few, who were farmers. Few moved with his family first to North Carolina and later to Georgia. Given a small tract of land in Georgia by his father, Few, who had little formal education, punctuated his farm tasks with reading. After serving at the state constitutional convention of 1777, Few entered the Georgia militia where he became a lieutenant colonel, specializing in guerilla tactics, before being elected to the state legislature and serving on the executive council.

Few was a tall (six feet) and slender man who married Catherine (Kitty) Nicholson (1764–1854) of New York with whom he had three daughters and a son. Although not a great orator, he was admitted to the bar without ever receiving formal training in law (he had listened to many cases and borrowed books from lawyers). Few was serving at the time of the Constitutional Convention, to which he had been appointed, as a member of Congress.

At the Convention

Few attended the first few weeks of the convention but spent most of his time during the summer of 1787 in New York on his congressional duties. As a consequence of this and of what appears to have been a timidity in the presence of men more educated than he (a French observer noted, "Il est tres timide et embarassant dans la societe, a moins qu'on ne lui parle d'affaires" [Farrand 1966, 3:238]), he is not recorded as having spoken a single time at the convention. He was present for the opening day of business on May 25, and he did sign the document.

In a short autobiography that he wrote in 1816, Few discussed the "incalculable difficulties" of the convention, especially the problems in addressing states' rights. He confirmed that the convention did not adopt Benjamin Franklin's proposal to bring in a chaplain each day to begin the meeting in prayer. Few observed that the convention had progressed on the "principle of accommodations" and "It was believed to be of the utmost importance to concede to different opinions so far as to endeavor to meet opposition on middle ground, and to form a Constitution that might preserve the union of the States" (3:423). He further observed that "after about three months' arduous labor, a plan of Constitution was formed on principles which did not altogether please anybody, but it was agreed to be the most expedient that could be devised and agreed to" (3:423).

Life after the Convention

Few served as a trustee of the University of Georgia, as one of Georgia's first two senators, and as a Georgia judge. In Congress he gravitated to the Democratic-Republican Party. Defeated in a reelection bid for the Senate, he later viewed the outcome favorably, observing that "if I had obtained that appointment I should have most probably spent the remainder of my days in the scorching climate of Georgia, under all the accumulating evils of fevers and Negro slavery, those enemies to humane felicity" (quoted in Whitney 1974, 90).

Few subsequently moved to New York in 1799 where the people elected him to the state legislature. He served in a number of governmental posts, including inspector of state prisons, and was respectively director of New York City's Manhattan Bank and of the City Bank in New York City. He was a strong proponent of manufacturing and was president of the National Institution for the Promotion of Industry. He died a wealthy man in New York on July 16, 1828, outlived among Constitutional Convention delegates only by James Madison. He was buried at Fishkill Landing (later named Beacon), New York in a Dutch Reformed cemetery. His grave was neglected and vandalized, and the Sons of the American Revolution and the Georgia Historical Society helped bring his body back to Augusta, Georgia where he was reinterred on October 19, 1973 at St. Paul's Episcopal Church.

Further Reading

Bradford, M. E. 1994. *Founding Fathers: Brief Lives of the Framers of the United States Constitution*. 2nd ed. Lawrence: University Press of Kansas.

Farrand, Max, ed. 1966. *The Records of the Federal Convention of 1787*. 4 vols. New Haven, CT: Yale University Press.

Sargent, Mildred Crow. 2004, 2006. *William Few, A Founding Father: A Biographical Perspective in Early American History*. 2 vols. New York: Vantage Press.

Whitney, David C. 1974. *Founders of Freedom in America: Lives of the Men Who Signed the Constitution of the United States and So Helped to Establish the United States of America*. Chicago: J. G. Ferguson Publishing.

THOMAS FITZSIMONS (1741–1811)
PENNSYLVANIA

Born in Ireland in 1741, Thomas Fitzsimons immigrated to Philadelphia in 1760. He started as a clerk, married Catharine Meade (1740–1810), and became a merchant. He is believed to have been the first Roman Catholic elected to public office in Pennsylvania, and he was, with Maryland's Daniel Carroll, one of two Catholics to sign the Constitution. In addition to serving as a member of Pennsylvania's provincial congress, he served as a militia captain during the Revolutionary War, was one of the directors of the Bank of America, represented Pennsylvania at the Continental Congress, served on the state's Council of Censors, and attended the Annapolis Convention as one of its representatives. Fitzsimons did not speak frequently at the convention, and most of what he said related fairly directly to his knowledge of mercantile affairs.

At the Convention

Fitzsimons was present on May 25. He is believed to have attended almost every session of the convention. However, his first recorded action took place on August 7 when he seconded a motion by Gouverneur Morris for a provision limiting the suffrage to freeholders (Farrand 1966, 2:201). Individuals like Morris, who hoped to give a more "high-toned" or "aristocratic" character to the new government, generally favored this provision.

Appropriately enough for a merchant, Fitzsimons offered his second recorded reaction to observations by Virginia's James Madison that it would be inconvenient to adopt a provision prohibiting vessels entering one state to pay duties in another. Fitzsimons agreed that this could be "inconvenient," but "thought it would be a greater inconvenience to require vessels bound to Philada. to enter below the jurisdiction of the State" (2:48). Significantly, the only committee on which Fitzsimons served at the convention was the committee appointed on August 25 to deal with commercial discrimination.

On September 6, Maryland's James McHenry reported in his notes that Fitzsimons had indicated in personal conversation that he favored adding a provision allowing Congress "to erect piers for protection of shipping in winter and to preserve the navigation of harbours" (2:529). On September 7, Fitzsimons further seconded a motion by fellow Pennsylvania delegate James Wilson requiring consent of both houses of Congress (and not simply the Senate) to treaties negotiated by the president. The convention defeated the motion by a vote of ten to one.

On September 10, Fitzsimons explained to fellow delegates that the proposal for ratification of the Constitution had omitted the words "for their approbation" so as "to save Congress from the necessity of an Act inconsistent with the Articles of Confederation under which they held their authority" (2:560). About the same time, when the convention was discussing the legitimacy of incidental state duties, Fitzsimons observed that such duties, like those on flour and tobacco, "never have been & never can be considered as duties on exports" (2:589). Finally, on September 14, when the delegates were discussing whether congressional expenditures could be published at stated times each year, Fitzsimons observed that "It is absolutely impossible to publish expenditures in the full extent of the term" (2:619).

Life after the Convention

Fitzsimons served as one of Pennsylvania's first delegates to the U.S. House of Representatives, where he served until 1795. He sat on committees dealing with finance and supporting the financial policies of Alexander Hamilton, who had represented New York at the Constitutional Convention. Fitzsimons founded the Insurance Company of North America and was president of the Philadelphia Chamber of Commerce. Generous to his friends, including Robert Morris, another delegate to the convention from Pennsylvania, Fitzsimons was brought to financial ruin by their inability to repay loans he had made to them and by his own speculation in western lands. He died in Philadelphia on August 26, 1811 and was buried in the city at the cemetery of St. Mary's Roman Catholic Church.

Further Reading

Bradford, M. E. 1994. *Founding Fathers: Brief Lives of the Framers of the United States Constitution*. 2nd ed. Lawrence: University Press of Kansas.

Burnett, Edmund C. 1938. "The Catholic Signers of the Constitution." In *The Constitution of the United States: Addresses in Commemoration of the Sesquicentennial of its Signing 17 September 1787*, edited by Herbert Wright, 40–54. Washington, DC: Catholic University of America.

Farrand, Max, ed. 1966. *The Records of the Federal Convention of 1787*. 4 vols. New Haven, CT: Yale University Press.

BENJAMIN FRANKLIN (1706–1790)
PENNSYLVANIA

With the possible exception of General Washington, Benjamin Franklin was the most widely known member of the Constitutional Convention of 1787. Born in Boston on January 17, 1706 (the fifteenth of seventeen children), at eighty-one years of age Franklin was also the convention's eldest, and probably its most widely traveled, member. Franklin had left

Boston as a youth for Philadelphia (and briefly for England). A self-educated man—described as one of the "least-schooled, and the most broadly educated" members of the convention (Carr 1990, 29), Franklin had arrived in Philadelphia with almost nothing and spent most of his life as a printer. Franklin had authored *Poor Richard's Almanack*, which was known for its witty aphorisms, and described his life in a famous autobiography published after his death. Inventor of the Franklin stove, bifocals, and the lightning rod, Franklin had established the first subscription library and helped found the University of Pennsylvania. Franklin had a common law marriage with Deborah (Debby) Read Rogers (1704–1774), but she did not like to travel, and they were separated for long periods of time.

Franklin had served as a representative to the Albany Congress where he had proposed a system of colonial alliance known as the Albany Plan of Union, represented the colonies in England in the disputes leading up to the Revolutionary War (where he took a verbal drubbing before Parliament), served on the five-man committee responsible for drafting the Declaration of Independence, served as postmaster general under the Continental Congress, presided over Pennsylvania's constitutional convention of 1776, helped negotiate the Treaty of Paris that ended the Revolutionary War, and later served as a diplomat to France, where he received almost universal adulation.

In 1787, Franklin was serving as president of Pennsylvania, and the next year he was chosen to head the nation's first antislavery society. It is unlikely that anyone in the former colonies, with the possible exception of Thomas Jefferson (then serving as an ambassador in France), would obtain Franklin's breadth of knowledge, although North Carolina's Hugh Williamson, a fellow convention delegate, may have come close.

Franklin had adopted the city of Philadelphia as his home, and he enjoyed entertaining a number of delegates to the convention at his residence on Market Street. Washington made a call shortly after arriving in town. A mural in the U.S. Capitol portrays Franklin at his home in Philadelphia entertaining Alexander Hamilton, James Wilson, and James Madison under his mulberry tree.

At the Convention

At the time of the convention, Franklin's health was not good. Although it does not appear that he arrived by this mode of conveyance every day, gout and kidney stones were among the problems that required him to be carried into the convention at least on May 28, in a sedan hoisted by four prisoners from the nearby Walnut Street jail. Franklin appears to have composed his own speeches, but his colleagues, usually James Wilson, usually delivered them on his behalf. Most of Franklin's most notable contributions to the convention were in the form of speeches and short vignettes rather than in debates with other delegates. Franklin often attempted to play the role of a conciliator.

Unable to attend the first session of the convention, Franklin agreed with other delegates from the Pennsylvania convention that Robert Morris would nominate George Washington as president of the convention (Farrand 1966, 1:4). Franklin was somewhat mortified, however, that Alexander Hamilton's nomination of William Jackson as convention secretary prevailed over Franklin's own hope that the position might go to his grandson, Temple Franklin (Hutson 1987, 1).

Congress

Franklin favored a unicameral legislature, like that in Pennsylvania. He had likened a bicameral legislature to a specimen of a snake that he owned with two heads (Isaacson 2003, 453). Madison attributed Pennsylvania's sole vote against the Virginia Plan's proposal for a bicameral Congress to Franklin's influence (1:48). This set something of a pattern whereby on many occasions delegates treated Franklin's proposals with respect because of his authorship, but were not thereby persuaded of their utility.

On June 11, Franklin expressed concern that the issue of representation in Congress was destroying the calm that was needed for deliberation. He had hoped that delegates to the convention might consider themselves to be "rather as a representative of the whole, than as an Agent for the interests of a particular State" although he now realized that this goal was no longer "to be expected" (1:197). Franklin's view, however, was that "the number of Representatives should bear some proportion to the number of the Represented; and that the decisions shd. be by the majority of members, not by the majority of States" (2:197–98). Franklin thought that there was little cause to fear that the large states would swallow the small, and he cited the union of England and Scotland to support this proposition (1:198). He believed, however, that if states were not represented proportionally, the minority might dominate. Franklin said that he would not oppose equalizing the states in regard to population if this were practical, but he did not think it was practical and observed that even if it could be done, boundaries would continually have to be changed as population altered. Franklin's speech on this subject has been characterized as "long, complex, and at times baffling" (Isaacson 2003, 450), and it did not appear directly to address the problem. He proposed that the smallest state should specify the amount of money and the number of troops it could supply and that each of the other states would agree to the same. In such circumstances (which, perhaps, Franklin thought impossible to fulfill), states could be equally represented in Congress. If Congress needed more than these requisitions, it could petition states to give more, leaving them, much as under the Articles of Confederation, to decide whether they could or would provide more (1:199–200). Immediately after having made this proposal (could Franklin therefore have intended for it to be ironic?), however, Franklin observed that the original decision to grant states equal representation in the First Continental Congress had stemmed from its inability to ascertain "the importance of each colony" (1:200).

Two days after he proposed that the convention should start the day with prayer, Franklin returned to the subject of state representation, and tried to appeal for compromise with a homely example. Observing that small states feared for their "liberties" and large ones feared for their "money," he observed, "When a broad table is to be made, and the edges [of the planks do not fit] the artist takes a little from both, and makes a good joint. In like manner here both sides must part with some of their demands, in order that they may join in some accommodating proposition" (1:488). His proposal was similar to what became the Connecticut Compromise but with some interesting wrinkles. He proposed that states would be represented equally in one house and that "in all cases or questions wherein the Sovereignty of individual States may be affected, or whereby their authority over their own Citizens may be diminished, or the authority of the General Government within the several States augmented, each State shall have equal suffrage" (1:489). Similarly, states would have an equal vote in the appointment of civil officers. However, on the issue of salaries and expenditures, states would be represented "in proportion to the Sums which their respective States do actually contribute to the treasury" (1:489). Franklin commended this approach as consistent with the rule that was used when a ship had many owners. Robert Yates later identified Franklin as the individual who introduced the motion in the Committee on Representation in Congress (appointed on July 2) that eventually resulted in the Great Compromise (1:523).

Franklin's presence on the committee indicated that he was considered to be one of the conciliatory voices on the subject at the convention—the only other committee to which he was appointed was the Committee on Sumptuary Legislation, appointed on September 13, which appears never to have met. Because this compromise involved the origination of money bills within the House, Franklin felt obligated to continue to vote for that measure in subsequent deliberations (1:543; also see 2:233). Franklin defended this provision, the utility of which James Madison and James Wilson had both questioned, by observing: "It was a maxim that those who feel, can best judge. This end would, he thought, be best attained, if money affairs were to be confined to the immediate representatives of the people" (1:546).

Just as he expressed concern over the magnitude of presidential salaries (see below), Franklin successfully proposed striking a provision that would have specified "liberal" salaries for member of Congress. Preferring the word "moderate," Franklin had observed "the tendency of abuses in every case, to grow of themselves when once begun," and, in an analogy especially apt for a largely Protestant audience, illustrated by the development of modest benefices enjoyed by the early Apostles as compared to those of later popes (1:216).

Similarly, Franklin later seconded a proposal by South Carolina's Charles Cotesworth Pinckney that would have disallowed members of the Senate from receiving salaries. Observing that the convention contained a number of "young men who would probably be of the Senate," he feared that "If lucrative appointments should be recommended we might be chargeable with having carved out places for ourselves" (1:427).

Toward the end of the convention, Franklin proposed that Congress should be entrusted with the power to cut canals (2:615). The convention rejected this proposal, leaving future Congresses to decide on the constitutionality of government corporations.

Presidency

Franklin prompted the convention to further discussion when delegates appeared reluctant (perhaps because of the presence of George Washington) to discuss James Wilson's proposal that the executive should be unitary (1:65).

Franklin introduced a far more novel proposal on June 2 when he suggested that the president should not receive a salary, although his expenses should be paid. More important than this suggestion, which received deference only out of regard for its author, was the logic by which Franklin attempted to justify this provision and the insight that it cast on Franklin's view of human nature. He observed that men were motivated by two powerful influences: "ambition and avarice; the love of power, and the love of money" (1:82). He feared the conjunction of these two motives to, as he indicated, "place before the eyes of such men a post of *honour* that shall at the same time be a place of *profit*, and they will move heaven and earth to obtain it" (1:82). Tracing factions to struggles for such objects, Franklin feared that they would stimulate "the bold and the violent, the men of strong passions and indefatigable activity in their selfish pursuits" (1:82). Franklin believed that there would be a natural pressure within government to increase the emoluments that presidents would receive. Indeed, he feared that this tendency would push the presidency toward monarchy. Again, his explanation says a great deal about his view of human nature and shows some affinity with those, like George Mason, who consistently advocated a republican ideology:

> There is a natural inclination in mankind to Kingly Government. It sometimes relieves them from Aristocratic domination. They had rather have one tyrant than five hundred. It gives them more of the appearance of equality among Citizens, and that they like. (2:83)

Franklin thought this descent into monarchy might be slowed, and that the nation could see that it did not nourish "the foetus of a King" by separating ambition from avarice. Acknowledging that some individuals would regard it as "utopian" to think that individuals would serve their nation without salary, Franklin cited the examples of sheriffs in England and Quaker committeemen who served without such compensation. He also pointed to Washington's service as commander in chief during the Revolutionary War (1:84). Franklin did not believe that the nation would ever "be without a sufficient number of wise and good men to undertake and execute well and faithfully the office in question" (1:85).

The irony of this speech is that Franklin appears to have written it with no thought that many individuals of merit, but without sufficient financial resources, would be unable to serve as president without a salary. This seeming equation of wealth and merit appears inconsistent with Franklin's acknowledgment elsewhere of the merit of the common people.

When the convention was discussing the possibility of investing the president with an absolute negative, Franklin argued that such a mechanism had not worked well in Pennsylvania. Indeed, in comments depicting atrocities by American Indians, he observed that the royal governors had used their veto to extort increases in their salaries (1:99). Franklin did indicate that he thought such a power would be less objectionable were the convention to vest it in the president in conjunction with a council, much as James Madison had previously proposed (1:99). Franklin continued to fear, however, that the executive would be constantly increasing in power, and, in this particular at least, his words were not especially reassuring about the long-range future. Undoubtedly anticipating, like many other delegates, that George Washington would serve as the nation's first president, Franklin observed:

> The first man, put at the helm will be a good one. No body knows what sort may come afterwards. The Executive will be always increasing here, as elsewhere, till it ends in monarchy. (2:103)

After the convention rejected the absolute veto, Franklin seconded a motion to grant the executive power to suspend legislation for a period still to be specified (1:103).

On July 20 Franklin indicated that he favored a provision for presidential impeachment, but his argument seems bizarre, in part because it seems to have been based upon a hereditary monarch rather than on an individual serving as chief executive for a fixed term. Arguing that "History furnishes one example only of a first Magistrate being formally brought to public Justice" [presumably England's Charles II, who was beheaded in 1649], Franklin advocated impeachment as preferable to assassination, which not only deprived an executive of his life but also of the possibility of vindicating his character. Franklin observed, "It wd. be the best way therefore to provide in the Constitution for the regular punishment of the Executive when his misconduct should deserve it, and for his honorable acquittal when he should be unjustly accused" (2:65). Shortly thereafter, Franklin cited King William, the former Prince of Orange, as someone whose power was diminished by accusations that he did not have the opportunity publicly to refute, as he would have had Parliament impeached him.

When George Mason reintroduced a motion limiting the president to one term, Franklin supported it with the observation that it was no disgrace in republican government for a ruler to return to live among the people. He argued that this was not, in fact, "to *degrade* but to *promote* them" (2:120). This prompted Gouverneur Morris to observe, with a touch of sarcasm, that "he had no doubt that our Executive like most others would have too much patriotism to shrink from the burden of his office, and too much modesty not to be willing to decline the promotion" (2:120).

On September 7, Franklin supported George Mason's proposal for a Council of State to consist of six persons from three different geographical regions appointed by the Senate to advise the president. Franklin said that he thought that "a Council would not only be a check on a bad President but be a relief to a good one" (2:542).

Judiciary

Franklin often added humor to the convention proceedings. One such occasion occurred on June 5 when he suggested that he would like to hear a suggestion for appointing judges other than by Congress or the president. He then told about procedures in Scotland where lawyers made the selection and, according to Franklin, "always selected the ablest of the profession in order to get rid of him, and share his practice" (1:120).

On July 18, Franklin was among those who supported a motion allowing for future increased in judicial salaries. He observed, "Money may not only become plentier [a time of inflation], but the business of the department may increase as the Country becomes more populous" (2:44–45).

Franklin supported the provision in the Constitution requiring the testimony of two witnesses to an overt act of treason. He observed that "prosecutions for treason were generally virulent; and perjury too easily made use of against innocence" (2:348).

Prayer

One of Franklin's most notable actions at the Constitutional Convention was calling for the convention to open with prayer. He proposed this on June 28 at a time when the dispute over representation for the large and small states was particularly intense. At a convention where members are perhaps best known for their faith in human reason, Franklin saw this disagreement as "a melancholy proof of the imperfection of the Human Understanding" (1:451). Indicating that the delegates had scoured history for examples, he wondered why no one had "hitherto once thought of humbly applying to the Father of lights to illuminate our understanding" (1:451).

Citing supplications that the colonists had made in the war against Great Britain, Franklin said that the longer he lived the more convinced he was "*that God governs in the affairs of men*" (1:451). Citing the observation (made by Jesus) that a sparrow could not perish without God's knowledge, the injunction that "except the Lord build the House they labour in vain that build it," and the example from the Old Testament of the Tower of Babel, Franklin proposed that the convention bring in a clergyman to lead each day's proceedings with prayer. When Hamilton suggested that it would be embarrassing to do this at this stage of the proceedings, Franklin was among those who observed that "the past omission of a duty could not justify a further omission—that the rejection of such a proposition would expose the convention to more unpleasant animadversions than the adoption of it: and that the alarm out of doors that might be excited for the state of things within would at least be as likely to do good as ill" (2:452). Still unsuccessful, Franklin seconded a motion by Virginia's Edmund Randolph requesting that a sermon be preached for the celebration of July 4. Even this motion appears to have failed, but Franklin's motion remains a frequently told story and is part of the lore of the convention. It seems ironic that a man known for his deism (albeit also for a close friendship with evangelist George Whitefield) would cite so many scriptural authorities, and it seems likely that, however he may have viewed the need for divine assistance, Franklin might have hoped that a convention that prayed together would be likely to stay together.

Defense of the Common Man

When James Madison proposed that the right to vote should be confined to "freeholders," Franklin responded that this would "be injurious to the lower class of Freemen" (2:208). He further observed that this group had shown its virtue and integrity in the Revolutionary War. Indeed, American seamen had refused to serve in the English navy in order to gain their freedom. Franklin wanted to assure that "Americans were all free and equal to any of yr. fellow Citizens" (2:208).

Franklin returned to this theme on August 10. Expressing "his dislike of every thing that tended to debase the spirit of the common people," Franklin observed:

> If honesty was often the companion of wealth, and if poverty was exposed to peculiar temptation, it was not less true that the possession of property

increased the desire for more property—Some of the greatest rogues he was ever acquainted with, were the richest rogues. (2:249)

Franklin argued that if the nation betrayed "a great partiality to the rich" it would not only lower the nation in the esteem of European thinkers but would also "discourage the common people from removing to this Country" (2:249).

Franklin displayed a similar attitude in regard to restricting the offices to which immigrants could qualify. Although he favored "a reasonable time," he observed that he "should be very sorry to see any thing like illiberality inserted in the Constitution" (2:236). Noting that America had many friends in Europe and that immigrants had served the nation favorably, he wanted America to remain on good terms with those who wanted to come here. He also observed that simply allowing immigrants to be eligible to hold offices did not guarantee that they would be elected to the same (2:239).

Ratification

On September 10, Franklin seconded a motion by Virginia's Edmund Randolph proposing that the convention send the Constitution to Congress for its approval and subsequently to state conventions that would have the power either to ratify the document or to propose amendments. This was not, of course, the manner in which the delegates proceeded.

One of Franklin's most notable speeches at the convention was given on the final day of convention deliberations. He subsequently circulated it in the form of a pamphlet. It is a model of Franklin's reasoning, and displays a worldly wisdom that must have had widespread appeal among those who questioned one or another aspect of the new government but who thought that it was an improvement over the Articles of Confederation.

Franklin began his speech by observing that "there are several parts of this constitution which I do not at present approve," but that he could not be sure that "I shall never approve them" (2:641). He explained that, although individuals found it difficult to admit mistakes, as he had aged, he had become more willing to doubt his own individual judgment. He was willing to accede to the document, flawed though it might be, because of what he hoped it could achieve:

I agree to this Constitution with all its faults, if they are such; because I think a general Government necessary for us, and there is no form of Government but what may be a blessing to the people if well administered, and believe farther that this is likely to be well administered for a course of years, and can only end in despotism, as other forms have done before it, when the people shall become so corrupted as to need despotic Government, being incapable of any other. (2:642)

Franklin thought it unrealistic to anticipate a perfect document:

For when you assemble a number of men to have the advantage of their joint wisdom, you inevitably assemble with those men, all their prejudices, their passions, their errors of opinion, their local interests, and their selfish views. (2:642)

He hoped that the document would "astonish our enemies" abroad who were expecting the confederation to fall apart much like the project on which builders of the Tower of Babel had worked (2:642). He further urged other delegates to swallow their reservations, like him, rather than reporting their own disappointments and stir opposition to the document. He proposed that the convention adopt the Constitution unanimously by the "consent of the States present" and offered a motion to this effect (apparently authored by the less popular fellow Pennsylvania delegate Gouverneur Morris) that would allow delegates the option of signing in witness to this unanimity rather than to their own individual consent (2:643). Perhaps a bit too clever, this ploy did not succeed in convincing all the remaining delegates to sign. Surprisingly, however, Franklin responded to a statement by South Carolina's General Pinckney by indicating that he thought it was "too soon to pledge ourselves before Congress and our Constituents shall have approved the plan" (2:647).

The Rising Sun

The final story in Madison's reports is based on a reminiscence about Franklin that confirms the image of the elder sage seeking to leave his mark on the mythology of a document under which he could expect to offer limited, if any, service. As president of the convention, George Washington had been seated in a Chippendale chair on the top slat of which had been painted a sun (this chair is one of the few original items still on display at Independence Hall). Observing that painters had found it difficult to distinguish a rising from a setting sun, Franklin observed:

I have . . . often and often in the course of this Session, and the vicissitudes of my hopes and fears as to its issue, looked at that behind the President without being able to tell whether it was rising or setting: But now at length I have the happiness to know that it is a rising and not a setting Sun. (2:648)

James McHenry of Maryland later reported that Franklin responded to a question by a lady of Philadelphia (a Mrs. Powel) as to what kind of government the convention had created by saying "A republic, if you can keep it" (3:85).

Impact on the Convention

Although Franklin has often been portrayed as an individual hobbled by physical illness and whose central ideas were largely rejected by the convention, his mind remained sharp during the convention, and he appears to have had a larger influence than is often recognized. Not only did he lend prestige to the event and foster necessary compromises, but many of his ideas were adopted. One study has shown that of twenty-seven recorded proposals that Franklin is known to have introduced or supported, sixteen (some of which were later modified or reversed) were approved, only six were rejected, and four were not acted upon (Carr 1990, 131). Franklin made one of his most quoted statements five months before his death when he wrote to Jean Baptiste Leroy, a former French neighbor, observing that "Our new Constitution is now established and has an appearance that promises permanency; but in this world nothing can be said to be certain except death and taxes" (quoted in Carr 1990, 142).

Life after the Convention

The knowledge that Franklin supported the document, like the knowledge that the document had the support of Washington, helped to convince individuals who might be wavering over the document's value. It was certainly difficult to cast aspersions on a body that had the assent of the two most distinguished men in the hemisphere. Franklin reiterated his support of the Constitution in a letter to the *Federal Gazette* (Philadelphia) on April 8, 1788 in which he compared the new Constitution to the Ten Commandments that Moses had brought down from Mt. Sinai, and the Antifederalists to those in ancient Israel who had opposed Moses.

Franklin's own death came on April 17, 1790 and was followed by a month of mourning in Congress. His massive funeral procession began at the Pennsylvania State House where he had signed the Declaration of Independence and the U.S. Constitution. Although his gravestone at Christ Church in Philadelphia (where visitors often throw pennies) simply bears his name and that of his wife, in his youth Franklin had composed a more engaging epitaph comparing himself to the books that he so loved:

> The Body of/ B. Franklin/ Printer;/ Like the Cover of an old Book,/Its Contents torn out,/ And stript of its Lettering and Gilding,/ Lies here, Food for Worms./ But the Work shall not be whlly lost:/For it will, as he believ'd, appear once more,/ In a new & more perfect Edition, Corrected and Amended/ By the Author. ("Benjamin Franklin's Funeral and Grave" n.d.)

Further Reading

"Benjamin Franklin's Funeral and Grave." n.d. The Electric Ben Franklin. http://www.ushistory.org/franklin/philadelphia/grave.htm. Accessed 7/17/2012.

Brands, H. W. 2000. *The First American: The Life and Times of Benjamin Franklin.* New York: Anchor Books.

Carr, William G. 1990. *The Oldest Delegate: Franklin in the Constitutional Convention.* Newark: University of Delaware Press.

Farrand, Max, ed. 1966. *The Records of the Federal Convention of 1787.* 4 vols. New Haven, CT: Yale University Press.

Gaustad, Edwin S. 2006. *Benjamin Franklin.* New York: Oxford University Press.

Hoffer, Peter Charles. 2011. *When Benjamin Franklin Met the Reverend Whitefield: Enlightenment, Revival, and the Power of the Printed Word.* Baltimore: The Johns Hopkins University Press.

Hutson, James H., ed. 1987. *Supplement to Max Farrand's The Records of the Federal Convention of 1787.* New Haven, CT: Yale University Press.

Isaacson, Walter. 2003. *Benjamin Franklin: An American Life.* New York: Simon & Schuster.

Lemay, J. A. Leo. 2006. *The Life of Benjamin Franklin.* Philadelphia: University of Pennsylvania Press, 2006.

Morgan, Edmund S. 2002. *Benjamin Franklin.* New Haven, CT: Yale University Press.

Pangle, Lorraine Smith. 2007. *The Political Philosophy of Benjamin Franklin.* Baltimore: The Johns Hopkins University Press.

Penegar, Kenneth Lawing. 2011. *The Political Trial of Benjamin Franklin: A Prelude to the American Revolution.* New York: Algora Publishing.

Wood, Gordon S. 2004. *The Americanization of Benjamin Franklin.* New York: Penguin Press.

Wright, Esmond. 1986. *Franklin of Philadelphia.* Cambridge, MA: Belknap Press.

Note: A project to publish all of Franklin's papers was begun in 1954 as a joint endeavor by the American Philosophical Society and Yale University Press, and is scheduled for completion in 2016. As of 2012, 40 of 47 anticipated volumes have been published.

Elbridge Gerry (1744–1814)
Massachusetts

Elbridge Gerry was born in Marblehead, Massachusetts to Thomas and Elizabeth Greenleaf Gerry on July 17, 1744. Gerry's father was a merchant who had immigrated from England. Members of the local clergy educated Gerry before he attended and graduated from Harvard College in 1762, after which he joined his father's business.

Gerry became involved in the revolution, becoming friends with Samuel Adams, serving on Marblehead's Committee of Correspondence, writing the Essex Resolves, chairing the Massachusetts Committee of Supply, and serving in the Second Continental Congress, where, however, he attended sporadically after his conduct was criticized in 1779 and 1780. Gerry was a small wiry man who was often likened to seabirds. When the colonists were voting for independence, Benjamin Harrison of Virginia, who was much more corpulent, claimed that were the British to hang Gerry for treason, Gerry "would dance in the air an hour or two" before dying (Billias 1990).

Gerry became further involved in developing the Northwest Territory, and in attempts to reduce the nation's standing army and to abolish the Society of the Cincinnati (Bradford 1981, 7). He developed a reputation for honesty, and a distaste for either pure popular democracy or rule by elites. While serving in the Continental Congress, Gerry married Ann Thompson (1753–1849). Three sons and six daughters survived the father, one of whom (Emily Louise) lived until 1894, the last known child of a signer of the Declaration of Independence.

Although he had signed both the Declaration of Independence and the Articles of Confederation, Elbridge Gerry of Massachusetts was one of three men who remained at the Constitutional Convention on September 17,

1787 and refused to sign the document, but his opposition could not have come as much of a surprise to those who listened to him closely. On May 30, just one day after his arrival, Gerry observed that it was necessary to distinguish "between a *federal* and *national* government" (Farrand 1966, 1:42). He observed that if the convention were intending to pursue the latter option, it might be exceeding its commission, since by his understanding, Congress had called the convention with the understanding that it would operate agreeably to its recommendations. Throughout the convention Gerry was continually concerned not simply about what proposals were best, but about which such proposals the people were likely to accept. Although he professed to be wary of direct democracy, as much as any delegate he appears to have been guided by his view of what the public wanted.

Congress

Selection of Members. James Madison, the putative author of the Virginia Plan, argued that it was essential for the people to elect members of at least one branch of Congress. By contrast, Gerry said that "he did not like the election by the people" (1:50). He did not think that the people actually trusted the legislators that they elected, although he had no objection if the people's election was so restrained "that men of honor & character might not be unwilling to be joined in the appointments" (1:50). He suggested that this might be accomplished by allowing the people to make nominations from which the Senate would choose.

By June 6, Gerry appears to have changed his position somewhat. He feared that the United States was running into an excess of democracy and indicated that the people in his home state of Massachusetts had recently selected some individuals of the legislature who had been convicted of crimes. Opposed both to monarchy and aristocracy, he now acknowledged that "It was necessary . . . that the people should appoint one branch of the Govt. in order to inspire them with the necessary confidence" (1:132). He apparently hoped that such a popular house could be balanced by another house chosen (as the Senate was initially to be) by the state legislatures thereof from nominees suggested by the people. Interestingly, Gerry indicated during this speech that "He was not disposed to run into extremes" (1:132). On June 7, after reviewing four methods that delegates had proposed for selecting senators, Gerry again recommended that this be done by state legislatures, adding to earlier arguments the hope that "The elections being carried thro' this refinement, will be most likely to provide some check in favor of the commercial interest agst. the landed; without which oppression will take place, and no free Govt. can last long when that is the case" (1:152). Later that day, Gerry observed that the people were more likely to favor schemes for paper money than the legislatures. He also argued that using interstate districts to select members of the Senate were impractical, would work against the small states, and would increase tensions within the districts themselves (1:155).

Representation. On June 11, Gerry indicated that he opposed considering property in apportioning congressional representation. He wondered why blacks "who were property in the South" should be entitled to any more representation "than the cattle & horses of the North" (1:201). On June 13, Gerry opposed allowing the Senate to originate money bills. He observed that "The other branch was more immediately the representatives of the people, and it was a maxim that the people ought to hold the purse-strings" (1:233).

On July 2 Gerry was one of the delegates who favored committing the issue of representation within Congress to a committee (1:515). The fact that Gerry was not only appointed to this committee (the only one on which he served during the convention) but selected as its chair indicated that fellow delegates probably considered him to be one of the more moderate members in respect to this issue. Gerry delivered the committee report on July 5. It recommended granting states one representative for every 40,000 persons in the lower house, with each state having at least one vote. It further provided that bills "for raising or appropriating money, and for fixing the Salaries of the Officers of the Governt. of the U. States shall originate in the 1st branch of the Legislature, and shall not be altered or amended by the 2d branch" and that states would have an equal vote in the Senate (1:526).

In responding to a question about the report, Gerry indicated that the conditions were meant to be mutually reinforcing and that "Those opposed to the equality of votes have only assented conditionally; and if the other side do not generally agree will not be under any obligation to support the Report" (1:527). Gerry later indicated that "Tho' he had assented to the Report in the Committee, he had very material objections to it" but believed that compromise was necessary if "secession" were to be avoided (1:532). Gerry did not favor splitting the large states. In what may have represented some backtracking in regard to slave representation, however, on July 6 he indicated that representation "ought to be in the Combined ratio of number of Inhabitants and of wealth, and not of either singly" (1:541). On July 11 he supported counting slaves as three-fifths of a person for purposes of representation rather than counting them equally (1:580). He subsequently favored using this same formula for both taxation and representation (1:601; see also 2:275 and 2:350).

Gerry had previously favored restricting the origination of money bills to the House, and he continued to insist that this was a vital part of the compromise his committee had offered. Acknowledging on July 6 that he "would not say that the concession was a sufficient one on the part of the small States," he said that "he could not but regard it in the light of a concession. It wd. make it a constitutional principle that the 2d. branch were not possessed of the Confidence of the people in money matters, which wd. lessen their weight & influence" (1:545). By July 14, Gerry was describing this measure as "the corner stone of the accommodation" (2:5).

Gerry indicated, however, that the "critical question" decided by the committee was to grant states equal representation in the Senate (1:550). Professing to favor a motion by South Carolina's Charles Pinckney giving states from two to five senators based on their populations, Gerry did not think this could be accomplished at the convention (2:5). Engaged in something of a chicken and egg debate (which should come first?) with Virginia's James Madison, Gerry indicated that he thought "it would be proper to proceed to enumerate & define the powers to be vested in the Genl. Govt. before a question on the report should be taken as to the rule of representation in the 2d. branch" (1:551). He did favor allowing senators to vote individually, rather than by state delegation, as a way of preventing "the delays & inconveniences that had been experience in Congs." (2:5).

Length of Terms. Consistent with the republican ideology of his day, Gerry favored annual elections for members of the House of Representatives. He argued that such elections were widely favored in the East and constituted "the only defence of the people agst. tyranny" (1:214–15). Madison said that the delegates should do what they considered best and not worry overmuch about public opinion. Gerry responded that by such reasoning the delegates might establish a limited monarchy, even though they knew that "the genius of the people was decidedly adverse to it" (1:215).

Representation of Western States. Gerry was among the delegates to the convention (Gouverneur Morris was another) who feared the dangers posed by admitting new states from the West. Saying on July 14 that "He was for admitting them on liberal terms," he indicated that he was "not for putting ourselves into their hands" (2:3). Reasoning that, like other men, they would abuse power if they had it and "will oppress commerce, and drain our wealth into the Western Country," he proposed limiting the number of new states "in such a manner, that they should never be able to outnumber the Atlantic States" (2:3).

Qualifications. Gerry favored excluding public debtors for election to office. Moreover, he favored a property qualification in the belief that "if property be one object of Government, provisions for securing it can not be improper" (2:123). He observed that, without qualifications, "we might have a Legislature composed of public debtors, pensioners, placemen & contractors" (2:125).

Gerry was similarly concerned about foreigners. He wanted to restrict future eligibility to Congress to natives, lest foreign governments conspire to influence U.S. policies (2:268).

Powers and Limits. As a merchant, Gerry was unwilling to trust Congress with the power to tax imports. He argued, "It might ruin the Country. It might be exercised partially, raising one and depressing another part of it" (2:307). Gerry's view of the powers of Congress was related to his concern for states' rights. He indicated that Congress could use a power over exports "to compel the States to comply with the will of the Genl Government, and to grant it any new powers which might be demanded" (2:362). He feared that the national government might become as oppressive over state governments as Great Britain had been over Ireland (2:362).

Gerry proposed adding the power to Congress of establishing post roads, as well as post offices (2:308). He believed that the Constitution should grant the power of concluding peace through treaties to the entire Congress rather than to the Senate, which he believed would be more subject to corruption (2:319). Gerry later argued that the Senate should have to vote for treaties of peace by larger majorities, because there was a greater danger that such treaties would sacrifice "the extremities of the Continent . . . than on any other occasions" (2:541). He also continued to fear that the Senate would be subject to foreign influence (2:548). Gerry joined South Carolina's John Rutledge in proposing that two-thirds of the senators should have to approve all treaties (2:549). Gerry thought that Congress should have power over public securities, and that it should be given specific power to issue letters of marque (2:326).

Although the notes are arguably subject to different interpretations, Gerry apparently indicated on August 21 that he thought states should retain both the power and the responsibility to pay off their debts. He believed this was needed to provide for the security of existing "public creditors," focusing both on "the merit of this class of citizens, and the solemn faith which had been pledged under the existing Confederation" (2:356). Gerry believed that if Congress assumed these obligations, the states that had already paid off most of their debts "would be alarmed, if they were now to be saddled with a share of the debts of States which had done least" (2:356). However on August 22, Gerry indicated that he favored some explicit constitutional statement regarding fulfillment of existing obligations "so that no pretext might remain for getting rid of the public engagements" (2:377). Observing on August 25 that "as the public had received the value of the literal amount, they ought to pay that value to some body," he expressed sympathy for those who had to sell their securities at a discount, and said that "If the public faith would admit, of which he was not clear, he would not object to a revision of the debt so far as to compel restitution to the ignorant & distressed, who have been defrauded" (2:413). On this occasion, he made a rare stand on behalf of stockjobbers—often derided at the time by republican spokesmen who associated them with "corruption"—who, he observed, "keep up the value of the paper" and without whom, "there would be no market" (2:413).

Gerry did not believe that it was the business of Congress to interfere with state control over slaves, but he indicated that he thought the delegates should "be careful not to give any sanction to" slavery (2:372). He favored provisions prohibiting Congress from adopting bills of attainder or ex post facto laws (2:375). In an argument that was almost the inverse of Madison's approach, Gerry thought that such provisions were more necessary at the national than at the state level since there would be fewer legislators in Congress than in the states, and they were therefore more to be feared (2:375). He later indicated that he also favored extending the ban on ex post facto laws to civil, as well as criminal, cases (2:617).

By the end of the convention, Gerry was becoming more and more suspicious of the government that the Constitution was creating. When the convention was considering a resolution to grant Congress power over places purchased for forts and the like, Gerry objected that Congress might attempt to use this power to "enslave any particular State by buying up its territory, and that the strongholds proposed would be a means of awing the State into an undue obedience to the Genl. Government" (2:510).

Other Matters. Gerry did not favor allowing members of Congress to accept any offices during their terms or for a year afterwards, fearing that "it would produce intrigues of ambitious men for displacing proper officers, in order to create vacancies for themselves" (1:388). He expounded at length on this subject on August 14, arguing that reposing confidence in legislators, rather than tying them down by law, "is the road to tyranny" (2:285). He feared that if the Senate were responsible for appointing ambassadors, as was then being considered, "they will multiply embassies for their own sakes" (2:285). Gerry observed, "If men will not serve in the Legislature without a prospect of such offices, our situation is deplorable indeed. If our best Citizens are actuated by such mercenary views, we had better chuse a single despot at once. It will be more easy to satisfy the rapacity of one than of many" (2:285). Gerry had apparently become increasingly concerned that the Senate as it had been constituted was too aristocratic, and he did not think the people would tolerate this (2:286). On September 3, Gerry indicated that if members of Congress were eligible for existing offices, they would use their power to drive existing office holders away to make way for themselves (2:491).

In the discussion of the length of Senate terms, Gerry favored terms of four or five years. He observed that less than one in a thousand persons in the United States favored monarchy. Acknowledging Madison's observation that the majority would violate justice when it had an incentive to do so, Gerry had hopes that "there would be a sufficient sense of justice & virtue for the purpose of Govt." (1:425).

When the convention proposed that the initial House of Representatives should consist of 65 members, Gerry indicated that he favored more. He thought that there would be less chance of corrupting a larger body. Consistent with his emphasis elsewhere at the convention on popular opinion, Gerry also believed that "The people are accustomed to & fond of a numerous representation, and will consider their rights as better secured by it" (1:569).

Gerry favored allowing members of the Senate to vote "per capita," or individually rather than (as at the convention) as a delegation. On July 14, he thus observed that this "would prevent the delays & inconveniences that had been experienced in Congs. and would give a national aspect & Spirit to the management of business" (2:5). The Convention accepted this idea on July 23 (2:95).

Gerry also favored allowing Congress to set the initial quorum for the House of Representatives somewhere between 33 and 50, out of the initial 65 seats (2:253). Possibly with a view to the Senate's anticipated role in foreign affairs, he thought there were occasions when the Senate should not be required to publish its proceedings (2:255–56). However, he later favored publication of all proceedings in the House of Representatives (2:613).

Gerry saw difficulties whether members of Congress collectively set their own salaries or whether the states set their salaries. He observed that state legislatures might attempt to turn their senators out of office by reducing their salaries (2:291).

Gerry did not favor requiring three-fourths majorities in Congress to override a presidential veto. He feared that this would grant too much power to too few senators who might combine with the president "and impede proper laws" (2:586). He argued that this likelihood was increased by the role of the vice president as president of the Senate.

Presidency

Council. Gerry indicated on June 1 that he favored "annexing a Council [to the Executive] in order to give weight & inspire confidence" (1:66). Consistent with his opposition to combining the executive and member of the judiciary in a Council of Revision, however, Gerry said that he disfavored "letting the heads of the departments, particularly that of finance have any thing to do in business connected with legislation. He mentioned the Chief Justice also as particularly exceptionable" (2:329). Gerry reasoned that judges would have too many judicial duties to accept others.

Selection. On June 2 Gerry indicated that he opposed legislative selection of the president as likely to lead to "constant intrigue" (1:80). In theory he liked the idea of an electoral college, but feared that "it would alarm & give a handle to the State partisans, as tending to supersede altogether the State authorities" (1:80). Gerry expressed less concern about the prospect of abolishing the states than about whether the states were yet ready for such a step, and he wanted to wait until the people would "feel more the necessity of it" (1:80). He continued to oppose direct elections even of electors, suggesting this time that the legislatures might nominate electors and let them make the choice (1:80). On June 9, Gerry suggested a plan whereby state governors would choose the president. He observed that "the Executives would be most likely to select the fittest men, and that it would be their interest to support the man of their own choice" (1:176).

Gerry offered a variant of this proposal on July 19. Vigorously opposed to allowing presidential re-eligibility if he were to be chosen by Congress, he also continued to oppose popular election as vesting selection in individuals who were uninformed and "would be misled by a few designing men" (2:57). He suggested that state governors should choose the electors who would choose the president. This plan would have the advantage of attaching state governments more strongly to the Union. He reiterated, "The popular mode of electing the chief Magistrate would certainly be the worst of all" (2:57; also see 2:100 and 2:109). He subsequently supported a plan whereby state legislators would choose 25 electors, who would select the president (2:58;

also see 2:63 for breakdown as to how these electors would be allocated). Gerry also proposed that presidential electors should neither be office holders nor be eligible to the presidency themselves (2:69; also see 2:521). On September 5, Gerry recommended that in cases where no individual got a majority of the electoral college, six senators and seven members of the House of Representatives chosen by a joint ballot should be entrusted with the eventual selection of the president (2:514). Gerry strongly opposed allowing the Senate, rather than the Congress as a whole, to select presidents in cases where no candidate got an electoral college majority (2:522).

Length of Term. Vigorously opposed to presidential selection by Congress, Gerry said that it would be better to give the president a term of 10, 15, or 20 years than to make the executive dependent on this branch (2:102). He specifically proposed a 15-year term (2:102). He later supported a motion offered by South Carolina's Charles Pinckney limiting the president to six years of service out of every twelve years (2:112). Gerry continued to oppose popular election. Identifying this mechanism as "radically vicious," he feared that it would give power to groups like the Society of the Cincinnati to "elect the chief Magistrate in every instance, if the election be referred to the people" (2:114).

Other Matters. Gerry opposed a tripartite executive. He believed that it would be inconvenient, especially in military matters. He likened such an executive to "a general with three heads" (1:97). When Pierce Butler of South Carolina suggested that the executive should have the power to suspend legislation for a time period still to be ascertained, Gerry observed that such a power "might do all the mischief dreaded from the negative of useful laws; without answering the salutary purpose of checking unjust or unwise ones" (1:104).

Gerry favored an impeachment mechanism for presidents, observing that "A good magistrate will not fear them. A bad one ought to be kept in fear of them" (2:66). He further thought this was a way of distancing the United States from the principle that the executive could do no wrong (2:66). Gerry seconded a motion by Virginia's George Mason to extend the grounds of impeachment of the president to "maladministration," a motion that Mason subsequently withdrew in place of the "other high crimes and misdemeanors" (2:550), the current constitutional language.

Gerry opposed allowing the vice president to preside over the Senate. He feared that the president and vice president would be too intimate. Gerry, who would later serve in this position under the presidency of James Madison, actually opposed having a vice president at all (2:536–37).

Gerry strongly opposed a motion that would allow the president power to declare war. He believed this to be inconsistent with government "in a republic" (2:318).

Judiciary

Although he had favored an executive council, Gerry opposed joining the executive with members of the judiciary in a Council of Revision as James Madison had proposed. Gerry believed that judges would already have the ability to void legislation that was unconstitutional (the power now known as judicial review) in their capacity as judges, and thought that this power was far different from that of making members of the judiciary "judges of the policy of public measures" (1:98). He also questioned giving so great a control over a body—the Congress—that he anticipated would consist of "the best men in the Community" (1:98). Later arguments indicate that Gerry might have shared in a suspicion of judges as a group. He thus observed on June 6 that "the Executive, whilst standing alone wd. be more impartial than when he cd. be covered by the sanction & seduced by the sophistry of the Judges" (1:139).

Gerry reiterated this view on July 21, when he opposed reconsideration of the Council of Revision. His critique of this proposal indicated that he viewed the judicial function as distinct from that of the other two branches:

> The motion was liable to strong objections. It was combining & mixing together the Legislative & the other departments. It was establishing an improper coalition between the Executive & Judiciary departments. It was making Statesmen of the Judges; and setting them up as the guardians of the Rights of the people. He relied for his part on the Representatives of the people as the guardians of their Rights & interests. It was making the Expositors of the Laws, the Legislators which ought never to be done. (2:75; also see 2:298)

Gerry suggested that the convention might follow the example of Pennsylvania and appoint an individual skilled in drafting laws to aid the legislature (2:75). He indicated, however, that he would prefer investing the president with an absolute veto than in mixing the powers of the two departments together in what might become "an offensive and defensive alliance agst. the Legislature" (2:78).

Gerry opposed a plan whereby the president would appoint judges with two-thirds of the Senate having the power to block such appointments. He did not believe that this plan as constructed would satisfy either the people or the states. He feared that the president would not be as informed of candidates throughout the Union as would members of the Senate, and he argued that appointments under the Articles of Confederation had been generally good (2:82). On September 7, Gerry reiterated his view that the responsibility expected from presidential appointments would be "chimerical" since the president could not possibly know everyone he appointed, and he could "always plead ignorance" (2:539).

On August 27, Gerry seconded a motion offered by Delaware's John Dickinson, which would have arguably undercut judicial independence. It would have allowed the president to remove judges on an application by Congress (2:428). On September 12, Gerry advocated guaranteeing the right to jury trials in civil cases. He thought such juries were a necessary guard against "corrupt Judges" (2:587). This was one of the reasons that Gerry made the proposal, seconded by Virginia's George Mason, on behalf of adding a bill of rights (2:588). Somewhat later, he joined South Carolina's Charles Pinckney in advocating adding the provision "that the liberty of the Press should be inviolably observed" (2:617). Gerry favored putting the same restraints on congressional interference with the obligations of contracts as has been imposed on the states (2:619).

Federalism

Gerry opposed Madison's proposal to allow Congress to veto state laws. Gerry observed that he "cd. not see the extent of such a power, and was agst. every power that was not necessary" (1:165). He suggested that Congress could remonstrate with state laws that it disapproved and could, if necessary, use force (1:165). He feared that such a negative would extend to regulation of the militia, which he thought the states should control. He further observed:

> The States too have different interest and are ignorant of each other's interests. The negative therefore will be abused. New States too having separate views from the old States will never come into the Union.(1:166)

On August 18, Gerry renewed his opposition to granting Congress control over state militia. He observed that such a decision would give the constitution "as black a mark as was set on Cain." He further observed, "He had no such confidence in the Genl. Govt. as some Gentlemen possessed, and believed it would be found that the States have not" (1:332). Again on August 23, Gerry said that he would just as soon see the citizens of his state disarmed "as to take the command from the States, and subject them to the Genl. Legislature." He observed that this "would be regarded as a system of Despotism" (2:385). He further asked whether anyone would think their liberty as secure "in the hands of eighty or a hundred men taken from the whole continent, as in the hands of two or three hundred taken from a single State" (2:386). When the convention was debating whether state or national governments should appoint officers of the militia, Gerry "warned the Convention agst pushing the experiment too far." He explained, "Some people will support a plan of vigorous Government at every risk. Others of a more democratic cast will oppose it with equal determination. And a Civil war may be produced by the conflict" (2:388).

On June 11, Gerry illumined his view of the relation between the nation and the states when he opposed requiring state officials to support the national constitution. He argued that "there was as much reason for requiring an oath of fidelity to the States, from Natl. officers, as vice. versa" (1:203). When the convention adopted a proposal on July 23 requiring that state officials pledge to uphold the national constitution, Gerry successfully proposed that national officials should have to take the same oath (2:87).

By contrast, Gerry's speech on June 29 appeared quite nationalistic. Then observing that "The States & the advocates for them were intoxicated with the idea of their *sovereignty*," Gerry indicated that he thought the Articles were dissolving. He further "lamented that instead of coming here like a band of brothers, belonging to the same family, we seemed to have brought with us the spirit of political negociators" (1:467).

When the convention discussed the possibility of allowing Congress to send troops into a state even without its request, Gerry showed considerable agitation. He said that he was "agst. letting loose the myrmidons [warriors] of the U. States on a State without its own consent" (2:317). With an eye to his own state, he argued that more blood would have been shed during Shays's Rebellion had the general government intervened.

Standing Armies

On August 18, Gerry rose to express his concern that the Constitution did not prohibit standing armies in times of peace. Referring, as he so frequently did, to public opinion, Gerry observed, "The people were jealous on this head, and great opposition to the plan would spring from such an omission"

(2:329). He clearly agreed with what he considered to be public sentiment and suggested that a limit of 3,000 men under arms might be appropriate in peacetime (2:329–30).

On September 5, Gerry tied his fear of standing armies in peacetime to his concern that military appropriations could be made for two-year periods. Again, he argued that "The people would not bear it" (2:509). He subsequently argued for annual publication of all public expenditures (2:618).

Gerry may have been an intense man, but he was not without a sense of humor. He is reported to have likened a standing army to an organ of the male anatomy with similar properties. He observed that such a standing organ was "an excellent assurance of domestic tranquility, but a dangerous temptation to foreign adventure" (quoted in Isaacson 2003, 456).

Other Matters

On August 20, Gerry opposed authorizing Congress to establish sumptuary laws regulating food and clothing purchases and the like. He argued quite practically that "the law of necessity is the best sumptuary law" (2:344).

Amendment and Ratification

Gerry indicated on June 5 that he favored including an amending process in the Constitution. He observed both that "the novelty & difficulty of the experiment requires periodical revision" and that "the prospect of such a revision would also give intermediate stability to the Govt." (1:122). He further thought that state experience confirmed the utility of such mechanisms.

On September 10, Gerry moved for a reconsideration of the amending clause. He feared that the provision whereby two-thirds of the states could request that Congress call a convention to propose amendments might be used to allow a majority of a convention "which can bind the Union to innovations that may subvert the State-Constitutions altogether" (2:557–58). He subsequently seconded a motion by Connecticut's Roger Sherman allowing Congress to propose amendments, which would not go into effect until the states ratified them (2:558).

Consistent with his distrust of election of governmental officials, Gerry said on June 5 that he feared allowing the people to ratify the Constitution. He observed that the people, at least those he knew in the eastern states, had "the wildest ideas of Government in the world" (1:123). He cited the desire of the people of Massachusetts to abolish the state senate and give all power to the more popular house. On July 23, Gerry reiterated his opposition to submitting ratification of the Constitution to the people:

> Great confusion he was confident would result from a recurrence to the people. They would never agree on any thing. He could not see any ground to suppose that the people will do what their rulers will not. The rulers will either conform to, or influence the sense of the people. (2:90)

On August 31, Gerry indicated that he did not think the Articles of Confederation could be dissolved except by "the unanimous Consent of the parties to it," by which he referred to the state government thereof (2:478). He further observed on September 10 that "If nine out of thirteen can dissolve the compact, Six out of nine will be just as able to dissolve the new one hereafter" (2:561). He thus seconded Alexander Hamilton's motion to send the Constitution first to Congress and then to the states, which would have authority to determine whether they were willing to join the new Union only when nine other states so consented (2:562). Gerry proposed a change in the amending clause that required Congress to call a convention on the application of two-thirds of the states (2:629). He was not successful, however, in striking a provision (only used to date in the case of the Twenty-first Amendment overturning national alcoholic prohibition) allowing amendments to be ratified by special state ratifying conventions.

Gerry's Decision Not to Sign

On September 15, Gerry presented eight reasons why he had decided not to sign the Constitution; most were issues on which he had previously taken positions. These included "the duration and re-eligibility of the Senate"; "the power of the House of Representatives to conceal their journals"; congressional control over "the places of election"; congressional power to set their own salaries; inadequate representation for the state of Massachusetts; representation of blacks according to the three-fifths ratio; his fear that Congress might use its power over commerce to establish monopolies; and his objection to the vice president's role in presiding over the Senate. He indicated that these objections would not alone have been sufficient for him to withhold his signature:

> If the rights of the Citizens were not rendered insecure 1. by the general power of the Legislature to make what laws they may please to call necessary and proper. 2. raise armies and money without limit. 3. to establish a tribunal without juries, which will be a Star-chamber as to Civil cases. (2:633)

He indicated that, under the circumstances, he favored calling a second convention (2:633).

Two days later, Gerry alluded to "the painful feelings of his situation and the embarrassment under which he rose to offer any further observations" (2:646). He feared that the nation was headed towards civil war. He observed that there were two parties within his own home state, "one devoted to Democracy, the worst he thought of all political evils, the other as violent in the opposite extreme" (2:647). He had hoped that the Constitution might have been proposed "in more mediating shape" but assured delegates that "if it were not otherwise apparent, the refusals to sign should never be known from him" (2:647).

Life after the Convention

Despite his opposition to the Constitution, Gerry also feared domestic strife. In enclosing the new Constitution to the Massachusetts General Court, along with his objections, Gerry noted that "I shall only add, that as the welfare of the union requires a better Constitution than the Confederation, I shall think it my duty as a citizen of Massachusetts, to support that which shall be finally adopted, sincerely hoping it will secure the liberty and happiness of America" (Bailyn 1993, 1:233). In contrasting his own support for the Constitution to that of Gerry's, South Carolina's Pierce Butler observed that "I shall not less admire his independent spirit, his disinterested conduct and his private worth because we differ on measures of great public concern" (Austin, 2:59–60). Once the states had ratified the Constitution, Gerry joined other Antifederalists in deciding to accept it and to continue to push for amendments protecting individual rights. Massachusetts elected Gerry to the first Congress under the new Constitution; Gerry defeated fellow delegate Nathaniel Gorham in this election.

Gerry served as a presidential elector for John Adams in 1797, but subsequently lost favor with Adams after he pursued a pro-French policy as one of three U.S. emissaries to France (the others were John Marshall and Charles Cotesworth Pinckney) to be caught up in the so-called XYZ Affair, in which the Americans turned aside French attempts to bribe them. Gerry continued to stay in France to negotiate after his colleagues had left. Later serving as an elector for Thomas Jefferson in the election of 1804, he was elected governor of Massachusetts in 1810. The term gerrymandering (referring to drawing district lines for partisan advantage) grew from this time period when a district that Gerry designed so as to favor his own party was shaped so bizarrely that it was likened to a salamander.

Gerry served briefly as vice president under James Madison before passing away in 1814. He was interred in the Washington, DC Congressional Cemetery beneath a monument that quoted him as saying, "It is the duty of every man, though he may have but one day to live, to devote that day to the good of his country" (Bradsher 2006, 30). The Gerry House, at 44 Washington Street in Marblehead, has been on the National Registry of Historical Places since 1973.

Further Reading

Austin, James. 2009. *The Life of Elbridge Gerry*. 2 vols. Boston: Wells and Lilly, 1828–1892; reprinted by Bedford, MA: Applewood Books.

Bailyn, Bernard, ed. 1993. *The Debate on the Constitution: Federalist and Antifederalist Speeches, Articles, and Letters during the Struggle over Ratification*. 2 vols. New York: The Library of America.

Billias, George Athan. 1976. *Elbridge Gerry: Founding Father and Republican Statesman*. New York: McGraw Hill.

———. 1990. "Elbridge Gerry." *Constitution* 2 (Spring–Summer): 68–74.

Bradsher, Greg. 2006. "A Founding Father in Dissent," *Prologue* 38 (Spring): 30–35.

Farrand, Max, ed. 1966. *The Records of the Federal Convention of 1787*. 4 vols. New Haven, CT: Yale University Press.

Isaacson, Walter. 2003. *Benjamin Franklin: An American Life*. New York: Simon & Schuster.

Morison, S. E. 1929. "Elbridge Gerry, Gentleman-Democrat." *The New England Quarterly* 2 (January): 6–33.

NICHOLAS GILMAN (1755–1814)
NEW HAMPSHIRE

Nicholas Gilman was born in Exeter, New Hampshire on August 3, 1755 to a family that had long-established roots within the state. His father was a relatively wealthy merchant who had served in the French and Indian War. Gilman served in the Revolutionary War and rose to the rank of assistant adjutant general, and was present at Valley Forge and Yorktown. He inherited a sizeable estate when his father died in 1783, the same year Gilman helped found the Society of the Cincinnati. Regarded as a handsome man,

Gilman was a lifelong bachelor who devoted much of the rest of his life to politics. From 1786 to 1788, Gilman represented New Hampshire in the Congress under the Articles of Confederation, and he was among those who voted to forward to the Constitution to the states for approval.

At the Convention

Gilman, and fellow delegate John Langdon, did not arrive at the Constitutional Convention to represent New Hampshire until July 23, a week after the delegates had resolved the issue of representation, and Langdon footed the bill for their expenses. Gilman was one of the youngest members, and his attendance seemed to make little difference. Although Gilman was one of the signers of the Constitution, he is not recorded as having made a single comment during convention deliberations.

Life after the Convention

Gilman served for eight years in the U.S. House of Representatives, where he established a reputation as a Democratic-Republican. During this time, he made only one recorded speech (Saladino 1999, 9:62). Although he had stepped down from office, in the 1805 race for New Hampshire Gilman supported John Langdon, his fellow delegate from New Hampshire to the Constitutional Convention, who succeeded in winning over Gilman's elder brother. The New Hampshire legislature subsequently appointed Gilman to the U.S. Senate where he served until his death in Philadelphia on May 2, 1814. Although he had initially supported Thomas Jefferson's administration, Gilman turned against Jefferson and his successor, James Madison, and opposed both the embargo against England and the War of 1812. Gilman is buried in the Exeter Cemetery in Exeter, New Hampshire.

Further Reading

"Nicholas Gilman." Find a Grave Memorial. http://www.findagrave.com/cgi-bin/fg.cgi?page=gr&GRid=4711. Accessed 7/6/2012.
Saladino, Gaspare J. 1999. "Gilman, Nicholas." In *American National Biography*, edited by John A. Garraty and Mark C. Carnes, 9: 62–63. New York: Oxford University Press.

Nathaniel Gorham (1738–1796)
Massachusetts

Born in Charlestown, Massachusetts on May 21, 1738, the son of a packet boat operator, Nathaniel Gorham was apprenticed to a Connecticut merchant before opening his own merchant house. Gorham was a successful merchant who had served his state and nation. He married Rebecca Call (1744–1812) in September 1763, and they had nine children, seven of whom lived into adulthood. Previous positions had included a stint from 1771 to 1775 in the Massachusetts legislature, service from 1774–1775 to the Massachusetts Provincial Congress, participation in the Massachusetts constitutional convention of 1779–1780, and two periods of service to the Congress under the Articles of Confederation, during which he served as president (its sixth).

Gorham was extremely concerned about Shays's Rebellion within Massachusetts and, in a development that might have shocked some of his fellow delegates, had written to Prussia's Prince Henry to see if he might be willing to serve as a U.S. king if the rebellion spread and the nation decided on a monarchy (Lettieri 1999, 9:306). Although this endeavor failed, Shays's Rebellion encouraged Gorham to push for a stronger national government.

At the Convention

Gorham began attending the Constitutional Convention on May 28, the day after his forty-ninth birthday, having stayed in New York for a time to help keep the Congress, of which he was president, running.

Likely because of the prominence he had achieved in Congress, the convention chose Gorham on May 30 by a vote of seven to one to chair the Committee of the Whole. He served in this role through June 19, taking a position at the front of the convention that George Washington otherwise occupied. Perhaps as a consequence, Gorham's first recorded comments at the convention were not made until June 22 during a discussion of congressional salaries. From that time forward, he participated in convention discussions on a fairly regular basis. In addition to chairing the Committee of the Whole, Gorham served on the committee for the original apportionment of

Congress which the convention created on July 6, on the important Committee of Detail that the convention formed on July 24, and on the Committee on Commercial Discrimination and the Committee on Interstate Comity and Bankruptcy that the delegates created on August 25 and 29.

Congress

Pay. Gorham opposed allowing the states to set the salaries of members of Congress. He observed that the state legislatures "were always paring down salaries in such a manner as to keep out of offices men most capable of executing the functions of them" (Farrand 1966, 1:372). He further opposed specifying this salary in the Constitution, "because we could not venture to make it as liberal as it ought to be without exciting an enmity agst. the whole plan" (1:372). He favored allowing Congress to "provide for their own wages from time to time; as the State Legislatures do" (1:372). Gorham opposed a motion that would require that members of both houses be paid the same. He pointed out that senators would need more since members "will be detained longer from home, will be obliged to remove their families, and in time of war perhaps to sit constantly" (2:293).

Eligibility for Other Offices. Gorham opposed a motion that would have prevented members of the House of Representatives from being ineligible to offices during their tenure and for one year after as "unnecessary & injurious" (1:375). He later argued that "the eligibility was among the inducements for fit men to enter into the Legislative service" (2:491).

Representation. On June 25, Gorham indicated that he favored a compromise in the representation of the small states and the large ones. He observed that in his state of Massachusetts, the large counties were not given representation "in an exact ratio to their numbers," and he expressed the view that a similar approach might be "expedient" in regard to Congress (1:405).

On June 29, Gorham made a strong speech directed to the small states urging them to consider the price of disunion. He observed that the smaller states would be far less capable of taking care of themselves in such a situation than the large ones. He observed that Delaware would lie at the mercy of Pennsylvania and that New Jersey would suffer from its lack of commerce. He also anticipated that the large states were through growing and might, like Massachusetts—which anticipated that Maine would become independent—split (1:462–63). He concluded that "a Union of the States [was] as necessary to their happiness, & a firm Genl. Govt. as necessary to their Union" (1:463). On July 6, Gorham repeated the idea that it would be good for the larger states to split, in which case their representation in Congress should be reduced. He favored a strong national government, and thought that a further division of the states would help accomplish this goal:

> He conceived that let the Genl. Government be modified as it might, there would be a constant tendency in the State Governmts. to encroach upon it: it was of importance therefore that the extent of the States shd. Be reduced as much & as fast as possible. The stronger the Govt. shall be made in the first instance the more easily will these divisions be effected; as it will be of less consequence in the opinion of the States whether they be of great or small extent. (1:540)

On July 6, the delegates appointed Gorham to the second of three committees designed to examine representation in Congress. This committee, chaired by Gouverneur Morris of Pennsylvania, proposed on July 9 a House of 56 members apportioned according to wealth and numbers (roughly one representative for every 40,000 inhabitants) with the number of representatives reapportioned to states if they broke up (1:559). In explaining this plan, Gorham observed that "The number of blacks & whites with some regard to supposed wealth was the general guide" (1:559). His explanation indicated that he must have supported Morris's reluctance to grant equal representation to equal numbers of persons in the western states. Gorham thus observed that "the Atlantic States having ye. Govt. in their own hands, may take care of their own interest, by dealing out the right of Representation in safe proportions to the Western States" (1:560). By July 11, Gorham indicated that if the current convention were perplexed as to how to apportion new states, the new government "under the full biass of those views" would be even more so; he thus favored fixing a standard (1:583).

Gorham had earlier indicated his support for the Three-fifths Clause as a provision "fixed by Congs. as a rule of taxation" and as "pretty near the just proportion" (1:580). He continued to support this provision on July 11. Acknowledging that the people of the eastern states might take some "umbrage" to allowing slaves to count as three-fifths of a person, he observed that when Massachusetts considered this proportion under the Articles of Confederation, "the only difficulty then was to satisfy them that the Negroes ought not to have been counted equally with whites instead of being counted in the ratio of three fifths only" (1:587).

It would appear that Gorham did not have particularly strong views against slavery. On August 25, Gorham seconded a motion by South Carolina's Charles Cotesworth Pinckney to extend the time that states could import slaves from 1800 to 1808 (2:415). When Connecticut's Roger Sherman objected that allowing a duty on slaves implied that they were property, Gorham preferred a more positive interpretation. Such duties were simply to be regarded "as a discouragement to the importation of them" (2:416).

The committee that reported the compromise granting differential modes of representation in the House and Senate also proposed barring the Senate from proposing money bills. Gorham indicated his agreement with this compromise on August 8 (2:224) and again on August 13 (2:297).

One of Gorham's more fascinating statements was made in the context of the formula for representation in the U.S. House of Representatives. When Madison objected that apportioning the House according to the rule of one for every 40,000 inhabitants would one day result in a House that was too big, Gorham asked, "It is not to be supposed that the Govt will last so long as to produce this effect?" He openly questioned, "Can it be supposed that this vast Country including the Western territory will 150 years hence remain one nation?" (2:221).

Long after the convention had settled on a formula for representation in the two houses and John Rutledge and Roger Sherman opposed a joint ballot for selecting the president, Gorham indicated that he thought the delegates were focusing too much on who the respective houses were representing:

> it was wrong to be considering, at every turn whom the Senate would represent. The public good was the true object to be kept in view—Great delay and confusion would ensue if the two Houses shd vote separately, each having a negative on the choice of the other. (2:402)

On the last day of the convention, Gorham was the delegate who proposed that his colleagues should change representation from a minimum of one representative for every 40,000 inhabitants to one for every 30,000 (2:643–44). Significantly, this motion proved the occasion for one of only two recorded speeches by George Washington—in favor of Gorham's proposition, which then passed unanimously.

Western Lands. Gorham, who spent much of his life speculating in Western lands, did not favor including an adjustment of western land claims within the new Constitution. He believed that Congress was already working on the subject and that "The best remedy would be such a Government as would have vigor enough to do justice throughout" (1:405). He argued that such a strengthened government would give the smaller states their "best chance" at justice (1:405).

Terms. Gorham favored granting each state two rather than three senators. He feared that a larger number of senators would find it difficult to decide on matters of peace and war. He also anticipated that new states would enter the Union and that existing states would split. As on other occasions at the convention, Gorham observed that "The strength of the general Govt. will lie not in the largeness, but in the smallness of the States" (2:94).

On June 25 Gorham proposed a four-year term for senators (1:408). On June 26, he proposed to lengthen this to a six-year term (1:421)—the solution that the convention eventually adopted. Both proposals were even numbers, allowing for equal numbers of terms to end each year.

Powers. Perhaps with a view to the disturbances that had rocked Massachusetts during Shays's Rebellion, Gorham thought that the national government needed to have power to quash rebellions within the states. He observed that if the government did not have this power, "an enterprising Citizen might erect the standard of Monarchy in a particular State, might gather together partisans from all quarters, might extend his views from State to State, and threaten to establish a tyranny over the whole & the Genl. Govt. be compelled to remain an inactive witness of its own destruction" (2:48). Acknowledging that individuals should be able to say what they wanted, he said that "If they appeal to the sword it will then be necessary for the Genl. Govt., however difficult it may be to decide on the merits of their contest, to interpose & put an end to it" (2:48).

Pointing to the British experience, Gorham also believed that Congress should have the power to regulate elections (2:240). Gorham feared that requiring a majority for a quorum in each house would lead to unnecessary delays.

Gorham favored striking a provision allowing Congress to emit bills of credit, but he also opposed specifically prohibiting such bills (2:309). He later argued that "an absolute prohibition of paper money would rouse the most desperate opposition from its partisans" and favored simply prohibiting states from issuing such money without congressional consent (2:439). At a time when the convention was suggesting that Congress should appoint the national treasurer, Gorham proposed that this should be done by joint ballot rather than by the houses jointly (2:314; also see 2:615). Gorham also moved to grant Congress power not only to "raise" but also to "support" armies (2:329). Gorham supported the provision granting Congress power to make uniform laws regarding bankruptcies and legislating in regard to damages arising "on the protest of foreign bills of exchange" (2:447).

Gorham did not see any need for a requirement that two-thirds of Congress should have to consent to navigation acts. He may have ruffled some feathers when on August 22 he observed that "the Eastern States had no motive to Union but a commercial one. They were able to protect themselves. They were not afraid of external danger, and did not need the aid of the Southn. States" (2:374). The next day, Gorham joined Virginia's James Madison in opposing a provision whereby treaties would have to be ratified by law—apparently by both houses. He observed that it would be difficult to get such previous ratification, which would make it difficult for American diplomats (2:392). Somewhat later in the day, however, he said that "it is necessary to guard against the Government itself being seduced" (2:393).

On August 29, Gorham again opposed a two-thirds requirement for navigation bills. Once again, he wondered what motives this would give the eastern states to join the Union. Although "he deprecated the consequences of disunion," he believed that the South would lose the most in such circumstances. He said that it was improbable that the northern states would combine against southern states (2:453).

Gorham did not see any necessity for allowing two-thirds of the Senate to make peace treaties without presidential consent. He observed that Congress would already have control over the "means of carrying on the war" (2:540; also see 2:549).

Other Matters. Gorham preferred to allow Congress to adopt legislation preventing abuses by debtors and others who might get elected to office in order to advance their own individual interests, rather than to rely on property qualifications for members of Congress or those who elected them (2:122). He thought a provision barring members with "unsettled accounts" from running from office would unfairly fall on "the commercial & manufacturing part of the people" (2:125). On August 8, he opposed a freeholder requirement for voting, observing that merchants and mechanics were just as qualified as small landowners. Moreover, "The people have been long accustomed to this right in various parts of America, and will never allow it to be abridged. We must consult their rooted prejudices if we expect their concurrence in our propositions" (2:216). Similarly, Gorham opposed applying durational citizenship requirements on immigrants retroactively: "When foreigners are naturalized it wd. seem as if they stand on an equal footing with natives" (2:270).

Gorham thought that requiring the nation to establish a capital in a place other than a city with an existing state capital could be evaded by a congressional refusal to construct buildings elsewhere (2:127). Gorham believed that the Constitution should specify the meeting time for Congress to avoid future disputes on the subject. He observed that the New England states had fixed such times, and that "no inconveniency had resulted" (2:198). He believed that state legislatures should meet at least once each year.

On August 10, Gorham opposed a provision that would have allowed a single member of Congress to ask for a roll-call vote. Based on his experience with such a mechanism in Massachusetts, he observed that members "stuffed the journals" with such requests and, that "they are not proper as the reasons governing the voter never appear along with them" (2:255).

Presidency

When the convention discussed a provision whereby Congress would select the president, Gorham wanted Congress to act by joint ballot. He thought that separate ballots would lead to "great delay, contention & confusion" (2:196). Acknowledging that a joint ballot would advantage the larger states, he thought this was preferable to disturbing the public tranquility.

Once the convention established the electoral college, Gorham said that he did not want the vice presidency going to the person with the second highest number of votes unless that individual had a majority. Otherwise, he feared that the office might go to "a very obscure man" (2:499). He did not, however, believe that a supermajority should be required for the presidential office (2:526–27).

Judiciary

On July 18, Gorham proposed that the president should appoint members of the judiciary with the advice and consent of the Senate. Gorham said that this measure, which was the eventual plan on which the convention settled, "had been long practiced" in Massachusetts (he later claimed the practice had been in effect for 140 years [2:44]) "& was found to answer perfectly well" (2:41). He defended this plan by saying that the president would look as widely as the Senate for judges, and that senators would be more likely to be attached to the seat of government and, as a public body, to "give full play to intrigue & cabal" (2:42). He observed that if senators "can not get the man of the particular State to which they may respectively belong, they will be indifferent to the rest" (2:42). He further observed, "The Executive would certainly be more answerable for a good appointment, as the whole blame of a bad one would fall on him alone" (2:43).

Gorham observed that national courts already operated in the states to deal with matters of piracy and commerce. He believed that "Inferior tribunals are essential to render the authority of the Natl. Legislature effectual" (2:46).

On July 21, Gorham opposed allying the judges with the executive in a Council of Revision. He observed, "As Judges they are not to be presumed to possess any peculiar knowledge of the mere policy of public measures. Nor can it be necessary as a security for their constitutional rights" (2:73). His solution was "to let the Executive alone be responsible, and at most to authorize him to call on Judges for their opinions" (2:73). Later in the day, Gorham observed that "the Judges ought to carry into the exposition of the laws no prepossessions with regard to them" (2:79). He also feared that the judges would outweigh the executive in numbers and that "instead of enabling him to defend himself" they "would enable the Judges to sacrifice him" (2:79).

In a discussion of judicial oaths, Gorham did not think they were particularly effective, but he sought to rebut the argument that such oaths would inhibit constitutional change. He opined that "A constitutional alteration of the Constitution, could never be regarded as a breach of the Constitution, or of any oath to support it" (2:88).

Gorham indicated on August 24 that he favored keeping a mechanism similar to that under the Articles of Confederation for resolving disputes among the states to granting this power to the Courts. He feared that such judges might be connected to the states that had claims in such cases (2:401).

On September 12, Gorham joined delegates who believed that it was impossible to specify within the Constitution conditions where civil juries should be required from cases where they would not be (2:587). Such reservations were among the reasons that the convention decided not to add a bill of rights.

Ratification

On July 23, Gorham used five different arguments to oppose allowing the existing Congress and state legislatures to ratify the new Constitution. He argued first that members chosen specifically for the purpose of ratifying a constitution would discuss the matter more candidly than those who stood to gain or lose power. He next observed that most state legislatures had two houses, both of which would have to approve. He further noted that some state legislatures excluded members of the clergy who were "generally friends to good Government" (2:90). He observed that legislatures would have plenty of other business, by which "designing men" would "find means to delay from year to year" (2:90). Finally, he noted the unlikelihood of getting unanimous state consent, especially when Rhode Island had not even sent delegates to the convention, and New York was enjoying commercial advantages under the existing system (1:90). Such arguments must have come with particular force from a man who was president of the Congress under the Articles of Confederation.

Gorham reiterated on August 31 his support for ratification of the Constitution by state conventions (2:476). He opposed a measure by Alexander Hamilton of New York that would have left it to the states to decide how many consenting votes should be necessary to the new Union. He feared that "the different and conditional ratifications will defeat the plan altogether" (2:560).

Life after the Convention

Gorham was selected as a member of the Massachusetts ratifying convention, but lost a bid to be elected to the new Congress to Elbridge Gerry, who had refused to sign the document. Gorham subsequently became involved in a massive land deal involving over six million acres. This led to his financial ruin and may have hastened his death by apoplexy on June 11, 1796. He was buried in the Phipps Street Burial Ground in Charlestown. One of his sons, Benjamin, subsequently served in Congress.

Further Reading

Farrand, Max, ed. 1966. *The Records of the Federal Convention of 1787*. 4 vols. New Haven, CT: Yale University Press.

Lettieri, Ronald J. 1999. "Gorham, Nathaniel." In *American National Biography*, edited by John A. Garraty and Mark C. Carnes , 9:306–7. New York: Oxford University Press.

Meister, Charles W. 1987. *The Founding Fathers*. Jefferson, NC: McFarland & Company.

Whitney, David C. 1974. *Founders of Freedom in America: Lives of the Men Who Signed the Constitution of the United States and So Helped to Establish the United States of America*. Chicago: J. G. Ferguson Publishing Company.

ALEXANDER HAMILTON (1755 OR 1757–1804)
NEW YORK

Alexander Hamilton was born in Nevis, in the British West Indies, in 1755 or 1757; his parents were never legally married, his father abandoned the family, and his mother died when Hamilton was eight. After serving as a merchant's apprentice, a minister's family helped bring Hamilton to the colonies where he was aided by William Livingston (a future delegate to the U.S. Constitutional Convention from New Jersey) before becoming a student at King's College, today's Columbia University.

Hamilton quickly became involved in the Revolutionary cause and wrote an influential pamphlet entitled "A Full Vindication of the Measures of the Congress from the Calumnies of their Enemies." He went on to serve as an aide-de-camp to General Washington and to fight at the battle of Yorktown. Delegates to the convention thus addressed him as "Colonel." Hamilton was a strong nationalist who was convinced early on that the government of the Articles of Confederation was inadequate. He had entered the field of law where he distinguished himself by his skills.

In 1780, Hamilton married Elizabeth (Betsey) Schuyler (1757–1854), the daughter of a wealthy businessman from a prominent New York family, with whom he had seven children who survived into adulthood. In a letter he wrote while still single to Henry Laurens, Hamilton indicated the kind of woman he sought:

> She must be young, handsome (I lay most stress upon a good shape), sensible (a little learning will do), well-bred . . . chaste and tender (I am an enthusiast in my notions of fidelity and fondness), of some good nature, a great deal of generosity (she must neither love money nor scolding, for I dislike equally a termagant and an economist).

Noting that he was indifferent to her political views—he was sure that he could "convert" her to his—he observed, "As to fortune, the larger stock of that the better" (quoted in Howard 2007, 159) Although he had been an ardent patriot, Hamilton was engaged in a number of cases defending the rights of loyalists and quickly distinguished himself for his legal skills.

Perhaps in part because he had been born and raised abroad rather than in one of the states, Hamilton was an avowed nationalist. He may well have been the first individual explicitly to call for a constitutional convention, a sentiment that he expressed in a letter of September 3, 1780 to James Duane (see Rossiter 1964, 36), even before the Articles of Confederation had been ratified. He tried at one point to apply military pressure on the Congress under the Articles before George Washington nixed the plan. On another occasion, Hamilton tried to get New York to ratify an amendment granting Congress power to enact import duties. He was a major figure at the Annapolis Convention, and went on to become an important figure at New York's ratifying convention.

Given this background, Alexander Hamilton must have been very frustrated at the Constitutional Convention. Fellow New York delegates John Lansing and Robert Yates, both favoring states' rights, constantly checked him at the convention. He left the convention for long periods. Still, he returned to sign the document and went on to argue for its adoption as one of three authors who wrote the *Federalist Papers* under the name of Publius.

Hamilton was a short man with red hair who dressed in dapper fashion. He was present when the convention opened on May 25. Maryland's James McHenry observed in his notes of May 29 that Hamilton asked whether the convention should conduct an inquiry as to "whether the united States were susceptible of one government, or required a separate existence connected only by leagues offensive and defensive and treaties of commerce" (Farrand 1966, 1:27).

Congress

On May 30, Hamilton introduced a resolution whereby "the rights of suffrage in the national Legislature ought to be proportioned to the number of free inhabitants" (1:36). On June 11, he further moved that the right of suffrage in the second branch should be the same as in the first (1:202). On June 21, Hamilton opposed state legislative selection of senators.

Also on June 21, Hamilton advocated a three-year term for members of the House of Representatives at a time when others were advocating annual or biennial terms. Hamilton reasoned that "there ought to be neither too much nor too little dependence, on the popular sentiments" (2:362). He indicated that septennial elections had not quenched "the democratic spirit" of the English constitution and that "Frequency of elections tended to make the people listless to them; and to facilitate the success of little cabals" (1:362).

Not unexpectedly, Hamilton opposed allowing states to pay members of Congress. He sagely observed, "Those who pay are the masters of those who are paid" (2:373). He further observed that states might pay unequally. Undoubtedly anticipating the need for future adjustments, Hamilton opposed fixing the wages within the Constitution (1:373).

Hamilton continued to support state representation in both houses of Congress on the basis of population. On June 29, shortly before he left the convention for an extended period, Hamilton indicated that he regarded the small state quest for equal representation in one or both houses to be "a contest for power, not for liberty" (1:466). He argued that the rights of the people individually, rather than the rights of the states as entities, should be the convention's central concern:

> The state of Delaware having 40,000 souls will *lose power*, if she has 1/10 only of the votes allowed to Pa. having 400,000: but will the people of Del: *be less free*, if each citizen has an equal vote with each citizen of Pa. (1:466)

Consistent with his focus on economics, Hamilton argued that the real distinction between states involved the "carrying & non-carrying States" rather than the distinction between the large and small ones (1:466). Hamilton feared that America could divide into partial confederacies that would ally with European governments and give them a foothold. Hamilton viewed the creation of a stronger government as thus a necessary measure for both domestic and foreign concerns, and he viewed the time as peculiarly ripe for positive actions:

> No Governmt. could give us tranquility & happiness at home, which did not possess sufficient stability and strength to make us respectable abroad. This was the critical moment for forming such a government. As yet we retain the habits of union. We are weak & sensible of our weakness. Henceforward the motives will become feebler, and the difficulties greater. It is a miracle that we were now here exercising our tranquil & free deliberations on the subject. It would be madness to trust to future miracles. A thousand causes must obstruct a reproduction of them. (1:467)

Hamilton did not take part in convention debates from June 30 through August 12. When he returned to the convention, he opposed specifying the number of years of citizenship and residency for members of Congress as "embarrassing the Govt. with minute restrictions" (2:268). He thought that an overly restrictive number of years would discourage immigration and wanted to leave to future Congresses the determination of how many years should be required.

On September 8, Hamilton supported a larger House of Representatives than the convention had provided. Favoring "a broad foundation" for this body, he observed that it "was on so narrow a scale as to be really dangerous, and to warrant a jealousy in the people for their liberties" (2:554).

Hamilton's Plan

By June 18, the convention had two major plans before it—the Virginia Plan and the New Jersey Plan. The first favored the large states and the second favored the smaller; the first called for a complete overhaul in the governmental system and the second stuck more closely to the existing Articles of Confederation. On this day, however, Hamilton took to the floor for an address that lasted the entire session. He observed that he had previously been largely silent out of deference to the "superior abilities age & experience" of others as well as because of "his delicate situation with respect to his own State, to whose sentiments as expressed by his Colleagues, he could by no means accede" (1:282). Proclaiming that the "crisis" obliged him to contribute his own efforts to forming a new constitution, he professed to be "unfriendly to both plans" (1:283), and especially to the New Jersey Plan. Convinced that "no amendment of the confederation, leaving the States in possession of their sovereignty could possibly answer the purpose," he took a more negative view of the nation's large extent than did James Madison, the putative author of the Virginia Plan. By contrast, Hamilton said that "he was much discouraged by the amazing extent of the Country in expecting the desired blessings from any general sovereignty that could be substituted" (1:283).

Hamilton thought that those who debated the meaning of federalism had become too subtle. He believed that a federal government was simply "an association of independent Communities into one" (1:283), and he did not believe such a system precluded direct action on individuals as well as on communities. The emergency dictated that the delegates act according to what they thought proper, and if states had not authority to ratify what they did, the people could assume this authority, presumably in state ratifying conventions.

Hamilton proceeded to the question, "what provision shall we make for the happiness of our Country?" (1:284) He thought the answer was a provision for a national government. Such a government would be based on five principles, which indicated that Hamilton had a realistic, perhaps even pessimistic, view of human motivations. These were:

- An active & constant interest in supporting it
- The love of power
- An habitual attachment of the people
- *Force* by which may be understood *a coertion of laws or coertion of arms*
- Influence. he did not [mean] corruption, but a dispensation of those regular honors & emoluments, which produce an attachment to the Govt. (1:284–85)

Hamilton did not think the current government had such supports. Under the Articles, states had developed "the esprit de corps" in favor of their individual interests rather than those of the nation as a whole (1:284). Under the Articles, power rested with the states and "the ambition of their demagogues is known to hate the control of the Genl. Government" (1:284). Moreover, the people were more firmly attached to their states than to national authority. Under the present system, state sovereignty "is immediately before the eyes of the people: its protection is immediately enjoyed by them. From its hands distributive justice, and all those acts which familiarize & endear Govt. to a people, are dispensed to them" (1:284). Under the Articles it was impossible to exert national force upon the states. Moreover the state governments had the dispensation of honors within their hands: "All the passions when we see, of avarice, ambition, interest, which govern most individuals, and all public bodies, fall into the current of the States, and do not flow in the stream of the Genl. Govt." (1:285).

Hamilton then offered a series of examples of past confederations including the Amphyctionic Council, the German confederacy, the reign of Charlemagne, the German Diet, and the Swiss cantons. He concluded that the only solution was to invest "such a compleat sovereignty in the general Govermt. as will turn all the strong principles & passions above mentioned on its side" (1:286).

Hamilton argued that the New Jersey Plan was inadequate on this account. He focused on the plan's need to requisition the states for money. He observed that experience proved such requisitions to be unreliable. He believed that the national government should rely instead on taxation of commerce, including exports (1:286). Hamilton also faulted the New Jersey Plan for proposing equal state representation within Congress. He observed that "It is not in human nature that Va. & the large States should consent to it, or if they did that they shd. long abide by it. It shocks too much the ideas of Justice, and every human feeling" (1:286). Hamilton did not believe that the New Jersey Plan provided for proper defense in peacetime. He also believed that the Congress proposed under this plan would represent "local prejudice" (1:287). He observed:

> It is agst. all the principles of a good Government to vest the requisite pow-
> ers in such a body as Cong. Two Sovereignties can not co-exist within the
> same limits. Giving powers to Congs. must eventuate in a bad Govt. or in
> no Govt. (1:287)

It was at this point that Hamilton returned to his concerns over the extent of the nation, and came close to suggesting that states, at least as semi-sovereign entities, should be abolished:

> The extent of the Country to be governed, discouraged him. The expence
> of a general Govt. was also formidable; unless there were such a diminu-
> tion of expence on the state of the State Govts. as the case would admit.
> If they were extinguished, he was persuaded that great economy might be
> obtained by substituting a general Govt. He did not mean however to shock
> the public opinion by proposing such a measure. On the other [hand] he
> saw no *other* necessity for declining it. (1:287)

Hamilton recognized the need for lesser administrative units, but not for the states qua states:

> Subordinate authorities he was aware would be necessary. There must
> be district tribunals: corporations for local purposes. But cui bono [to
> whose benefit?], the vast & expansive apparatus now appertaining to the
> States. (1:287)

Hamilton wondered however how representatives would be drawn "from the extremes to the center of the Community" (1:287). Indeed, "this view of the subject almost led him to despair that a Republican Govt. could be established over so great an extent" (1:288). Still, "He was sensible at the same time that it would be unwise to propose one of any other form" (1:288).

As to his private views, Hamilton "had no scruple in declaring, sup-ported as he was by the opinions of so many of the wise & good, that the British Govt. was the best in the world; and that he doubted much whether any thing short of it would do in America" (1:288). He knew that the public did not currently agree, but he observed that public opinion was progressing, and anticipated that it would one day recognize the British system as "the only Govt. in the world 'which unites public strength with individual security'" (1:288). Whereas Madison stressed the multifarious factions that arise within society, Hamilton saw a primary division between "the few & the many" (1:288), and he thought that government needed to be devised so as to protect both classes. In England, the House of Lords performed this balancing function:

> Having nothing to hope for by a change, and a sufficient interest by means of their property, in being faithful to the National interest, they form a permanent barrier agst. every pernicious innovation, whether attempted on the part of the Crown or of the Commons. (1:288–89)

Hamilton did not believed that the proposed Senate would be adequate to these purposes. He thought that the seven-year term then under discussion would not give that body adequate "firmness" in the face of "the amazing violence & turbulence of the democratic spirit" (1:289). Similarly, Hamilton did not have confidence in the proposed executive. Again, England provided an example of what was needed:

> The Hereditary interest of the King was so interwoven with that of the Nation, and his personal emoluments so great, that he was placed above the danger of being corrupted from abroad—and at the same time was both sufficiently independent and sufficiently controuled, to answer the purpose of the institution at home. (1:289)

He therefore favored service for life in both the Senate and the chief executive offices.

Hamilton knew that his listeners would wonder whether the government he was proposing qualified as a republican government. He answered that it would so qualify "if all the Magistrates are appointed, and vacancies are filled, by the people, or in a process of election originating with the people" (1:290).

Hamilton then proceeded to outline his plan. It called for a bicameral Congress, with the members of the lower house elected to three-year terms and senators to serve during good behavior. The president would also be elected by the people and would serve during good behavior. He would have a veto on all laws, would direct war, would make treaties, would appoint the heads of departments, and could pardon all offenses other than treason (1:292). The Senate would declare war and advise on and approve treaties.

Members of the judiciary would serve during good behavior. All U.S. officers would be subject to impeachment. The general government would appoint the governors of each state who would have power to veto state laws. States would further be prohibited from having any land or sea forces, and their militia would be under national control.

Two days after Hamilton's speech, Connecticut's William Johnson observed that although Hamilton "has been praised by every body, he has been supported by none" (1:363). Hamilton seemed to understand his position. On June 26, he apparently indicated, or at least this is how Madison interpreted his remarks, that he did not himself favor republican government (he said however that he was "as zealous an advocate for liberty as any man whatever" (1:424), but recognized that he needed to address his remarks to those that did in the hopes that they would "tone their Government as high as possible" (1:424). The rest of his remarks followed up on the theme of the speech by which he had introduced his plan of government. He pointed out that as long as liberty existed, the distribution of property would vary, and such inequality would result in distinctions between rich and poor that were mirrored in Roman society by the distinction between patricians and plebeians. Hamilton thought that the House of Representatives would be the guardian of the poor and the Senate of the rich (1:424).

Human Nature

One of the fascinating aspects of Hamilton's plan was the way that it attempted to rely on human motives for the support of government. New York delegate Robert Yates cited Hamilton as having said that "the science of policy is the knowledge of human nature" (1:378). Hamilton cast further light on this view in opposing the provision limiting members of Congress from accepting other offices. After observing that "We must take man as we find him, and if we expect him to serve the public must interest his passions in doing so" (1:376). Hamilton cited David Hume's view that the "corruption" in Great Britain was essential to the operation of the system there (1:376).

Federalism

Hamilton had gone just about as far as anyone at the convention in suggesting that the states be abolished or reorganized. Apparently responding to a comment by Pennsylvania's James Wilson who had indicated that he did not favor the establishment of a national government "that would swallow up the

State Govts. as seemed to be wished by some gentlemen" (1:322), Hamilton had to explain himself the day after his long-winded speech, but it is likely that his explanation aroused even greater suspicion:

> He had not been understood yesterday. By an abolition of the States, he meant that no boundary could be drawn between the National & State Legislatures; that the former must therefore have indefinite authority. If it were limited at all, the rivalship of the States would gradually subvert it. Even as Corporations the extent of some of them as Va. Massts. &c. would be formidable. *As States*, he thought they ought to be abolished. But he admitted the necessity of leaving in them, subordinate jurisdictions. (1:323)

On June 19, Hamilton joined Wilson in disagreeing with Maryland's Luther Martin who believed that independence had put individual states in a "state of nature," in which each was on an equal footing. Although admitting that states were now on an equal footing, Hamilton "could see no inference from that against concerting a change of the system in this particular" (1:325). He believed that small states would be protected by the fact that the three largest states were "separated from each other by distance of place, and equally so by all the peculiarities which distinguish the interests of one State from those of another" (1:325). He also pointed out that states did not fall simply into the category of "large" and "small" but that there were all kinds of gradations in size between these.

In opposing a motion whereby state legislatures would select one branch of Congress, Hamilton feared that this "would increase that State influence which could not be too watchfully guarded agst." (1:358–59). In what might well have been a case of wishful thinking, Hamilton said that there was always the possibility that under the new system "the State Govts. might gradually dwindle into nothing," and that delegates should beware of engrafting the national government onto that which "might possibly fail" (1:359).

Hamilton opposed allowing states to pay members of Congress because he wanted to avoid dependency of that body on them. He observed that state governments were distinct from the people of the states (1:373–74).

Presidency

On June 2, Hamilton seconded the motion by Benjamin Franklin of Pennsylvania that the president should serve without pay, but it was clear that he did so as a way of honoring its author rather than because Hamilton agreed with the proposal (1:85). On June 4 Hamilton moved that the president should have an absolute veto of legislative acts, but in doing so, he observed that the British king, who had similar authority, had not exercised it since the American Revolution (1:98). On September 12, Hamilton indicated that the provision in the New York legislature to override the governor by a two-thirds vote had proven to be ineffectual (2:585).

Hamilton said on September 6 that he preferred the electoral college mechanism to the previous proposal of allowing members of Congress to select the president for a single term. He referred to the previous plan negatively as one in which:

> the President was a Monster elected for seven years, and ineligible afterwards; having great powers, in appointments to office, & continually tempted by this constitutional disqualification to abuse them in order to subvert the Government—Although he should be made re-eligible, Still if appointed by the Legislature, he would be tempted to make use of corrupt influence to be continued in office. (2:425)

Because he feared that such corruption might also occur between the president and the Senate, Hamilton favored allowing the individual with the highest number of electors to be president rather than having this choice devolve on the Senate (2:525).

Critique of Madison's Extended Republic

On June 6, Hamilton made some notes on a speech that Madison gave, in which Madison argued that large districts were less likely to allow factions and demagogues to predominate. Interestingly, Hamilton, with whom Madison would join forces in writing *The Federalist*, appended a note indicating that "An influential demagogue will give an impulse to the whole—Demagogues are not always *inconsiderable* persons—Patricians were frequently demagogues—Characters are less known & a less active interest taken in them—" (1:147).

Prayer

After he fell out of political powers, Hamilton appears to have turned to religion for consolation (Adair and Harvey 1955). In 1802, he proposed the establishment of a "Christian Constitutional Society," and he received communion on his deathbed from an Episcopal bishop after making a clear profession of faith. Earlier in life, Hamilton was often associated, correctly or not, with impiety. These associations might have been formed in part from Hamilton's objection to Benjamin Franklin's motion that each day of the convention be opened in prayer. Despite later stories stating that Hamilton objected to the impropriety of calling in foreign aid, Madison's notes suggested that Hamilton was among those who argued that "however proper such a resolution might have been at the beginning of the convention, it might at this late day, 1. bring on it some disagreeable animadversions. & 2. lead the public to believe that the embarrassments and dissentions within the convention, had suggested this measure" (1:452).

Amendment and Ratification

On September 10, Hamilton seconded a motion to reconsider the amending provision which called, up to this point, for Congress to call a convention to propose amendments on the application of two-thirds of the states. Whereas Elbridge Gerry of Massachusetts had favored reconsideration for fear that the national government might invade the powers of the states, Hamilton had a different concern. He favored "an easier mode for introducing amendments" (2:558). Fearing that state legislatures would only apply for conventions with a view toward increasing their own powers, Hamilton wanted Congress to be able to propose amendments on its own: "The National Legislature will be the first to perceive and will be most sensible to the necessity of amendments, and ought also to be empowered, whenever two thirds of each branch should concur to call a Convention" (2:558). Hamilton subsequently seconded a motion by James Madison that closely resembles the current amending mechanism (2:559).

Curiously, Hamilton thought that Congress should have to approve the new Constitution. He further proposed allowing states to decide whether they felt comfortable entering into a union to which only nine states had consented (2:560).

Hamilton urged all members of the convention to sign the Constitution. Indicating that the plan proposed was far from what he desired, Hamilton still thought the choice was clear:

A few characters of consequence, by opposing or even refusing to sign the Constitution, might do infinite mischief by kindling the latent sparks which lurk under an enthusiasm in favor of the convention which may soon subside. No man's ideas were more remote from the plan than his own were known to be; but it is possible to deliberate between anarchy and

Convulsion on one side, and the chance of good to be expected from the plan on the other. (2:646)

Life after the Convention

Hamilton was the chief author of *The Federalist*, and was responsible for recruiting James Madison and John Jay as coauthors. This work explained and defended the government that the Philadelphia Convention had proposed. In these papers, Hamilton emerged as a particularly powerful critic of the weaknesses of the Articles of Confederation. He was also a proponent of strong presidential powers and of the power of judicial review, whereby courts can invalidate legislation that they consider to be unconstitutional. Hamilton also successfully led the Federalist forces at New York's ratifying convention.

Washington subsequently appointed Hamilton to be the first secretary of the treasury. Much as in the English model of government he so admired, Hamilton practically converted this into a position of prime minister. In this capacity, Hamilton proposed stretching the powers of the new government to their utmost by assuming state debts and establishing a national bank; he was a powerful defender of the idea of implied powers, which federal courts later affirmed in the case of *McCulloch v. Maryland* (1819). Hamilton took a leading role in suppressing Pennsylvania's Whisky Rebellion. He founded the Federalist Party, which put him at odds with James Madison and Thomas Jefferson, who founded the rival Democratic-Republican Party. Hamilton authored essays under the name of Pacificus, supporting Washington's decision to proclaim American neutrality in the conflict between Great Britain and France (with James Madison responding, under the name Helvidius, for a more pro-French position). Hamilton resigned from the cabinet in 1795 and returned to his law practice but continued to advise Washington's administration. At one point, in an attempt to refute charges that as secretary of the treasury, he had misused his office, Hamilton admitted to an affair with Maria Reynolds, the wife of an individual who was attempting to blackmail him.

At odds with the Federalist administration of John Adams whom he had tried to maneuver out of the presidency in 1796, when the presidential electors for Thomas Jefferson and Aaron Burr (the intended vice president) were tied in the election of 1800, Hamilton advocated Jefferson as the lesser of two evils. This, and subsequent comments about Burr's character, which Hamilton made when Burr ran for governor of New York in 1804, eventually led to a duel with Burr at Weehawken, New Jersey on July 11, 1804 that left Hamilton mortally wounded (like his son Philip, who also died in a duel); he died the next day.

Hamilton's home in modern-day Harlem, known as The Grange, has twice been moved but is a designated national park site that is open to the public. The Schuyler Mansion of his parents-in-law in Albany is also a state historic site that is open to the public. As befits his role as the first secretary of the treasury, his picture is on the ten-dollar bill. His devoted wife survived him by 50 years.

Further Reading

Adair, Douglass, and Marvin Harvey. 1955. "Was Alexander Hamilton a Christian Statesman?" *William and Mary Quarterly*, 3rd Ser., 12 (April): 308–29.

Brookhiser, Richard. 1999. *Alexander Hamilton: American*. New York: Free Press.

Chernow, Ron. 2004. *Alexander Hamilton*. New York: The Penguin Press.

Ely, James W., Jr. 2001. "Hamilton, Alexander." In *Great American Lawyers: An Encyclopedia*, edited by John R. Vile, 1: 318–24. . Santa Barbara, CA: ABC-CLIO.

Farrand, Max, ed. 1966. *The Records of the Federal Convention of 1787*. 4 vols. New Haven, CT: Yale University Press.

Federici, Michael P. 2012. *The Political Philosophy of Alexander Hamilton*. Baltimore: The Johns Hopkins University Press.

Ferguson, E. James. 1983. "Political Economy, Public Liberty, and the Formation of the Constitution." *William and Mary Quarterly*, 3rd Ser., 40 (July): 389–412.

Frazer, Gregg L., 2009. "Alexander Hamilton, Theistic Rationalist." In *The Forgotten Founders on Religion and Public Life*, edited by Daniel L. Dreisbach, Mark David Hall, and Jeffrey H. Morrison, 101–24. Notre Dame, IN: University of Notre Dame Press.

Frisch, Morton J. 1999. *Alexander Hamilton and the Political Order: An Interpretation of His Political Thought and Practice*. New York: Free Press.

Howard, Hugh. 2007. *Houses of the Founding Fathers*. New York: Artisan.

McCraw, Thomas K. 2012. *The Founders and Finance: How Hamilton, Gallatin, and Other Immigrants Forged a New Economy*. Cambridge, MA: Belknap Press of Harvard University Press.

Rossiter, Clinton. 1964. *Alexander Hamilton and the Constitution*. New York: Harcourt, Brace & World, Inc.

Vile, John R., ed. 2001. *Great American Lawyers: An Encyclopedia*. 2 vols. Santa Barbara, CA.: ABC-CLIO.

Walling, Karl. 2003. "Alexander Hamilton and the Grand Strategy of the American Social Compact." In *The American Founding and the Social Compact*, edited by Ronald J. Pestritto and Thomas G. West, 199–230. Lanham, MD: Lexington Books.

Note: The Papers of Alexander Hamilton, in 27 volumes, were published from 1954 to 1987 by Columbia University Press.

WILLIAM CHURCHILL HOUSTON (1746–1788)
NEW JERSEY

William Churchill Houston was born into a family of small planters in South Carolina's Sumner District in 1746. He attended the University of New Jersey (today's Princeton) where he was quickly recruited to teach at the grammar school, and where he later taught mathematics and natural philosophy and served as the College's treasurer and part-time administrator before undertaking the study of law. Houston married Jane Smith of Long Island, who bore him two sons and three daughters. Prior to attending the Constitutional Convention, Houston had served in the New Jersey state militia, in the New Jersey legislature, as a delegate to the Continental Congress where he was deputy secretary (Charles Thomson was the secretary) from 1785 to 1786, as a clerk of the New Jersey Supreme Court, and as a delegate to the Annapolis Convention.

Afflicted with the tuberculosis that would soon kill him, Houston was present at the Constitutional Convention on May 25 but left by June 6. He is not recorded as having made any statements during this time. Houston died in 1788 but had signed the report of his delegation to the New Jersey legislature. Houston's authorship of an address that he delivered in Trenton in 1784 entitled "Whether the Liberty of the Press Ought to Extend so Far as to Justify the Publishing of the Name of a Person, with Strictures on His Conduct, by an Anonymous Author, or with a Fictitious Signature" suggests that he would have been a strong supporter of First Amendment protections of speech and press. In his speech, Churchill took firm positions in favor of allowing truth as a defense against libel and of allowing individuals to publish pamphlets anonymously.

Houston died on August 12, 1788 and was buried at the Second Presbyterian Churchyard in Philadelphia. His wife died in 1796 and his father in 1805.

Further Reading

Bradford, M. E. 1984. *Founding Fathers: Brief Lives of the Framers of the United States Constitution.* 2nd ed. Lawrence: University Press of Kansas.

Clemens, Paul G. E. "Houston, William Churchill." In *American National Biography*, edited by John A. Garraty and Mark C. Carnes, 11: 281–83. New York: Oxford University Press.

Glenn, Thomas Allen, 1803. *William Churchill Houston, 1746–1788*. Norristown, PA: Privately printed.

"Houston, William Churchill," 1950. *Biographic Directory of the American Congress, 1774–1749*, 1335. Washington, DC: U.S. Government Printing Office.

William Houstoun (1757–1812)
Georgia

William Houstoun was born in Savannah, Georgia around 1755 to 1757. His father, Sir Patrick Houstoun, was a baronet who immigrated to Georgia with his wife and served on the council of the royal governor. William was privately educated before attending the English Inns of Court. On his return to the United States, he was able to secure the properties of his Tory brothers and was clearly a member of the landed elite. Elected to the Georgia legislature in 1782, Houston subsequently served in the Continental Congress, where he earned a reputation as an ardent supporter of southern interests. He was married to Mary Bayard of New York (who died in 1808) and served as a trustee for the University of Georgia.

In an unflattering character sketch that he wrote of Houstoun, fellow Convention delegate William Pierce observed that "Nature seems to have done more for his corporeal than [for his] mental powers. His Person is striking, but he has done of the talents requisite for the Orator, but in public debate is confused and irregular" (Farrand 1966, 3:97).

At the Convention

Houstoun was seated at the convention on June 1, but he did not participate extensively in convention deliberations, and he left before the document was signed. On July 2, Houstoun was recorded as having voted against a motion to grant each state a single senator (1:510), thus dividing his state since Abraham Baldwin had voted the other way. Houston was subsequently appointed to the Committee to Reconsider Proportional Representation that was created on July 9, the only such convention committee on which he served. He may not have been happy with the results since, the next day, he joined South Carolina's General Pinckney in unsuccessfully urging that Georgia's representation in the first Congress be raised from three to four representatives (1:568)—the committee on which Houstoun had served had already raised representation from two to three.

Although associated with love for his state, Houstoun feared that a federal guarantee to the states against domestic violence might perpetuate bad constitutions, among which he counted that of Georgia. Expressing the hope that this constitution "would be revised & amended," he also observed that it might be difficult for the general government to decide between contending parties (2:48).

Presidency

On July 20, the convention was debating a plan proposed by Elbridge Gerry of Massachusetts, whereby there would be twenty-five presidential electors with each state having from one to three. Houstoun seconded a motion by Oliver Ellsworth of Connecticut to add one elector each to New Hampshire and Georgia—each of which had, along with Delaware, been allocated one vote (2:64).

On July 23, Houstoun proposed reconsideration of the proposal for allowing state legislatures to choose presidential electors. His reasoning reflected Georgia's location on the periphery of the nation. He thus pointed to "the extreme inconveniency & the considerable expense, of drawing together men from all the States for the single purpose of electing the Chief Magistrate" (2:95). With a similar objective, the next day Houstoun proposed that state legislatures should select the president, arguing for "the improbability, that capable men would undertake the service of Electors from the more distant States" (2:99). Although the convention did not choose this method of legislative selection, it did take Houstoun's concern into account in the eventual design of the electoral college, which specifies that electors meet within individual states to cast their ballots rather than assembling collectively at the nation's capital.

On July 17, Houstoun joined Gouverneur Morris of Pennsylvania in successfully postponing a motion that the presidential term be seven years (2:32). That same day he succeeded in getting a motion adopted that would strike presidential re-eligibility to a second term (2:33).

Life after the Convention

Houstoun was plagued by illness during the convention and is believed to have left, probably in late July, or after fellow delegate William Few arrived after August 6. Houstoun married in 1788 and subsequently spent much of his life in New York living a fairly private life. He died in Savannah, Georgia on March 3, 1813 but was buried in St. Paul's Chapel in New York City in 1812. Houston (a variant spelling) Street in Manhattan, New York was named after him.

Further Reading

Bradford, M. E. 1981. *Founding Fathers: Brief Lives of the Framers of the United States Constitution*. 2nd ed. Lawrence: University Press of Kansas.

Farrand, Max, ed. 1966. *The Records of the Federal Convention of 1787*. 4 vols. New Haven, CT: Yale University Press.

"Houstoun, William," 1950. *Biographical Dictionary of the American Congress, 1774–1949*, 1335. Washington, DC: U.S. Government Printing Office.

JARED INGERSOLL (1749–1822)
PENNSYLVANIA

Jared Ingersoll Jr. was born in New Haven, Connecticut on October 24, 1749. His father was a lawyer who favored the Loyalists during the revolution. After Ingersoll graduated from Yale, his father sent him to London where he studied law at the Middle Temple before going to Paris and then returning during the American Revolution to establish a law practice in Philadelphia. Ingersoll represented Pennsylvania at the Continental Congress from 1780 to 1781. He married Elizabeth Pettit in 1781, and they had four children, three of whom survived into adulthood.

At the Convention

Pennsylvania's Jared Ingersoll was seated at the Constitutional Convention on May 28, 1787, and he signed the document on September 17. Unlike some who were somewhat more equivocal about their signing of the document, Ingersoll said that he "did not consider the signing, either as a mere attestation of the fact, or as pledging the signers to support the Constitution at all events; but as a recommendation, of what, all things considered, was the most eligible" (Farrand 1966, 3:647). He was not appointed to any committees at the convention, and he was otherwise silent.

An Undelivered Speech

There is, however, a draft of a speech, once attributed to Maryland's Luther Martin or to Connecticut's Roger Sherman, in Ingersoll's handwriting, which he appears to have prepared for delivery sometime after June 19. Such an attribution seems consistent with the speech's somewhat apologetic beginning in which the author attributes his silence to "my Inferiority, to the members of this hon[orab]le convention, in an acquaintance with the political history of this Country" and to the fact that "a laborious application to the business of my profession has not afforded me much Opportunity for attendance here in order to collect Information, nor time for reflecting on the few Ideas with which my Mind was stored relative to the Object of our present meeting" (Hutson 1987, 101).

Ingersoll saw the dilemma of the convention as that of being able "to introduce a System unexceptionable in itself & relatively so, authorized & yet efficacious" (Hutson 1987, 101). He identified the central issue as that of whether the convention would settle on a "national" or a "federal" government (101). Ingersoll further attempted to trace the cause of the nation's problems. He believed that many of these problems were attributable not so much to the weakness of Congress as to the situation that the nation faced after winning independence. Many of these problems he traced to British pride and to the interest of European nations to keep the United States weak.

Ingersoll identified three powers that Congress should exercise: the power to get sufficient revenue to discharge its debts; the power to regulate foreign and internal commerce; and the power to fix the currency. Ingersoll expressed doubts as to whether Congress also needed to be granted "physical power" to carry its will into execution or whether it needed power to act directly upon individual citizens.

In addressing this question, Ingersoll thought it necessary to examine abstract principles, practical concerns, and what the convention was authorized to do. In looking at abstract principles, Ingersoll developed an argument as to why, even if the convention were starting from scratch, a federal government might be preferable to a unitary one. His central theme was diversity. Laws needed to differ for:

> the Fisheries & Manufacturers of New-England, The Flour Lumber Flaxseed & Ginseng of New York New Jersey Pennsylvania & Delaware The Tobacco of Maryland & Virginia the Pitch Tar, Rice & Indigo & Cotton of North Carolina South Carolina & Georgia. (Hutson 1987, 103)

Similarly there were differences between slave states and free, as well as those that stemmed from "the Climate, Produce, Soil, & even Genius of the people" (Hutson 1987, 103).

Ingersoll feared that "the present System," by which he appeared to be speaking of the proposals under consideration by the convention, might be much "more objectionable than a general Government" (Hutson 1987, 104). He observed that those opposed to a "general government" would also oppose the proposals under consideration, citing criticisms that had already been raised within the convention itself to the effect that the new government would result either in monarchy or the abolition of the states. Ingersoll himself had doubts about the plan under consideration: "I cannot but think that the present System is much more objectionable than a general Government" (Hutson 1987, 104). Ingersoll continued:

> others will say & I must be of the Number that this Government is consonant to no principle whatever, on the principle of the Union it is too much on the Idea of a general Government it is too little—that it has all the expence of a National Government without its *energy*—will give equal Alarm, equal opportunity to excite prejudice, without affording any dignity to Government or securing Obedience to obtaining any of the primary Objects of Government, that an eternal contest will be excited between the several Governments & this monstrous sluggard, that the activity of the latter will be able to thwart the overgrown lubber [?], that all that can be expected from it is securing a Revennue, the whole of which will be absorbed in the collection that so much might be obtained nearly in the present system & a great part of the expence saved that it is [?]. (Hutson 1987, 104)

Unfortunately, the speech soon becomes difficult to follow (perhaps because it was not complete), addressing what the people might be likely to accept but failing to examine, as promised, what the convention was authorized to do. What is most notable about the speech is the candid observation that the very attitudes that propelled the nation to war against Britain (attitudes similar to those that the British philosopher Edmund Burke had identified during the Revolutionary War) were now making it difficult—impractical—to form a new government in which the national government was given too much power:

> The people of the United-States, excited to Arms by the insidious designs of the then Mother Country have become admirers of liberty warmly & passionately so—they snuff Tyranny in every tainted Gale—they are

jealous of their liberty—they are pleased with their present Governments, they think them as energetick as they ought to be framed, they are continually planning subdivisions of the present Governments, they are complaining of the expence of the present Governments—they are jealous of designs to introduce a Monarchy, under specious pretences & different names . . . they are apprehensive of designs to abridge the liberties of the common people . . . they are prejudiced each against the neighboring State—of no humour to coalesce. (Hutson 1987, 104–5).

The lesson would appear to be that the delegates should do more to work to strengthen the present system than to alter it. The writer of this speech would appear especially unlikely to favor the proposed congressional veto of state laws or any other measures that might be associated with a national bureaucracy. Again, it is important to remember that the speech began by observing that the current plight of the nation might not be as attributable to the weakness of the general government as to the animosity of European powers.

Pennsylvanians were, of course, at the forefront of the movement toward a stronger central government, a stronger presidency, and a reconfigured Congress based on proportional representation—witness the influence of Gouverneur Morris and James Wilson. Perhaps this is the reason Ingersoll never delivered his speech. If it had been delivered, this speech would arguably have been as strong as any such speech at the convention in portraying the continuation of significant state powers, not simply as practical necessity, but as desirable in and of itself as a way of adapting to the wide variety of local interests. If, in fact, Ingersoll was the author of this speech, it would appear that convention deliberations would have been even stronger had he participated.

Life after the Convention

Ingersoll continued his legal work (his clients included Stephen Girard and William Blount), was a trustee of the University of Pennsylvania, and served in a number of governmental positions to which Federalists appointed him. These included serving as Pennsylvania's attorney general, as Philadelphia's city solicitor, and as judge. Ingersoll ran for vice president in 1812 with New York's governor DeWitt Clinton, but the two lost to James Madison and Elbridge Gerry (all the candidates except Clinton had attended the Constitutional Convention). Ingersoll argued a number of cases before the U.S. Supreme Court including *Chisholm v. Georgia* (1793), which dealt with a suit brought against a state, and *Hylton v. United States* (1796), involving a federal tax on carriages,

Ingersoll died on October 31, 1822, financially ruined by his speculation in western lands, and was buried in the cemetery of the First Presbyterian Church in Philadelphia. His son, Charles Jared Ingersoll, served in the U.S. Congress from 1813 to 1815 and again from 1841 to 1849, and another son, Joseph Reed Ingersoll, served as a U.S. minister to England during the administration of Millard Fillmore.

Further Reading

Farrand, Max, ed. 1966. *The Records of the Federal Convention of 1787.* 4 vols. New Haven, CT: Yale University Press.

Hutson, James H. 1987. *Supplement to Max Farrand's The Records of the Federal Convention of 1787.* New Haven, CT: Yale University Press.

Keene, Ann T. 2010. "Jared Ingersoll Jr." *American National Biography* Online. http://www.anb.org/articles/07/07–00821.html. Accessed 6/24/12.

Whitney, David C. 1974. *Founders of Freedom in America: Lives of the Men Who Signed the Constitution of the United States and So Helped to Establish the United States of America.* Chicago: J. G. Ferguson Publishing Company.

Daniel of St. Thomas Jenifer (1723–1790)
Maryland

Born in Charles County, Maryland in 1723 to a wealthy planter family, Jenifer grew up at the family plantation named Retreat. Establishing himself as both a planter and a merchant, Jenifer occupied a number of posts in the colonial government, including service on the commission that established the Mason-Dixon Line between the North and the South. As the conflict with the British arose, Jenifer hesitatingly joined the patriot side and served both as president of Maryland's committee of safety and of the Maryland Senate. A friend of George Washington, Jenifer had attended the meeting at Mt. Vernon designed to settle issues of navigation between the states of Maryland and Virginia.

From 1782 to 1788, Jenifer tried to bring fiscal stability to Maryland in his service as the intendant of revenue.

At the Convention

Jenifer, who arrived at the convention on June 2, often found that he and Luther Martin were the only two Maryland delegates in attendance. Because Martin was a strong proponent of states' rights who ultimately refused to sign the Constitution and Jenifer was a nationalist who signed it, the two often split the state's vote. The two did join on July 6 in urging postponement of the vote related to state equality in the Senate until a committee appointed to look into the matter had made its report (Farrand 1966, 1:543). It would have been highly likely that, as a representative of a relatively small landlocked state, Jenifer would have agreed with Martin on the necessity for equal state representation. Jenifer missed a vote on the issue on July 2 (1:510). On August 6, he was reported by James McHenry to have responded privately to criticisms by Martin by saying that he had voted with him against the new system until he realized that it was useless to oppose it; on this same occasion, he stated that mere amendments of the Articles of Confederation would prove inadequate (2:190–91). There were other signs of tension between Jenifer and Martin (see 3:85).

Jenifer's best-known position at the convention may have been his first. On June 12, he was recorded as favoring a three-year term for members of the U.S. House of Representatives, a motion that Virginia's James Madison seconded. Jenifer had favored a three-year term in preference to terms of one or two years on the basis that "too great frequency of elections rendered the people indifferent to them, and made the best men unwilling to engage in so precarious a service" (1:214). Although Jenifer's motion succeeded at the time, the convention later voted to reduce the term of service from three years to two.

On June 23, Jenifer observed that the senators of Maryland, who served five-year terms, were prohibited from holding other offices. He said that "this circumstance gained them the greatest confidence of the people" (1:390). On August 31, Jenifer joined fellow delegates James McHenry and Daniel Carroll in urging adoption of a provision prohibiting states from obligating vessels going to or from one state from paying duties in another. Jenifer was reported as having agreed to Carroll's assertion that "this was a tender point in Maryland" (2:481).

Life after the Convention

After the convention, Jenifer advocated for the Constitution in his home state. He died in Annapolis, Maryland on November 16, 1790, a lifelong bachelor who provided that his slaves would be freed in 1796. Jenifer willed all his French books to Virginia's James Madison. He is believed to have been buried in the Ellersie Estate Cemetery in Port Tobacco, Maryland.

Further Reading

Farrand, Max, ed. 1966. *The Records of the Federal Convention of 1787*. 4 vols. New Haven, CT: Yale University Press.

Hoffman, Ronald. "Jenifer, Daniel of St. Thomas." 1999. In *American National Biography*, edited by John A. Garraty and Mark C. Carnes, 11: 931–33. New York: Oxford University Press.

William Samuel Johnson (1727–1819)
Connecticut

William Samuel Johnson was born on October 7, 1727 in Stratford, Connecticut. His father Samuel Johnson was an Anglican pastor who would later head King's College (today's Columbia University). Johnson studied Latin and Greek at an early age, earned two degrees from Yale, with Harvard and Oxford later awarding him honorary degrees.

After turning from the study of theology to that of law, Johnson married a wealthy woman, Ann Beach (1729–1796), whose dowry helped launch him into a highly successful legal career. The people elected him to the Connecticut legislature, the Stamp Act Congress, and to the governor's council. Subsequently sent to England to represent Connecticut in the growing dispute with England, he made the acquaintance of Benjamin Franklin. Unlike Franklin, Johnson opposed the colonial decision to split with the mother country, declined appointment to the Continental Congress, and did not take an oath of allegiance to the new state government until 1779.

At the Convention

Johnson was, however, elected to the Congress under the Articles of Confederation. In the same month that the Constitutional Convention began, Johnson was asked to fill the shoes that his father once filled as president of King's College. Although he was one of the most educated men at the Constitutional Convention, he was not among the more active participants. He is chiefly known for his role in effecting the Connecticut Compromise and the compromise related to slave importation, taxation, and duties. During the convention, he served on committees to look into the slave trade and navigation (August 22), interstate comity and bankruptcy (August 29), and, as discussed below, he chaired the Committee of Style and Arrangement (September 8) and was appointed to a Committee on Sumptuary Legislation (September 13). Coming relatively late in the convention, these appointments might suggest either that Johnson was more available and/or that he had risen in the eyes of his fellow delegates as the convention progressed.

Sovereignty

Johnson was seated at the convention on June 2, after the Virginia Plan had been sent to the Committee of the Whole for consideration. Johnson's first recorded comments took place on June 21, after William Paterson had introduced the New Jersey Plan and Alexander Hamilton had outlined his own plans for a new government. What is fascinating about Johnson's first speech is that it focused not so much on the effect each plan would have had on state representation, but on state sovereignty itself. Johnson observed that the primary difference between the Virginia Plan and the New Jersey Plan was that the latter was "calculated to preserve the individuality of the States" (Farrand 1966, 1:355). Although the authors of the Virginia Plan had not professed the destruction of the states as an object, critics had made this accusation, and Hamilton had advanced the idea of abolishing the states as desirable.

According to Johnson, the issue thus posed was whether the Virginia Plan's allocation of "general sovereignty and jurisdiction" in the central government was compatible with allowing the states to retain "a considerable, tho' a subordinate jurisdiction" (1:355). If the proponents of the Virginia Plan could demonstrate that these two goals were compatible, it would relieve proponents of the New Jersey Plan. Johnson said the issue for consideration was therefore:

Whether in case the States, as was proposed, shd. retain some portion of sovereignty at least, this portion could be preserved, without allowing them to participate effectually in the Genl. Govt., without giving them each a distinct and equal vote for the purpose of defending themselves in the general Councils. (1:355)

Johnson's speech evoked a response from Pennsylvania's James Wilson who noted his "respect" for him.

Johnson further expostulated on the differences between the Virginia and New Jersey Plans on June 29. Almost like a schoolteacher, Johnson attempted to demonstrate to each side the arguments of the other. Supporters of the Virginia Plan, Johnson believed, were viewing the situation from the perspective of a single political society, whereas proponents of the New Jersey Plan were viewing it from the perspective of a society of states. Johnson correctly perceived that a compromise might be achieved by combining the two ideas:

In some respects the States are to be considered in their political capacity, and in others as districts of individual citizens, the two ideas embraced on different sides, instead of being opposed to each other, ought to be combined; that in *one* branch the *people*, ought to be represented; in the *other*, the *States*. (1:461–62)

Just four days before adoption of the Connecticut Compromise, as the convention was discussing how slaves should be counted, Johnson indicated his preference for providing for representation in the lower house of Congress on the basis of population, which he thought would also provide a good measure of wealth. In contrast to many northern delegates, Johnson was willing to count slaves on an equal basis with whites, rather than counting them by the discounted three-fifths formula (1:593).

On August 20, the convention was debating the definition of treason against the United States. Johnson appeared to take an academic position in suggesting that treason could not take place both against the national government and the states since sovereignty "can be but one in the same community" (2:346). He joined Wilson in proposing that the phrase "or any of them" thus be struck out after the words "United States" (1:346), but continued to insist that any treason that would occur, under the Articles or under the new Constitution, would be against the whole rather than against particular states (1:347).

Congress

On August 22, Johnson opposed a limitation prohibiting Congress from passing ex post facto, or after the fact, laws. He believed the clause was "unnecessary" and implied "improper suspicion" of that body (2:376).

Three days later, in a view that would be especially compatible with his emphasis on sovereignty, Johnson said that it would not be necessary to indicate that the new Congress would assume the debts of the old. He observed that "Changing the Government cannot change the obligation of the U—S— which devolves of course on the New Government" (2:414).

On August 29, Johnson joined James Wilson in attempting to explain the Full Faith and Credit Clause, after North Carolina's Hugh Williamson asked for explanation. Johnson and Wilson believed that it provided that "Judgments in one States should be the ground of actions in other States, & that acts of the Legislatures should be included, for the sake of Acts of insolvency &c" (2:447; also see 2:488). That same day, Johnson indicated that he believed the faith of the existing Congress should be recognized in granting Vermont its independence of New York (2:456). The next day, he introduced language exempting this process from the consent of the new Congress (2:463).

On September 13, Johnson seconded a motion by Virginia's George Mason for the appointment of a Committee on Sumptuary Legislation (1:606). Although the motion was subsequently agreed to and Johnson was appointed as one of its five members, it does not appear that the committee issued any subsequent report.

Judiciary

On August 24, Johnson seconded a motion by South Carolina's John Rutledge striking out a mechanism, similar to one used under the Articles of Confederation, for resolving disputes among the states. Presumably he agreed with Rutledge that the establishment of a national judiciary would make such a mechanism unnecessary (2:401).

Johnson appears to have made at least a small mark on the actual language of the U.S. Constitution on August 27 when he successfully proposed that the federal judicial power should extend to cases of "equity" as well as "law" (2:428). In Britain these two areas of law, the first of which was designed to provide for more just and flexible remedies than those that were available in the regular courts of law, were distinct. That same day, Johnson was also responsible for inserting the words "this Constitution and the" before the word "laws" so that what would become Article III of the new Constitution vested judicial power to all cases "in Law and Equity, arising under this Constitution, ["and" later deleted] the Laws of the United States" (2:430).

Ratification

Although Pennsylvania's Gouverneur Morris was the primary mover on the committee, the convention appointed Johnson to chair the Committee of Style. In his capacity as chair, Johnson reported the committee recommendations that the Constitution should be "laid before" the U.S. Congress and then submitted to ratifying conventions in each of the states (2:608). This resolution further provided that nine states should be sufficient to ratify the document, and that once they had done so, Congress should fix a day for the electors to meet and for the new Constitution to commence.

Life after the Convention

Johnson returned to the Continental Congress in New York after the convention and accepted the presidency of King's College that had been previously offered to him. This did not keep him from attending the Connecticut ratifying convention, where he supported adoption of the new Constitution. In describing the difficulty of using force against the states, Johnson indicated that the convention had chosen a different route:

> They have framed a new nation out of the individual States. . . . The force which is to be employed, is the energy of law, and their force is to operate only upon individuals, who fail in their duty to their country. (quoted in McCaughey 1980, 226)

He further observed at the convention:

> I cannot but impute it to a signal intervention of divine providence, that a convention from States differing in circumstances, interest, and manners should be so harmonious in adopting one grand system. If we reject a plan of government, which with such favorable circumstances is offered for our acceptance, I fear our national existence must come to an end. (quoted in McCaughey 1980, 226–27)

Similarly, Johnson accepted a position as one of Connecticut's first two senators—it helped that King's College and the nation's first capital were both in New York City. Johnson remained in the Senate for only two years, where he supported the admission of Vermont (where he had investments, and where a city was named in his honor), and the congressional assumption of state debts, from which he and his sons profited financially. Shortly after Congress adopted the latter bill, part of Hamilton's fiscal package, Johnson resigned and devoted full time to his responsibilities as a college president. Ill health forced him to resign in 1800, but in 1801, five years after the death of his first wife, he married a widowed sister-in-law, Mary Brewster Beach (1735–1827). He died in Stratford, Connecticut on November 14, 1819, at the age of ninety-two, the oldest age of any of the men who signed the Constitution.

Further Reading

Andrews, William Given. 2012. *William Samuel Johnson and the Making of the Constitution*. Whitefish, MT: Kessinger Publishing; reprint of 1887 original.
Calhoun, Robert M. 1999. "Johnson, William Samuel." In *American National Biography*, edited by John A. Garraty and Mark C. Carnes, 12: 144–45. New York: Oxford University Press.
Farrand, Max, ed. 1966. *The Records of the Federal Convention of 1787*. 4 vols. New Haven, CT: Yale University Press.
McCaughey, Elizabeth P. 1980. *From Loyalist to Founding Father: The Political Odyssey of William Samuel Johnson*. New York: Columbia University Press.
Whitney, David C. 1974. *Founders of Freedom in America: Lives of the Men Who Signed the Constitution of the United States and So Helped to Establish the United States of America*. Chicago: J. G. Ferguson Publishing Company.

RUFUS KING (1755–1827)
MASSACHUSETTS

Rufus King was born in present-day Scarboro, Maine (then Massachusetts) on March 24, 1755 to the family of a merchant. Educated at Harvard, he served briefly in the Revolutionary War before studying law under Theophilus Parsons, chief justice of the Massachusetts Supreme Court, and being admitted to the Massachusetts bar. Although he was an able attorney, he spent most of his life in public office. King represented Massachusetts in the

Congress under the Articles of Confederation, where he introduced the first resolution opposing slavery in the Congress and was influential in excluding slavery from the area northwest of the Ohio River. Just a year prior to the convention, King had been described as "an uncommonly handsome man in face and form" who "had a powerful mind, well cultivated, and was a dignified and graceful speaker" (William Sullivan, as quoted in Brush 1926, 26). Historian Edward Bancroft believes he may have been "the most eloquent orator" at the convention (Brush 1926, 31). King had married Mary Alsop (1769–1819) just a little over a year before the convention began, and five of their seven children survived into adulthood.

At the Convention

Rufus King was present at the convention when it began work on May 25, he was there for the signing on September 17, and he was active in between. He served on a record six committees: the Committee on the Original Apportionment of Congress (July 6); the Committee to Reconsider Representation, which he chaired (July 9); the Committee on State Debts and Militia (August 18); the Committee on the Slave Trade and Navigation (August 22); the Committee on Postponed Matters (August 31); and the Committee of Style and Arrangement (September 8).

Rules and Records

King made an important contribution to Convention deliberations on May 28 when he suggested that the rules proposed by Virginia's George Wythe and the committee Wythe chaired be so modified that delegates could not call for roll-call votes during the proceedings. King observed that "as the acts of the Convention were not to bind the Constituents it was unnecessary to exhibit this evidence of the votes." Perhaps more importantly, he feared that such a record might make it more difficult for delegates to change their votes as they changed their minds during convention deliberations (Farrand 1966, 1:10). On the final day of the convention, King made the last recorded motion when he proposed that the Journals of the convention should either be destroyed or entrusted to the president. Otherwise, he feared that "a bad use would be made of them by those who would wish to prevent the adoption of the Constitution" (2:648).

Congress

Representation. On May 30, King observed that he did not think that the House should be apportioned according to state contributions. He was concerned, first that monies might be so collected by the government as to make it difficult to know how much states had contributed, and second that such funds would vary too much to make them a good standard (1:36). On June 11, he further observed that, if the national government were to rely on taxes on imports, this would work particular hardship on such non-importing states as Connecticut and New Jersey (1:197). On June 11, King also introduced a motion that representation in the new Congress should be "according to some equitable ratio of representation" rather than as under the Articles of Confederation (1:196).

King further elaborated on his views on June 30. Expressing willingness to accept a plan proposed by Pennsylvania's James Wilson under which each state would have at least one senator but would otherwise be represented according to population, King thought that it was more important to see that men were represented than states: "if we were convinced that every *man* in America was secured in all his rights, we should be ready to sacrifice this substantial good to the phantom of *State* sovereignty" (1:489). King indicated that he thought that granting states equal suffrage in the Senate was to found government "in a vicious principle of representation" that was likely to shorten its life (2:490).

On July 6, King opposed setting the number of representatives at one for every 40,000 voters on the basis that increases in population would one day result in a House with too many members. He was also concerned that recent legislation allowed states northwest of the Ohio River to enter when they had populations equal to that of Delaware, giving new states greater representation than that to which they would otherwise be entitled (1:541). On July 14, King seconded a motion by Elbridge Gerry to limit future representation of the western states to no more than that currently possessed by those in eastern states (2:3).

King joined the southern delegates in agreeing that their slaves should be counted as three-fifths of a person in apportioning state representation in the House of Representatives (see, however, the section on slavery below).

He thought that this would be a fair trade for "preferential distinctions in Commerce & other advantages" that the northern states could expect from union (1:562). He observed that eleven of the thirteen states had agreed to the three-fifths formula for apportioning taxes, and that representation and taxation should go together (1:562).

King attempted to incorporate compromises between the East (North) and South in the report of the committee that proposed that the House be composed of 65 members. Indeed, King said that he believed the chief fault line at the convention was not between the large and small states but between those of the East and those of the South. He explained the work of his committee:

> For this reason he had been ready to yield something in the proportion of representatives for the security of the Southern. No principle would justify giving them a majority. They were brought as near an equality as was possible. He was not averse to giving them a still greater security, but did not see how it could be done. (1:566)

When Robert Morris objected on July 11 to fixing the standard of representation and favored allowing future Congresses to make adjustments as it chose, King said that he believed that "there was great force" in Morris's objections but that "he would however accede to the proposition for the sake of doing something" (1:582). He expressed further reservations later in the day, observing that he thought his committee had probably given the southern states more than they would be entitled to under the Three-fifths Clause (1:586). The next day, King noted that there was nothing that could keep the southern states in the Union if they did not want to stay, and he expressed the view that Congress should be able to vary the Three-fifths Clause if in the future it found that "the foregoing Rule of Taxation is not in a just proportion to the relative Wealth and population of the several States" (1:597). King was among those who resisted a last-minute attempt at the convention (September 15) to readjust representation in the House by granting North Carolina and Rhode Island each an additional seat (2:623). However, King joined Maryland's Daniel Carroll in seconding a motion, supported in a rare speech by George Washington and subsequently adopted, changing the minimum formula of representation to one representative for every 30,000 persons rather than one for every 40,000 (2:644).

King correctly observed that it would be difficult to allow for state legislative selection of members of the U.S. Senate unless this body were either to be "very numerous, or *the idea of proportion among the States was to be disregarded*" (1:51). King reasoned that unless there were a minimum of 80 to 100 senators, the smallest state (Delaware) would not be entitled to a single one.

On June 21, King indicated that he favored popular election of members of the House of Representatives. He feared that if such selection were left to state legislatures, they "wd. constantly choose men subservient to their own views as contrasted to the general interest" (1:359). The following day, King opposed allowing states to pay members of Congress for the same reason (1:372).

On the very eve of a compromise on representation in Congress, King continued to oppose equal state representation in the Senate. He thought that the government being formed would be "a General and National Government" that would operate directly on individuals rather than on state governments (1:6). He did not believe that granting states equality was consistent with "just principles." Indeed, "He preferred the doing of nothing, to an allowance of an equal vote to all the States. It would be better he thought to submit to a little more confusion & convulsion, than to submit to such an evil" (2:7). He did not follow up on the point or make it clear in which cases the third branch would operate, but he suggested during this speech that it might be possible to construct a Congress of three houses (2:7). After the Great Compromise was effected, King was among those who favored allowing senators to vote individually rather than by states (2:94).

Qualifications and Limitations. When the convention debated a resolution on June 22 preventing members of Congress from accepting appointments to other offices during this service or for one year after, King fretted that the delegates "were refining too much." Not only did he think such a provision would "discourage merit," but he also feared that it would provide the president with an excuse for bad appointments (1:376). King repeated his argument the following day, further pointing to examples that appeared to show that "the idea of preventing intrigue and solicitation of offices was chimerical" (1:387).

On July 26, King opposed a proposal that would have required that members of Congress own property. He believed that this "would exclude the monied interest, whose aids may be essential in particular emergencies to the public safety" (2:123).

Powers. King favored granting Congress power over elections. He observed that many delegates still seemed to support the idea of "erecting the Genl. Govt. on the authority of the State Legislatures" even though this had proven "fatal to the federal establishment" (2:241).

King did not think that Congress should be able to move to another site without adopting a law for this purpose (2:261). He favored providing that the national government would assume existing state debts, appealing not only to "considerations of justice and policy" but also as a way of garnering support for the new Constitution; otherwise, he feared opposition to the new Constitution from state creditors (2:328). He thought that if Congress did assume state debts, states should in turn give up their "unlocated lands" (2:328).

King wanted to grant the sole power to punish treason to the national government (2:348). He seemed to think that states could, however, punish similar offenses as "high misdemeanors" (2:348). Moreover, he did not think delegates could draw a clear line between treason against an individual state and against the states collectively (2:349).

A committee on which King served proposed granting Congress power to organize, arm, and discipline the militia while allowing states to appoint and train it. King attempted to defend this report by distinguishing among the terms organizing, arming, and disciplining (2:385). King favored allowing Congress to appoint the national treasurer by a joint ballot rather than allowing this officer to be appointed and confirmed like other officers recognized in the Constitution (2:614). Late in the convention (September 14), King opposed a motion by James Madison allowing Congress to create corporations. King feared that "The States will be prejudiced and divided into parties by it," citing conflicts that had erupted in Philadelphia and New York City over the establishment of a national bank under the Articles of Confederation (2:616).

On September 15, King opposed a motion to grant Congress, rather than the president, the power to pardon treason. King argued that this revision would be inconsistent with the idea of separation of powers. He further observed, "A Legislative body is utterly unfit for the purpose. They are governed too much by the passions of the moment" (2:626). Consistent with amendments that have been proposed to this power, however, King suggested that it might be appropriate to require Senate concurrence in such pardons (2:627).

Other Matters. On August 7, King indicated that he thought it unnecessary to establish in the Constitution a fixed meeting time each year for Congress. He did not think that Congress would need to meet each year. In his view, the objects of Congress would be chiefly focused on "commerce & revenue," and, once these were settled, there would not be much to do. He further observed that "A great vice in our system was that of legislating too much" (1:198). On September 7, King reiterated his view that the Senate should not have to sit constantly. Consistent with his view that Congress could legislate too much, he expressed concern about the multiplication of offices "which must increase the expense as well as influence of the Government" (2:539).

King favored a motion setting a bare majority of the first Congress as necessary for a quorum but allowing future Congresses to increase them or not as Congress grew. He feared that "the future increase of members would render a majority of the whole extremely cumbersome," but he apparently thought such adjustments would be subject to a presidential veto (2:253). King did not favor requiring majorities of two-thirds of the Senate to approve treaties; he believed that requiring the president and the Senate jointly to approve treaties would provide sufficient protection (2:540).

Presidency

On June 4, King joined with James Wilson and Alexander Hamilton in expressly favoring an absolute executive veto (1:108; Ernst 1968, 96). King subsequently supported a proposal for a conditional executive veto rather than associating the presidency with members of the judiciary in a Council of Revision (1:98). On June 6, he observed that the virtue of executive unity was as applicable to revisionary power as to other powers to be wielded by the executive (1:139).

King indicated on July 19 that he did not like the idea of making the president ineligible for reelection. King reasoned that "he who has proved himself to be most fit for an Office, ought not to be excluded by the constitution from holding it" (2:55).

King believed that the people could choose a president, but he thought that "an appointment by electors chosen by the people for this purpose, would be liable to fewest objections" (2:56). He opposed a plan whereby electors would be chosen by lot, observing that "We ought to be governed by reason, not by chance" (2:106). He later argued that the electoral college helped balance the influence of the large and the small states (2:514), and he introduced the motion preventing members of Congress from serving in the capacity of electors (2:521). He favored allowing Congress as a whole to select the president when no candidate received a majority rather than leaving this choice to the Senate alone (2:522).

When the delegates voted on July 19 against a seven-year presidential term, King expressed concern that they might "shorten the term too much"

(2:59). On July 24, King followed motions by Luther Martin for a presidential term of eleven years and a motion by Elbridge Gerry for a term of fifteen years by proposing that the president serve for twenty years, but King's comment, that "This is the medium life of princes," suggests that he was being ironic (2:102).

King feared the impeachment mechanism as undermining executive independence. He thought that such a mechanism was only proper in the case of officials who served "during good behavior" rather than for limited terms, and thought it particularly inappropriate for the president to be tried by members of Congress (2:67–68). When the convention did establish an impeachment mechanism for members of the executive branch, King joined Madison in opposing a provision that would suspend the executive until the charges were tried (2:612).

Judiciary

On June 4, King opposed associating members of the judiciary with the presidency in a Council of Revision. He observed that "the Judges ought to be able to expound the law as it should come before them, free from the bias of having participated in its formation" (1:98).

When fellow delegates were debating whether Congress should be able to establish federal courts below that of the Supreme Court or whether they should simply take appeals from existing state courts, King added a touch of realism by observing that it would be less costly to establish inferior federal tribunals than to multiply appeals (1:125).

Federalism

King's views on federalism were often tied to his comments, described above, relative to how states should be represented in the new system. King delivered an important speech on June 19 in which he discussed the nature of the government being contemplated. He objected to the term "sovereignty" being applied to the states:

> The States were not "sovereigns" in the sense contended for by some. They did not possess the peculiar features of sovereignty. They could not make war, nor peace, nor alliances, nor treaties. Considering them as political Beings, they were dumb, for they could not speak to any foreign Sovereign whatever. They were deaf, for they could not hear any propositions

from such Sovereign. They had not even the organs or faculties of defense or offense, for they could not of themselves raise troops, or equip vessels, for war. (1:323)

Similarly, the union of states comprised not only "the idea of a confederation" but "also of consolidation" (1:323). He continued: "If the States therefore retained some portion of their sovereignty, they had certainly divested themselves of essential portions of it. If they formed a confederacy in some respects—they formed a Nation in others" (1:324). Although King said that he did not favor annihilating the states, he said that he "thought that much of their power ought to be taken from them" (1:324).

In this same speech, King made an impassioned plea for continuing with the Virginia Plan rather than with simply patching up the Articles of Confederation as William Paterson had proposed in the New Jersey Plan. Notes that King prepared for his speech indicate he argued that even though Congress had not authorized such a plan, the Virginia Plan was authorized by "The public Expectations, & the public Danger" (1:332). He further argued that the Virginia Plan was "no crude and undigested plan, the Child of narrow and unextensive views, brought forward und[er] the auspices of Cowardice & Irresolution" but "a measure of Decision," the "foundation of Freedom & of national Glory." It was, he said, "no idle Experiment, no romantic Speculation," but a measure that "forces itself upon wise men" (1:332).

Because King put greater emphasis on the rights of individuals than the rights of states, he did not favor equal representation of the states in one or both houses of Congress. On June 30, however, King indicated that he did not think that "a full answer had been given to those who apprehended a dangerous encroachment" on state jurisdiction (1:492–93). He believed that the Constitution could be so devised as to provide for such security, as the English had provided for the security of Scotland when the two nations united. King expressed special concern (1:493) over the intemperate language of Delaware's Gunning Bedford, who had previously suggested that the small states might seek an alliance with foreign powers, but Yates's notes indicate that King may have in part prompted this response when he indicated that if states were granted equal suffrage in the Senate, then "our business here is at an end" (1:499; Ernst 1968, 103). King's contrast of "our common Country" to "some foreign land" indicates that he had a keen sense of national patriotism (1:493).

On August 28, King introduced a motion for the provision that the convention eventually incorporated into Article I, Section 10 of the Constitution, prohibiting states from interfering with private contracts (2:439); initially defeated, the proposal reemerged from the Committee of Style of which King was a member (Ernst 1968, 112). That same day, he opposed prohibiting congressional taxation of exports (2:442). When Gerry objected that the federal power to exercise power over property used for forts could undermine the states, King moved to insert the words "by the consent of the Legislature of the State" after "purchases" (2:510).

Slavery

After the convention fixed the rule for representation in the House according to the rule previously adopted for taxation, King wanted to know how this would affect slave representation, and he came out swinging against the institution of slavery. He said, "The admission of slaves was a more grating circumstance to his mind" (2:220). Observing that the delegates had tied the hands of the legislature in regard both to slave importation and the taxation of exports, he questioned, "Is this reasonable?" (2:220). Believing that the two great objects of Union were internal and external defense, he believed these agreements injured both:

> Shall all the States then be bound to defend each; & shall each be at liberty to introduce a weakness which will render defence more difficult? Shall one part of the U.S. be bound to defend another part, and that other part be at liberty not only to increase its own danger, but to withhold the compensation for the burden? If slaves are to be imported shall not the exports produced by their labor, supply a revenue the better to enable the Genl. Govt. to defend their Masters? (2:220)

A unique mix of moralistic and practical concerns, King ended this speech by observing that "either slaves should not be represented, or exports should be taxable" (2:220). King later observed that the northern and middle states would not think it fair if slaves were the only imports exempted from federal duties (2:373). King served on the committee that proposed allowing states to import slaves until 1808 in exchange for securing the power to tax them, and he believed the two parts of the compromise were linked together (2:416).

Ratification

On June 5, King observed that according to the Articles of Confederation, state legislatures were competent to ratify the new Constitution. He believed, however, that it would be more expeditious for conventions within the states to do so since such conventions would meet in a single body at a time when most state legislatures were bicameral and because state legislators slated "to lose power, will be most likely to raise objections" (1:123). King repeated this view on July 23, indicating as an additional advantage of popular ratification that it would "get rid of the scruples which some members of the States Legislatures might derive from their oaths to support & maintain the existing Constitutions" (2:92). King proposed the motion that limited the application of the new Constitution only to the states that ratified it (2:475). As the convention progressed, King became even more persuaded of the desirability of ratifying the Constitution by state conventions. He thus remarked on August 31 that:

> striking out "convenient" as the requisite mode was equivalent to giving up the business altogether. Conventions alone, which will avoid all the obstacles from the complicated formation of the Legislatures, will succeed, and if not positively required by the plan, its enemies will oppose that mode. (2:476)

Observing that Massachusetts, which he represented, contained a provision making its constitution unalterable until 1790, he observed that "this was no difficulty with him. The State must have contemplated a recurrence to first principles before they sent deputies to this Convention" (2:477). King thought it would be respectful to Congress to submit the Constitution to it without requiring that it approve or disapprove of it, and he suggested that the approval of nine states would be adequate for the new Constitution to go into effect (2:561). To require congressional approval or to allow states to decide on the appropriate number required to ratify would throw everything into confusion and risk losing everything (2:563).

Life after the Convention

King represented Massachusetts at the ratifying convention, where he was an effective advocate for the new Constitution. In one speech he made a particularly powerful appeal for the new document. Pointing to the failure of the Articles of Confederation to get states to pay their quotas, he said that it was essential that the government be able to operate directly on individuals:

It has been objected to the proposed constitution, that the power is too great, and by this constitution is to be sacred. But if the want of power is the defect in the old confederation, there is fitness and propriety in adopting what is here proposed. . . . It is an objection in some gentlemen's minds, that Congress should possess the power of the purse and the sword. But, sir, I would ask, whether any government can exist, or give security to the people, which is not possessed of this power. . . . To conclude, sir, if we mean to support an efficient federal government, which under the old confederation can never be the case, the proposed constitution is, in my opinion, the only one that can be substituted. (quoted in Ernst 1968, 115–6)

Despite his efforts at the Constitutional Convention and in the state's ratifying convention, his marriage in 1786 to Mary Alsop of New York (the only daughter of a merchant, she was sixteen when they were married) with whom he would have seven children, changed his residency. After Massachusetts ruled that he was ineligible to represent that state in the U.S. Senate, the people of New York elected him to their legislature, which selected him as one of its first two senators. King became a strong Federalist and joined Alexander Hamilton in authoring essays in support of the Jay Treaty. King served from 1796 to 1803 under three U.S. presidents as a minister to Great Britain, a post that he resumed at the request of president John Quincy Adams from 1825 to 1826 but had to give up because of declining health. He served again as a U.S. senator from New York from 1813 to 1825, in which capacity he opposed the Missouri Compromise, and he was twice defeated as a candidate for vice president (both times running with Charles Cotesworth Pinckney), once defeated for governor, and once defeated as a candidate for president on the Federalist ticket.

King died in Jamaica, New York on April 29, 1827 and was interred at the Grace Episcopal Church Cemetery in that city. Today the King Manor Museum in Jamaica, New York honors his legacy and that of his descendants with particular emphasis on King's opposition to slavery.

Further Reading

Brush, Edward Hale. 1926. *Rufus King and His Times*. New York: Nicolas L. Brown.
Ernst, Robert. 1968. *Rufus King: American Federalist*. Chapel Hill: The University of North Carolina Press.
Farrand, Max, ed. 1966. *The Records of the Federal Convention of 1787*. 4 vols. New Haven, CT: Yale University Press.
Siry, Steven E. 1999. "King, Rufus." In *American National Biography*, 12: 711–12. New York: Oxford University Press.

JOHN LANGDON (1741–1819)
NEW HAMPSHIRE

Born near Portsmouth, New Hampshire on June 26, 1741, John Langdon served as an apprentice to a merchant and soon became a merchant and shipbuilder reputed to be the wealthiest man in New Hampshire. An ardent patriot, Langdon helped seize gunpowder from the British in December of 1774 and was soon thereafter elected to the legislature, where he served from 1776 to 1781 as the speaker. The previous year he had served in the Continental Congress where he helped build the first ship for the U.S. Navy. Langdon personally advanced money to finance troops to face the armies of General John Burgoyne and participated in a number of battles as well, but he also advanced his fortune as a Continental agent for New Hampshire. Langdon married Elizabeth (Betsy) Sherburne (1751–1813), and they had a daughter, Elizabeth Langdon Elwyn.

Langdon was president of New Hampshire from 1784 to 1786 and fronted the money to pay himself and Nicholas Gilman (the state's representatives to Congress) to attend the Constitutional Convention. Because the trip awaited his own financing, however, he and Gilman did not arrive at the Constitutional Convention until July 23. They thus arrived a week after the convention's critical decision regarding representation in Congress.

At the Convention

On July 26, Langdon supported a motion by Pennsylvania's James Wilson to strike a provision that would have prevented individuals with unsettled accounts from serving in Congress. Langdon supported Wilson's very practical arguments that this would give too much power to auditors, who might delay settling accounts in order to exclude individuals from office (Farrand 1966, 2:125). Later that day, Langdon supported a motion by Virginia's George Mason preventing the seat of the national government from being moved to a city that was serving as a state capital. However, he expressed concern that a state might evade this requirement by moving its capital to the national capital after public buildings were constructed in the latter (2:127).

On August 14, Langdon opposed having states pay the salaries of members of Congress. Not only did he foresee difficulty in establishing the amount of such payment, but he felt it would be unjust to "distant States" with greater expenditures for their members' travel costs (2:290–1).

When the convention was discussing whether to grant Congress power to "emit bills," that is, whether to print paper money, as it had done under the Articles of Confederation, Delaware's George Read said that the words "would be as alarming as the mark of the Beast in Revelations [sic]" (2:310). Langdon added that he would "rather reject the whole plan than retain the three words [and emit bills]" (2:310).

When Elbridge Gerry of Massachusetts objected to a provision allowing Congress to send troops into a state when the legislature could not request the same, Langdon supported the provision. He observed that "The apprehension of the national force, will have a salutary effect in preventing insurrections" (2:317). Similarly, Langdon opposed Gerry's attempt to limit the size of standing armies in peacetime. On this occasion, Langdon said that he "saw no room for Mr. Gerry's distrust of the Representatives of the people" (2:330). Similarly supporting a motion by Virginia's George Mason entrusting Congress with the power to regulate the militia and the states to appoint their officers, Langdon said that "He saw no more reason to be afraid of the Genl. Govt than of the State Govts. He was more apprehensive of the confusion of the different authorities on this subject, than of either" (2:331). On a later day, Langdon indicated that he did not share the concerns of other delegates as to which powers were exercised by the states and which were to be exercised by the national governments:

> The General & State Govts. were not enemies to each other, but different institutions for the good of the people of America. As one of the people he could say, the National Govt. is mine, the State Govt is mine—In transferring power from one to the other—I only take out of my left hand what it cannot so well use, and put it into my right hand where it can be better used. (2:386)

In later supporting allowing two-thirds majorities in Congress to negative state laws, Langdon said "He considered it as resolvable into the question whether the extent of the National Constitution was to be judged of by the Genl or the State Governments" (2:391).

Again opposing a motion by Elbridge Gerry that would apportion direct taxes on the states until the first meeting of Congress, on the basis of the number of representatives that they had in the first branch, Langdon said his opposition stemmed from his belief that this would be unreasonably hard on New Hampshire (2:350). Acknowledging that he was at a disadvantage since he was not present when the representation for New Hampshire was apportioned, Langdon indicated on August 21 that if it had been given extra representatives to which it was not entitled, then "he did not wish for them" (2:358). By contrast on September 15, Langdon indicated that he thought that both Rhode Island and New Hampshire were entitled to an extra representative in the U.S. House (2:622).

Langdon expressed concern on August 21 that states were to this point left free to tax exports. He thought that this would work to the disadvantage of New Hampshire and other non-exporting states and thought that was unacceptable. Also pointing to fears that northern interests would attempt to oppress those from southern states, he proposed as a remedy that two-thirds or three-fourths majorities should be required for such commercial regulations (2:359). He also favored prohibiting states from taxing exports of other states that left their harbors (2:361).

By contrast, Langdon thought that Congress should be entrusted with the power to prohibit slave importation: "He cd. not with a good conscience leave it with the States who could then go on with the traffic" (2:373). However, when Connecticut's Roger Sherman objected that allowing the taxation of slave imports classified them as property, Langdon joined Rufus King of Massachusetts in indicating that he thought this was a necessary part of the compromise (2:416).

Langdon wanted to leave the status of debts against the United States just where they were under the Articles (2:413). He further favored leaving Congress the option of admitting new states into the Union with fewer privileges than the original states (2:454). Langdon was concerned that if Vermont did not join the union and remained exempt from taxes, this could hurt New Hampshire (2:456). Langdon expressed concern over the clause preventing ships from one state paying duties in another, believing that there may be cases where the general government needed to adopt such regulations to deal with smuggling (2:481). Langdon feared that a provision allowing states to lay duties for the costs of inspection could be abused (2:589). Similarly, he thought that states should have nothing to do with regulating tonnage, since this was an aspect of trade committed to Congress (2:625).

When the delegates were still considering allowing Congress to select the president, Langdon proposed that they should do this by joint ballot rather than by individual houses, even though he did not believe this would help his home state. Langdon said that he feared that a negative vote by the Senate "would hurt the feelings of the man elected by the votes of the other branch" (2:402).

In part because he arrived late, Langdon appeared to have a penchant for addressing relatively minor details of the Constitution, many dealing with commercial matters, rather than for tackling larger questions. He appeared less concerned than some delegates over the respective relations between the national government and the states in general, but continued to concern himself with some of the particulars of this relationship.

Life after the Convention

Langdon returned to Congress after the convention, served again as his state's president, and worked for ratification of the Constitution, which he initially thought would be ratified more quickly than proved to be the case (see Mayo 1970, 206–12). He served as one of New Hampshire's first two senators and had the honor, as Senate pro tempore, to count the votes that elected George Washington as president. Initially a supporter of Hamilton's fiscal programs, Langdon found himself drawn, in part by his Anglophobia and his opposition to the Jay Treaty, to the Democratic-Republican Party of Thomas Jefferson. Langdon subsequently returned to New Hampshire to serve in the state legislature and in a number of terms as governor where he helped get the state capital moved to Concord and stopped slave importation through Portsmouth. In 1805 fellow delegate Nicholas Gilman supported him in a successful race for governor over Gilman's older brother. Langdon turned down the opportunity to run as James Madison's vice president in 1812 but was active in the American and New Hampshire Bible Societies.

Langdon died in Portsmouth on September 18, in 1819 (his wife preceded him in death in 1813) and was buried in its Old North Cemetery. Their daughter inherited and occupied their commodious Georgian-style house in Portsmouth until 1833. The house is now open to the public between June 1 and October 15.

Further Reading

Daanen, Jeroen. n.d. "A Biography of John Langdon 1741–1819." American History: From Revolution to Reconstruction. http://www.let.rug.nl/usa/biographies/john -langdon/. Accessed 7/5/2012.

Farrand, Max, ed. 1966. The Records of the Federal Convention of 1787. 4 vols. New Haven, CT: Yale University Press.

Mayo, Lawrence Shaw. 1970. *John Langdon of New Hampshire*. Port Washington, NY: Kennikat Press.

Van Atta, John R. 1999. "Langdon, John." In *American National Biography*, edited by John A. Garraty and Mark C. Carnes, 13: 138–39. New York: Oxford University Press.

JOHN LANSING (1754–1829)
NEW YORK

John Lansing was born in Albany in 1754, the descendant of Dutch immigrants. He is believed to have been the wealthiest man in the state with vast landholdings and numerous slaves. He read law under Robert Yates, who also attended the Constitutional Convention, and with James Duane. A military secretary to General Philip Schuyler during the revolution, Lansing had served six terms in the New York legislature prior to being elected to serve at the convention. At the time of the convention, he was allied with New York governor George Clinton and was serving as the mayor of Albany. Lansing married Cornelia Ray, with whom he had 10 children.

None of New York's three delegates to the Constitutional Convention especially liked the direction that it took. Along with Robert Yates, John Lansing was one of two members who left before the convention ended and therefore did not sign the document. Although Alexander Hamilton, the state's third delegate, did so, he was convinced that the new government was not strong enough. Lansing did not speak frequently at the convention. His central contribution to debates at the convention was to support the New Jersey Plan, which he believed was more consistent with the purpose of the convention and more likely to be accepted by the states than the more visionary Virginia Plan, which Lansing believed imperiled state sovereignty.

At the Convention

Convention records indicate that Lansing was seated on Saturday, June 2 (Farrand 1966, 1:76). His first recorded action occurred nearly two weeks later after William Paterson presented the New Jersey Plan, when Lansing and some unnamed "gentlemen" argued for postponing a meeting of the Committee of the Whole so that supporters would have more time to examine and defend the new plan (1:242). On this occasion he observed that "the two systems [that of the New Jersey and Virginia Plans] are fairly contrasted. The one [the New Jersey Plan] now offered is on the basis of amending the federal government, and the other [the Virginia Plan] to be reported as a national government, on propositions which exclude the propriety of amendment" (1:246).

The following day, June 16, Lansing developed his ideas in greater detail. Interestingly, he led off in defense of the New Jersey Plan, with Paterson following. Lansing portrayed the New Jersey Plan as sustaining "the sovereignty of the respective States" whereas the Virginia Plan, with its provision for a congressional negative on state laws, destroyed it (1:249). Although Lansing had concerns about the perceived derogation of state sovereignty, he focused not so much on the undesirability of the Virginia Plan in and of itself but on the "want of power in the Convention to discuss & propose it" and "the improbability of its being adopted" (1:249). Arguing that the convention was exceeding its power by even considering the Virginia Plan, Lansing said that his own state "would never have concurred in sending deputies to the convention, if she had supposed the deliberations were to turn on a consolidation of the States, and a National Government" (1:249). As to ratification, Lansing did not think the states were likely to ratify proposals that exceeded the convention's mandate and pointed to previous difficulties under the Articles of Confederation in extending congressional powers. He believed it even less likely that the states would approve a plan of government like that advocated in the Virginia Plan:

> The States will never feel a sufficient confidence in a general Government to give it a negative on their laws. The Scheme is itself totally novel. There is [no] parallel to it to be found. The authority of Congress is familiar to the people, and an augmentation of the powers of Congress will be readily approved by them. (1:250)

Lansing further elaborated his views on June 20, when he restated his opinion that the convention had no authority to adopt the Virginia Plan and that the people would not follow the convention in ratifying it. As to the first point, he observed that, whether elected by state legislatures or by the people, the delegates were there not to represent people as individuals but "as forming a sovereign State" (1:336). Although some believed that necessity could warrant exceeding convention instructions, Lansing and other delegates did not agree on such a necessity (1:336). Pennsylvania's James Wilson had argued that since the convention was only making recommendations, it should recommend what it would, but Lansing feared that such proposals, if rejected by the people, "will be a source of great dissentions" (1:336). For his part, he did not believe that it was likely that states that currently possessed sovereignty were likely to part with it.

Lansing went on to answer a number of other arguments that delegates had raised. He did not believe that equal representation in Congress was equivalent to the system of rotten boroughs in England. He believed any configuration of Congress would result in the representation of state prejudices. If, as Alexander Hamilton had asserted, there was no commonality of interests among the large states and interests were relatively uniform, then it could not matter if small states retained their equality. Lansing did not believe that Congress would have sufficient "leisure" to oversee the laws of individual states and void those that Congress thought to be inappropriate. He further argued that Congress was not competent to do so and likened such oversight to that which the British had exercised in America prior to independence. A government like that proposed by the Virginia Plan would require greater influence on the part of the national government than the states would give. As long as the states existed, they could be expected to protect themselves. Their reluctance would be expanded by the novelty of the new system and by their inability to predict its consequences: "The system was too novel & complex. No man could foresee what its operation will be either with respect to the Genl. Govt. or the State Govts. One or other it has been surmised must absorb the whole" (1:338). In Yates's notes of the speech, which provide a useful supplement to Madison's, Lansing was recorded as asking, "Fond as many are of a general government, do any of you believe it can pervade the whole continent so effectively as to secure the peace, harmony and happiness of the whole?" (1:345).

Although the convention voted to proceed with its discussion of the Virginia Plan, Lansing remained unconvinced. On June 28, he introduced a motion to restore representation in the first branch of Congress to that which existed under the Articles of Confederation, under which states were equally represented (1:445).

Life after the Convention

Despite the progress that the proponents of equal state representation in the Senate were making, Lansing and Yates subsequently left the convention on July 10 and returned to New York to oppose it, authoring an open letter to Governor Clinton expressing their opposition (3:246–47). Along with Melancton Smith, Lansing was one of the primary opponents of ratification of the Constitution at the New York ratifying convention. He introduced numerous amendments and unsuccessfully attempted to condition New York's ratification on their adoption.

Lansing served for eleven years on the New York Supreme Court and then served from 1801 to 1814 as chancellor of the state, where he was widely respected for his integrity but which resulted in him becoming a defendant in a case in which he was sued by John Van Ness Yates. After retiring from the bench at the mandatory age of sixty, Lansing resumed his legal practice. In 1824 New Yorkers chose him as a presidential elector for Georgia's William Crawford, and in 1826 he published an account of some of his cases. After leaving a hotel room in New York City, he mysteriously disappeared after going to post a letter in December 1829. His wife Cornelia died five years later.

Further Reading

Bradford, M. E. 1994. *Founding Fathers: Brief Lives of the Framers of the United States Constitution*. Lawrence: University Press of Kansas.

Farrand, Max, ed. 1966. *The Records of the Federal Convention of 1787*. 4 vols. New Haven, CT: Yale University Press.

Hanyan, Craig. 1999. "Lansing, John." In *American National Biography*, edited by John A. Garraty and Mark C. Carnes, 13: 180–81. New York: Oxford University Press.

Strayer, Joseph Reese, ed. 2002. *The Delegate from New York or Proceedings from the Federal Convention of 1787 from the Notes of John Lansing Jr*. Clark, NJ: Lawbook Exchange.

Westbury, Susan. 2001. "Robert Yates and John Lansing Jr.: New York Delegates Abandon the Constitutional Convention." *New York History* 82 (October): 312–35.

WILLIAM LIVINGSTON (1723–1790)
NEW JERSEY

In 1723, William Livingston was born in Albany New York to Philip and Catharine Livingston, one of the state's most wealthy and powerful families. As a boy, he spent a year with a Moravian missionary family living with the Mohawk Indians. He subsequently graduated from Yale where he mastered a number of languages and developed a love for writing. He returned to New York where he studied under two different lawyers before joining the bar, where he developed a highly successful practice (Klein 1958). In addition to serving as a member of New York's colonial legislature, Livingston wrote in a variety of media, but was particularly critical of what he believed was the desire of the Episcopal Church to establish itself over its rivals.

His wealth allowed Livingston to decide to retire at the age of forty-nine. He then moved to the state of his wife, Susannah French (1723–1789) in Elizabethtown, New Jersey and built a house in 1772–1773 that he named "Liberty Hall." Shortly thereafter, he and his family befriended Alexander Hamilton who had come from the West Indies.

Duty called Livingston out of retirement in New Jersey. He was elected to the Continental Congress, served as a militia commander, and then was continually elected governor from 1776 to 1790, when he died in Elizabethtown.

At the Convention

Livingston divided his duties as a delegate to the Constitutional Convention with his responsibilities as state governor and rarely participated in convention debates. He was seated on June 5 and signed the Constitution on September 17. As the putative author and introducer of the New Jersey Plan, William Paterson took a much more active role in the convention than the state's governor.

Livingston served as chairman of the Committee on State Debts and Militia that the convention appointed on August 18 and was a member of the Committee on Slave Trade and Navigation that the delegates created on August 22 (interestingly, when in New York, Livingston had freed his own two slaves and joined an antislavery society). Delegates also appointed Livingston to the Committee on Sumptuary Legislation that was formed on September 13 but which appears never to have met.

Because the only records of Livingston's participation come from the motions that came out of the committees that he chaired, our most extensive knowledge of Livingston's role at the Constitutional Convention is found in a letter that Virginia's James Madison wrote on February 12, 1831 in answer to a query about Livingston's role. Madison observed that Livingston had not taken "an active part in its debates" but that he had served on some committees, "where it may be presumed he had an agency and a due influence" (Farrand 1966, 3:496). Madison specifically cited the respect Livingston gained as a result of "the celebrity of his name" (3:496).

As to whether Livingston "had a leaning to the federal party [that is, to the group at the convention favoring increased national powers] and principles," Madison was uncertain. He observed that, given Livingston's silence, he could only surmise what he might have thought from how the state of New Jersey cast its votes:

> The votes of N. Jersey corresponded generally with the Plan offered by Mr. Patterson [sic]; but the main object of that being to secure to the smaller States an equality with the larger in the structure of the Govt, in opposition to the outline previously introduced, which had reversed the object, it is difficult to say what was the degree of power to which there might be an abstract leaning. (3:496)

Madison further observed, "With those . . . who did not enter with debate, and whose votes could not be distinguished from those of their State colleagues, their opinions could only be known among themselves, or to their particular friends" (3:496). Madison ended by noting, "My acquaintance with Gov Livingston was limited to an exchange of the common civilities, and these to the period of the Convention" (3:496). It would appear to be the nation's loss that this highly articulate governor did not participate more actively in convention debates.

Life after the Convention

Livingston was pleased that New Jersey was the third state to ratify the Constitution and that it did so unanimously. In as message to the New Jersey legislature of August 19, 1788, Livingston said, "We are arrived at that auspicious period which, I confess, I have often wished that it might please Heaven to protract my life to see. Thanks to God that I have lived to see it" (quoted in Sedwick 1833, 422). As New York's chancellor, Livingston administered the first presidential oath to George Washington.

Livingston was the father of Brockholst Livingston, who was later appointed to the U.S. Supreme Court. He also fathered Sarah Van Brugh Livingston, who married John Jay, the Court's first chief justice.

Livingston died on July 25, 1790 and was succeeded in the governor's position by William Paterson, who had also attended the Constitutional Convention. Livingston was buried first in New Jersey, later in Manhattan, and finally in the Greenwood Cemetery in Brooklyn, New York. Livingston's New Jersey house, Liberty Hall, expanded from 14 rooms to a 50-room Victorian mansion and is now a museum, operated by Kean University.

Further Reading

Bradford, M. E. 1994. *Founding Fathers: Brief Lives of the Framers of the United States Constitution*. Lawrence: University Press of Kansas.

Farrand, Max, ed. 1966. *The Records of the Federal Convention of 1787*. 4 vols. New Haven, CT: Yale University Press.

Klein, Milton M. 1958. "The Rise of the New York Bar: The Legal Career of William Livingston." *William and Mary Quarterly*, 3rd Ser., 15 (July): 334–58.

———. 1993. *The American Whig: William Livingston of New York*. Rev. ed. New York: Garland Publishing.

Livingston, William. 1979—. *The Papers of William Livingston*. 5 vols. Trenton: New Jersey Historical Commission.

Sedwick, Theodore, Jr. 1833. *A Memoir of the Life of William Livingston*. New York: J. & J. Harper. Nabu Public Domain reprint.

JAMES MADISON JR. (1751–1836)
VIRGINIA

Often dubbed the "father" of the U.S. Constitution, Virginia's James Madison was certainly one of the most intellectual and influential delegates at the Constitutional Convention. Born on March 16, 1751 at Port Conway, Virginia, the son of planter James Madison and Eleanor Conway Madison, Madison attended boarding school before going to the College of New Jersey (today's Princeton) where he studied theology and law, without directly pursuing either occupation. Madison, barely one hundred pounds and five feet

four inches (some say five feet six) tall, graduated early and worked himself into a virtual state of exhaustion, staying an extra six months at Princeton to do further study under president John Witherspoon (the only clergyman who would sign the Declaration of Independence) before returning home.

Returning to Virginia, Madison was elected to the Orange County Committee of Safety in 1774 and to the state's constitutional convention in 1776. In addition to managing his family's plantation in Orange, Virginia, Madison spent most of his life as a career politician. He served from 1778 to 1779 as a member of the Governor's Council of Virginia, from 1780 to 1783 as a member of the Congress under the Articles of Confederation, from 1784 to 1786 as a member of the Virginia legislature, and from 1787 to 1788 as a member of Congress. In Congress Madison had been instrumental in Virginia's accession of the old Northwest, and in Virginia he had opposed the jailing of dissident ministers and had helped enact the Statute for Religious Freedom.

As an elected official, Madison became increasingly convinced of the inadequacy of the Articles of Confederation and of injustices at the state level. Not informed by governor Patrick Henry of his appointment to the Mount Vernon Conference in time to attend, Madison was one of the prime movers at the Annapolis Convention. He followed up this service with work to get the Virginia legislature to issue a call for the Constitutional Convention. In addition to the important role that he played in the convention debates, Madison took the most comprehensive notes of the convention's proceedings. In a preface that he drafted but never completed, Madison described his method as follows:

> In pursuance of the task I had assumed I chose a set in front of the presiding member, with the other members of my right & left hands. In this favorable position for hearing all that passed, I noted in terms legible & in abreviations & marks intelligible to myself what was read from the Chair or spoken by the members; and losing not a moment unnecessarily between the adjournment & reassembling of the Convention I was enabled to write out my daily notes during the session or within a few finishing days after its close in the extent and form preserved in my own hand on my files. (Vile 2005, 888)

Madison further observed:

> In the labour & correctness of doing this, I was not a little aided by prac-
> tice, and by a familiarity with the style and the train of observation & rea-
> soning which characterized the principal speakers. It happened, also that I
> was not absent a single day, nor more than a casual fraction of an hour in
> any day, so that I could not have lost a single speech, unless a very short
> one (Vile 2005, 888).

Without his notes, the simple record of ayes and nays that the official secretary, William Jackson, took would be relatively worthless. Madison, however, provided that his notes would not be published until after his death,
and he lived a long time.

At the Convention

The Virginia Plan

Prior to attending the convention, Madison had asked his friend Thomas Jefferson to send him books on government from Europe, where Jefferson was
serving as an ambassador to France. Madison in turn reviewed these books,
focusing on the history of previous republic, and writing two essays. One
focused on "Ancient and Modern Confederacies." The other was entitled
"The Vices of the Political System." In this essay, he analyzed the situation
under the Articles of Confederation and possible remedies. He envisioned a
stronger national government over a large land mass as a means of increasing
the number of factions, or interest groups, and therefore moderating their
influence so as to protect individual rights.

Although governor Edmund Randolph presented the Virginia Plan to
the convention on May 29, the ideas of this plan correspond so closely to
ideas that Madison expressed in letters he wrote just prior to the convention
that scholars generally attribute chief authorship to him. The sheer audacity
of the plan, which was used to set the initial agenda of the convention, is
perhaps its most intriguing fashion. Instead of simply adding to the powers
of Congress, the plan proposed a whole new system. The plan proposed a
new government divided into three branches rather than one. It proposed
dividing Congress into two houses, the first to be elected directly by the
people and apportioned according to population and the second to be chosen by members of the first branch from among nominees proposed by the
states. Given Madison's belief that the Senate should be a relatively small

body to check excesses of the House, it is not altogether clear whether, as the Virginia Plan promised, this would have allowed for proportional state representation in this body or whether (as seems more likely) it would simply have given each state the opportunity to nominate individuals for such posts.

Rather than enumerating the powers of Congress, as had the Articles of Confederation, Madison proposed to invest Congress with the power "to legislate in all cases to which the separate States are incompetent, or in which the harmony of the United States may be interrupted by the exercise of individual Legislation" (Farrand 1966, 1:21). In another prized provision, Madison hoped to give Congress power "to negative all laws passed by the several States, contravening in the opinion of the National Legislature the articles of Union" (1:21). As late as August 27, Madison was still arguing for the efficacy of a congressional veto of state laws (2:440). In a provision about which he would shortly after express doubts (see 1:54), the Virginia Plan also provided that the national government could use force against states that failed to perform their duties.

The Virginia Plan initially called for the legislature to select a national executive for a single term. In combination with members of the judiciary, the Virginia Plan called for vesting the executive with the power to examine and veto all laws of the states or of Congress, with Congress having the power to override such a veto by an unspecified supermajority. Congress would appoint members of the national judiciary who would serve during good behavior and try impeachments of national officers. The Virginia Plan further provided for the admission of new states, for guaranteeing them a republican form of government, and for an amending provision. The new plan was to go into effect when ratified by state conventions.

A day after Hamilton's long speech of June 18 proposing a plan of government that called for stronger powers than either the Virginia or New Jersey Plans, Madison delivered a lengthy speech of his own designed to urge the convention to continue with its consideration of the Virginia Plan. He began by arguing that the government under the Articles of Confederation was not completely federal and that the Virginia Plan was not therefore proposing a complete alternative. Madison argued that the New Jersey Plan could not adequately preserve the Union against threats from abroad or guard against threats to national authority at home. He also argued that the government proposed under the New Jersey Plan would be inadequate in preventing "trespasses of the States on each other" (1:317), securing internal tranquility within the states (1:318), obtaining good legislation and administration within the states (1:318), or securing the Union against foreign influences (1:319). Madison urged the smaller states to reconsider their attachment to the New Jersey Plan. The timing may or may not have been significant, but it was Madison's speech, rather than the more extreme and more noticed speech by Hamilton, that directly preceded the convention's decision to continue with consideration of the Virginia rather than the New Jersey Plan.

Long after other delegates had given in to demands by the smaller states, Madison continued to insist on the injustice of equal state representation in one or both houses of Congress; he believed that he was fighting for a basic principle and not just for the interest of his own state (then the most populous of the thirteen). In a long speech on June 28, in which Madison ransacked the history of previous republics for illustrations and support, he argued that the matter involved "fundamental principles" (1:446). Madison's tone was not as belligerent as that of many other delegates, and so the timing may have been merely coincidental, but shortly after this speech Benjamin Franklin proposed that the convention should open each session with prayer (1:451). The next day, Madison continued to implore his fellow delegates against incorporating a principle of representation that was "confessedly unjust, which cd. never be admitted, & if admitted must infuse mortality into a Constitution which we wished to last forever" (1:464). On the day after, Madison somewhat prophetically attempted to convince delegates that the real principle of division was not that between the large states and the small ones, but between the northern and southern interests (1:476). Madison reiterated this theme on June 30 (1:485–86), and on July 13 (1:601).

On June 30, Madison said he was willing to accept an idea, which Pennsylvania's James Wilson proposed, whereby states would have a minimum of one senator for every 100,000 people with representation otherwise according to population. He only felt he could agree to such a plan, however, if the delegates granted senators independence from the states. Otherwise he feared that the Senate would be "only another edition of Congs." (1:490), that is, of the woefully weak Congress under the Articles of Confederation. On July 9, Madison floated another plan whereby states would be represented according to free population in the House of Representatives and according to the sum of both free persons and slaves in the Senate (1:562). On July 14, Madison expressed willingness to accept a proposal by South Carolina's Charles Pinckney whereby existing states would have one to five delegates in the Senate (2:5).

On July 14, Madison seemed to offer another proposal. He suggested:

In all cases where the Genl. Governt. is to act on the people, let the people be represented and the votes be proportional. In all cases where the Governt. is to act on the States as such, in like manner as Congs. now act on them, let the States be represented & the votes be equal. This was the true ground of compromise if there was any ground at all. (2:8–9)

Madison almost immediately, however, appeared to take back this concession by denying that there was "a single instance in which the Genl. Govt. was not to operate on the people individually" (2:9). Madison continued with a list of evils that would flow from equal state suffrage in the Senate:

1. The minority could negative the will of the majority of the people. 2. They could extort measures by making them a condition of their assent to other necessary measures. 3. They could obtrude measures on the majority by virtue of the peculiar power which would be vested in the Senate. 4. The evil instead of being cured by time, would increase with every new State that should be admitted, as they must all be admitted on the principle of equality. 5. The perpetuity it would give to the preponderance of the Northn. agst. the Soutn. Scale was a serious consideration. (2:9)

Madison may have had the stronger arguments (contemporary critics still complain about the unrepresentative nature of the U.S. Senate), but the convention defeated his proposal with the acceptance of the Great Compromise on July 16.

On the day after that, Madison suffered yet another devastating defeat. He had continued to argue that his proposed congressional negative of state laws was "essential to the efficacy & security of the Genl. Govt." and that "nothing short of a negative" could control "the propensity of the States to pursue their particular interests in opposition to the general interest" (2:27). Gouverneur Morris of Pennsylvania responded that such a negative "would disgust all the States" (2:28), and the convention defeated this proposal by a vote of seven to three.

Federalism

One of the enigmas of James Madison is attempting to ascertain and reconcile his positions on issues related to federalism at the Constitutional Convention with those that he later took as a leader of the Democratic-Republican Party and as an author of the Virginia Resolutions of 1798. Madison's primary concern at the Constitutional Convention was that that of state encroachments on the national government. In comparing the Virginia and New Jersey Plans on June 21, Madison thus observed that he thought that:

> There was 1. less danger of encroachment from the Genl. Govt. than from the State Govts. 2. that the mischief from encroachments would be less fatal if made by the former, than if made by the latter. (1:356)

He attempted to illustrate his points by reference to past confederacies. He went so far as to suppose that the national government should exercise indefinite power and that the states should be "reduced to corporations dependent on the Genl. Legislature" (1:357). He hypothesized that, even in such an extreme case, he did not believe that the national government would have an incentive to "take from the States [any] branch of their power as far as its operation was beneficial, and its continuance desirable to the people" (1:357).

In addition favoring a broad grant to Congress to legislate over matters over which individual states were incompetent, Madison favored granting Congress power "to grant charters of incorporation where the interest of the U.S. might require & the legislative provisions of individual State may be incompetent" (2:615). He also wanted to grant Congress the power "to establish an University, in which no preferences or distinctions should be allowed on account of religion" (2:616).

As a politician Madison would later question some broad exercises of federal power. Near the end of the convention, however, he indicated that "He was more & more convinced that the regulation of Commerce was in its nature indivisible and ought to be wholly under one authority" (2:625).

Congress

On May 30, Madison said that his belief in proportional representation stemmed from his conviction that "whatever reason might have existed for the equality of suffrage when the Union was a federal one among sovereign States, it must cease when a national Governt. should be put into the place" (1:37). A day later, he said that the popular election of at least one branch of Congress was "essential to every plan of free government" (1:49). Although he favored "the policy of refining the popular appointments by successive filtrations" (1:50), he believed that the legislature should be kept close to the people. As he put it, "the great fabric to be raised would be more stable and durable if it should rest on the solid foundation of the people themselves, than if it would stand merely on the pillars of the Legislatures" (1:50). When the convention settled on an initial House of Representatives consisting of 65 members, Madison suggested that this number should be doubled (1:568).

On July 26, Madison cautioned against excluding individuals from Congress who were in debt, although he was willing to consider excluding those who did not account for public money (2:122). Similarly, he worked against a provision requiring that members have "landed" property. He observed that "every class of Citizens should have an opportunity of making their rights be felt & understood in the public Councils;" this included members of "the landed[,] the commercial & the manufacturing" interests (2:124).

Madison, however, opposed a proposal to consolidate individuals in districts across state lines for the selection of senators, believing that this would disadvantage members of the smaller states (1:52). That same day, Madison professed to have brought "a strong bias in favor of enumeration and definition of the powers necessary to be exercised by the national Legislature." However, he also said that he had increasing doubts about the practicality of such enumeration and that "he should shrink from nothing which should be found essential to such a form of Govt. as would provide for the safety, liberty and happiness of the Community" (1:53).

When Delaware's John Dickinson proposed on June 7 that state legislators should select members of the Senate, Madison objected that this would require either a deviation "from the doctrine of proportional representation" or require a number of senators too large for it to perform its moderating function. Applying his theory of factions, Madison observed:

> The more the representatives of the people therefore were multiplied, the more they partook of the infirmaties of their constituents, the more liable they became to be divided among themselves either from their own indiscretions or the artifices of the opposite factions, and of course the less capable of fulfilling their trust. (1:152)

Madison reiterated his support for an absolute congressional veto of state acts on June 8. He viewed this veto as an alternative to the use of national force against states, which he had earlier labeled as impractical. Citing an astronomical analogy, Madison said, "The prerogative of the

General Govt. is the great pervading principle that must controul the centrifugal tendency of the States; which, without it, will continually fly out of their proper orbits and destroy the order & harmony of the political system" (1:165). Later that same day, Madison did suggest that there might be "some emanation of the power from the Natl. Govt. into each State so far as to give temporary assent" (1:168); he also proposed that the convention might vest this power in the Senate rather than in the entire Congress. As late as August 23, Madison was still trying to revive the idea of a congressional veto over state laws (2:390).

The original Virginia Plan did not specify the length of congressional terms. On June 12, Madison seconded a motion to set terms of members of the House of Representatives at three years. He hoped this term would prevent "instability" and would give legislators, many of whom he estimated would spend a year preparing for and traveling to and from the seat of government, adequate time to learn their duties (1:214; also see 1:361). He answered Gerry's argument that the people preferred annual elections by saying that the delegates should exercise their best judgments and hope that public opinion would follow (1:215). Madison initially favored a seven-year term for U.S. senators (1:218), although he later did not express opposition to a term of nine years (1:423).

Madison argued that congressional pay, for both members of the House and the Senate, should be fixed and paid by the national government in order to prevent undue dependency on the states. Madison feared that allowing the states to pay senators would "make the Senate like Congress, the mere Agents & Advocates of State interests & views, instead of being the impartial umpires & Guardians of justice and general Good" (1:428). On a number of occasions, Madison expressed the hope that such pay might be stabilized by settling on an exchange rate based on the average price of wheat or some other common commodity (2:216; also see 1:373). Madison, the author of the Twenty-seventh Amendment, proposed as part of the Bill of Rights but not ratified until 1991, thought that it would be "indecent" for members of Congress to set their own salaries (1:374), and he opposed allowing members to accept offices that had been created or augmented while they were in office—the basis of the current emoluments clause (1:380; 1:386). He unsuccessfully proposed that the Constitution might restrict Congress by "fixing at least two extremes not to be exceeded by the Natl. Legislre. in the payment of themselves" (2:291).

Madison was among those who consistently favored the origination of money bills from either house of Congress. He argued that the Senate would also be a representative institution and that it would be composed of more capable men (1:233). He further believed that, however senators were restricted, they would exercise similar powers in amending money bills (1:234). When the restriction of money bills was tied into the Great Compromise on congressional representation, Madison continued to insist that he "could not regard the exclusive privilege of originating money bills as any concession on the side of the small States" (1:527). Again on August 13, Madison argued that at the very least the Senate should have power to *reduce* sums appropriated by the House (1:276).

Madison thought that congressional meeting times could be fixed by law rather than needing to be fixed within the Constitution (2:198). If such a time were to be fixed, he thought that May would be more appropriate than December, when travel would be more difficult (2:199).

Madison apparently favored confining the right to vote to freeholders (2:208). He feared that those without such property might be too dependent upon their patrons.

Madison opposed long residency requirements for members of Congress, fearing that they might leave new western states without adequate representation (2:217). He had the foresight to realize that if states were guaranteed one representative for every 40,000 persons, rather than making this a minimum, there would eventually be an "excessive" number of House members (2:221). Madison opposed a 14-year residency requirement for members of the Senate on the basis that "it will give a tincture of illiberality to the Constitution: because it will put it out of the power of the Natl Legislature even by special acts of naturalization to confer the full rank of Citizens on meritorious strangers & because it will discourage the most desirable class of people from emigrating to the U.S." (2:236). Madison repeated this position for minimal residency requirements for members of the Senate (2:268), arguing with special vehemence against an argument by Connecticut's Roger Sherman that the national government was under no obligation to honor pledges made by the states (2:270–71).

Madison favored allowing Congress to regulate elections (2:240), but opposed allowing Congress to set voting qualifications. He feared that by such means "A Republic may be converted into an aristocracy or oligarchy" (2:250). Similarly, he thought that it should require a two-thirds vote for Congress to expel one of its own members (2:254).

Madison thought it was essential to find a centrally located place for the nation's new capital (probably favoring a spot in or near Virginia). He argued:

As the powers & objects of the new Govt. would be far greater, more private individuals wd. have business calling them to the seat of it, and it was more necessary that the Govt should be in that position from which it could contemplate with the most equal eye, and sympathize most equally with, every part of the nation. (2:261)

Madison thought that the power of taxing exports was appropriate, but that the United States should do this collectively rather than individually (2:306); he favored requiring consent of two-thirds of the states to such embargoes than prohibiting them completely (2:363). He believed that the time might come when the national government might also need to enact complete embargoes (2:361). He opposed prohibiting the emission of bills on the credit of the United States but apparently favored prohibiting making them legal tender (2:309). He supported allowing Congress to define felonies on the high seas so as to promote "uniformity" and "stability" in the law (2:316).

Similarly, Madison was the delegate who proposed granting Congress the power to "declare" rather than to "make" war (2:318). He argued that Congress should have the power to regulate the militia, believing that such a power "did not seem in its nature to be divisible between two distinct authorities" (2:332; also see 2:386–87). He was apparently willing for states to appoint lower officers (2:388). Madison saw provisions for an effective militia as a way to guard against the danger of large standing armies (2:388), and he was willing to include language in the Constitution designed to indicate concern over standing armies (2:617).

Madison argued against a narrow definition of treason. He believed that Congress should have "more latitude" and that "it was inconvenient to bar a discretion which experience might enlighten, and which might be applied to good purposes as well as be abused" (1:345). He apparently favored limiting the definition of treason to acts committed against the United States rather than leaving open the possibility of double punishment from state and national authorities (2:346). Madison did not favor requiring supermajorities in Congress to regulate navigation, believing that existing constitutional checks would be adequate to protect the states (2:451–52).

Judiciary

On June 5, Madison argued against granting Congress, or any other numerous body, the power to select judges, although he suggested that the Senate might appropriately exercise such a function (1:120; also see

1:232). Madison favored dispersing federal courts throughout the nation as a way of keeping down the number of appeals and of avoiding verdicts by "the biased directions of a dependent Judge, or the local prejudices of an undirected jury" (1:124). Madison offered a rather novel proposal for judicial appointments (a kind of legislative veto), by suggesting that the president might appoint judges subject to confirmation of one-third of the Senate (2:42), or disapproval by two-thirds (2:44). Madison argued that, with such a check, the executive was the more appropriate appointing authority. By his arguments, the executive would be better able to select fit individuals, and would (after adoption of the Great Compromise giving states equal representation in the Senate) be more likely to represent a majority than a minority of the people (2:80–81). Madison eventually modified his proposal, in accord with the present Constitution, so that a majority of the Senate could reject such nominees.

As in the case of members of Congress, he favored tying increases in judicial salaries to the price of a commodity like wheat (2:45). Madison proposed that judicial jurisdiction should extend "to all cases arising under the Natl. laws; And to such other questions as may involve the Natl. peace & harmony" (2:46). He thought, however, that the courts should be limited "to cases of a Judiciary Nature," explaining that "The right of expounding the Constitution in cases not of this nature ought not to be given to that Department" (2:430).

Presidency

When, on June 1, the convention first debated whether the presidency should be singular or plural, Madison suggested that it might first be wise "to fix the extent of the Executive authority" (1:66). He proposed that it should have power to carry out congressional laws, to appoint officers not otherwise provided for, and to exercise other powers that Congress delegated to it. Notes taken by New York's Alexander Hamilton suggest that Madison argued that allowing for a plural executive would prevent "contention" and be closer to "republican genius" (1:72). Notes by Georgia's William Pierce from the same day suggest that Madison may simply have been advocating that a single executive should be aided by a Council of Revision (1:74).

Madison advocated separation of the legislative and executive branches. To this end, he thought it essential that the legislature should not select the presidency. He gave at least tepid support to a proposal by fellow Virginian and friend James McClurg for appointing the president "during good behavior" (2:34–35), but he seemed more concerned about the principle of separation of powers. Madison was especially wary of the "tendency in our governments to throw all power into the Legislative vortex" (2:35).

On July 19, Madison repeated his concern that legislative and executive powers should be exercised independently. Agreeing with James Wilson that the people were "the fittest" to make such a decision, he feared that they might not have knowledge of candidates outside their own states and that conflict would occur because suffrage was more "diffusive" in the North, which had fewer slaves. This led Madison to advocate some form of electors, independent of Congress (2:57).

On June 2, Madison opposed a proposal to allow states to petition for removal of the presidency, in part because it put states of differing populations in similar situations and in part because he did not think it wise to mix state and national institutions (1:86). He opposed, however, an absolute executive veto, partly on the basis that he thought it contradicted the national temper (1:100). At one point, Madison favored three-fourths rather than two-thirds congressional majorities to override presidential vetoes. He believed this was necessary both "to defend the Executive Rights" and "to prevent popular or factious injustice" (2:587).

Similarly, in discussions of an impeachment mechanism, Madison favored some provision "for defending the Community agst the Incapacity, negligence or perfidy of the chief Magistrate" (2:65). He thought such a mechanism was particularly necessary in the case of an institution, like the presidency, that would be vested in a single individual. Madison objected to impeachments on the grounds of "maladministration," believing the term to be too vague and "equivalent to a tenure during the pleasure of the Senate" (2:550). Similarly, Madison opposed suspending the president from office during impeachment trials, believing that such a suspension "Will put him in the power of one branch only" (2:612).

Madison reaffirmed the need to combine the executive with a Council of Revision. He felt that combining the executive with the judiciary would help both to "support" and "control" the former (1:138). He further argued that allying the executive and members of the judiciary would be much different than allying the presidency and the legislative branch, as he thought the British had done (2:77). Losing out on his plan for a Council of Revision, near the end of the convention, Madison supported Mason's idea for a Council of State (2:542).

As observed above, Madison feared that legislative selection of the president would lead the latter to be unduly dependent on the former. On

July 25, Madison reviewed the various mechanisms that had been proposed for presidential selection, and said that he liked popular election the best. He feared, however, that direct election would overly advantage the large states and those in the North, where suffrage was more widespread. Fellow delegates agreed with his critique, rather than his preference for popular selection, and voted to allow Congress to choose the president. When presidential selection was still to be left to Congress, Madison argued that the two houses should vote jointly rather than giving each house a veto over the other (2:403). Madison, however, favored a system that made "eventual resort to any part of the Legislature improbable" (2:513).

Slavery

Madison recognized that the problem of race was a problem of a minority being kept in subjection by the majority. Thus on June 6, he said, "We have seen the mere distinction of colour made in the most enlightened period of time, a ground of the most oppressive dominion ever exercised by man over man" (1:135). He made no apparent effort to eliminate slavery at the convention, however, suggesting at one point that states should be represented by the population of free persons in one house and by the number of such persons and slaves in the other. He did strongly oppose the motion extending the right of states to import slaves from 1800 to 1808, noting that "Twenty years will produce all the mischief that can be apprehended from the liberty to import slaves. So long a term will be more dishonorable to the National character than to say nothing about it in the Constitution" (2:415). In discussing slave duties, Madison further observed that he "thought it wrong to admit in the Constitution the idea that there could be property in men" (2:417).

Extended Republic

At a time when many Antifederalists held the view, which the philosopher Charles Louis de Secondat Baron de Montesquieu of France espoused, that republican government would be impossible in a government the size of that which the Constitution was creating, Madison argued that an extended democratic republic was not only feasible, but could actually serve as a guard against faction. Madison expressed this view on June 6 when he cited "the security of private rights, and the steady dispensation of Justice" as among the key objects of government (1:134). Here, as in Federalist No. 10, Madison connected oppression with small states. The remedy followed accordingly:

The only remedy is to enlarge the sphere, & thereby divide the community into so great a number of interests & parties, that in the 1st place a majority will not be likely at the same moment to have a common interest separate from that of the whole or of the minority; and in the 2d. place, that in case they shd. have such an interest, they may not be apt to unite in the pursuit of it. (1:136)

Amendment

The Virginia Plan had rather vaguely called for the necessity of an amending provision. Madison gave a clearer idea of what he favored on September 10 when he proposed that:

The Legislature of the U—S—whenever two thirds of both Houses shall deem necessary, or on the application of two thirds of the Legislatures of the several States, shall propose amendments to this Constitution, which shall be valid to all intents and purposes as part thereof, when the same shall have been ratified by three fourths at least of the Legislatures of the several States, or by Conventions in three fourths thereof, as one or the other mode of ratification may be proposed by the Legislature of the U.S. (2:559)

When this provision was amended to allow for states to require Congress to call a convention to propose amendments, Madison indicated that he "did not see why Congress would not be as much bound to propose amendments applied for by two thirds of the States as to call a Convention on the like application." He continued by observing that "He saw no objection however against providing for a Convention for the purpose of amendments, except only that difficulties might arise as to the form, the quorum &c which in Constitutional regulations ought to be as much as possible avoided" (2:629–30).

Ratification

Madison thought the proposal for ratifying the Constitution through state conventions was essential. He feared that if state legislatures ratified, the parties would be able to make a breach of the Constitution by one party a way of absolving the allegiance of all. He wanted the Constitution to be "ratified in the most unexceptionable form, and by the supreme authority of the people themselves" (1:123). On July 23, Madison argued that "the difference between a system founded on the Legislatures only, and one founded on the people, to be the true difference between a league or treaty, and a *Constitution*" (2:93). Madison proposed at one point that the Constitution might be ratified by seven or more states with at least 33 seats (the majority of 66) in the House of Representatives (2:475). He continued to insist on popular ratification:

> The people were in fact, the fountain of all power, and by resorting to them, all difficulties were got over. They could alter constitutions as they pleased. It was a principle in the Bill of Rights, that first principles might be resorted to. (2:476)

Committee Work

Madison served on four committees at the Constitutional Convention. He was on the committee, appointed on July 9, which reconsidered the original apportionment of the U.S. House of Representatives and increased that number from 56 to 65. He was a member of the committee created on August 22 that devised a compromise regarding the slave trade and navigation. Committee assignments would appear to indicate that he rose in the estimation of his colleagues as the convention proceeded. He was thus appointed both to the Committee on Postponed Matters that the delegates created on August 31, and to the Committee of Style and Arrangement, which delegates appointed on September 8. He did not, however, chair any of the committees on which he served.

Life after the Convention

Madison distinguished himself, along with Alexander Hamilton and John Jay, as a leading Federalist by serving as one of three authors of *The Federalist Papers*, which defended and advocated ratification of the proposed Constitution. Madison's essays on republican government (No. 10) and on separation of powers (No. 51) are regarded as classics and are often taken as embodiments of the central underlying philosophy of the Constitution. Elected to the Virginia ratifying convention, Madison successfully applied cool reason to beat back the powerful rhetoric of Patrick Henry opposing the new Constitution.

The biggest threat to the new Constitution came from those who argued for a second convention, which Madison feared might undo the work of the first. To avoid this contingency, and in possible response to letters he was receiving from his friend, Thomas Jefferson, Madison agreed to support a bill of rights once the new Constitution was adopted. Machinations by governor Patrick Henry kept Madison from getting a spot in the U.S. Senate. Narrowly defeating future president James Monroe, Madison was elected to the House of Representatives (he served there until 1797) where he took the lead in the formulation of the Bill of Rights. Madison generally worded these rights so as to protect rights of citizens without undermining the authority of the new national government. Madison did not succeed in getting an amendment that would restrict state powers over civil liberties—a development that would wait until Supreme Court interpretations (largely in the twentieth century) of the Fourteenth Amendment, which was ratified in 1868. Congress accepted the arguments of Roger Sherman and added amendments to the end of the Constitution rather than integrating them into the original text.

Madison was a close confidant of George Washington at the beginning of his administration. He helped draft his inaugural address, helped write the House response to the address, and then authored Washington's response to the response! Although they worked together on The Federalist Papers, Madison became increasingly suspicious of Alexander Hamilton, Washington's secretary of state, and his program for the new government. Madison opposed the establishment of the U.S. Bank, but ultimately joined a compromise with Hamilton providing for the location of the capital near Virginia in exchange for federal assumption of paper currency at face value. As Madison's hostility to Hamilton increased, his relationship was strained. Increasingly siding with secretary of state Thomas Jefferson, Madison questioned Washington's proclamation of neutrality toward France, with which the United States had signed a treaty.

In the Adams administration, Madison accordingly secretly authored the Virginia Resolution of 1798, which opposed the Alien and Sedition Acts of the Adams administration (Jefferson wrote the corresponding Kentucky Resolution). Somewhat contrary to the positions Madison had taken at the Constitutional Convention, he advocated the right of states to interpose themselves against federal legislation. Madison served again in the Virginia state legislature from 1799 to 1800.

A strong friend of Thomas Jefferson, whose Democratic-Republican Party he supported, Madison was selected as a Jeffersonian elector in 1800. Madison served as Jefferson's secretary of state from 1801–1809, a period during which the United States purchased the Louisiana Territory and in which Jefferson declared a highly unpopular embargo that unsuccessfully attempted to bring Great Britain to heel. Madison's buxom wife, Dolley Todd Madison (1768–1849), a former widow whom he married in 1794 when he was forty-three, was a popular hostess during this time and into Madison's presidency. Madison was elected president in 1808 (defeating Charles Cotesworth Pinckney who had also attended the Constitutional Convention as a delegate from South Carolina) and served for two terms, the second of which witnessed the War of 1812 and the burning of the nation's capital. Madison respected the civil liberties of opponents at a time when some New England Federalists contemplated disunion. He sought to preserve Jefferson's memory after Jefferson's death and served for a time as rector of the University of Virginia, which Jefferson had founded.

Called out of retirement from his farm in 1820, Madison cochaired Virginia's state constitutional convention. His friend Thomas Jefferson, who Charles Ingersoll called "the god of his idolatry" (quoted in Broadwater, 2012, 207) died (as did John Adams) on July 4, 1826, and when William Few died in 1828, Madison was the last surviving member of the convention that he so influenced. Madison commented, "Having outlived so many of my contemporaries, I ought not to forget that I may be thought to have outlived myself" (quoted in Broadwater, 206).

Madison died on June 28, 1836 at Montpelier, where he was buried on the grounds. A granite obelisk was added in 1857 and Dolley, who died in 1849, was moved from the Congressional Cemetery in Washington DC in 1858, where she was buried behind him in a grave marked by a similar, but smaller, monument. Madison's notes and papers on the convention were published in 1840 and remain the best single source of information about its proceedings. Numerous towns and cities, and a university in Virginia's Shenandoah Valley, have been named in Madison's honor. Madison's house, Montpelier, was long owned by the Dupont family and has been painstakingly restored to its eighteenth century appearance, and is now open to the public.

In his old age Madison had become increasingly concerned about the controversies over slavery that were racking the country, and he tried to distinguish his own careful appeals to fellow states in the Virginia Resolutions from the theory of concurrent majorities that John C. Calhoun of South Carolina and others were espousing that would allow a single state to nullify a federal law (Ford 1994, 51–55). Appealing as it were from beyond the grave, his "Advice to My Country" was first published in the National Intelligencer in 1850. Sounding a nationalistic note similar to that which he had consistently advocated at the convention, but not always consistently followed thereafter, Madison implored his countrymen to cherish the Union:

The advice nearest to my heart and deepest in my convictions is that the Union of the States be cherished and perpetuated. Let the open enemy to it be regarded as a Pandora with her box opened; and the disguised one, as the Serpent creeping with his deadly wiles into Paradise. (Meyers 1973, 576)

Further Reading

Banning, Lance. 1983. "James Madison and the Nationalists, 1780–1783." *William and Mary Quarterly*, 3rd Ser., 40 (April): 227–55.

———. 1995. *The Sacred Fire of Liberty: James Madison and the Founding of the American Republic*. Ithaca: Cornell University Press.

Bence, Evelyn. 2008. *James Madison's Montpelier: Home of the Father of the Constitution*. Orange, VA: The Montpelier Association.

Bigler, Philip, and Annie Lorsbach. 2009. *Liberty and Learning: The Essential James Madison*. Harrisonburg, VA: The James Madison Center.

Broadwater, Jeff. 2012. *James Madison: A Son of Virginia and Founder of the Nation*. Chapel Hill: The University of North Carolina Press.

Brookhiser, Richard. 2011. *James Madison*. New York: Basic Books.

Burstein, Andrew, and Nancy Isenberg. 2010. *Madison and Jefferson*. New York: Random House.

Chadwick, Brtuce. 2010. *Triumvirate, The Story of the Unlikely Alliance That Saved the Constitution and United the Nation*. Napierville, IL: Sourcebooks.

Collins, J. J. 2012. *James Madison: The Father of the Constitution (1751–1836)*. CreateSpace Independent Publishing Platform.

Connelly, William F., Jr. 2010. *James Madison Rules America: The Constitutional Origins of Congressional Partisanship*. Lanham, MD: Rowman & Littlefield.

Conniff, James. 1975. "On the Obsolescence of the General Will: Rousseau, Madison, and the Evolution of Republican Political Thought." *Western Political Quarterly* 28 (March): 32–58.

DeRose, Chris. 2011. *Founding Rivals: Madison vs. Monroe, the Bill of Rights, and the Election That Saved a Nation*. Washington, DC: Regnery.

Farrand, Max, ed. 1966. *The Records of the Federal Convention of 1787*. 4 vols. New Haven, CT: Yale University Press.

Ford, Lacy K., Jr. 1994. "Inventing the Concurrent Majority: Madison, Calhoun, and the Problem of Majoritarianism in American Political Thought." *Journal of Southern History* 60 (February): 19–58.

Gutzman, Kevin R. C. 2012. *James Madison and the Making of America*. New York: St. Martin's Press.

Hobson, Charles F. 1979. "The Negative on State Laws: James Madison, the Constitution, and the Crisis of Republican Government." *William and Mary Quarterly*, 3rd Ser., 36 (April): 214–35.

Kernell, Samuel. 2003. *James Madison: The Theory and Practice of Republican Government*. Stanford, CA: Stanford University Press.

Koch, Adrienne. 1950. *Jefferson and Madison: The Great Collaboration*. New York: Oxford University Press.

Kramer, Larry D. 1999. "Madison's Audience." *Harvard Law Review* 112 (January): 611–79.

Labunski, Richard. 2006. *James Madison and the Struggle for a Bill of Rights*. New York: Oxford University Press.

Matthews, Richard K. 1995. *If Men Were Angels: James Madison and the Heartless Empire of Reason*. Lawrence: University Press of Kansas.

Meyers, Marvin, ed. 1973. *The Mind of the Founder: Sources of the Political Thought of James Madison*. Indianapolis: Bobbs-Merrill Company, Inc.

Miller, William L. 1992. *The Business of May Next: James Madison and the Founding*. Charlottesville: University Press of Virginia.

Morgan, Robert J. 1988. *James Madison and the Constitution and the Bill of Rights*. New York: Greenwood Press.

Rakove, Jack N. 1990. *James Madison and the Creation of the American Republic*. Glenville, IL: Scott, Foresman.

Read, James H. 1995. "'Our Complicated System': James Madison on Power and Liberty." *Political Theory* 23 (August): 452–74.

Robertson, David Brian. 2005. "Madison's Opponents and Constitutional Design." *The American Political Science Review* 99 (May): 225–43.

Rosen, Gary. 1999. *American Compact: James Madison and the Problem of Founding*. Lawrence: University Press of Kansas.

Rutland, Robert A. 1987. *James Madison: The Founding Father*. New York: Macmillan Publishing.

Rutland, Robert A., ed. 1994. *James Madison and the American Nation, 1751–1836*. New York: Charles Scribner's Sons.

Sheldon, Garrett Ward. 2001. *The Political Philosophy of James Madison*. Baltimore: Johns Hopkins University Press.

Siemers, David J. 2002. *Ratifying the Republic: Antifederalists and Federalists in Constitutional Time*. Stanford, CA: Stanford University Press.

Smith, James Morton, ed. 1995. *The Republic of Letters: The Correspondence Between Thomas Jefferson and James Madison*. 3 vols. New York: W. W. Norton & Company.

Spencer, Mark G. 2002. "Hume and Madison on Faction." *William and Mary Quarterly*, 3rd Ser., 59 (October): 869–96.

Vile, John R. 2005. *The Constitutional Convention of 1787: A Comprehensive Encyclopedia of America's Founding*. 2 vols. Santa Barbara, CA: ABC-CLIO.

Vile, John R., William D. Pederson, and Frank J. Williams, eds. 2008. *James Madison: Philosopher, Founder, and Statesman*. Athens: Ohio University Press.

Weiner, Greg. 2012. *Madison's Metronome: The Constitution, Majority Rule, and the Tempo of American Politics*. Lawrence: University Press of Kansas.

Zuchert, Michael P. 2003. "The Political Science of James Madison." In *History of American Political Thought*, edited by Bryan-Paul Frost and Jeffrey Sikkenga, 149–66. Lanham, MD: Lexington Books.

Zvesper, John. 1984. "The Madisonian Systems." *Western Political Quarterly* 37 (June): 236–56.

Note: The Papers of James Madison, begun by the University of Chicago (the first volume was published in 1962), has been continued by the University of Virginia. As of 2012, 35 of a projected 48 volumes have been published. The rest should be completed by 2026.

Alexander Martin (1740–1807)
North Carolina

Alexander Martin was born in 1740 in Hunterdon County, New Jersey to the family of a Presbyterian minister who had immigrated there from Ireland. Martin earned both a bachelor's and a master's degree from the College of New Jersey (today's Princeton) and moved, as did most of his siblings, to North Carolina where he was both a merchant and an attorney. He was a justice of the peace and briefly served as a judge. On one occasion, a crowd of westerners associated with the Regulator Movement beat him. He later served in the North Carolina legislature and helped defend Charleston against British attacks. Subjected to a court martial for cowardice at the battle of Germantown, Martin was not convicted but resigned. He was elected to the North Carolina legislature and served from 1782 to 1785 as state governor.

At the Convention

Martin was present when the convention opened in May 25, and he appears to have stayed until late August. However, he did not serve on any convention committees, and his public participation appears to have been limited to seconding three motions. On June 23 he seconded a motion by James

Madison of Virginia to prohibit members of the House of Representatives from being eligible for offices during their service and for one year afterwards (Farrand 1966, 1:386). On July 10, Martin joined South Carolina's General Pinckney in proposing that North Carolina be granted six U.S. representatives instead of the five that were proposed (1:568). Again on July 26, Martin seconded a motion, this one by Virginia's George Mason, that would limit the nation's new capital from being located in the same city as the capital of any state until such time as the necessary building could be constructed (2:127). Significantly, in each case, Martin seconded a motion of a fellow southerner.

Fellow delegate Hugh Williamson, the intellectual leader of the North Carolina delegation, wrote a letter dated July 8, 1787 to future Supreme Court justice James Iredell explaining Martin's reticence to participate in the proceedings. He observed:

> I am inclined to think that the great exertions of political wisdom in our late Governor [Martin], while he sat at the helm of our State, have so exhausted his fund, that time must be required to enable him again to exert his abilities to the advantage of the nation. (3:55)

On August 20, Martin wrote to the North Carolina governor to tell him that he would be leaving the convention in early September. In this letter he observed that "the Deputation from the State of North Carolina have generally been unanimous on all great questions, and I flatter myself will continue so until the Objects of their mission be finished" (3:72–73).

Life after the Convention

Martin supported ratification of the Constitution in North Carolina but was not elected to the state's ratifying conventions. He served as the state's first governor under the Constitution, a position he occupied for three subsequent terms, during the last of which he helped establish the state's capital in Raleigh. In 1791, Martin hosted George Washington at his Danbury estate in North Carolina. The state legislature chose Martin as a U.S. senator in 1792. Although generally aligned in the Senate with the Democratic-Republican Party, he supported the Alien and Sedition Acts in 1798. He went on to serve as a trustee of the University of North Carolina and as speaker of the North Carolina Senate. He died in 1807 (his mother, who lived with him, died four days later at the age of 90) and was buried at his Danbury estate. A lifelong bachelor, Martin acknowledged paternity of Alexander Strong Martin.

Further Reading

Bradford, M. E. 1981. *Founding Fathers: Brief Lives of the Framers of the United States Constitution.* 2nd ed. Lawrence: University Press of Kansas.

Craige, Burton. 1987. *The Federal Convention of 1787: North Carolina in the Great Crisis.* Richmond, VA: Expert Graphics.

Farrand, Max, ed. 1966. *The Records of the Federal Convention of 1787.* 4 vols. New Haven, CT: Yale University Press.

Mitchell, Memory F. 1964. *North Carolina's Signers: Brief Sketches of the Men Who Signed the Declaration of Independence and the Constitution.* Raleigh: Division of Archives and History, North Carolina Department of Cultural Resources.

LUTHER MARTIN (1744–1826)
MARYLAND

Born near New Brunswick, New Jersey in 1744 to a farm family, Martin attended the College of New Jersey (now Princeton University) before becoming a schoolmaster of the Free-School of Queen Anne's County in Maryland. He later studied for the bar, to which he was admitted after an examination by George Wythe and John Randolph of Virginia. Partly because of his enthusiasm for the patriot cause, Martin was elevated as attorney general of Maryland and served in this post consecutively for more than 27 years (a record) and later again for a brief time.

Martin married Maria Cresap (who died in 1796) in 1783. Two of their children died at young ages. Of the three daughters who survived into adulthood, one had to be confined to an insane asylum and another eloped at the age of fifteen with a man named Richard Keene, who had been reading law with Martin, and who became the subject of five splenic letters that Martin collected in a book ironically called *Modern Gratitude*! Known for improvident spending and excessive drinking, Martin may have been even better known for his prolix rhetoric—one scholar says his arguments were characterized by "their orotundity, antiquarian scholarship, otiose circumambient development, and irresistible conclusion" (Bradford 1994, 112).

At the Convention

Martin attended the convention in part because members of the state legislature feared leaving lest the state adopt a paper money scheme. Martin was seated at the Constitutional Convention on June 9. He left on September 4 before the convention was completed, but after it was clear that it departed too much from his sentiments for him to consent to it.

Martin's first recorded position at the convention was a motion to strike the requirement that state officials pledge to uphold the new Constitution. He observed that if such an oath were contrary to the pledge they had taken to support their state constitutions, the oath would be "improper," whereas if it coincided with this pledge, such prior oaths would be "sufficient" (Farrand 1966, 1:203).

Federalism and Representation

On June 19, Martin argued, consistent with social contract theory, that the American Revolution had "placed the 13 States in a state of nature towards each other." He believed that the states had therefore entered the Articles of Confederation on the basis of equality, and he said that he could never agree to a plan that did not provide for equal state representation in Congress (1:324). Even after the convention had rejected the New Jersey Plan for the Virginia Plan, Martin indicated that he opposed a number of the latter plan's provisions. He thus observed that he would support the state governments over the national government, and that he could see no reason to divide Congress into two houses (1:340). Martin believed that the American people had entrusted "the security of their lives, liberties & property" to the state governments (1:341). The people had accordingly formed the federal government for limited purposes and continued to be on guard against it:

> The federal Govt. they formed, to defend the whole agst. foreign nations, in case of war, and to defend the lesser States agst the ambition of the larger: they are afraid of granting powers unnecessarily, lest they should defeat the original end of the Union; lest the powers should prove dangerous to the sovereignties of the particular States which the Union was meant to support; and expose the lesser to being swallowed up by the larger. (2:341)

Martin elaborated on his view of the relationship between the nation and the states in a speech of more than three hours that he delivered on June 27. Madison's summary indicates that Martin delivered the speech with his usual exuberance, and that Madison was only able to record its central points:

> The General Govt. was meant merely to preserve the State Governts: not to govern individuals: that its powers ought to be kept within narrow limits; that if too little power was given to it, more might be added; but that if too much, it could never be resumed: that individuals as such have little to do but with their own States; that the Genl. Govt. has no more to apprehend from the States composing [the Union] while it pursues proper measures, that a Govt. over individuals has to apprehend from its subject: that to resort to the Citizens at large for their sanction to a new Governt. will be throwing them back into a State of Nature: that the dissolution of the State Govts. is involved in the nature of the process: that the people have no right to do this without the consent of those to whom they have delegated their power for State purposes. (1:437)

Martin continued to argued that states remained in the state of nature, and hence of equality, relative to one another. Clearly unable to record everything, Madison observed that Martin had "read passages from Locke, Vattel, Lord Summers—Priestly" (1:437) in support of his argument from the state of nature. Martin accused the three largest states of seeking to enslave the ten smaller ones. He opposed the veto that Madison had proposed over state laws and suggested that it would be better to carve up the large states than to join small ones together (1:438). Madison observed that Martin was "too much exhausted" to finish his speech. In his notes of the speech, New York's Robert Yates recorded that Martin said that he would not accept a government organized on the principles of the Virginia Plan "for all the slaves of Carolina or the horses and oxen of Massachusetts." He further records that Martin charged that the "feeling" that the large states professed on behalf of justice "are only the feelings of ambition and the lust of power" (1:441).

When he resumed his speech on the following day, Martin continued to argue that the general government had been formed on behalf of the states rather than for the people, and he continued to fear that small states would be enslaved if they were not represented equally. He said that "it will be in vain to propose any plan offensive to the rulers of the States, whose influence over the people will certainly prevent their adopting it" (1:445). He also stated that he would rather see the formation of partial confederacies between the large states and the small ones than give sanction to the plan being considered (1:445). This is one of the few occasions on which Yates's notes were more complete than Madison's, perhaps reflecting the latter's exasperation with Martin's arguments. In addition to the arguments above, Yates observed that Martin expressed a clear preference for government by the states on the basis that the general government "is too remote for their good. The people want it nearer home" (1:454). Toward the end of his speech, Yates cited Martin as saying that "we are already confederated, and no power on earth can dissolve it but by the consent of *all* the contracting powers—and four states, on this floor, have already declared their opposition to annihilate it" (1:455).

When Elbridge Gerry later argued against the idea of state sovereignty, Martin "remarked that the language of the States being, Sovereign & independent, was once familiar & understood; though it seemed now so strange & obscure" (1:468). He further quoted passages from the Articles of Confederation to prove his point. When on June 30, New Jersey's Jonathan Dayton objected that the plan of government being proposed was "an amphibious monster," Martin, in apparent agreement, said that he could "never confederate if it could not be done on just principles" (1:490). On July 2, he reiterated that "no modifications whatever could reconcile the Smaller States to the least diminution of their equal Sovereignty" (1:511). However, Martin was appointed that day to the committee to compromise on representation in Congress, and this seems to have served to moderate his views. Thus, on July 14, Martin said that although he neither liked the idea of a bicameral Congress nor the idea of unequal representation in the lower house, he "was willing . . . to make trial of the plan, rather than do nothing" (2:4). He quickly established an even more forceful defense of his new position, however, in declaring that "He had rather there should be two Confederacies, than one founded on any other principle than an equality of votes in the 2d branch at least" (2:4). Martin later carried his state in singular opposition to allowing members of the Senate to vote "per capita" as "departing from the idea of the *States* being represented in the 2d. branch" (2:95). Similarly, on August 14, Martin argued: "As the Senate is to represent the States, the members of it ought to be paid by the States" (2:292).

On June 21, Martin seconded a motion by South Carolina's Charles Pinckney to allow for election of members of the House of Representatives in the manner that states chose rather than requiring that this be done by popular election (1:358). On June 23, Martin seconded a motion offered by

James Madison that restricted members of Congress from accepting offices during their tenure or for one year after for offices established or the emoluments of which were increased during their terms (1:386).

When during a discussion of whether to restrict office holding to individuals with debts or unsettled accounts, fellow Maryland delegate Daniel Carroll proposed striking out the prohibition on those with unsettled accounts, Martin replied that this would leave it in the interest of such candidates "to keep their accounts unsettled as long as possible" (2:125). On August 17, Martin expressed opposition to allowing the national government to subdue rebellion within the state without the consent of the legislature as giving Congress "a dangerous & unnecessary power" (2:317). The next day, Martin proposed limiting the number of troops in peacetime to a limited, but yet to be specified, number (2:330). Although Martin favored limiting direct taxes, he favored a mechanism, similar to that under the Articles of Confederation, whereby Congress would requisition the states and that only in cases where states failed to comply would it then "devise and pass acts directing the mode, and authorizing the collection of the same" (2:359).

Martin opposed congressional superintendence over state militia. He argued both that states would never concede this power and that, if they did so, "the militia would be less attended to by the Genl. than by the State Governments" (2:387). Martin and Carroll also introduced a motion preventing Congress from using its power over commerce to favor ports of some states over those of others (2:417). On August 29, Martin introduced a motion to require two-thirds majorities of Congress to enact commercial regulations (2:449).

When the convention was debating a provision on August 29 whereby new states could not be admitted into the Union without the consent of those already present, Martin said that this would "alarm" the landlocked states. He feared that the provision could be used to deny independence to Vermont, trying to establish a separate identity from Massachusetts, or Frankland (meaning Franklin), the current state of Tennessee, which was attempting to secure its independence from North Carolina (2:455). He reiterated this argument the following day and used it as a launching pad to reiterate the value of state sovereignty. Directing his argument toward the nationalistic James Wilson, Martin observed: "In the beginning, when the rights of the small States were in question, they were phantoms, ideal beings. Now when the Great States were to be affected, political Societies were of a sacred nature" (2:464). Somewhat injudiciously, Martin matched a threat by Gouverneur Morris that large states would leave the Union if they were split without their consent with a threat that small states would leave if the Constitution forced them to guarantee existing large state boundaries (2:464). Martin unsuccessfully offered a motion providing for the admission of new states within their existing territories, but Morris's motion, providing for both state and national consent, succeeded in passing instead.

Presidency

On July 19, at a time when the convention was still anticipating that Congress would choose the president, Martin moved to reinstate a provision making a president ineligible for reelection (2:52 and 2:58). He reintroduced this opposition on July 24 (2:101) and followed by proposing that the president serve for an 11-year term (2:102). On August 27, Martin introduced a motion requiring that the president should not be able to issue reprieves or pardons until after individuals have been convicted, but he withdrew the motion after Pennsylvania's James Wilson indicated that it might sometimes be necessary to issue pardons beforehand, as in cases where this was necessary to get the names of accomplices (2:426).

Judiciary

On June 20, Martin expressed his view that extending the national judiciary into the states would prove to be "ineffectual, and would be viewed with a jealousy inconsistent with its usefulness" (1:341). Arguing on July 17 against the congressional negative of state laws, Martin indicated that he thought the new government could depend on state courts since they "would not consider as valid any law contravening the Authority of the Union, and which the legislature would wish to be negatived" (2:27).

Martin appears to have been partly responsible for the introduction of the Supremacy Clause in the New Jersey Plan, but the version he introduced was apparently designed to see that state judges would still enforce state constitutions and bills of rights (albeit not state laws) in cases where they conflicted with the national constitution (See Clarkson and Jett 1970, 114–15; Farrand 1966, 2:29). Martin may also have regarded judicial enforcement as an alternative to Madison's proposed congressional negative of state legislation (see Kauffman 2008, p. 53). Seeking to rely on state, rather than on federal courts, Martin argued that lower federal tribunals "will create jealousies & oppositions in the State tribunals, with the jurisdiction of which they will interfere" (2:45–46).

Martin favored vesting the Senate, rather than the president, with the power to appoint federal judges. He argued that "Being taken from all the States it wd. be best informed of characters & most capable of making a fit choice" (2:41).

Martin strongly opposed associating judges with the executive in a Council of Revision. In the process of expressing his opposition, however, he indicated that not only did he doubt that judges had understanding superior to other public officials, but also that he anticipated that judges would, in their judicial capacity, exercise the power to declare laws to be unconstitutional:

> A knowledge of mankind, and of Legislative affairs cannot be presumed to belong in a higher degree to the Judges than to the Legislature. And as to the Constitutionality of laws, that point will come before the Judges in their proper official character. In this character they have a negative on the laws. Join them with the Executive in the Revision and they will have a double negative. (2:76)

Martin further observed that judges would lose the confidence of the public "if they are employed in the task of remonstrating agst. popular measures of the Legislature," and he wondered how many judges would serve on such a council (2:77).

On August 20, Martin proposed that individuals convicted of treason could be convicted not only on the testimony of two witnesses but also "on confession in open court" (2:349–50). Interestingly, Martin later defended Aaron Burr against prosecution for treason during the Jefferson administration. On August 30, Martin failed to get a motion adopted that would have the U.S. Supreme Court decide on all claims respecting the governing of U.S. territory or property (2:466); delegates thought that the Constitution already offered protection in regard to such matters.

Slavery

On August 21, Martin, who was himself a slave owner, proposed allowing the taxation of slaves. He made three arguments: two were practical, and one was based on morality. He observed that the Three-fifths Clause would give states an incentive to import slaves and that "slaves weakened one part of the Union which the other parts were bound to protect" (2:364). He also observed, however, that "it was inconsistent with the principles of the revolution and dishonorable to the American character to have such a feature in the Constitution" (2:364). Perhaps with a view to how earlier service on the committee to adjust state representation had moderated his views, the next day the convention placed Martin on the committee to adjust the issue of slave trade and navigation.

Bill of Rights

In presenting his reasons for opposing the Constitution to the Maryland legislature, Martin said that he had opposed suspension of the writ of habeas corpus and the presence of standing armies, but Madison's notes do not record any of his comments on the subject (such notes would not, of course, reflect Martin's individual votes within his state delegation on such issues). Martin offered a rather novel, albeit not unconvincing, explanation as to why he had not supported a committee to propose such a bill:

> A very few days before I left the Convention, I shewed to an honorable member sitting by me a proposition, which I then had in my hand, couched in the following words; "Resolved that a committee be appointed to prepare and report a bill of rights, to be prefixed to the proposed Constitution," and I then would instantly have moved for the appointment of a committee for that purpose, if he would have agreed to second the motion, to do which he hesitated, not as I understand from any objection to the measure, but from a conviction in his own mind that the motion would be in vain. (quoted by Clarkson and Jett 1970, 133, citing the *Maryland Journal*, 21 March 1788, 391).

Martin had apparently left the convention by September 12 (Clarkson and Jett 1970, 133–34), when the states voted ten to zero against George Mason's proposal for a committee to draft a bill of rights (2:588).

Interestingly, Martin suggested to the Maryland legislature that he opposed the provision prohibiting religious oaths:

> there were some members so unfashionable as to think, that a belief of the existence of a Deity, and of a state of future rewards and punishments would be some security for the good conduct of our rulers, and that, in a Christian country, it would be at least decent to hold out some distinction between the professors of Christianity and downright infidelity or paganism. (3:227)

As he presented his view to the state legislature, Luther's critique does not seem to recognize that an oath specifying adherence to Christianity would also have excluded adherents of Judaism (presumably lumped in with proponents of "infidelity or paganism") from national public office.

Ratification

Martin opposed allowing state conventions to ratify the Constitution (1:341). He reiterated this opposition on August 31:

> He argued the danger of commotions from a resort to the people & to first principles in which the Governments might be on one side & the people on the other. He was apprehensive of no such consequences however in Maryland, whether the Legislature or the people should be appealed to. Both of them would be generally against the Constitution. (2:476).

Martin followed these observations by proposing, along with Daniel Carroll, who together with Martin carried Maryland as the only state favoring this mechanism, that all the states should have to ratify the Constitution before it when into effect (2:477). He soon thereafter observed that he did not believe the states would ratify the Constitution "unless hurried into it by surprise" (2:478).

Life after the Convention

Shortly after arriving back in Maryland, Martin delivered his extensive criticism of the Constitutional Convention and its work in what the Maryland legislature later printed as *The Genuine Information*. This was in turn reprinted in 1838, along with notes by Robert Yates, as the *Secret Proceedings and Debates of the Convention*. Martin almost always interpreted the convention proceedings with a jaundiced eye as a conspiracy by those who favored the powers of the large states and of the national government. He was especially critical of the convention's secrecy and was concerned about what he considered the undue erosion of state power. Still, his analysis is quite useful in confirming a number of particulars that scholars know about the convention from other sources. and in filling in some details that would not otherwise be known.

In 1801, the *Baltimore American* quoted Martin as saying that "from the moment the constitution of the United States was adopted by the requisite number of states until this time, my conduct has been perfectly uniform: from that moment I ceased my opposition to the constitution" (quoted in Kauffman 2008, 133). Although Martin never accepted a position in the new national government, he did establish himself as one of the greatest attorneys of his day, arguing such cases as *Fletcher v. Peck* (1810), involving the sale by Georgia of its western lands; defending his longtime friend (and one-time fellow Antifederalist) Samuel Chase in an impeachment trial sanctioned by Thomas Jefferson and conducted in 1804 by the House of Representatives; defending Aaron Burr in a trial for treason (also pursued by Jefferson) in Richmond, Virginia in 1807; and serving as one of the attorneys unsuccessfully arguing that Maryland could tax the national bank in *McCulloch v. Maryland* (1819). Ironically, Jefferson (whom he often opposed) described the man who was such a defender of state's rights at the Constitutional Convention as a "Federalist bulldog." He continued to have a reputation for drinking, on one occasion apparently tipping his hat to a stray cow that he found wandering the streets of Baltimore (Kauffman 2008, 127).

Stricken by a stroke in 1819, the Maryland bar passed a resolution assessing each member of the bar $5 for his support. Aaron Burr subsequently took Martin into his house where he died on July 10, 1826, just days after the deaths of Thomas Jefferson and John Adams. Martin was buried in the cemetery of St. John's Trinity Church in Manhattan.

Further Reading

Biswell, Christian, and Brannon P. Denning, 2001. "Luther Martin." In *Great American Lawyers*, edited by John R. Vile, 2:498–504. Santa Barbara: ABC-CLIO.

Bradford, M. E. 1994. *Founding Fathers: Brief Lives of the Framers of the United States Constitution*. 2nd ed. Lawrence: University Press of Kansas.

Clarkson, Paul S., and R. Samuel Jett. 1970. *Luther Martin of Maryland*. Baltimore, MD: Johns Hopkins Press.

Farrand, Max, ed. 1966. *The Records of the Federal Convention of 1787*. 4 vols. New Haven, CT: Yale University Press.

Kauffman, Bill. 2008. *Forgotten Founder, Drunken Prophet: The Life of Luther Martin*. Wilmington, Delaware, ISI Books.

Reynolds, William L., II. 1987. "Luther Martin, Maryland, and the Constitution." *Maryland Law Review* 47 (Fall): 291–321.

Secret Proceedings and Debates of the Convention Assembled at Philadelphia, in the Year 1787, For the Purpose of Forming the Constitution of the United States of America. 1838. Cincinnati: Alston Mygatt.

GEORGE MASON (1725–1792)
VIRGINIA

A Virginia planter, George Mason was born on December 11, 1725 to George Mason III and Ann Thomas Mason, a fourth-generation Virginian, who had amassed a plantation of over 5,000 acres and 300 slaves. George's father drowned in 1735. George, who was educated by private tutors, was strongly influenced both by his mother and by an uncle, John Mercer of Marborough, an attorney with an impressive library. Although he was a planter rather than an attorney, Mason was chosen as a justice of the Fairfax County Court in 1749, was soon after elected a vestryman, and married Ann Eilbeck from across the Potomac in Maryland. The couple worked from 1744 to 1758 on Gunston Hall, an impressive brick Georgian-style plantation in Virginia that is now open to the public. Ann died in 1773, leaving her husband with nine children; he married Sarah Brent in 1780, when he was fifty-four and she was fifty.

Mason served in the Virginia House of Burgesses from 1758 to 1761. However, Mason was a private man who appeared to accept public office more from a sense of public duty than from a feeling of personal enjoyment. Adverse to compromise, he once stated that "I would not forfeit the approbation of my own mind for the approbation of any man, or all the men upon earth" (Henriques,1989, 191). Mason has been described as having "a sturdy frame and brown hair, hazel eyes, and bushy eyebrows" (Meister 1987, 174). Gout frequently served as a rationale for dodging such service and seems to have endowed Mason with a somewhat dyspeptic personality.

Mason participated little in public affairs in the 1760s and early 1770s, but in July 1774 he did help draft the Fairfax Resolves, which articulated the colonial position of no taxation without representation. He was subsequently elected to the Virginia Convention where he was the chief author of the Virginia Declaration of Rights, which influenced subsequent declarations (including the Declaration of Independence) throughout the colonies. In 1777 he was appointed to a commission charged with rewriting the laws of Virginia. In 1785 he participated in the Mt. Vernon Conference that served as one of the stepping stones to the Constitutional Convention (Bradford 1994, 148–56), but the governor apparently did not notify him in time of his selection to the Annapolis Convention for him to attend. Mason's trip of approximately 120 miles to Philadelphia to attend the Constitutional Convention was the longest that he made during his life. He did, however, have a long-running interest in the Ohio Company, and helped defend its claims to western lands.

At the Convention

George Mason was one of only three delegates who attended the Constitutional Convention from start to finish and yet still refused to sign the document. The fact that Mason attended the entire session, and that he began on a hopeful note, indicates that he probably did not anticipate being one of three dissenters. Thus, writing to his son on June 1, Mason observed:

> I have the pleasure to find in the convention, many men of fine republican principles. America has certainly, upon this occasion, drawn forth her first characters; there are upon this Convention many gentlemen of the most respectable abilities, and so far as I can discover, of the purest intentions. (Farrand 1966, 3:32).

Given such a hopeful start and a dramatic declaration more than a month into Convention deliberations that "he would bury his bones in this city rather than expose his Country to the Consequences of a dissolution of the Convention without any thing being done" (1:533), it seems almost tragic that Mason did not sign the Constitution. As late as August 10 Mason had indicated "He thought the Constitution as now moulded was founded on sound principles, and was disposed to put into it extensive powers" (2:252). Twenty-one days later, however, he declared "that he would sooner chop off his right hand than put it to the Constitution as it now stands" (2:479), and indicated that if the document were not amended, he would favor calling yet another convention.

Although he began the convention with hope, he left fearing that the Constitution created there would embody aristocracy and/or lead to anarchy. He was also concerned about the omission of a Bill of Rights and subsequently went on to oppose the convention in his home state, beginning a rift with his longtime neighbor and friend, George Washington. The fact that Mason remained at the convention rather than leaving early, however, undoubtedly contributed to changes that made the document more palatable to Antifederalists than it would otherwise have been.

Mason was present for the first day of convention proceedings on May 25. On the next day of convention business, May 28, Mason went on record, seconding a motion by Rufus King of Massachusetts, as opposing recording convention votes under individual names. He had two reasons—first, he feared that this would make it more difficult for delegates to change their mind, and second, he feared that a record of such votes might later "furnish handles to the adversaries of the Result of the Meeting" (1:10). The latter argument clearly reveals that Mason hoped to be able to support the convention's work.

As a Virginian, it is likely that Mason knew about, and may have had a part in shaping, the Virginia Plan, which Edmund Randolph introduced on May 29 and which scholars generally attribute to James Madison. On May 30, Mason said that he believed the Articles of Confederation was deficient in being unable to act against "delinquent States." Like Madison, he believed the solution was to grant a new government power to act directly on individuals (1:34). On July 18, Mason supported the congressional guarantee of republican government in the states by observing, "If the Genl Govt. should have no right to suppress rebellions agst. particular States, it will be in a bad situation indeed. As Rebellions agst. itself originate in & agst. individual States, it must remain a passive Spectator of its own subversion" (2:47).

On June 20, Mason compared the Virginia and New Jersey Plans and came down strongly in favor of the former. Indicating that both plans called for increasing the power of Congress, Mason did not think it likely that the people would entrust such powers to a unicameral body. He believed the people were attached both to the principle of republicanism and to bicameralism (1:339). He further observed that the New Jersey Plan might require military coercion, whereas the Virginia Plan would give Congress power to act on individual citizens. Mason's voice may have had particular effect, as he favored the Virginia Plan as a way of preserving, rather than of abolishing, state government: "he never would agree to abolish the State Govts. or render them absolutely insignificant. They were as necessary as the Genl. Govt. and he would be equally careful to preserve them. He was aware of the difficulty of drawing the line between them, but hoped it was not insurmountable" (1:340).

Congress

Mason favored the election of members of the House of Representatives by the people—even to the extent of discounting slaves in the apportionment of state representation (1:581). As one who would later express reservations about the Senate, it is telling that Mason referred on May 31 to the House as "the grand depository of the democratic principle of the Govt.," as "our House of Commons" (1:48). Admitting that "we had been too democratic," he seemed more concerned that "we sd. incautiously run into the opposite extreme" (1:49). He portrayed the House as a body that would represent "the rights of every class of people" (1:49). Noting that the posterity of the rich would someday be scattered among the lower classes, he argued that "Every selfish motive therefore, every family attachment, ought to recommend such a system of policy as would provide no less carefully for the rights—and happiness of the lowest than of the highest orders of Citizens" (1:49). Mason repeated this view on June 21 (1:359). On July 10, he indicated that he favored a House of more than 65 members both so that its members would have "all the necessary information relative to various local interests" and so that they would "possess the necessary confidence of the people" (1:569).

Mason favored biennial elections for the House of Representatives, but the reason he gave for biennial as opposed to annual elections was quite practical. He believed that annual elections would advantage the middle states, which would be more likely to be able to get and keep their representatives in a centrally located capital (1:362). Mason favored a minimum age of twenty-five for members of the House, arguing that individuals old enough to vote (twenty-one) were not yet mature enough to make laws (1:375). Mason was among the delegates who favored disqualifying members of Congress for other offices for a year after they left Congress. Indeed, he referred to this mechanism, designed to prevent corruption, as "a corner stone in the fabric" (1:376). Mason thought that Madison's emoluments clause—limiting ineligibility only to offices created during a legislator's tenure—was "but a partial remedy for the evil" (1:387). Mason also believed that the Constitution should specify that Congress must meet at least once a year, and he anticipated that it would have "inquisitorial" as well as law-making powers (2:199).

Although he conceived of Congress, especially the House, as a mirror of the people, Mason was concerned about demagoguery. He accordingly proposed on July 26 that members of Congress should have to own a certain amount of landed property. He was particularly concerned that individuals with "unsettled accounts" would use their congressional offices to advance their own personal interests (2:121). Similarly, Mason did not believe that the House should have a veto on treaties (2:197).

Mason, who favored a six-year term, appears to have believed that the Senate would represent a different class of people than the House of Representatives. He accordingly favored property qualification for senators (1:428). Although Mason favored a large House, he opposed a motion providing for three senators from each state as both too expensive and as creating a body that was too numerous (2:94). Mason believed that under the new system, "the Senate did not represent the *people*, but the *States* in their political character" (2:273). It was thus appropriate that "the pursestrings should be in the hands of the Representatives of the people" (2:274). Mason seemed consistent in his fear of the Senate, reenforcing his view that it should not have the power to originate money bills by observing in an almost paranoid tone that it "could already sell the whole Country by means of Treaties" (2:297).

Mason was a member of the five-person committee appointed on July 2 to bridge the gap between the large states and the small states on representation in Congress. On July 5, Mason expressed his willingness to accept the Great Compromise, providing for states to be represented by population in the U.S. House of Representatives and equally in the U.S. Senate. On the next day, he indicated that "He was a friend to proportional representation in both branches; but supposed that some points must be yielded for the sake of accommodation" (1:544). Mason favored that part of the Connecticut Compromise limiting the origination of money bills to the House of Representatives. His reasoning showed a continuing suspicion of the Senate. He argued that, should senators "have the power of giving away the peoples money, they might soon forget the Source from whence they received it. We might soon have an aristocracy" (1:544; also see 2:233). On August 9, Mason said that he would withdraw his support for the Connecticut Compromise unless it continued to exclude the Senate from the origination of money bills (2:234).

Some members of the convention were willing to allow the House of Representatives to decide how and when to apportion itself, but Mason thought it was essential to provide a fixed rule. His observations indicate that he was among those who feared that individuals would generally be unwilling to part with power:

> From the nature of man we may be sure, that those who have power in their hands will not give it up while they can retain it. On the Contrary we know they will always when they can rather increase it. (1:578)

Like many other southerners, Mason anticipated that the South would grow more quickly than other parts of the nation, and he feared that, without mandatory reapportionment, the North would hold onto its power. Reminding fellow delegates of opposition in some eastern states to admitting western states on an equality with those in the East (a principle that Mason, and most other southern delegates who spoke at the convention on the subject, thought to be essential), Mason tied the interests of the South and West together (1:578–79). Indeed, on July 11, Mason announced that he could not vote for the Constitution unless it provided for continuing adjustments to representation in the House (1:578).

Mason favored a seven-year (rather than a three-year) residency for members of the House of Representatives. He observed that he "was for opening a wide door for emigrants; but did not chuse to let foreigners and adventurers make laws for us & govern us" (2:216). Similarly, Mason favored a residency requirement for members of the Senate, especially in light of its relatively few members (2:218). Were it not for the contributions that foreigners had made during the revolution, Mason indicated that he would have favored a qualification of native birth for members of the Senate (2:235; also see 2:271).

Mason thought that it was essential to have at least a majority of Congress in order to constitute a quorum. He was especially concerned that states at the periphery of the nation might find their interests ignored if members of the central states could vote for measures by less than such a majority (2:251–52). In such a case, the nation might be "governed by a Juncto" (2:252). Mason favored a provision requiring a two-thirds vote of Congress to expel a member (2:254), and he thought it essential for Congress to publish its proceedings (2:260). Mason unsuccessfully pushed for a requirement, favored mostly by fellow southerners, prohibiting Congress from enacting navigation acts prior to 1808 without the consent of two-thirds majorities (2:631). Mason was a member of the Committee on Commercial Discrimination appointed on August 25, which proposed that Congress should not have power to favor one port over another.

Because he did not believe it was possible to foresee all contingencies, Mason was willing to allow the Congress to have the power to emit, or issue, paper money (2:309). He did not believe the nation could have won the Revolutionary War without such power. Mason objected to providing that Congress "shall" pay the debts as being too strong and possibly impossible to honor (2:412–13). He served on the Committee on State Debts and Militia that the convention appointed on August 18, which recommended that Congress would have the power to assume state debts without being obligated to do so. Mason opposed the contracts clause on the basis that its wording was too restrictive (2:440).

Mason was among those who favored allowing Congress, rather than the president, to appoint the secretary of the treasury: "if [the money belonged to the] people, the legislature representing the people ought to appoint the keepers of it" (2:315). Mason also supported the provision entrusting Congress with the power to "declare" rather than to "make" war (2:319).

Mason feared large standing peacetime armies. Believing that the states "will never concur in any one system, if the displining of the Militia be left in their hands," he favored granting this power to Congress (2:326), while allowing the states to appoint officers for the militia (2:330). He did not think it would be prudent to prevent the government from ever diverting funds from public creditors to other purposes, but thought that it might be wise to put a limit on the time for which individual taxes were levied" (2:327). Mason twice pushed unsuccessfully for the congressional power to enact sumptuary laws, believing that "No Government can be maintained unless the manners be made consonant to it" (2:344; also see 2:606).

Mason favored strict construction of congressional powers. When James Wilson observed that Congress would have the power to create "mercantile monopolies" as part of its power to regulate commerce, Mason not only expressed opposition to such monopolies but also indicated that he did not think Congress would have the power to create them (2:616).

Nation's Capital

Consistent with his fear of aristocratic tendencies, Mason was quite concerned that members of Congress might develop interests separate from those of their constituents. He accordingly moved that the nation's capital should not be located in the capital of an existing state. He believed this would result in disputes over jurisdiction between the two governments and lend "a provincial tincture to ye Natl. deliberations" (2:127). Perhaps Mason also hoped that a new capital might be located, as it eventually was, on the Potomac River, near his home.

Presidency

Like many other proponents of the Virginia Plan, Mason initially favored a seven-year executive term, with the executive being ineligible so as not to lead to possible intrigue with the legislative branch (1:68). He expressed similar concerns about providing a way of making the president accountable without making it overly dependent on the legislature—"a violation of the fundamental principle of good Government" (1:86).

Although he professed on June 1 to favor the proposal by Pennsylvania's James Wilson for direct election of the president, Mason thought it was impractical (1:69). On July 17, he argued that "it would be as unnatural to refer the choice of a proper character for chief Magistrate to the people, as it would, to refer a trail of colours to a blind man" (2:31). Mason did not denigrate the capacities of the common people, however, but their knowledge of individuals who would seek the presidential office. As he explained, "The extent of the Country renders it impossible that the people can have the requisite capacity to judge of the respective pretensions of the Candidates" (2:31). Mason also shared Elbridge Gerry's fear that popular election "would throw the appointment into the hands of the Cincinnati, a Society for the members of which he had a great respect; but which he never wished to have a preponderating influence in the Govt." (2:119).

At a time when Congress was slated to elect the president for six-year terms, Mason supported a resolution that would allow the president to serve only six of every twelve years (2:112). He believed this would prevent executive/legislative intrigue when sitting presidents were seeking reappointment. He also thought it was essential that "the great officers of State, and particularly the Executive should at fixed periods return to that mass from which they were at first taken, in order that they may feel & respect those right & interests [of the people]" (2:119–20). He later supported a single seven-year term (2:120).

Perhaps with a view to the colonial experience under Britain's King George III, Mason was suspicious of executive power. On June 4, he expressed concern over the possibility that the convention would create an "elective" monarchy (1:101). Opposing an absolute executive veto of congressional legislation, he observed that it would be better "to enable the Executive to suspend offensive laws, till they shall be coolly revised, and the objections to them overruled by a greater majority than was required in the first instance" (1:102). On July 17, Mason opposed a motion for presidents to serve "during good behavior." He argued that this "was a softer name only for an Executive for life" and "that the next would be an easy step to hereditary Monarchy" (2:35). Mason favored a mechanism for impeachment as an assurance that no one, including the president, would be above the law (2:65). He appears to have been responsible for substituting the words "other high crimes & misdemeanors" for "maladministration" (2:550). Ma-

son added the words "giving them aid and comfort" to the definition of treason (2:349), and he also favored allowing Congress to override presidential
vetoes by two-thirds rather than by three-fourths majorities (2:586).

Mason, who had apparently missed the vote settling on a single executive (see 1:101), was particularly hesitant to give broad powers to a single
individual. He later advocated an "Executive in three persons" [although
this may be merely coincidental, the formula sounds much like those used
to describe the Christian view of the Trinity] (1:111), with one representing each of the three major regions—North, Middle, and South—of the
nation (1:113). Acknowledging that a single executive was known for "the
secrecy, the dispatch, the vigor and energy which the government will
derive from it," he attributed such praise to "monarchical writers" and suggested that advocates of republican government relied instead on "the love,
the affection, the attachment of the citizens to their laws, to their freedom,
and to their country" (1:112).

Fellow delegate James Madison had favored a Council of Revision
blending the executive and the judiciary. Mason appears to have favored
this council as opposed to one combining the president and members of
his cabinet. One reason that Mason advanced for a plural presidency was
to give it greater weight in such a body (1:111–12). He emphasized the
need to keep the power of the purse and the power of the sword in separate
hands (1:139–40). He thought that allying members of the judiciary with the
executive would "give a confidence to the Executive, which he would not
otherwise have, and without which the Revisionary power would be of little
avail" (2:74). He further thought that combining the executive and judicial
powers would "discourage demagogues" from attempting to pass unjust
legislation (2:78). He saw nothing inappropriate about allowing judges to
review the justice, as well as the constitutionality, of legislation (2:78).

When the convention devised the electoral college, Mason observed
that it had helped remove "the danger of cabal and corruption." However,
he feared an early version of the plan on the basis that 19 out of 20 times,
it would leave presidential selection in the Senate, which he considered "an
improper body for the purpose" (2:500; also see 2:512). On September 5,
Mason observed that "He would prefer the Government of Prussia to one
which will put all power into the hands of seven or eight men, and fix an
Aristocracy worse than absolute monarchy" (2:515). Mason helped persuade
fellow delegates to move the power of selection from the Senate to the
House of Representatives (2:527).

Mason was not pleased with the institution of the vice presidency. He indicated that he thought it was "an encroachment on the rights of the Senate; and that it mixed too much the Legislative & Executive, which as well as the Judiciary departments, ought to be kept as separate as possible" (2:537). He suggested establishing a Privy Council as a substitute. Like the plural presidency he had suggested earlier, this council would have representatives from each of the three major sections of the United States (two from each). One reason he favored such a council was his belief that it "would prevent the constant sitting of the Senate which he thought dangerous, as well as keep the departments separate & distinct" (2:537; also see 2:541–42).

Judiciary

In discussing the presidential nomination of judges, Mason argued that the mode of judicial selection should depend in part on the impeachment mechanism. He did not think it would be appropriate for the president to select judges if they in turn would sit in judgment on his impeachment. He also feared that executives would favor individuals from their own state (2:42). Mason continued to oppose executive appointments of judges (presumably favoring appointment by Congress) even after this power was tempered by a power of confirmation in the Senate (2:83). His opposition may have stemmed from his continuing concerns about the aristocratic nature of this body.

Mason anticipated, and apparently favored, the exercise of judicial review—the power of courts to declare laws to be unconstitutional. Indeed, he was willing to give the judges even greater powers. In defending a Council of Revision that would ally the judges with the executive, he observed:

> They could declare an unconstitutional law void. But with regard to every law however unjust oppressive or pernicious, which did not come plainly under this description, they would be under the necessity as Judges to give it a free course. He wished the further use to be made of the Judges, of giving aid in preventing every improper law. Their aid will be the more valuable as they are in the habit and practice of considering laws in their true principles, and in all their consequences. (2:78)

Mason believed that it would be necessary to have a system of lower federal courts, rather than simply relying on state courts that were in place (2:46). He may have changed his mind on this point, or he may have opposed the subsequent delineation of federal judicial jurisdiction. In either event, at the end of the convention Mason charged: "The Judiciary of the United States is so constructed and extended, as to absorb and destroy the judiciaries of the several states; thereby rendering law as tedious, intricate and expensive, and justice as unattainable, by a great part of the community, as in England, and enabling the rich to oppress and ruin the poor" (2:638).

States' Rights

Although he thought the national government under the Articles of Confederation was deficient, Mason favored states' rights. On June 7, he spoke out in favor of state legislative selection of senators. He observed that:

> whatever power may be necessary for the Natl. Govt. a certain portion must necessarily be left in the States. It is impossible for one power to pervade the extreme parts of the U.S. so as to carry equal justice to them. The State Legislatures also ought to have some means of defending themselves agst encroachment of the Natl. Govt. (1:155)

Similarly, on August 20, in supporting a provision allowing punishment for treasons against individual states, Mason observed, "The United States will have a qualified sovereignty only. The individual States will retain a part of the Sovereignty" (2:347). Mason derisively referred on August 21 to those who favored "reducing the States to mere corporations," and opposed congressional taxation of exports on the basis that it might allow a majority of states to oppress the minority (2:362–63). Mason had reservations about granting Congress power to void state legislation. Thus, on August 23, he questioned: "Are all laws whatever to be brought up? Is no road nor bridge to be established without the Sanction of the General Legislature? Is this to sit constantly in order to receive & revise State Laws?" (2:390).

Although he was outvoted on both issues, Mason thought that states should have the right to declare embargoes and to level export taxes (2:440–41). Mason's support for two-thirds majorities in Congress to regulate commerce stemmed from his fear, undoubtedly stimulated by the Jay-Gardoqui Negotiations over rights to navigate the Mississippi River, that Congress could work against certain regional interests:

> If the Govt. is to be lasting, it must be founded in the confidence & affections of the people, and must be so constructed as to obtain these. The *Majority* will be governed by their interests. The Southern States are

the *minority* in both Houses. Is it to be expected that they will deliver themselves bound hand & foot to the Eastern States, and enable them to exclaim, in the words of Cromwell on a certain occasion—"the lord hath delivered them into our hands." (2:451)

On June 12, however, Mason supported Madison's motion that members of Congress be paid out of the national treasury. He observed that otherwise different states would provide for different salaries, and some might be so parsimonious as to leave the office open not to those "who were most fit to be chosen, but who were most willing to serve" (1:216).

Mason opposed limiting voting to freeholders on the basis that some states had already gone further than that. He thought that "A power to alter the qualifications would be a dangerous power in the hands of the Legislature" (2:202). Although he favored property qualifications for running for certain offices, Mason argued that "every person of full age and who can give evidence of a common Interest with the community shd. be an Elector" (2:207).

Amendment

When some members questioned the need for a constitutional amending process, Mason observed both that such a process was needed and that it would be wise to provide a means of amending the Constitution in cases where the legislature did not assent:

> The plan now to be formed will certainly be defective, as the Confederation has been found on trial to be. Amendments therefore will be necessary, and it will be better to provide for them in an easy, regular and Constitutional way than to trust to chance and violence. It would be improper to require the consent of the Natl. Legislature, because they may abuse their power, and refuse their consent on that very account. (1:203)

Two days before the Constitution was signed, Mason was influential in providing for the still unused mechanism whereby two-thirds of the states can petition Congress to call a constitutional convention. This proposal stemmed from Mason's fear that Congress might otherwise fail to propose such amendments on its own:

> As the proposing of amendments is in both the modes to depend, in the first immediately, and in the second, ultimately, on Congress, no amendments of

the proper kind would ever be obtained by the people, if the Government should become oppressive, as he verily believed would be the case. (2:629)

Slavery

Mason owned many slaves, but he had a strong moralistic streak that was evident in a speech of August 22. Although Mason's speech reflected racist assumptions of the superiority of white settlers over blacks, no one at the convention but Gouverneur Morris offered a more extensive criticism of slavery:

> Slavery discourages arts & manufactures. The poor despise labor when performed by slaves. They prevent the immigration of Whites, who really enrich & strengthen a Country. They produce the most pernicious effect on manners. Every master of slaves is born a petty tyrant. They bring the judgment of heaven on a Country. As nations can not be rewarded or punished in the next world they must be in this. By an inevitable chain of causes & effects providence punishes national sins, by national calamities. (2:370)

Tragically, although he influenced the decision to allow minimal taxation of them (2:417), Mason did not succeed in efforts to ban the continuing importation of slaves. Mason also unsuccessfully opposed the three-fifths compromise as "unjust" (2:581).

Bill of Rights

Mason, the primary author of the Virginia Declaration of Rights, is probably best known at the Constitutional Convention for his support of a bill of rights. There is some irony in this since, as observed above, Mason was often fearful of constitutional provisions, like the ex post facto clause or a ban on standing armies in peacetime, that seemed too restrictive. Moreover, Mason actually offered his proposal for a bill of rights *in opposition to* a provision suggested by North Carolina's Hugh Williamson and Elbridge Gerry of Massachusetts to provide for trial by juries in civil cases. Mason appears to have favored an earlier kind of bill of rights announcing general principles phrased as "oughts" that would not necessarily be enforceable, as are current provisions, in courts of law. In supporting a response by Massachusett's Nathaniel Gorham to Williamson's and Gerry's proposal for trial by jury, which stated "It is not possible to discriminate equity cases from those in which juries are proper" (2:587), Mason thus observed:

A general principle laid down on this and some other points would be sufficient. He wished the plan had been prefaced with a Bill of Rights, & would second a Motion if made for the purpose—It would give great quiet to the people; and with the aid of the State declarations, a bill might be prepared in a few hours. (2:588)

When Connecticut's Roger Sherman observed that the new Constitution would not repeal state bills, Mason argued, "The Laws of the U.S. are to be paramount to State Bills of Rights" (2:588). Absent a showing of areas where the new Constitution would restrict rights beyond those that the states were already offering, this response does not appear altogether responsive to Sherman's observation.

Mason cast further light on what his proposed bill of rights might have looked like on September 14. Noting that he did not believe it would be possible absolutely to prohibit standing armies in time of peace, he nonetheless moved to add words before the section giving Congress power to organize, arm, and discipline the militia: "And that the liberties of the people may be better secured against the danger of standing armies in time of peace" (2:617). Similarly, he renewed his plea to strike the clause prohibiting ex post facto laws on the basis that it "was not sufficiently clear that the prohibition meant by this phrase was limited to cases of a criminal nature—and no Legislature ever did or can altogether avoid them in Civil cases" (2:617). This suggests again that Mason preferred a bill of rights with fairly general declarations that the people could cherish, rather than with precisely worded provisions that courts could enforce.

Still, Mason later praised the Bill of Rights that James Madison introduced in Congress. Mason observed, "I have received much Satisfaction from the Amendments to the federal Constitution, which have lately passed the House of Representatives (quoted in Senese 1989, 80). Perhaps he never saw anything as quite perfect, since after observing that he hoped the Senate would adopt the rights, he added, "With two or three further Amendments . . . I cou'd cheerfully put my Hand & Heart to the new Government" (80).

Ratification

Even before he seems to have decided to oppose the document, Mason thought that it was essential for the people to ratify the document through conventions rather than by existing state legislatures. He thought that legislators did not have sufficient authority to do so, and he feared that if legislatures were allowed to ratify, then they would also claim the power to dissolve (2:88). Mason believed the new Constitution should go into effect when ratified by nine or more states (2:477).

In expressing his reservations about signing the Constitution, Mason advocated yet another convention. Without such a further meeting, he could not sign:

> Mason . . . followed Mr. Randolph in animadversions on the dangerous power and structure of the Government, concluding that it would either end in monarchy, or a tyrannical aristocracy; which, he was in doubt. But one or other, he was sure. This Constitution had been formed without the knowledge of idea of the people. A second Convention will know more of the sense of the people, and be able to provide a system more consonant to it. It was improper to say to the people, take this or nothing. As the Constitution now stands, he could neither give it his support or vote in Virginia; and he could not sign here what he could not support there. With the expedient of another Convention as proposed, he could sign. (2:632)

Mason expressed his objections to the new Constitution to his colleagues and later circulated his observations in pamphlet form. His objections included many familiar themes and some new ones. These consisted of the Constitution's lack of a declaration of rights; its failure to secure the protection of the common law; concern that the House of Representatives was not large enough to provide adequate representation; fear of the Senate's power to alter money bills; apprehension of the powers vested in the Senate; fear that the federal judiciary would swallow that of the states; concern about the failure to have a constitutional council; concern over the office of the vice presidency; concern over the president's unrestricted power to grant pardons for treason; fear that declaring treaties to be the supreme law of the land gave too much power to the Senate; apprehension that Congress would abuse its power to enact navigation acts without supermajorities; fears of monopolies in trade and commerce; concern over the absence of provisions providing for freedom of the press, trials in civil cases, and opposing standing armies in peacetime; concern over stripping states from taxing exports; opposition to the ex post facto clause; fear that the new government had created an aristocracy that could lead to tyranny; and displeasure over the failure to prohibit slave importation (2:637–40).

Mason sometimes let his pique get the better of him. In contrast to the many accolades that others bestowed on the delegates who attended the Constitutional Convention, Mason was quoted by one contemporary as having claimed that "the Convention, generally speaking, was made up of block-heads from the northern, coxcombs [dandies] from the southern, & office-seekers from the middle states" (quoted in Tarter 1991, 284).

Life after the Convention

Mason, who had been chosen from a neighboring county, and Patrick Henry were the leading opponents of the new Constitution at the Virginia ratifying convention. Mason warmed somewhat to the Constitution after the adoption of the Bill of Rights. Although he never healed the rift with his neighbor, George Washington, or accepted any public offices under the new government, he frequently entertained members of the new government as they passed through his neighborhood, and he established himself back in good graces with James Madison and Thomas Jefferson (Leibiger 1993, 467).

Mason died on October 7, 1792 at his beloved Gunston Hall where he was buried on the grounds. An expanding public university in northern Virginia is named in Mason's honor, and the National Park Service dedicated a memorial to him in Washington, DC in April 2002.

Further Reading

Bradford, M. E. 1994. *Founding Fathers: Brief Lives of the Framers of the United States Constitution*. 2nd ed. Lawrence, Kansas: University Press of Kansas.

Conley, Patrick T., and John P. Kaminski, eds. 1992. *The Bill of Rights and the States: The Colonial and Revolutionary Origins of American Liberties*. Madison, Wisconsin: Madison House.

Dreisbach, Daniel L. 2011. "George Mason." In *America's Forgotten Founders*, 2nd ed., edited by Gary L. Gregg II and Mark David Hall, 39–54. Wilmington, DE: Intercollegiate Studies Institute.

Farrand, Max, ed. 1966. *The Records of the Federal Convention of 1787*. 4 vols. New Haven, CT: Yale University Press.

Ganter, Herbert Lawrence. 1937. "The Machiavellianism of George Mason." *William and Mary Quarterly*, 3rd Ser., 17 (April): 239–64.

Henri, Florette. 1971. *George Mason of Virginia*. New York: Atheneum.

Henriques, Peter P. 1989. "An Uneven Friendship: The Relationship between George Washington and George Mason." *The Virginia Magazine of History and Biography* 97 (April): 185–204.

Leibiger, Stuart. 1993. "James Madison and Amendments to the Constitution, 1787–1789: 'Parchment Barriers.'" *The Journal of Southern History* 59 (August): 441–68.

Lynch, Jack. 2004. "Mirroring the Mind of Mason." *Colonial Williamsburg* 26 (Spring): 52–55.

Mason, George. 1970. *The Papers of George Mason, 1725–1792*, edited by Robert A. Rutland. 3 vols. Chapel Hill: University of North Carolina Press.

Meister, Charles W. 1987. *The Founding Fathers*. Jefferson, NC: McFarland & Company, Inc.

Miller, Helen H. 1975. *George Mason: Gentleman Revolutionary*. Chapel Hill: University of North Carolina Press.

Rutland, Robert A. 1961. *George Mason: Reluctant Statesman*. New York: Rinehart and Winston, Inc.

———. 1981. "George Mason: The Revolutionist as Conservative." In *The American Founding: Politics, Statesmanship, and the Constitution*, edited by Robert A. Rossum and Gary L. McDowell. Port Washington, NY: Kennikat Press.

Senese, Donald J., ed. 1989. *George Mason and the Legacy of Constitutional Liberty: An Examination of The Influence of George Mason on the American Bill of Rights*. Fairfax County, VA: Fairfax County Historical Commission.

Tarter, Brent. 1991. "George Mason and the Conservation of Liberty." *The Virginia Magazine of History and Biography* 99 (July): 279–304.

JAMES MCCLURG (1746–1823)
VIRGINIA

Born in Elizabeth City County, Virginia in 1746 to the family of a physician, James McClurg entered the same occupation. After receiving his undergraduate education at the College of William and Mary, McClurg went to the University of Edinburgh where he wrote a respected thesis and received his medical degree. McClurg served for a time during the revolution as a surgeon for the militia and was appointed as a professor of anatomy and medicine at William and Mary, where he may or may not have taught. McClurg was serving as a member of the Virginia Council of State when he was recruited to attend the Constitutional Convention after Patrick Henry and Richard Henry Lee had declined their appointments. He was married to Elizabeth Seldon.

At the Convention

McClurg was present on the opening day of business on May 25, but he left sometime toward the end of July or early August and did not return. A man of relatively little governmental experience compared to other convention delegates and one whose silence within his delegation was matched only by that of George Washington and John Blair, McClurg must have felt especially daunted by his better known Virginia colleagues. Writing to James Madison after he had left the convention in August of 1787, McClurg observed:

> If I thought that my return could contribute in the smallest degree to it's Improvement, nothing should keep me away. But as I know that the talents, knowledge, & well-establish'd character, of our present delegates, have justly inspired this country with the most entire confidence in their determination; & that my vote could only *operate* to produce a division, & so destroy the vote of the State, I think that my attendance now would certainly be useless, perhaps injurious. (Hutson 1987, 205)

It is interesting to speculate as to how McClurg thought his presence might have split the Virginia delegation. His scanty comments certainly offer little with which to work. He does not appear to have openly spoken until July 17, at which time he proposed substituting service by the president during "good behavior" rather than for a term of seven years. His motives may, however, have been mixed as his resolution directly followed a convention decision to make the president, whom the convention was still expecting Congress to select, re-eligible for election. In this context, it is likely that McClurg was in fact (perhaps at the instigation of Madison) attempting to point to the difficulty that such dependency on the legislature might bring— better to be chosen for life than to remain subject to the legislature (Farrand 1966, 2:33). Referring specifically to the president's re-eligibility, McClurg said that the president "was put into a situation that would keep him dependent for ever on the Legislature; and he conceived the independence of the Executive to be equally essential with that of the Judiciary department" (2:33). Further responding to objections that his proposal would lead to monarchy, McClurg stated that he:

> Was not so much afraid of the shadow of monarchy as to be unwilling to approach it; nor so wedded to Republican Govt. as not to be sensible of the tyrannies that had been & may be exercised under that form. It was an

essential object with him to make the Executive independent of the Legislature; and the only mode left for effecting it, after the vote destroying his
ineligibility a second time, was to appoint him during good behavior. (2:36)

The next day, McClurg seconded a motion by fellow Virginian James
Madison, who had helped recruit him for the convention, providing that
Congress should guarantee states against both domestic and foreign violence (2:48). He did not take part in resulting debates as to whether states
needed such help or whether states needed congressional guarantees against
domestic violence.

Madison recorded that McClurg, like him, favored both a single executive (1:97) and a congressional veto of state laws (1:168). Indeed, in a letter
he sent to Madison after he had left the convention, McClurg observed:

> I have still some hope that I shall hear from you of ye reinstatement of ye
> Negative—as it is the only mean [sic] by which the several Legislatures
> can be restrain'd from disturbing ye order & harmony of ye whole, & ye
> Governmt. Render'd properly national, & one. (3:73).

Perhaps even more bravely, McClurg had asked on July 20 whether consideration should be given "to determine on the means by which the Executive
is to carry the laws into effect, and to resist combinations agst. them." He
asked, "Is he to have a military force for the purpose, or to have the command of the Militia, the only existing force that can be applied to that use?"
(2:69). Although Pennsylvania's James Wilson agreed that delegates should
address this issue, it is not clear that anyone did so. If McClurg were in fact
pointing to a specific issue, it is possible, but by no means certain, that Mc-
Clurg considered that the question he had posed would, if he were present,
have further divided the Virginia delegation.

Life after the Convention

President Washington appointed McClurg, a man of considerable financial means, as one of the original directors of the U.S. Bank, but passed
him up in favor of Edmund Randolph for secretary of state. After his
service at the convention, McClurg served again on the Virginia Council
of State and three times as mayor of Richmond, but fellow citizens continued to regard him chiefly for his expertise as a medical doctor. He died in
Richmond, Virginia on July 9, 1823 and was buried in the cemetery at St.
John's Episcopal Church.

Further Reading

Bradford, M. E. 1994. *Founding Fathers: Brief Lives of the Framers of the United States Constitution.* Lawrence: University Press of Kansas.

Farrand, Max, ed. 1966. *The Records of the Federal Convention of 1787.* 4 vols. New Haven, CT: Yale University Press.

Hutson, James H., ed. 1987. *Supplement to Max Farrand's The Records of the Federal Convention of 1787.* New Haven, CT: Yale University Press.

Tyler, Lyon G. 1911. "The Medical Men of Virginia." *William and Mary College Quarterly Historical Magazine* 19 (January): 145–62.

JAMES MCHENRY (1753–1816)
MARYLAND

James McHenry was born to a merchant family at Ballymena, Ireland in 1753. His parents, who later followed and set up a store in Baltimore, sent him to America in 1771 in hopes that it would improve his health. McHenry appears to have attended the Newark Academy in Delaware and to have studied medicine under Benjamin Rush.

McHenry eagerly volunteered for the Continental Army in 1774 and served as a surgeon for a Pennsylvania battalion. Captured and paroled, he was freed from this restriction and rejoined the army, serving as a surgeon at Valley Forge and subsequently serving as a secretary to George Washington, Alexander Hamilton, and the Marquis de Lafayette. He was present at the battle of Yorktown. McHenry served from 1781 to 1786 as a member of the Maryland senate and from 1783 to 1785 as a delegate to the Continental Congress. He married Margaret (Peggy) Caldwell (1762–1833) in 1784, and they had four children; they lived at an estate named Fayetteville, after General Lafayette.

At the Convention

McHenry took his seat as a Maryland delegate to the Constitutional Convention on May 28, but upon hearing news that his younger brother was ill, he left the convention on June 1 (Farrand 1966, 1:75). He is next recorded as taking notes of conversations with fellow delegates from Maryland on August 7, the day after fellow delegate John Mercer was seated (2:176). Fortunately, McHenry's notes give us insight into his view of a number of issues that the convention had discussed, and may be combined with what he said throughout the remainder of the convention.

Notes of August 7

These notes indicate that McHenry was strongly opposed to the provision (proposed as part of the Connecticut Compromise) that limited the origination of money bills to the House of Representatives. Whereas debates on the floor of the convention centered on whether this provision would be of any value—with proponents saying that it was a major concession and opponents claiming that it was simply inconsequential—McHenry, and fellow delegate Daniel Carroll, apparently believed that the provision could actually prove dangerous. McHenry observed:

> That lodging in the house of representatives the sole right of raising and appropriating money, upon which the Senate had only a negative, gave to that branch an inordinate power in the constitution, which must end in its destruction. That without equal powers they were not an equal check upon each other. (2:211)

McHenry's notes indicate that he and Carroll also opposed the provision requiring a two-thirds vote of Congress for navigation acts, although his explanation appears to point in the other direction—with concern being expressed that trade might otherwise be controlled by four states (2:211). McHenry and Carroll were greatly concerned over the congressional power to levy taxes and to regulate interstate commerce: "We almost shuddered at the fate of the commerce of Maryland should we be unable to make any change in this extraordinary power" (2:211).

McHenry feared possible ratification of the new Constitution by nine states was contrary to the commission that Maryland had given to him and other commissioners, as well as to the unanimity requirement for constitutional amendments under the Articles of Confederation. He observed:

> If we relinquished any of the rights or powers of our government to the U.S. of America, we could no otherwise agree to that relinquishment than in the mode our constitution prescribed for making changes or alterations in it. (2:212)

According to McHenry's account, as he and Carroll talked, Daniel of St. Thomas Jenifer entered the room. Although Jenifer agreed that the delegates from Maryland should act "in unison," according to McHenry, he "seemed to have vague ideas of the mischiefs of the system as it stood in the report." McHenry then volunteered his view that the plan being contemplated was too expensive:

> An army and navy was to be raised and supported, expensive courts of ju-dicature to be maintained, and a princely president to be provided—That it was plain that the revenue for these purposes was to be chiefly drawn from commerce. That Maryland in this case would have this resource taken from her, without the expences of her own government being lessened.—That what would be raised from her commerce and by indirect taxation would far exceed the proportion she would be called upon to pay under the pres-ent confederation. (2:212)

John Mercer, who later left without signing the Constitution, then joined the conversation and indicated that he was convinced that the delegates needed to construct a better system than the one proposed (2:212). It would thus appear that McHenry and the rest of the Maryland delegation were leaning against the new Constitution, although it may be significant that Luther Martin, who would be the state's most prominent critic of the Con-stitution, was not reported to be in attendance.

Other Comments

Consistent with his earlier notes, on August 13, McHenry condemned the provision for the origination of money bills as "an extraordinary subterfuge, to get rid of the apparent force of the Constitution" (2:280). On August 21, McHenry seconded a motion by Luther Martin relating to direct taxation. The two wanted to have the states collect such taxes and resort to other means only in cases where states did not meet these requisitions on their own (2:359).

McHenry took a position that seemed to foresee the doctrine of implied powers when on August 21, he suggested that Congress would have the right to declare embargoes under its power to declare war (2:362). On August 22, McHenry joined Elbridge Gerry in supporting a ban on congressional adop-tion of bills of attainder or ex post facto laws (2:375).

On August 25, McHenry and General Pinckney proposed a complicated resolution that would have prohibited Congress from collecting duties or imposts within the states unless the state legislatures should first fail to do so. They also introduced the provision stipulating that all duties, imposts, and excises be uniform throughout the United States (2:418).

McHenry joined Madison on August 27 in supporting a provision that would prohibit any judicial increases during a judge's term of office (2:429).

On August 31, McHenry told the convention, as he had told his fellow delegates privately, that they were under oath to support the mode of ratification that was specified under the Articles of Confederation rather than the method that fellow delegates were proposing (2:476). In discussing the provision preventing vessels entering one state from having to pay duties in another, McHenry offered the view that this restriction would "not shreen a vessel from being obliged to take an officer on board as a security for due entry &c" (2:481).

In notes that he took on September 4, McHenry indicated that it did not appear that the Constitution granted Congress power to erect lighthouses or clean harbors for purposes of navigation. He further indicated that he thought this was a power that should be shared by the states collectively rather than by a single state. He then asked, "Is it proper to declare all the navigable waters or rivers and within the U.S. common high way?" (2:504). Records indicate that McHenry waited until September 15 to introduce a motion prohibiting the government from restraining states from laying duties for the purpose of erecting lighthouses or clearing harbors (2:625).

On September 8, McHenry moved that the president should be given power to convene either house of Congress (2:553).

Signing the Constitution

We know more about McHenry's thoughts on the basis of his own notes than from the notes of others, and the occasion of the signing of the Constitution on September 17 proved to be no exception. Although Madison does not record that he said anything, McHenry wrote that "Being opposed to many parts of the system I made a remark why I signed it and mean to support it" (2:649). He does not say whether he made this remark publicly or privately, but he continues, not with a single remark but with three arguments. The first appears to summarize the more frequently cited speech that Benjamin Franklin made on the same occasion but indicates that McHenry's own objections appear to have been even stronger. McHenry thus observed:

> I distrust my own judgment, especially as it is opposite to the opinions of a majority of gentlemen whose abilities and patriotism are of the first cast;

and as I have had already frequent occasions to be convinced that I have not always judged right. (2:649)

McHenry's second argument was that if future alterations were needed, the Constitution had an amending process to accommodate them. Finally, he thought the existing situation called for some expedient:

> Comparing the inconveniences and the evils which we labor under and may experience from the present confederation, and the little good we can expect from it—with the possible evils and probable benefits and advantages promised us by the new system, I am clear that I ought to give it all the support in my power. (2:650)

Life after the Convention

McHenry delivered a speech on November 29, 1787 to the Maryland constitutional convention in which he made similar arguments. After summarizing what he remembered of the Philadelphia convention's deliberations, he stated that:

> Many parts of this proposed Constitution were warmly opposed, other parts it was found impossible to reconcile to the Clashing Interest of different States—I myself could not approve of it throughout, but I saw no prospect of getting a better—the whole however is the result of that spirit of Amity which directed the wishes of all for the general good, and where those sentiments govern it will meet I trust, [with?] a Kind and Cordial reception.

McHenry served in the Maryland ratifying convention and was elected back to the Maryland legislature. He served under presidents George Washington and John Adams as secretary of war, but was eventually fired by Adams who believed that McHenry, whose inefficiencies as an administrator others had noticed, was also taking too much direction from Alexander Hamilton, who was undermining the Adams administration. McHenry retired at the age of forty-six. He was a Mason and he served in retirement as president of the Baltimore Bible Society. The Baltimore fort, whose defense against the British during the War of 1812 is recorded in the *Star Spangled Banner*, is named after McHenry. He died in Maryland on May 3, 1816, and was interred in the Westminster Presbyterian Churchyard in Baltimore.

Further Reading

Browne, Gary L. 1988. "Federalism in Baltimore." *Maryland Historical Magazine* 83 (Spring): 50–57.

Farrand, Max, ed. 1966. *The Records of the Federal Convention of 1787*. 4 vols. New Haven, CT: Yale University Press.

McHenry, James. "James McHenry's Speech to Maryland State House of Delegates." Teaching American History.org. http://teachingamericanhistory.org/library/index.asp?document=2326. Accessed 9/9/2012.

Steiner, Bernard C. 1907. *Life and Correspondence of James McHenry*. Cleveland: Burrows Brothers. Reprinted 2007, Whitefish, MT: Dessington Publishing.

Whitney, David C. 1974. *Founders of Freedom in America: Lives of the Men Who Signed the Constitution of the United States and So Helped to Establish the United States of America*. Chicago: J. G. Ferguson Publishing Company.

John Mercer (1759–1821)
Maryland

John Mercer was born in Strafford County, Virginia on May 17, 1759 to a landholding family, Colonel John Mercer (a lawyer) and his wife Ann Roy Mercer. Mercer was first educated at home and then at the College of William and Mary before studying law under Thomas Jefferson, who was then governor, but whose trust he never appears to have earned. Mercer served in a number of positions during the Revolutionary War and participated in the battle of Yorktown.

After serving in the Virginia House of Delegates and the Continental Congress, where he strongly opposed the expansion of federal powers, Mercer married Sophia Sprigg (1766–1812) in 1785, and they had three children. He moved to her estate in Maryland, where the legislature selected him as a delegate to the Constitutional Convention. A man of resources who later lost money in western land speculation, Mercer was nonetheless concerned about the dangers of aristocracy. At twenty-eight, Mercer was the second youngest member of the convention.

At the Convention

Mercer was not seated at the Constitutional Convention until August 6, and he appears to have left after August 17, but he was an active participant during his attendance. Notes that fellow delegate James McHenry took on August 7 give the first glimpse into Mercer's thoughts. According to McHenry, Mercer indicated that he would go along with attempts by his fellow delegates to change the proposals but that:

> He would wish it to be understood however, that he did not like the system, that it was weak—That he would produce a better one since the convention has undertaken to go radically to work, that perhaps he would not be supported by any one, but if he was not, he would go with the stream. (Farrand 1966, 2:212)

Mercer somewhat clarified these words when, during a discussion of the provision for electing members of the House of Representatives on August 8, he was recorded as expressing "his dislike of the whole plan, and his opinion that it never could succeed" (2:215).

Congress

Mercer's first specific criticism, which he raised on August 8, centered on the direct election of members of the House. He said that he "did not object so much to an election by the people at large" as long as they had "some guidance." According to Madison's notes, Mercer "hinted" that state legislatures should first nominate the candidates (2:216).

On that same day Mercer joined Virginia's James Madison in criticizing a proposal requiring that members of the House of Representatives reside for seven years in the state that elected them. He observed that this requirement would be greater than that under the existing Articles of Confederation and said that "It would interweave local prejudices & State distinctions in the very Constitution which is meant to cure them" (2:217). He further pointed to disputes that had arisen in Maryland as to the meaning of "residence" (2:217), and feared that the substitution of the term "inhabitant" might exclude individuals who returned from a state after an absence but were clearly conversant with its affairs (2:218). On August 13, Mercer seconded a motion that Pennsylvania's Gouverneur Morris advanced to limit the application of the residency requirement to any individuals who were citizens at the time the Constitution was adopted (2:270). He went on to characterize a disability on existing citizens as "a breach of faith" (2:272).

Like fellow delegate James McHenry, Mercer believed that the provision allowing the House of Representatives to originate money bills was both weighty and dangerous. Indeed, he thought that it would give the House of Representatives such an advantage "that it rendered the equality of votes in the Senate ideal & of no consequence" (2:224).

On August 10, Mercer indicated that he thought a congressional quorum should not require a majority. He feared that setting the quorum too high would enable some members to "secede" and thus prevent business from being done. He favored allowing Congress to set its own quorum, as the British Parliament did (2: 251). He subsequently seconded a motion, offered by Gouverneur Morris, that set an initial quorum at half of the membership (33 of 65 in the House and 14 of 28 in the Senate) but allowed Congress to decide whether this number needed to be raised as membership grew (2:252–53).

When, on August 11, Madison offered a motion allowing the Senate to keep certain of its proceedings secret, Mercer objected that this implied that it would conduct something other than legislative business, which he did not believe would be appropriate (2:259). That same day, Mercer said it was necessary to specify where the first Congress would meet because he did not think the two houses would be able to come to an agreement on this point (2:262).

On August 16, Mercer strongly opposed the idea of granting Congress the power to tax exports. He argued that "Such taxes were impolitic, as encouraging the raising of articles not meant for exportation" (2:307). He further observed that, under the Articles, the states had the right to tax both imports and exports and that they should only be expected to sacrifice one of these powers. As to arguments that the South was most in need of naval protection, Mercer somewhat defensively argued: "Were it not for promoting the carrying trade of the Northn States, the Southn States could let their trade go into foreign bottoms, where it would not need our protection" (2:308). He ended by commenting that by taxing its own tobacco, Virginia had given an advantage to that grown in Maryland.

Although generally wary of increased national powers, Mercer seconded a motion by Elbridge Gerry of Massachusetts granting Congress power over "post-roads" as well as post offices (2:308). Professing himself to be "a friend of paper money," Mercer did not believe it was consistent with the current temper of the people. Consistent with his own view of its propriety, however, he did not want to prohibit Congress from issuing it all together. In observations consistent with his view of influence that is explained in the following section, Mercer observed:

> It was impolitic also to excite the opposition of all those who were friends of paper money. The people of property would be sure to be on the side of the plan, and it was impolitic to purchase their further attachment with the loss of the oppose class of Citizens. (2:309)

Fear of Aristocracy and Support of Executive Authority

One of Mercer's most notable speeches occurred on August 14 during discussion of whether members of Congress should be eligible during their terms for other offices. Proponents of this restriction believed that it would lead to an aristocracy. Although he was concerned about aristocracy, Mercer apparently believed that the president needed to be able to make appointments from Congress (he appears to have been contemplating something like the present-day parliamentary system where members of the cabinet are drawn from parliament) in order to resist aristocratic tendencies.

Mercer began his speech by observing that "It is a first principle of political science, that whenever the rights of property are secured, an aristocracy will grow out of it" (2:284). He believed this was true even in "elective governments" since "the rulers being few can & will draw emoluments for themselves from the many" (2:284). He believed that state governments had already become aristocratic and that "public measures are calculated for the benefit of the Governors, not of the people" (2:284). He further believed that the people were dissatisfied with this system. What was the solution? Much as Alexander Hamilton of New York had argued elsewhere at the convention, Mercer believed that governments depended on "force or influence" (2:284). However, he thought that the convention had not entrusted the executive with sufficient amounts of either. Mercer seems to have envisioned a mixed government like that in England, where the executive would weigh in against aristocrats on the side of the people. To this end, he suggested that the president needed to be buttressed by a council, consisting of members of Congress:

> The Legislature must & will be composed of wealth & abilities, and the people will be governed by a Junto. The Executive ought to have a Council,

being members of both Houses. Without such an influence, the war will
be between the aristocracy & the people. He wished it to be between the
Aristocracy & the Executive. Nothing else can protect the people agst.
those speculating Legislatures which are now plundering them throughout
the U. States. (2:284–85)

This appears to be the incubus of an alternate plan that Mercer had told
McHenry he had in view.

Mercer further elaborated on his views later in the day when the
convention was discussing whether congressional disabilities should be
extended to state appointments. Mercer feared that if congressmen were so
ineligible, the most influential men would stay home "& prefer appointments
within their respective States" (2:289). Mercer recognized that a parchment
would have limited influence over the lives of men:

It is a great mistake to suppose that the paper we are to propose will govern
the U. States? It is The men whom it will bring into the Govent. and interest in maintaining it that is to govern them. The paper will only mark out
the mode & the form—Men are the substance and must do the business.
All Govt. must be by force or influence. (2:289)

Absent granting the government substantial force, Mercer thought that it
was imperative to grant it influence.

Mercer's concern for influence appears to have been reflected in his
opposition to allowing the Senate to ratify treaties. He argued on August 15
that this power belonged, as in Britain, to the executive. However, he further
observed that "Treaties would not be final so as to alter the laws of the land,
till ratified by legislative authority" (2:297).

Mercer's attempt to bolster executive powers was also reflected in his
approval of the idea of a Council of Revision granting the executive and
members of the judiciary power, subject to override by congressional supermajorities, to invalidate laws. In expressing this view, however, Mercer
opposed the idea that members of the judiciary should have the power to invalidate laws because they believed them to be unconstitutional, the power
that is today known as judicial review:

It is an axiom that the Judiciary ought to be separate from the Legislative:
but equally so that it ought to be independent of that department. The
true policy of the axiom is that legislative usurpation and oppression may

be obviated. He disapproved of the Doctrine that the Judges as expositors of the Constitution should have authority to declare a law void. He thought laws ought to be made well and cautiously made, and then to be uncontroulable. (2:298).

On August 17, Mercer seconded a motion allowing the national treasurer to be appointed by the president like other officers rather than being appointed by Congress (2:315).

Mercer's last recorded act at the convention was on August 17, a month before the document was signed. On this occasion, he seconded a motion by fellow delegate Luther Martin opposing striking a provision that would require a state legislature to request help before Congress could introduce troops into a state to suppress rebellion there (2:317). Mercer was clearly concerned about preserving state sovereignty.

Life after the Convention

It is not surprising to find that Mercer opposed adoption of the Constitution and worked against it at the Maryland state ratifying convention. Although he did not succeed in blocking Maryland's ratification, his insistence on accompanying ratification with proposed amendments appears to have influenced subsequent deliberations in neighboring Virginia. Antifederalists subsequently elected him to the Maryland state legislature and to the U.S. House of Representatives where he aligned with the Democratic-Republicans in opposition to Alexander Hamilton's fiscal policies. Mercer was twice elected as governor, in which capacity he helped to eliminate property qualifications for voting. He died seeking medical attention in Philadelphia on August 30, 1821 and was initially buried in a vault at St. Peters Church in that city before being moved to his estate in Cedar Park, Maryland.

Further Reading

Bradford, M. E. 1994. *Founding Fathers: Brief Lives of the Framers of the United States Constitution*. Lawrence: University Press of Kansas.

Farrand, Max, ed. 1966. *The Records of the Federal Convention of 1787*. 4 vols. New Haven, CT: Yale University Press.

Stiverson, Gregory A. 1988. "Maryland's Antifederalists and the Perfection of the U.S. Constitution." *Maryland Historical Magazine* 83: 18–35.

THOMAS MIFFLIN (1744–1800)
PENNSYLVANIA

Thomas Mifflin was born in Philadelphia, Pennsylvania in 1744. A member of a merchant Quaker family (the denomination later expelled him because of his military activity), he attended the College of Philadelphia (today's University of Pennsylvania), traveled abroad for a year, and served as a clerk before becoming a merchant. He was chosen to serve in the Pennsylvania colonial legislature and joined the patriot side. Elected to serve in the Continental Congress, Mifflin became an aide-de-camp to George Washington, who appointed him as quartermaster-general of the Continental Army, a position in which Mifflin does not appear to have been very effective. With his political connections, Congress promoted Mifflin to the rank of major general, in which capacity he was linked to General Thomas Conway in the "Conway Cabal," in what was alleged to have been an attempt to displace Washington from his position as commander in chief of the colonial forces. In 1767 Mifflin married a cousin, Sarah (Sally) Morris; their daughter Emily married the son of a signer of the Declaration of Independence.

Retaining popularity within his home state where he portrayed himself as a man of the common people (he later supported the Democratic-Republican Party), Mifflin represented Pennsylvania in Congress under the Articles of Confederation. He served for about a year as its president.

At the Convention

Thomas Mifflin was seated at the Constitutional Convention on May 28. Because of his previous military service, fellow delegates addressed him as "general." He is believed to have attended almost every session of the convention, and he signed the document, but he is not recorded as giving a single speech. In light of accusations that would later be raised against Mifflin, it may be ironic, but it is otherwise difficult to draw much from his only recorded action, that of seconding a motion on August 14 by Charles Pinckney proposing that members of Congress who accepted offices would have to resign their seats (Farrand 1966, 2:284).

Life after the Convention

As he aged, Mifflin's reputation for patriotism and for public speaking was replaced by suspicions that he was too free with, and too little accountable for, public money and that he was unable to control an alcohol problem. After the convention ended, Mifflin succeeded Benjamin Franklin as president of the state and went on to head the convention that wrote a new state constitution. He served for nine years as Pennsylvania's governor, was then elected to the state legislature, and died almost penniless on January 20, 1800 in Lancaster, where he was buried in the cemetery of the Trinity Lutheran Church.

Despite the offices that he held after serving at the convention, it would appear that Mifflin's service in Philadelphia came at a time when his powers were already ebbing. Clearly capable of great things, he evidenced little such greatness at the convention. Not only did Mifflin not speak there, but he is not reported as having served on any committees. Fortunately, he was a member of a brilliant delegation that was well able to represent the interests of both the state and the nation without counting on him to make more extensive contributions.

Further Reading

Farrand, Max, ed. 1966. *The Records of the Federal Convention of 1787*. 4 vols. New Haven, CT: Yale University Press.

Rossman, Kenneth R. 1952. *Thomas Mifflin and the Politics of the American Revolution*. Chapel Hill: University of North Carolina Press.

Whitney, David C. 1974. *Founders of Freedom in America: Lives of the Men Who Signed the Constitution of the United States and So Helped to Establish the United States of America*. Chicago: J. G. Ferguson Publishing Company.

GOUVERNEUR MORRIS (1752–1816)
PENNSYLVANIA

Gouverneur Morris was one of the most vocal and influential members of the Constitutional Convention. A committed nationalist, he is perhaps best known as the member of the Committee of Style and Arrangement who gave the final polish to the Constitution. In this capacity, he authored its preamble, which substituted the words, "We the People," for a list of states and eloquently described the goals of the new document.

Morris was born on January 31, 1752 on the family estate at Morrisania, New York, the current site of the Bronx. Morris's father died when his son was only ten. Initially educated by tutors, Morris attended King's College (today's Columbia University), studied law under William Smith, and was admitted to the New York bar by age twenty. Morris served as a member of New York's provincial congress from 1775 to 1777, during which time he also served in the New York constitutional convention where he appears to have been influential. As a delegate from New York to the Continental Congress, Morris signed the Articles of Confederation. He also inspected the dismal situation that George Washington and his men faced at Valley Forge and served as an associate to Robert Morris (not related), the superintendent of finance. At the end of his term, he remained in Philadelphia.

At the Convention

Morris was thirty-five years old when he served as one of Pennsylvania's delegates to the Constitutional Convention. He was notable for his florid speech and a wooden leg that had resulted from a carriage accident in 1780. He had also largely lost the use of an arm from a burn in another accident, but standing over six feet tall, his physical disabilities did nothing to detract from his reputation as a lady's man. Morris missed the month of June attending to business in New York. Dubbed the "eternal speaker" (Bush 2011, 58), he was still recorded as giving the most speeches at the convention and playing an important part in the rest of the convention's proceedings.

Early Comments

On May 30, the day after Edmund Randolph presented the Virginia Plan and the convention met as a Committee of the Whole, Morris seconded the resolutions constituting the Virginia Plan as well as a substitute motion that Randolph introduced proposing that a merely "federal" union "will not accomplish the objects proposed by the articles of confederation" (Farrand 1966, 1:30). That same day, Morris explained that a federal government was "a mere compact resting on the good faith of the parties" whereas a national government had "a *compleat* and compulsive operation" (1:34).

Morris seconded Madison's proposal that an "equitable ratio of representation" should be established in Congress (1:36). When delegates from Delaware indicated that they might not be able to continue if the convention considered changing the states' equal representation in Congress, Morris observed that this change in representation was "so fundamental an article in a national Govt. that it could not be dispensed with" (1:37). Maryland's James McHenry reported that Morris believed the convention would either accept "a supreme government now" or a "despot" in 20 years (1:43). Morris left the convention on May 31 to deal with his estate at Morrisania and to take care of business for Robert Morris, and he did not return until July 2.

Congress

Senate. Morris did not allow his absence to keep him from withholding his opinions about the convention's seeming impasse over representation in the Senate shortly after he returned. Although he opposed its report, Morris initially favored the appointment of a committee to resolve this issue. He also favored a radically more aristocratic Senate than most of the other delegates were contemplating. Like them, Morris conceived of the Senate's primary role as that of checking the excesses of the House of Representatives. To do this, he thought its members would require "*abilities* and *virtue*" (1:512). Members of the Senate should have a personal interest in checking the democratic excesses of the House. They should have "great personal property" and "an aristocratic spirit" and they should be independent (1:512). Morris believed that this required that they have life tenure. Because he envisioned a Senate that would represent wealth, Morris did not favor paying its members. Moreover, he favored executive appointment, rather than state or congressional selection.

Morris professed not to care how senators were apportioned: "The members being independt. & for life, may be taken as well from one place as from another" (1:513). He feared that existing proposals were too dependent on the states. The only security against encroachments of the House would be "a select & sagacious body of men, instituted to watch agst. them on all sides" (1:514).

Morris proposed that the members of the Senate should vote per capita, that is, by casting individual votes instead of voting as states (2:94). He initially favored giving each state three senators (2:94). Morris expressed doubts as to whether the Senate should have any role in the making of treaties (2:392). When the convention established that a two-thirds majority of the Senate would be required to approve treaties, however, he did not favor exempting treaties of peace (2:548).

Representation. When the Committee of Eleven proposed on July 5 that representation should be apportioned according to population in the House and equally in the Senate, Morris objected that this plan was too state centered. Morris professed to be attending the convention as "a Representative of America," indeed, as "a Representative of the whole human race" (1:529). Morris thought it best not to worry about public sentiment but to recommend what is "reasonable & right" in the hope that "all who have reasonable minds and sound intentions will embrace it (1:529).

In somewhat intemperate language that seemed to respond to earlier threats of Delaware's Gunning Bedford that small states might seek foreign allies, Morris anticipated that if the large states formed a government on their own, factions would form within the smaller states to join them, and "If persuasion does not unite it, the sword will" (1:530). Repeating that "State attachments, and State importance have been the bane of this Country," Morris said, "We cannot annihilate, but we may perhaps take the teeth out of the serpent" (1:530).

Like Virginia's James Madison, Morris saw little value in the "concession" by the small states prohibiting money bills from originating in the Senate. Openly espousing the Senate's aristocratic function, Morris feared that such a restriction "will take away the responsibility of the 2d branch, the great security for good behavior" (1:45). Morris was still advocating this opinion on August 8 (2:224), and on the following day, accused George Mason of trying to scare the smaller states into continuing support for this provision, lest they lose their right to equal state representation (2:234). Morris may have undercut his argument for the need for both houses to be able to originate money bills when he argued on August 13 that the Senate veto on money bills would give it just as much power as if it had the power to originate such measures (2:276).

Morris said on July 7 that he favored "supporting the dignity and splendor of the American Empire" (1:552). He feared that a Senate overrepresenting the small states would be an obstacle to these objectives and thought that the small states were pressing an unfair advantage:

The small States aware of the necessity of preventing anarchy, and taking advantage of the moment, extorted from the large ones an equality of votes. Standing now on that ground, they demand under the new system greater rights as men, than their fellow Citizens of the large States. The proper answer to them is that this same necessity of which they formerly took advantage does not now exist, and that the large States are at liberty now to consider what is right, rather than what might be expedient. (1:552)

Morris objected that the scheme of representation in the House of Representatives did not include property, which he considered to be "the main object of Society" (1:533). In a position that evoked strong opposition from many southern delegates, Morris further argued that "the rule of representatives ought to be so fixed as to secure to the Atlantic States a prevalence in the National Councils" (1:533). Morris opposed requiring Congress to reapportion itself on a regular basis, repeating that he feared "the danger of throwing such a preponderancy into the Western Scale" (1:571). He later argued:

The Busy haunts of men not the remote wilderness, was the proper School of political Talents. If the Western people get the power into their hands they will ruin the Atlantic interest. The Back members are always most adverse to the best measures. (1:583)

Morris did not think it possible to stop western migration, but he did not favor throwing "the power into their hands" (2:454). He proposed that the admission of new states should require approval by two-thirds of Congress, but he substituted a motion, to which the convention agreed, that no new states should be formed within existing states without their consent (2:455). He apparently attempted to protect New York's interest with respect to the actions of Vermont (2:463).

Consistent with his view that the legislature should have considerable discretion, Morris did not think the Constitution needed to specify the frequency of congressional meetings (2:198). He did, however, favor establishing a quorum for Congress at 33 for the House and 14 for the Senate (a majority plus one). He feared that if the number were set lower, members might absent themselves in order to prevent such a quorum from being able to conduct business (2:252). Morris thought that the Constitution could entrust the power of expelling members to such a majority

(2:254). He also believed that members of Congress should be allowed to accept other offices, so long as they had to vacate their seats in order to take them (2:286). He was especially concerned about the possibility that the Constitution could be so worded as to prevent the appointment of the individual most qualified to conduct a war simply because he was a congressman (2:289). Morris believed that the national government should pay the salaries of members of Congress. In light of his prior comments on representation of the western states, one might question his newly professed concern about putting an "unequal burden" on such states, as well as the realism of his belief that "there could be no reason to fear that they would overpay themselves" (2:290).

On July 6, the convention appointed Morris to the committee to come up with a plan of apportionment for the House. He chaired the Committee of Five, which suggested an initial allocation of 56 members, apportioned according to what they believed would be one representative for every 40,000 inhabitants, albeit not altogether disregarding wealth, apparently a reference to slaves (1:560; also see 1:567). Morris further served on the Committee of Eleven, which reconsidered this number and arrived at the new number of 65. He was concerned that these proposals raised conflicts between the North and South. It is not altogether clear that he poured oil on this water when he observed that while southern states might supply more of the money for future wars, the northern states would spill more of their blood (1:567).

Slavery. Morris initially opposed the Three-fifths Clause for representation of slaves. He thought that counting slaves as partial persons conflicted with the convention's earlier agreement to consider them as wealth (1:582). Morris also observed that the people of Pennsylvania would "revolt at the idea of being put on a footing with slaves. They would reject any plan that was to have such an effect" (1:583).

On July 11, Morris observed that "he could never agree to give such encouragement to the slave trade as would be given by allowing them a representation for their Negroes, and he did not believe those States would ever confederate on terms that would deprive them of that trade" (1:588). The next day, proposing to leave future allocations of representation to Congress, Morris observed that he did not think that either side could accept the existing compromise: "it is in vain for the Eastern States to insist on what the Southn States will never agree to. It is equally vain for the latter to require what the other States can never admit; and he verily belived the people of Pena. will never agree to a representation of Negroes" (1:593).

Morris continued to oppose the three-fifths compromise on July 13: "If Negroes were to be viewed as inhabitants, and the revision was to proceed on the principle of numbers of inhabts. they ought to be added in their entire number, and not in the proportion of 3/5. If as property, the word wealth was right, and striking it out would produce the very inconsistency which it was meant to get rid of" (1:604).

Morris argued that the main distinction in the nation was between the "maritime" and the "interior & landed interest" (1:604). In a speech that seemed to anticipate Abraham Lincoln's idea that the Union could not survive half slave and half free (without Lincoln's emphasis on the necessity of union), Morris argued, that if North and South were so radically different, perhaps they should consider separating:

> If it be real, instead of attempting to blend incompatible things, let us at once take a friendly leave of each other. There can be no end of demands for security if every particular interest is to be entitled to it. (1:604)

Harkening back to a dispute in the Continental Congress, Morris further feared that the southern states would join with new states in the West to war against Spain for the control of the Mississippi River (1:604).

Morris returned to the theme of slavery on August 8 by suggesting that the term "free" be inserted before a provision designed to allocate one representative for every 40,000 inhabitants. Morris gave perhaps the convention's strongest speech against slavery. As on other occasions, his candor appears to have overtaken his sensitivity to the interest of fellow delegates:

> He never would concur in upholding domestic slavery. It was a nefarious institution—It was the curse of heaven on the States where it prevailed. Compare the free regions of the Middle States, where a rich & noble cultivation marks the prosperity & happiness of the people, with the misery & poverty which overspread the barren wastes of VA. Maryd. & the other States having slaves. (2:221)

Morris further observed:

> The admission of slaves into the Representation when fairly explained comes to this: that the inhabitant of Georgia and S.C. who goes to the Coast of Africa, and in defiance of the most sacred laws of humanity tears away his fellow creatures from their dearest connections & dam(n)s them to the most cruel bondages, shall have more votes in a Govt. instituted for

the protection of the rights of mankind, than the Citizen of Pa or N. Jersey who views with a laudable horror, so nefarious a practice. (2:222)

Morris proclaimed that "He would sooner submit himself to a tax for paying for all the Negroes in the U. States. than saddle posterity with such a Constitution" (2:223), but he does not appear to have offered a concrete proposal to this effect. Although he later withdrew the motion, Morris proposed listing the two Carolinas and Georgia in the Constitution as the states with permission to continue to import slaves so that it would "be known also that this part of the Constitution was a compliance with those States" (2:415).

Other Matters. Morris thought that it would be wiser to establish requirements for electors than for members of Congress. He was particularly concerned about a proposal that would bar individuals with unsettled accounts from accepting offices. He asked "What will be done with those patriotic Citizens who have lent money, or services or property to their Country, without having been yet able to obtain a liquidation of their claims? Are they to be excluded?" (2:121). Interestingly, he observed that delegates should heed not only the ancient precept not to "be righteous overmuch" by also guard against "being wise over much" (2:122). Morris did not believe it was necessary to prohibit citizens from voting for nonresidents for Congress, since they would rarely elect them (2:217). He favored restricting the vote to freeholders (2:201; also see 2:217). He supported a motion raising the required residency for members of the House of Representatives from three years to seven (2:216). Similarly, he moved to increase the required number of years of citizenship for senators from four to fourteen years (2:235). However, Morris proposed that the citizenship requirement should not affect anyone who was currently a citizen (2:270), although he did not think it necessary to make a similar exception for those then under the age of twenty-five (2:271).

In responding to an emotional appeal by Pennsylvania's James Wilson, an immigrant, for liberality toward immigrants, Morris said that it was important for the delegates to "be governed as much by our reason, and as little by our feelings as possible" (2:237). Ironically, he followed with a highly emotional example of the practice, which he attributed to American Indians, of sharing their wives with guests! Perhaps unintentionally, Morris further called into question his own earlier characterization of himself as a citizen of the world:

As to those philosophical gentlemen, those Citizens of the World, as they called themselves, He owned he did not wish to see any of them in our public

Councils. He would not trust them. The men who can shake off their attachments to their own Country can never love any other. These attachments are the wholesome prejudices which uphold all Governments. (2:238).

Powers. The day after the convention finally settled on the Connecticut Compromise, Morris moved to reconsider the whole issue of representation (2:25). The delegates appear to have politely ignored him. After Connecticut's Roger Sherman proposed that Congress should be prevented from interfering in the internal police affairs of the states, Morris was unsympathetic. In his view, "The internal police, as it would be called & understood by the States ought to be infringed in many cases, as in the case of paper money & other tricks by which Citizens of other States may be affected" (2:26). In a similar vein, Morris favored direct taxation by the national government instead of a system of "quotas & requisitions, which are subversive of the idea of Govt." (2:26). Morris opposed Madison's plan for a negative on state laws, however, "as likely to be terrible to the States, and not necessary, if sufficient Legislative authority should be given to the Genl. Government" (2:27).

Morris might have reflected the view of more timid delegates when, on July 18, he indicated that he would have reservations about the Guarantee Clause if it were to be interpreted so as to provide that Congress would have to guarantee the existing government of Rhode Island. Known for its legislative measures favoring debtors by inflating currency, it was the sole state that did not send delegates to the convention (2:47).

On August 9, Morris supported congressional oversight of congressional elections, fearing that, otherwise, "the States might make false returns and then make no provisions for new elections" (2:241). Morris opposed the restriction, introduced by Southern delegates, prohibiting Congress from taxing exports. He believed that such taxes would constitute "a necessary source of revenue" and indicated that he favored them over direct taxes which might push the people "into Revolts" (2:307). He later favored a provision specifying that taxes on exports would have to go to the benefit of the entire nation. He feared that otherwise the Atlantic states might force the western states into the arms of Great Britain by taxing navigation on the Mississippi River (2:442).

Morris favored granting Congress power to "emit bills on the credit of the U. States"; he reasoned that "If the United States had credit such bills would be unnecessary; if they had not unjust & useless" (2:309). He wanted wide powers to restrict counterfeiting (2:315) and thought that Congress should have power to put down insurrections within states, even without a request from the states. He complained that "We are acting a very strange part. We first form a strong man to protect us, and at the same time wish to tie his hands behind him. The legislature may surely be trusted with such a power to preserve the public tranquility" (2:317). Morris feared that the prohibition of export taxes might be interpreted to prohibit general embargoes that might be needed in time of war (2:360). Morris opposed national sumptuary laws (as proposed by Virginia's George Mason) on the grounds that they "tended to create a landed Nobility, by fixing in the great-landholders and their posterity their present possessions" (2:344). He favored allowing Congress to make regulations to provide for uniform bankruptcy laws (2:489). He opposed a statement in the Constitution disfavoring standing armies for fear that it would set "a dishonorable mark of distinction on the military class of Citizens" (2:617).

Morris was far less attached to state governments than many other delegates. However, he opposed a provision prohibiting states from interfering with private contracts as going too far. Believing both that judges could guard against abuses, he observed that "within the State itself a majority must rule, whatever may be the mischief done among themselves" (2:439). In an ultimate irony, Morris introduced the provision specifying that states could not be deprived of their equal representation in the Senate without their consent (2:631).

Presidency

Morris thought the executive branch was quite important: "Make him too weak: The Legislature will usurp his powers: Make him too strong. He will usurp on the Legislature" (2:105). During the ten-day adjournment of the convention beginning on July 26 to allow the Committee of Detail to do its work, Morris vacationed at Valley Forge with George Washington, whom he idolized, and who Morris anticipated would be the first to occupy the presidency.

When the convention considered a provision for congressional appointment of the presidency, Morris objected. He favored popular election, believing that the people "will never fail to prefer some man of distinguished character, or service; some man, if he might so speak, of continental reputation." By contrast, he believed that legislative selection was likely to be "the work of intrigue, of cabal, and of faction," likened to "the election of a pope by a conclave of cardinals" (2:29). He further believed that legislative selection would lead to undue dependency of the presidency on that body.

After the convention initially settled on July 17 on the selection of the presidency by Congress, Morris seconded a motion by Virginia's James McClurg to strike the provision for a seven-year term and to substitute an appointment "during good behavior" in its place (2:33). He apparently believed that such tenure would obviate the problem of legislative intrigue that he had previously identified. He denied that this was likely to lead to monarchy, professing that the chief obstacle to such government was "to establish such a Repub. Govt. as wd. make the people happy and prevent a desire of change" (2:36). Morris also believed that it was wise to prevent frequent rotation in the presidency as "a change of men is ever followed by a change of measures," and this would contribute to governmental instability (2:112). Moreover, a president who anticipated that he would not be reelected to the presidency would try to keep the door open to the legislature (2:113).

Of all the modes of selecting the president, Morris argued that legislative appointment was the worst. His fear was that it would make the president the "mere creature" of Congress (2:103). Somewhat prophetically, he observed that legislatures typically split into two parties and that such parties would seek to influence presidential selection (2:104).

Morris appears to have been one of the originators of the idea that the president should be chosen by electors chosen by the states (2:404). This institution was largely formulated by the Committee on Postponed Matters that the convention established on August 31, and of which Morris was a member. Although he did not serve as the Committee's chairman, Morris emerged as a primary defender of this proposal on the floor of the convention (2:500; also see 2:512). When Elbridge Gerry objected that the newly created vice president should not preside over the Senate because of the "close intimacy" that would exist between the president and him, Morris bluntly responded that "The vice president then will be the first heir apparent that ever loved his father" (2:537).

When the convention reconsidered presidential re-eligibility to office on July 29, Morris observed that "It has been a maxim in political Science that Republican Government is not adapted to a large extent of Country, because the energy of the Executive Magistracy can not reach the extreme parts of it" (2:52). Noting the wide extent of the United States, Morris portrayed the executive branch as the branch that would have to check Congress. His description sounds a bit like the later arguments that Andrew Jackson and Woodrow Wilson would make on behalf of the presidency:

It is necessary that the Executive Magistrate should be the guardian of the people, even of the lower classes, agst. Legislative tyranny, against the Great & the wealthy who in the course of things will necessarily compose—the Legislative body. . . . The Executive therefore ought to be so constituted as to be the great protector of the Mass of the people. (2:52)

In this same speech, Morris further argued that the president should be vested with the power to make key appointments. Morris opposed the restriction on presidential re-eligibility on the basis that if the "love of fame," which he considered to be "the great spring to noble & illustrious actions" is closed, the executive would be tempted "to make the most of the Short space of time allotted him, to accumulate wealth and provide for his friends" (2:53).

Morris favored popular election as the check on the executive rather than legislative impeachment:

If he is to be the Guardian of the people let him be appointed by the people? If he is to be a check on the Legislature let him not be impeachable. Let him be of short duration, that he may with propriety be re-eligible. (2:53)

When the convention insisted that presidents should be impeachable, Morris pushed to have offenses "enumerated & defined" (2:65). Indeed, he admitted to having changed his mind on the subject, now arguing for such impeachment by observing that "This Magistrate is not the King but the prime-Minister. The people are the King" (2:69). An objection by Morris resulted in a motion by George Mason substituting the words "other high crimes & misdemeanors" for the word "maladministration" (2:550). Morris further supported the view that the Senate would be a more appropriate body to try presidential impeachments than would the smaller Supreme Court (2:551). Curiously (such a measure would appear to undermine independence and give the initiative to those initiating impeachment charges), he also supported a proposal that would have suspended an individual from office until that person could be tried (2:612).

On August 7, Morris seconded a proposal by Delaware's George Read designed to give the president an absolute veto over congressional legislation (2:200), and Morris supported this measure again on August 15 (2:299). He observed: "The most virtuous citizens will often as members of a legislative body concur in measures which afterwards in their private capacity they will be ashamed of. Encroachments on the popular branch of the Government ought to be guarded against" (2:299). He voted late in the convention in favor of a provision that it take three-fourths rather than two-thirds of Congress to override a presidential veto, observing that "The excess rather than the deficiency of laws was to be dreaded" (2:585). When Mason opined that the larger majority might serve as an obstacle to the repeal of bad laws, Morris argued that legal instability was a greater danger (2:586).

Judiciary

Just as he had feared the intrigues that congressional selection of the president might generate, so too Morris feared the intrigues that would be generated if judges were required to sit on impeachment trials (2:42). Morris seconded the proposal, eventually incorporated into the Constitution, by Nathaniel Gorham of Massachusetts that the president should appoint judges with the advice and consent of the Senate (2:44), although he later indicated that he favored vesting absolute appointment power in the president (2:82). Morris strongly opposed senatorial appointment of judges. He believed that it would be "too numerous for the purpose; as subject to cabal; and as devoid of responsibility" (2:389). By contrast, Morris defended the system of presidential appointment and senatorial confirmation: "as the President was to nominate, there would be responsibility, and as the Senate was to concur, there would be security" (2:539).

Morris was the individual who first explained that it would be unfair to appoint judges for life and prevent them from receiving any pay increases during their tenure (2:44). He observed that if new judges received more than those on the bench, the latter might simply resign and seek reappointment (2:430). Similarly, he thought it was inconsistent to say that judges served during good behavior and allow the president to remove them on the application of Congress (2:428). Morris thought that it was essential to have a system of lower federal courts (2:46), and he was willing to allow judges to participate in a Council of Revision, assessing the validity of laws before they went into effect (2:75; also see 2:78). On August 20, Morris renewed the call for a Council of State to consist of the chief justice of the U.S. Supreme Court and of various secretaries of executive departments (2:342–44), which appears to be something of a precursor to the present cabinet. Explaining the action of the Committee on Postponed Matters in not proposing such a council, however, Morris observed that the committee had "judged that the Presidt. by persuading his Council—to concur in his wrong measures, would acquire their protection for them" (2:542).

Location of the Capital

When Virginia's George Mason argued for the establishment of the nation's capital in a city other than one already housing a state government, Morris said that he did not "dislike the idea" but indicated that he feared such a requirement in the Constitution would lead to opposition in Philadelphia and New York City, both of which hoped to be such a site (2:127). Later in the convention, Morris said that it exhibited improper "distrust" to believe that the government would never leave New York (2:261). In a position that stretched, if it did not break, the idea of enumerated powers, Morris argued that the power of the national government over the seat of government would give it power, without further enumeration, to establish a national university (2:616).

Amendment

When the delegates discussed the provision requiring Congress to call a convention for proposing amendments upon the request of Congress, Morris unsuccessfully suggested that "the Legislature should be left at liberty to call a Convention, whenever they please" (2:468). Somewhat ironically, Morris introduced the provision specifying that states could not be deprived of their equal representation in the Senate without their consent (2:631). The delegates subsequently entrenched this provision against constitutional amendment.

Ratification

Morris favored ratification of the Constitution by the people acting in conventions. He did not believe that existing state legislatures had adequate authority to ratify (2:92). When this plan was initially rejected, Morris proposed that "the reference of the plan be made to one general Convention, chosen & authorized by the people to consider, amend, & establish the same" (2:93). This motion died for lack of a second. Morris later proposed that a smaller number of states should be required to ratify the new Constitution if these states were contiguous than if they were not (2:468). On August 31, he proposed striking out the requirement for ratification by conventions in favor of allowing states to ratify the document in a manner of their own choosing (2:475), but he appears to have changed his mind by day's end: "his object was to impress in stronger terms the necessity of calling Conventions in order to prevent enemies to the plan, from giving it the go by" (2:478). His strategy may have been tactical, but he responded to George Mason's call for a second convention by saying that he favored the idea of yet another Convention in the hope that it "will have the firmness to provide a vigorous Government, which we are afraid to do" (2:479).

Morris attempted to word the resolution approving the Constitution so that delegates would simply sign "in witness" to the fact that the states had been unanimous in approving the document rather than as testifying to their own support for it, but this wording was insufficient to persuade Elbridge Gerry of Massachusetts and George Mason and Edmund Randolph of Virginia to sign. On the day that the delegates signed the Constitution, Morris indicated that he had objections, but that, like Benjamin Franklin, he considered the plan adopted to be the best possible that could be attained and that "he should take it with all its faults" (2:645). He said that he was yielding his concerns to the will of the majority and observed: "The moment this plan goes forth all other considerations will be laid aside—and the great question will be, shall there be a national Government or not? and this must take place or a general anarchy will be the alternative" (2:645). In January 1788, in a comment long falsely attributed to Robert Morris, Gouverneur Morris observed that:

> This paper has been the subject of infinite investigation, disputation, and declamation. While some have boasted it as a work from Heaven, others have given it a less righteous origin. I have many reasons to believe that it is a work of plain, honest men, and such, I think, it will appear. Faulty it must be, for what is perfect? But if adopted, experience will, I believe, show that its faults are just the reverse of what they are supposed to be.(3:243)

In 1802, Morris observed that "I not only took it as a man does his wife, for better, for worse, but what few men do with their wives, I took it knowing all its bad qualities" (quoted in Brookhiser 2003, 92).

Life after the Convention

Morris did not participate in the ratification debates and in fact declined an invitation by Alexander Hamilton to contribute to writing *The Federalist Papers*. The year after the Constitution was signed, Morris went to Europe as an agent for Robert Morris. When Washington became president, he appointed Morris as his agent in Great Britain, and he then served from

1792 to 1794 as the American ambassador to France, where he attempted to give aid to the royal family. Morris served as a Federalist senator from the state of New York from 1800 to 1803 and was later chairman of the Erie Canal Commission.

Morris married Ann (Nancy) Cary Randolph (1774–1837) of Virginia on December 25, 1809; their son Gouverneur Morris Jr. became a railroad magnate and a Republican who opposed slavery. Responding to criticism of his choice of mates (Ann had been accused of having had a child by her sister's husband in 1793, whom he, in turn, had been acquitted of murdering), Morris once observed that "if the world were to live with my wife, I should certainly have consulted its taste; but as that happens not to be the case, I thought I might, without offending others, endeavor to suit myself" (quoted in Bush 2011, 62).

Ironically, the great proponent of national unity was one of the leading proponents of the Hartford Convention, which considered northern disunion during the War of 1812, although he was again supporting union by the time of his death on November 6, 1816 in Morrisania. He was buried in the cemetery at St. Ann's Episcopal Church in the Bronx, which Gouverneur Morris Jr. built in honor of his mother, who died on May 28, 1837.

Further Reading

Adams, William Howard. 2003. *Gouverneur Morris: An Independent Life*. New Haven, CT: Yale University Press.

Brookhiser, Richard. 2003. *Gentleman Revolutionary: Gouverneur Morris, The Rake Who Wrote the Constitution*. New York: Free Press.

Bush, John K. 2011. "Gouverneur Morris." In *America's Forgotten Founders*, 2nd ed., edited by Gary L. Gregg II and Mark David Hall, 55–66. Wilmington, DE: Intercollegiate Studies Institute.

Crawford, Alan Pell. 2000. *Unwise Passions: A True Story of a Remarkable Woman— and the First Great Scandal of Eighteenth-Century America*. New York: Simon & Schuster.

Farrand, Max, ed. 1966. *The Records of the Federal Convention of 1787*. 4 vols. New Haven, CT: Yale University Press.

Finkelman, Paul. 1988. "The Pennsylvania Delegation and the Peculiar Institution: The Two Faces of the Keystone State." *The Pennsylvania Magazine of History and Biography* 112 (January): 49–71.

Kirschke, James J. 2005. *Gouverneur Morris: Author, Statesman, and Man of the World*. New York: Thomas Dunne Books.

Miller, Melanie Randolph. 2008. *An Incautious Man: The Life of Gouverneur Morris.* 2nd ed. Wilmington, DE: Intercollegiate Studies Institute.

Morris, Gouverneur. 2012. *To Secure the Blessings of Liberty: Selected Writings of Gouverneur Morris*, edited by J. Jackson Barlow. Indianapolis: Liberty Fund.

Whitney, David D. 1974. *Founders of Freedom in America: Lives of the Men Who Signed the Constitution of the United States and So Helped to Establish the United States of America.* Chicago: J. G. Ferguson Publishing Company, 1974.

Robert Morris (1734–1806)
Pennsylvania

Born on January 31, 1734 in Liverpool, England to an ironmonger who later became a Maryland tobacco agent, Morris came to the United States in 1747 and as a Philadelphia merchant earned a fortune that made him one of the richest men in America. He married Mary (Molly) White (1749–1827) of Maryland in 1769, and they had seven children. A loyal patriot, Morris served as a Pennsylvania representative to the Continental Congress where he signed both the Declaration of Independence and the Articles of Confederation. His greatest service to the nation occurred from 1781 to 1783, when he served as the superintendent of finance, often using his personal credit to obtain supplies for the Continental Army. He also founded the Bank of North America during his term. After resigning as superintendent, Morris resumed his work as a merchant and helped outfit the *Empress of China*, the first ship to go to and from China from the United States. Long a strong nationalist, in 1786 Morris served as a delegate to the Annapolis Convention.

At the Convention

On the convention's opening day of business, Morris nominated George Washington as the president and subsequently escorted him to the presiding chair. Morris also had Washington as a house guest and accompanied him on a number of trips during this period. Madison observed on May 28 that

Gouverneur Morris (no relation), Robert Morris, and other Pennsylvania delegates thought "that the large States should unite in firmly refusing to the small States an equal vote, as unreasonable, and as enabling the small States to negative every good system of Government, which must in the nature of things, be founded on a violation of that equality" (Farrand 1966, 1:11).

Morris did not, however, take an active part in convention deliberations. Perhaps he considered that his own abilities were in the area of finance rather than oratory. On June 25, Morris wrote to his son describing members of the convention as "gentlemen of great abilities . . . many of whom were in the first Congress, and several that were concerned in forming the Articles of Confederation now about to be altered and amended" (3:49). On June 7, he seconded a motion by James Wilson proposing that the people should elect members of the U.S. Senate as well as the House of Representatives (1:151). Similarly, on June 25, he seconded a motion proposing that senators serve "during good behavior" (1:409). On August 13, James Wilson observed that Morris, Fitzsimons, and he were all foreign born (2:269). Morris signed the Constitution on September 17.

Life after the Convention

After he signed the Constitution, Pennsylvania selected Morris as one of its first two senators. He served on a record number of committees and was influential in the negotiations that led to the eventual placement of the nation's capital in the District of Columbia. Heavily engaged in western land speculation, sometimes involving millions of acres, Morris subsequently went bankrupt and was confined for a time in debtor's prison. He died in 1806 in the city he had adopted and was buried, with other Framers, in the yard of Christ Church. In his will, Morris opined:

> I have to express my regret at having lost a very large fortune acquired by honest industry, which I had long hoped and expected to enjoy with my family during my own life and then to distribute amongst those of them that should outlive me. Fate has determined otherwise and we must submit to the decree, which have done with patience and fortitude. (quoted in Rappleye 2010, 515).

Part of one of Morris's houses is incorporated in the Robert Morris Inn in Oxford, Maryland, which is still open for business.

Further Reading

Bouton, Terry. 2007. *Taming Democracy: "The People," the Founders, and the Troubling Ending of the American Revolution.* New York: Oxford University Press.

Farrand, Max, ed. 1966. *The Records of the Federal Convention of 1787.* 4 vols. New Haven, CT: Yale University Press.

Goodrich, Charles A. 1856. *Lives of the Signers to the Declaration of Independence,* 233–44. New York: William Reed & Co.

Rappleye, Charles. 2010. *Robert Morris: Financier of the American Revolution.* New York: Siimon & Schuster.

Sumner, William Graham. 1891. *The Financier and the Finances of the American Revolution.* 2 vols. New York.

Ver Sterg, Clarence L. 1954. *Robert Morris: Revolutionary Financier with an Analysis of His Early Career.* Philadelphia: University of Pennsylvania Press.

Whitney, David C. 1974. *Founders of Freedom in America: Lives of the Men Who Signed the Constitution of the United States and So Helped to Establish the United States of America.* Chicago: J. G. Ferguson Publishing Company.

Young, Eleanor M. 1950. *Forgotten Patriot: Robert Morris.* New York: Macmillan.

Note: The Papers of Robert Morris, edited by E. James Ferguson et al., were published in nine volumes by the University of Pittsburgh Press from 1973 to 1999.

WILLIAM PATERSON (1745–1806)
NEW JERSEY

William Paterson was born in Ireland on Christmas Eve 1745. His father, a merchant, brought him to the United States when he was two years old. Paterson studied at the College of New Jersey (today's Princeton), in a building just across the street from a store that his father owned. Paterson earned both an undergraduate and a master's degree, but his career languished until the American Revolution when he joined the patriot side and went on to become the state's attorney general (Haskett 1950). Paterson became a secretary of the Provisional Congress and had a hand in drafting the New Jersey constitution. Paterson married Cornelia Bell (1755–1783) and lived on as estate near Raritan, New Jersey. After Cornelia died, Paterson married Euphemia (Affa) White (1746–1832), one of her close friends. Paterson served as a delegate to the Annapolis Convention. At the Constitutional Convention, Paterson is primarily remembered as introducing the author of the New Jersey Plan, which favored both the smaller states and required fewer changes in the relationship between the national government and the states than had the Virginia Plan.

At the Convention

Paterson, a modest but well-liked man who was only five feet, two inches tall, was present for the convention's opening day of the business on May 25. His first recorded comment, on June 5, was prophetic in that he argued for deciding how states would be represented in Congress before deciding on the adoption of a clause whereby Congress would guarantee a republican form of government to the states (Farrand 1966, 1:121). Similarly, on June 9, Paterson moved to resume discussion of the subject of representation in Congress. Soon thereafter, he indicated that he thought the idea of proportional representation threatened "the existence of the lesser States" (1:177). He further pointed out that the convention had been called to revise the Articles, and he said that if the delegates exceeded this call, "we should be charged by our constituents with usurpation" (1:178). Paterson did not think the people had given warrant to exchange a "federal" government for "a national Govt." (1:178), and he thought the delegates were bound by the people's wishes: "We must follow the people; the people will not follow us" (1:178).

Paterson further argued that a federal government presupposed the equality of the states, and "If we are to be considered as a nation, all State distinctions must be abolished, the whole must be thrown into hotchpot [a legal term where property of an intestate decedent is combined and then divided equally], and when an equal division is made, then there may be fairly an equality of representation" (1:178). Likening states to individuals, Paterson said there was no more reason for states paying more money to have more votes in Congress than for rich people to have more votes. Paterson pointed to colonial resistance to the Galloway Plan on the basis that a parliament with only a third of the representatives from the New World would not have done justice to their interests. Paterson further questioned

whether a government formed to act directly for the people had to necessarily be selected by the people (as opposed to the state legislatures).
Commending the existing Articles of Confederation, Paterson argued, "No
other amendments were wanting than to mark the orbits of the States with
due precision, and provide for the use of coercion, which was the great
point" (1:179). Responding to Pennsylvania's James Wilson, Paterson said
that if the large states chose to confederate among themselves, they were
free to do so, but they had no power to compel the smaller states to do so.
Paterson did not mince words. As to New Jersey, it "will never confederate
on the plan before the Committee. She would be swallowed up. He had
rather submit to a monarch, to a despot, than to such a fate. He would
not only oppose the plan here but on his return home do everything in his
power to defeat it there" (1:179).

Whereas many delegates took positions on key issues throughout the
convention, Paterson introduced most of his ideas in the New Jersey Plan.
Most of what we know about his views come from this plan and his explanation of it.

Introduction of the New Jersey Plan

On June 14, Paterson asked the convention for a postponement of business so that delegates from New Jersey and other states could devise and
propose a purely federal plan. He presented this plan on the following day
in the form of nine propositions. The first proposition advocated revising,
correcting, and enlarging the Articles of Confederation, in accord with the
task that had been assigned to the convention so "as to render the federal
Constitution adequate to the exigencies of Government, & the preservation
of the Union" (1:242). The second proposition called for granting five new
powers to Congress but not for altering its unicameral structure. The first
three powers were all related. They included the power to levy duties or
imposts, to make rules for the foregoing, and to be able to alter these rules.
Paterson also proposed that Congress should have power to regulate trade
among the states and with foreign nations and to see that punishments for
violations of such rules would be judged by the courts of the states, subject
to correction by the federal judiciary (1:243). The third proposition would
have continued the existing system of requisitioning the states according to
their white citizens and three-fifths of other persons with the understanding that, if the states did not comply, Congress could "direct the collection
thereof in the non complying States" subject to approval by an unspecified

supermajority of Congress. The fourth proposition called for a plural executive to be elected by Congress for a nonrenewable term and removable by Congress on application of a majority of state governors. The executive would have power over the military but would not be permitted personally to command troops. Paterson's fifth proposition called for the executive branch to appoint the federal judiciary (the Virginia Plan had called for appointments to be made by Congress) and included the power to hear impeachments of federal officials. The sixth proposition is recognizable as the origin of the current Supremacy Clause recognizing Congress's acts as the supreme law of the land. The last three propositions called for a provision to admit new states, for a uniform law regarding naturalization, and for recognition that individuals who violated the law in another state would be treated just like state citizens in the same circumstances (1:245).

Justification for the New Jersey Plan

Paterson sought to justify the New Jersey Plan on June 16. He argued that the plan was in closer accord both with the commission of the convention and the sentiments of the people. Indeed, Paterson observed that "Our object is not such a Governmt. as may be best in itself, but such a one as our Constituents have authorized us to prepare, and as they will approve" (1:250). Paterson further argued that states were on equal footing under the Articles of Confederation and that no alteration could be made in these Articles without the unanimous consent of the states. He argued that "If the sovereignty of the States is to be maintained, the Representatives must be drawn immediately from the States, not from the people" (1:251). Again Paterson suggested that the only way to "cure the difficulty" is to throw "the States into hotchpot" (1:251).

Paterson observed that delegates had objected to the idea of coercing states, but he doubted that coercion would be any easier under the Virginia Plan than under the plan he had presented: "Its efficacy will depend on the quantum of power collected, not on its being drawn from the States, or from the individuals; and according to his plan it may be exerted on individuals as well as according that of Mr. R[andolph]." (1:251).

Paterson further questioned the need for a bicameral Congress. Paterson thought that representatives from different states would be adequate checks on one another. He did not think that the people were complaining about the actions of Congress but simply about the inadequacy of powers in this body: "With proper powers Congs. will act with more energy & wisdom than the proposed Natl. Legislature; being fewer in number, and more secreted & refined by the mode of election" (1:251). Paterson further projected that the Congress under the Virginia Plan could have 180 members in one house and half again as many in the other, and that it would be far too expensive to have a Congress this size.

Other Matters

The Committee of the Whole decided to proceed with the central outline of the Virginia Plan rather than with the New Jersey Plan. Interestingly, Paterson seconded a motion on June 30 urging the delegation from New Hampshire (another small state) to do its best to get to the convention, probably hoping for the arrival of reinforcements.

The only committee on which Paterson served during the convention was the 11-man committee, established on July 2, which formulated the Connecticut Compromise providing for representation in the House of Representatives according to population and equally in the Senate. When a subsequent committee suggested further modifications, Paterson professed to be uncertain whether he thought it important that money bills should originate in the House of Representatives, but absolutely certain that "the small States would never be able to defend themselves without an equality of votes in the 2d. branch." Not surprisingly, he drew this as a line in the sand, which he did not think could be crossed: "There was no other ground of accommodation. His resolution was fixt. He would meet the large States on that Ground and no other" (1:551).

When another committee recommended a House composed of 56 members to be apportioned among the states according to population and wealth, Paterson objected that this formula was too vague. Although his own plan had called for counting slaves in the proportion to be fixed for ascertaining taxes, Paterson objected to including them for purposes of representation in a mix of persuasive practical and theoretical considerations:

> He could regard Negroes slaves in no light but as property. They are no free agents, have no personal liberty, no faculty of acquiring property, but on the contrary are themselves property, & like other property entirely at the will of the Master. Has a man in Virga. a number of votes in proportion to the number of his slaves? and if Negroes are not represented in the States to which they belong, why should they be represented in the Genl. Govt. What is the true principle of Representation? It is an expedient by

which an assembly of certain individls. chosen by the people is substituted in place of the inconvenient meeting of the people themselves. If such a meeting of the people was actually to take place, would the slaves vote? they would not. Why then shd. they be represented. (2:561)

Paterson further observed that allowing for representation of the slaves would give further encouragement to the slave trade, and pointed to the ignominy of the institution by the fact that its supporters had refused to use the term "slaves" in the Articles of Confederation (1:561).

On July 16, the day that the convention finally acceded to the Connecticut Compromise, Paterson, either apparently misunderstanding or purposely misconstruing (O'Connor 1986, 157 believes the latter) a motion by Edmund Randolph as a motion to adjourn *sine die*, or indefinitely, and not simply for the day, seconded the motion and proposed that the delegates be released from secrecy and be able to consult their constituents. He reiterated that "No conciliation could be admissible on the part of the smaller States on any other ground than that of an equality of votes in the 2d. branch" (2:18).

On July 19, Paterson supported a proposal to grant states from one to three electors in the choice of the president (2:56). On July 23, Paterson further supported a motion proposing that the Constitution be referred for ratification to state legislators (2:88).

He left that same day, the day that delegates from New Hampshire finally arrived, for New Jersey in what may well be a sign of his "underlying modesty and rectitude about his duties" (Degnan 1998, 238). Paterson returned in September to sign the Constitution (O'Connor 1986, 160–1).

Life after the Convention

After signing the Constitution, Paterson went on to serve as one of his state's senators (supporting Alexander Hamilton's proposals for economic reform), as the state governor, and, finally, as an associate justice of the U.S. Supreme Court, to which George Washington appointed him. Appropriately enough, Paterson had served in the first Congress to draft the Judiciary Act of 1789, where his role in formulating the law appears second only to that of Oliver Ellsworth, who chaired the committee.

As a justice, Paterson was responsible for riding the massive southern circuit. In *Vanhorne's Lessee*, Paterson referred to the Constitution as "the work or will of the People themselves, in their original, sovereign, and unlimited capacity." He further noted that "the Constitution is the sun of the political system, around which all Legislative, Executive and Judicial bodies must revolve" (quoted by Degnan 1998, 250).

As governor, Paterson also issued the charter for the city named in his honor. Injured in a carriage accident, Paterson's health declined and he died at the home of a daughter (who had married into the Rennselaer family) in Albany, New York on September 9, 1806. Originally buried in the Rennselaer family vault at their manor house, after that was demolished, his body was moved to the family plot at Menands.

Further Reading

Cushman, Clare. 1995. *The Supreme Court Justices: Illustrated Biographies, 1789–1995.* Washington, DC: Congressional Quarterly.

Degnan, Daniel. 1998. "William Paterson: Small States' Nationalist." In *Seriatim: The Supreme Court before John Marshall*, edited by Scott Douglas Gerber, 231–59. New York: New York University Press.

Farrand, Max, ed. 1966. *The Records of the Federal Convention of 1787.* 4 vols. New Haven, CT: Yale University Press.

Haskett, Richard C. 1950. "William Paterson, Attorney General of New Jersey: Public Office and Private Profit in the American Revolution." *William and Mary Quarterly*, 3rd Ser., 7 (January): 26–38.

O'Connor, John E. 1986. *William Paterson: Lawyer and Statesman, 1745–1806.* New Brunswick, NJ: Rutgers University Press.

William Pierce Jr. (1753–1789)
Georgia

Born as the youngest of three sons of Elizabeth and Matthew Pierce in York County, Virginia, in 1753, Pierce used the suffix Jr. to distinguish himself from an uncle. Pierce briefly studied art under Charles Willson Peale in Maryland before coming to Williamsburg, Virginia. Within a year he joined forces fighting for the patriot cause and later attended the College of William and Mary where he was a member of Phi Beta Kappa, which was then chiefly a debating society. He served in the revolution as an aide-de-camp to General Nathaniel Greene, was recognized by Congress for his valor, and received land for his service to Virginia. He subsequently headed a trade company in Savannah, married Charlotte Fenwick (b. 1766), the daughter of a South Carolina planter by whom he had four sons, one of whom

(William Leigh) survived into adulthood. Pierce was elected first to the Georgia Assembly and then to the Confederal Congress. He was a member of the Society of the Cincinnati, a veterans' organization.

In a letter from New York dated May 19, 1787, before the start of the Constitutional Convention, William Pierce observed that he favored "powers equal to a prompt and certain execution, but tempered with a proper respect for the liberties of the People. I am for securing their happiness, not by the will of a few, but by the direction of the Law" (Hutson 1987, 9). In this same letter, he said that it was necessary to pay respect "to the temper of the People" and indicated that he thought this temper was incompatible with the establishment of a monarchy (Hutson 1987, 9). He recorded that he opposed the exercise of "dictatorial power," and that "Unless we can settle down into some permanent System very shortly, our condition will be as fickle and inconsistent, as that of the Romans; and our political schemes be nothing more than chimeras and disorders" (Hutson 1987, 10). Clearly, Pierce recognized that the convention he would attend would be an important one. He concluded his letter, in his own idiosyncratic spelling, by observing that "The Statesman and the Phylosopher have their attention turned towards us: the oppressed and wretched look to America" (Hutson 1987, 10).

At the Convention

Pierce was seated at the convention on May 31 and stayed until sometime at the end of June. Pierce's most distinctive contribution to knowledge of the convention was a set of character sketches of all but two of the delegates that was originally published in the *Savannah Georgian* in 1828, later published in the *American Historical Review* (see Farrand 1966, 3:87–97), and published numerous times since. These sketches reveal an individual of considerable literary accomplishment and powers of observation. He identified himself as a soldier in the Revolutionary War, spoke of his interest in the general welfare, mentioned his ambition, and spoke with pride of having sat in what he described, with perhaps a bit of hyperbole, as "the wisest Council in the World" (3:97). On occasion, his notes are useful supplements to those of James Madison and other members.

Pierce's notes of the first day indicate that he believed it was necessary to know "how the Senate should be appointed" before deciding on how the first branch would be selected. His notes continue with his view that it would be necessary to balance the powers of the state and national governments:

It appeared clear to me that unless we established a Government that should carry at least some of its principles into the mass of the people, we might as well depend upon the present confederation. If the influence of the States is not lost in some part of the new Government we never shall have any thing like a national institution. But in my opinion it will be right to shew the sovereignty of the State in one branch of the Legislature, and that should be in the Senate. (1:59).

Pierce followed up on these thoughts on June 6 when he said that he "was for an election by the people as to the 1st. branch & by the States as to the 2d. branch; by which means the Citizens of the States wd. be represented both *individually & collectively*" (1:137).

On June 12, Pierce successfully proposed that members of the House of Representatives should be paid out of the national treasury rather than by the individual states (1:216). That same day, Pierce proposed that the term of senators should be three years. At the time, the convention was considering a seven-year term; Pierce pointed out that such a term had caused "great mischief" in Great Britain where it has been "reprobated by most of their patriotic Statesmen" (1:218).

Pierce reiterated the need to balance state and national interest on June 29 in following up a speech by Madison. He observed that members of Congress had represented the interests of their states. Pointing out that the federal government under the Articles of Confederation was "no more than a compact between states," he observed:

We are now met to remedy its defects, and our difficulties are great, but not, I hope, insurmountable. State distinctions must be sacrificed so far as the general government shall render it necessary—without, however, destroying them altogether. Although I am here a representative from a small state, I consider myself as a citizen of the United States, whose general interest I will always support. (1:474)

As a member of a state that needed national help in repelling Indian attacks, Pierce's position may have enabled him to take a more nationalistic view than that of delegates from states where such a dependency was less obvious.

Life after the Convention

Pierce left the convention sometime after June 29 after he felt that "all the first principles of the new Government were established" (Hutson, 1987,

182). Intending to engage in a duel with John Auldjo, a partner in one of his firms who was visiting New York, Alexander Hamilton, who was Auldjo's designated second and would later die in such an encounter with Aaron Burr, mediated to avoid this. Pierce then went back to Congress where he pled for national help for Georgia against Indian threats.

Pierce's early departure would appear to have been a genuine loss to the convention. Explaining to St. George Tucker in a letter of September 18, 1787 (the day after the delegates signed the Constitution), why he had not stayed at the convention and signed the document, he referred to "a piece of business so necessary that it became unavoidable." He further indicated that he supported the document:

> I approve of its principles, and would have signed it with all my heart, had I been present. To say, however, that I consider it as perfect, would be to make an acknowledgement immediately opposed to my judgment. Perhaps it is the only one that will suit our present situation. The wisdom of the convention was equal to something greater; but a variety of local circumstances, the inequality of states, and the dissonant interests of the different parts of the Union, made it impossible to give it any other shape or form. ("Notes" 1898, 314)

Pierce elaborated on his views by using nautical analogies:

> The condition of America demands a change; we must sooner or later be convulsed if we do not have some other government than the one under which we at present live. The old Federal Constitution is like a ship bearing under the weight of a tempest; it is trembling, and just on the point of sinking. If we have not another bark to take us up we shall all go down together. There are periods in the existence of a political society that require prompt and decisive measures; I mean that point of time between a people's running into anarchy and an anxious state of the public mind to be rescued from its approaching mischiefs by the intervention of some good and efficient government. ("Notes" 1898, 314)

Further expressing his view that the new Constitution "is the ark that is to save us," he opined that "as individuals in society . . . give up a part of their national rights to secure the rest, so the different states should render a portion of their interests to secure the good of the whole" ("Notes" 1898, 314). Pierce further argued that "when there are restraints on power, to prevent its invading the positive rights of a people, there is no necessity for any such thing as a Bill of Rights" ("Notes" 1898, 315). Pierce did confess to some concerns as to whether the executive department, which had been greatly enlarged after he left the convention was "too highly mounted to preserve exactly the equilibrium" ("Notes" 1898, 316), but he also confessed that he was "at a loss to know whether any government can have sufficient energy to effect its own ends without the aid of a military power" ("Notes" 1898, 317).

Pierce helped persuade Congress to send the Constitution to the states for ratification, and he helped print the Constitution in his home state and worked for its ratification. He delivered an oration on July 4, 1788, which was in part a plea for ratification of the new Constitution. Pierce's life took a decidedly downward turn after the convention when both his business and his health failed. He died shortly thereafter on December 10, 1789 in Savannah. His son and namesake, who was born after his death, studied at Princeton and at the Litchfield Law School and subsequently wrote a long poem decrying the War of 1812 and what he believed to be the decline in statesmanship that it represented (Pierce 1813).

Further Reading

Bradford, M. E. 1981. *Founding Fathers: Brief Lives of the Framers of the United States Constitution.* 2nd ed. Lawrence: University Press of Kansas.

Farrand, Max, ed. 1966. *The Records of the Federal Convention of 1787.* 4 vols. New Haven, CT: Yale University Press.

Fore, Sam. "William Pierce (1753–1789)." The New Georgia Encyclopedia. http://www.georgiaencyclopedia.org/nge/Article.jsp?id=h-3698. Accessed 10/10/2012.

Jones, Charles C. *Biographical Sketches of the Delegates from Georgia to the Continental Congress.* Boston: Houghton, Mifflin and Company, 1891.

Leffler, Richard, John P. Kaminski, and Samuel K. Fore, eds. 2012. *William Pierce on the Constitutional Convention and the Constitution.* Dallas, TX: Harlan Crowe Library.

"Notes of Major William Pierce on the Federal Convention of 1787." 1898. *American Historical Review* 3 (January): 310–34.

Pierce, William Leigh. 1813. *The Year: A Poem, in Three Cantoes.* New York: David Longworth at the Shakespeare-Gallery. Nabu Public Domain reprint.

Vile, John R. *Members of "the Wisest Council in the World": An Examination of William Pierce's Character Sketches of Delegates Who Attended the Constitutional Convention of 1787.* Forthcoming.

———. "William Pierce and Political Rhetoric." *Colonial Williamsburg Journal* (Winter 2014; forthcoming).

Wier, Robert M. 2000. "Pierce, William Leigh." *American National Biography* Online. http://www.anb.org/articles/01/01-00731.html. Accessed 7/4/2012.

Charles Cotesworth Pinckney (1746–1825)
South Carolina

Charles Cotesworth Pinckney was born on February 25, 1746 to Charles and Elizabeth (Liza) Lucas Pinckney. The former was an interim chief justice of South Carolina, and the latter was one of the most accomplished women of her day, managing her father's plantations after his death and later doing the same when her husband died in 1758; she helped introduced the growing of indigo, which was used to make blue dye and became a major staple, into the colony. Pinckney had 16 years of formal education. He was schooled at Christ Church College at Oxford College where he sat under the lectures of the great English jurist, William Blackstone, at the Temple in London, and at the Royal Military Academy in Caen, France.

Upon his return to South Carolina, Pinckney entered a very successful law practice and was soon appointed as deputy to the state's attorney general. He also married Sarah (Sally) Middleton (1756–1784), the daughter of a wealthy plantation owner, and thus became the brother-in-law to Edward Rutledge and Arthur Middleton, both of whom signed the Declaration of Independence. The Pinckneys had three children. After Sarah's death, Pinckney married Mary Stead (1751–1812), a wealthy heiress for whom he had done legal work. No children resulted from this second union.

An early supporter of colonial independence, Pinckney helped draft South Carolina's first constitution. Pinckney rose to the rank of brigadier general during the Revolutionary War. The British imprisoned him after the surrender of Charleston, but he adamantly refused to follow a number of fellow South Carolinians and go over to the British side, declaring that "If I had a vein that did not beat with love for my country, I myself would open it" and proclaiming that he would answer any such request "as is becoming an American officer, a man of honor, and a devotee to the freedom and dependence of his country" (quoted in Meister, 220). He made friends with George Washington during the Revolutionary War and had his trust throughout his life. Pinckney's law practice continued to flourish after the war. A book that highlights Pinckney observed that although he "was not handsome . . . his broad shoulders gave him a commanding appearance" and that "He had dark eyes, a Roman nose, and a wide mouth posed to laugh" (Meister 1987, 215). Known for his love of good food, he was also described as "portly" (Meister 1987, 218).

At the Convention

Charles Cotesworth Pinckney arrived at the Constitutional Convention on May 17 and was present on the opening day of business on May 25. He sought to protect his state's interest and participated in a fair number of debates, chiefly focusing on protecting the state's slave interest and on preventing import taxes.

Federalism

Pinckney's first recorded action at the Constitutional Convention was on May 30 when he seconded a motion by Delaware's George Read proposing an introductory motion to accompany the Virginia Plan for "a more effective government consisting of a Legislative, Judiciary, and Executive" (Farrand 1966, 1:30). Although this motion recognized the need for greater centralized powers, Read proposed it as a substitute for an earlier motion calling for the establishment of "a national government" (1:30). It would thus appear that the resolution Pinckney supported was designed to give a somewhat less nationalistic cast to the proposal under consideration. Pinckney was on record the same day as doubting whether members of the convention were authorized either by the act of Congress creating it or by their state commissions to discuss "a System founded on different principles from the federal Constitution [the designation for the government under the Articles of Confederation]" (1:35).

On June 6, Pinckney indicated that he "wished to have a good national Govt. & at the same time to leave a considerable share of power in the States" (1:137). He also expressed doubts about the feasibility of electing either house of Congress through popular election. He believed that the legislature typically exercised better judgment than the people and illustrated with his experience from his home state of the former opposing, and the latter favoring, the issuance of paper money. He attributed this to the fact that members of the legislature had "some sense of character and were restrained by that consideration" (1:137). He also believed that state governments would exercise greater jealousy of their powers and be ready "to thwart the National Govt. if excluded from a participation in it" (1:137). On

June 21, Pinckney noted that he "was for making the State Govts. a part of the General System" and further observed, "If they were to be abolished, or lose their agency, S. Carolina & other States would have but a small share of the benefits of Govt." (1:360)

Congress

Selection of Members. Pinckney opposed allowing the people to select members of either branch of Congress, favoring state legislative appointment of such delegates instead. Not only was this consistent with his view of federalism, but it also reflected his distrust of the people (Zahniser 1967, 92). Speaking at the convention on June 6, General Pinckney thus observed that:

> An election of either branch by the people scattered as they are in many States, particularly in S. Carolina was totally impracticable. He differed from gentlemen who thought that a choice by the people wd. be a better guard agst. bad measures, than by the Legislatures. A majority of the people of S. Carolina were notoriously for paper money as a legal tender; the Legislature had refused to make it a legal tender. The reason was that the latter had some sense of character and were restrained by that consideration. The State Legislatures also he said would be more jealous, & more ready to thwart the National Govt. if excluded from a participation in it. (1:137)

Consistent with this view, Pinckney moved on June 21 to allow members of the House of Representatives to be selected "in such manner as the Legislature of each State should direct" (1:358). He argued that this would allow the legislatures to "accommodate the mode to the conveniency & opinions of the people," that it would avoid undue influence by the larger counties, and that it would prevent disputed elections from having to be appealed to the legislature where it would cause trouble and expense (1:358). The convention defeated this motion by a vote of six to four to one.

Origination of Money Bills. Pinckney opposed the idea of limiting the origination of money bills to the House of Representatives. He said that this distinction had been a source of controversy between the two branches within his home state and had proven relatively easy to evade (1:234). He later argued that this was not really a concession on the part of the small states (1:546).

Ineligibility to Offices. On June 23, Pinckney opposed the provision that would have made members of the House of Representatives ineligible to accept state offices. He thought that this would prove inconvenient and that it would attain little (1:386). Using a biblical analogy, he also suggested that such a provision would be setting up a kingdom divided against itself (1:386).

Terms. When the convention was discussing the terms of senators on June 25, Pinckney supported terms of four years rather than for six or for good behavior. He was concerned about what today is sometimes called the "beltway syndrome," through which representatives who spend long time in the nation's capital are thought to lose contact with their constituents:

> A longer term wd. fix them at the seat of Govt. They wd. acquire an interest there, perhaps transfer their property & lose sight of the States they represent. Under these circumstances the distant States wd. labour under great disadvantages. (1:409)

Pinckney repeated this argument the following day (1:421).

Pay and Qualifications. Pinckney revealed his aristocratic proclivities on June 26 when he proposed that senators should serve without pay. He reasoned that "as this branch was meant to represent the wealth of the Country, it ought to be composed of persons of wealth; and if no allowance was to be made the wealthy alone would undertake the service" (1:426–27). On July 26, he further moved to extend property and citizenship qualifications not only to members of Congress but also to members of the other two branches (1:122).

After the convention defeated Pinckney's motion that senators should serve without pay by a six to four vote, Pinckney advocated allowing states to pay the salaries of their senators and to recall them home. Notes indicate that Pinckney observed that "such a restriction would also discourage the ablest men from going into the Senate" (1:429). This could mean that Pinckney actually hoped that the best men would remain in service at the state level. He had previously reported that he "was for making the States as much as could be conveniently done a part of the Genl. Gov't" (1:429).

Representation. On July 2, Pinckney reluctantly supported the appointment of a committee of a member from each state to resolve the issue of state representation in Congress (1:511). He actually preferred a motion by Benjamin Franklin on June 30, however. It would have provided for equal state representation in one house and would have granted each state an equal vote when matters of state sovereignty were in question.

Pinckney was concerned when a committee raised the initial number of representatives in the House from 56 to 65 members, and his concern was motivated by regional considerations. He feared that the new allocation was less favorable to the southern states. He did not expect these states to be represented equally, but thought they needed to be brought closer to equality than the proposed allocation (1:567). He proposed raising the number of representatives from North Carolina from five to six, those from South Carolina from five to six, and Georgia's from three to four (1:568; also see 2:219).

Pinckney further tried on July 11 to strike the Three-fifths Clause so as to provide equal representation for slaves and free persons (1:580). Pinckney wanted a specific formula, however, rather than a general reference to representation on the basis of wealth. He feared that otherwise "property in slaves" would be "exposed to danger" (1:594).

Powers and Limits. On August 18, when the delegates were discussing whether it was appropriate to have troops in time of peace, Pinckney questioned whether the nation would have to wait until it was attacked before raising such troops (2:330). He also favored allowing the Congress to regulate and discipline the militia, citing his own military experience to indicate that the dissimilarity among state militia "had produced the most serious mischiefs" during the Revolutionary War (2:330). On this issue, "he saw no room for such distrust of the Genl. Govt." (2:331; also see 2:386).

Slavery

In addition to supporting full representation for states that allowed for slavery, Pinckney worked in other ways to protect the institution. On July 23, he said that he would be duty bound to vote against the Constitution if it did not provide "some security to the Southern States agst. an emancipation of slaves, and taxes on exports" (2:95).

Pinckney discoursed more fully on the subject on August 22, just after his cousin had attempted to justify slavery by appealing to historical practice. The General observed that his influence and that of other southern delegates would not be enough to achieve southern ratification of the Constitution if slavery were not protected. He did not believe that his state and Georgia could do without slaves, and he argued that the only reason other southern states were not insistent on slave importation is that they believed their own slaves would rise in value if imports ceased. Ignoring arguments about the morality or immorality of slavery, he further argued for the economic benefits of continuing importation:

> The importation of slaves would be for the interest of the whole Union. The more slaves, the more produce to employ the carrying trade; The more consumption also, and the more of this, the more of revenue for the common treasury. (2:371)

At his state's ratifying convention, Pinckney highlighted his role in permitting the continuation of the slave trade for another 20 years, observing that in combatting "the religious and political prejudices of the Eastern and Middle States, and with the interested and inconsistent opinion of Virginia" that "I am . . . thoroughly convinced . . . that the nature of our climate, and the flat, swampy situation of our country, obliges us to cultivate our land with negroes, and that without them South Carolina would soon be a desert waste" ("Debates in the Legislature" 1788).

Pinckney thought that slaves should be subject to the same taxes as other imports, but repeated that if slave imports were prohibited, his state would not ratify the new Constitution (2: 372). Unlike his cousin, the general did not think it was likely that his state would stop such imports on its own, at least not permanently (2:373). The general eventually succeeded in moving the prohibition of slave imports from the year 1800 to 1808 (2:415). He somewhat cynically conceded that one reason he was willing to accept a tax on incoming slaves was that this would acknowledge that they were considered to be property (2:416). He subsequently supported a motion designed to see that all duties and imposts were enacted uniformly throughout the United States (2:418).

Although Pinckney thought it would be best for the South if there were no federal regulation of commerce, he nonetheless opposed fettering this with requirements for supermajorities. He partly based this argument on the good faith and liberality that he had observed in the eastern states (2:449–50).

On August 30, Pinckney, who had supported the disestablishment of the Anglican Church within his own state, supported the prohibition of religious tests as a condition for office (2:468). On September 14, he opposed the appointment of the national treasurer by joint ballot. Appealing as he often did to his experience in South Carolina, Pinckney indicated that such a mechanism had resulted in bad appointments there but that the legislature refused to accept reports of faults of their own officer (2:614).

Judiciary

Given Pinckney's extensive legal training, he said little at the convention related to the judiciary, but he clearly thought judges were important. On August 27, Pinckney opposed a motion to prohibit pay raises for sitting judges. He reasoned, "The importance of the Judiciary will require men of the first talents: large salaries will therefore be necessary, larger than the U.S. can allow in the first instance" (2:429). He did not think it would be proper for more recently appointed judges to have higher salaries than those who had been on the bench for some time (2:430).

Ratification

On July 16, the day the Connecticut Compromise, Pinckney appears to have misunderstood a motion by Edmund Randolph to adjourn for the day as a motion to adjourn the convention. He observed that he "could not think of going to S. Carolina, and returning again to this place" (2:18). He also thought it was unlikely that, if the states were consulted, they would be able to agree to any plan before it was completed.

Life after the Convention

Charles Cotesworth Pinckney participated in his state's ratifying convention, where he supported the Constitution. He vigorously defended the Constitution's provisions for treaty making and ratification. Affirming his respect for the worthy individuals who had drafted the Articles of Confederation, Pinckney observed that:

> his respect for them could not prevent him from being thoroughly sensible of the defects of the system they had established; sad experience had convinced him that it was weak, inefficient, and inadequate to the purposes of good government; and he understood that most of the framers of it were so thoroughly convinced of this truth, that they were eager to adopt the present Constitution ("Debates in the Legislature" 1788).

In 1790, Pinckney helped write a new constitution for South Carolina. He declined a number of appointments by Washington as a Supreme Court justice and as secretary of state or secretary of war, but he did agree to be an envoy to France where he was one of three American participants in the notorious XYZ Affair involving a French attempt to demand bribes as a condition for negotiation. After returning home, Pinckney was placed third in command, behind Washington and Hamilton, in preparation for a possible war with France.

Although he opposed the Alien and Sedition Acts of 1798, Pinckney supported the Federalist Party and ran unsuccessfully as a vice presidential candidate in 1800 and as a presidential candidate in both 1804 and 1808 (he did not carry his home state in either election but was widely admired for his patriotism). Pinckney helped found the University of South Carolina and served on its board of trustees. In his later years, Pinckney served as president of the Society of the Cincinnati, a group of Revolutionary War veterans, and as president of the Charleston Bible Society. With Richard Furman, a Baptist minister, he also mounted a campaign against dueling (he had once served as a second in such an altercation) and for the propagation of the gospel among slaves. Pinckney died in Charleston on August 16, 1825 and was buried at the city's St. Michael's Episcopal Church, where his epitaph notes that he "Maintained the principles of the Constitution."

Further Reading

"Debates in the Legislature and in Convention of the State of South Carolina on the Adoption of the Federal Constitution." January 16–19, 1788. Constitution Society. http://www.constitution.org/rc/rat_sc-l.htm. Accessed 7/15/2012.

Farrand, Max, ed. 1966. *The Records of the Federal Convention of 1787*. 4 vols. New Haven, CT: Yale University Press.

Meister, Charles W. 1987. *The Founding Fathers*. Jefferson, NC: McFarland & Company.

Williams, Frances Leigh. 1978. *A Founding Family: The Pinckneys of South Carolina*. New York: Harcourt Brace Jovanovich.

Zahniser, Marvin R. 1967. *Charles Cotesworth Pinckney: Founding Father*. Chapel Hill: University of North Carolina Press.

CHARLES PINCKNEY (1757–1824)
SOUTH CAROLINA

The reality and the myth of Charles Pinckney are somewhat difficult to separate. He falsely claimed to be twenty-five years old (rather than his real age of twenty-nine) at the convention so that individuals would think that he, and not New Jersey's twenty-six-year-old Jonathan Dayton, was

the youngest member. Scholars are still debating the content and the influence of the plan that he introduced just after the Virginia Plan that was later apparently considered by the Committee of Detail. It seems clear that a version of the Constitution that he claimed to have proposed was not in fact the one that he offered in the early days of the convention, but numerous suggestions that he made at the convention do appear to have found their way into the final document.

Pinckney was born on October 16, 1757 to the family of a lawyer and planter in Charleston, and related to many other prominent men in the state; his cousin Charles Cotesworth Pinckney also represented South Carolina at the Constitutional Convention. Pinckney read law with his father and went on to achieve success at the South Carolina bar. Pinckney took an early lead in the movement for revolution against England, helping to serve on a three-person state executive committee and later helping to draft a new state constitution. He fought in the Revolutionary War, during which the British captured and imprisoned him for a time. He subsequently served as a delegate to the Continental Congress, where he had argued for strengthening the national government. Princeton awarded him an honorary degree for his congressional service in 1787, an honor it bestowed that same year on Virginia's James Madison.

Just before the Constitutional Convention, Pinckney married Mary (Polly) Eleanor Laurens (1770–1794), the daughter of a wealthy Charleston merchant, Henry Laurens, who had previously served as president of the Continental Congress. Pinckney and his wife had three children, but she died in 1794. Analyzing Pinckney's only known portrait, which shows him sitting and thus gives little clue to his height, his biographer observes that it shows him with a round face, a high forehead, "intense eyes and a broad, fine nose above slightly feminine lips" (Matthews 2004, 39).

At the Convention

Pinckney was present on the opening day of the convention, and on that day, he moved that the convention create a Rules Committee. He was subsequently one of three individuals appointed (along with Virginia's George Wythe and New York's Alexander Hamilton) to this committee (Farrand

1966, 2:2). Wythe, the chair of the committee and the nation's first law professor, probably had the most important role on the committee, but it was nonetheless important in establishing a set of rules designed to promote reason and deliberation at the convention.

The Pinckney Plan

Madison's notes indicate that Pinckney introduced his plan on May 29, the same day that Edmund Randolph introduced the Virginia Plan, and, perhaps because Pinckney's plan followed Randolph's proposal, it was referred along with this plan to the Committee of the Whole. As best as can be reconstructed, the plan called for a bicameral Congress consisting of a Senate and a House of Delegates. State legislatures were to select members of the House of Delegates who would in turn select senators to four-year terms either from their own ranks or from among the people at large (3:605). The nation was to be divided into four districts for this purpose.

The Senate was to choose the president every four years. His powers would include power to correspond with state executives, execute the laws, serve as commander in chief of the armed forces, and convene the legislature. He was to be aided by a Council of Revision consisting of various department heads (3:606).

Congress would have exclusive power to raise military forces, to regulate interstate and foreign trade, to establish a post office, coin money, and so forth. The legislature would also have the power to appoint major offices and to institute a federal judicial court. Two-thirds majorities would be required for regulating trade, levying imposts, and raising revenue (3:608). The House of Delegates would have the power of impeachment, and the Senate and federal judges would judge such impeachments.

The plan further provided for the later addition of powers by the consent of an unspecified number of states. It also provided for trial by jury, freedom of the press, and a prohibition of religion tests (3:609).

Federalism

On May 30, the day after Edmund Randolph introduced the Virginia Plan, Pinckney asked him whether he intended to abolish state governments altogether (1:33–34). In the same vein, Pinckney expressed concern the next day about granting Congress power "in all cases to which the State

Legislatures were individually incompetent" (2:53). Pinckney thought that this language was too vague.

On June 8, however, Pinckney indicated that he favored a congressional negative over state laws "which they shd. judge to be improper" (1:164). Moreover, he argued:

> That such a universality of the power was indispensable necessary to render it effectual; that the States must be kept in due subordination to the nation; that if the States were left to act of themselves in any case, it wd. be impossible to defend the national prerogatives, however extensive they might be on paper; . . . that this universal negative was in fact the corner stone of an efficient national Govt . . . (1:164).

Pinckney renewed his support for the negative of state laws on July 17 (2:28), and again on August 23. On the latter occasion, he proposed that such a negative would require a two-thirds vote of both houses of Congress (2:390). He further suggested that state governors (perhaps appointed by Congress) should be able to exercise such power and suggested that this might be done if another convention were to be called (2:391).

On August 9, Pinckney indicated that he opposed congressional oversight of the times, places, and manner of their elections. He thought that the states should be relied on for this purpose (2:240). He favored allowing Congress to subdue rebellion in the states without an application from their legislatures (2:317). Pinckney thought that many state debts were so related to national purposes that they should be considered as expenditures on behalf of the nation as a whole (2:327).

Congress

Consistent with reconstructions of Pinckney's Plan, on May 31, he apparently proposed to divide the nation into four divisions, from which senators would be chosen (1:59). On June 7, Pinckney observed that if senators were to be chosen by state legislatures, and that if each state were to have at least one, the Senate would consist of at least 80 members, a number he thought was too high (1:150). However, he argued later in the day that members of the Senate "ought to be permanent & independent," and that appointment by state legislatures would enhance this likelihood. In a precursor to the Connecticut Compromise, he also proposed that states should be divided into three classes, granting the smallest states one senator, the medium size states, two, and the large states, three (1:155; also see 1:169). Still later he proposed a Senate of 36 persons, with states having from one to five members (2:5).

Representation. Pinckney generally sided with the large states on the issue of representation. He was realistic, perhaps even skeptical of the motives of the small ones. His tone on June 16 was almost cynical: "Give N. Jersey an equal vote, and she will dismiss her scruples, and concur in the Natil. system (1:255). On this occasion, he further argued that the convention had the power to go to whatever length it needed it making recommendations "to remedy the evils which produced this Convention" (1:255).

On July 2, Pinckney said that he thought it would be "inadmissible" to grant states equal votes in the Senate. He recognized, however, that larger states "would feel a partiality for their own Citizens & give them a preference, in appointments" (1:510). He appeared to argue that the difference between northern and southern states was greater than that between the large and small states. Still, he suggested, consistent with his earlier proposal to divide states into three groups, that the small states should be granted "some but not a full proportion" (1:511).

In his state's ratifying convention, Pinckney indicated that he had accepted the Great Compromise. He observed that "Though he was at first opposed to this compromise, yet he was far from thinking it an injudicious one," and went on to observe that "The different branches of the legislature being intended as checks upon each other, it appeared to him they would more effectually restrain their mutual intemperances under this mode of representation than they would have done if both houses had been so formed upon proportionable principles" (Debates in the Legislature" 1788).

Origination of Money Bills in the House. On July 6, he argued that the provision stipulating that money bills should originate in the House was of little substance (1:545). He later argued that "if the Senate can be trusted with the many great powers proposed, it surely may be trusted with that of originating money bills" (2:224; also see 2:263).

Selection of Members. On June 6, Pinckney opposed popular election of members of the first branch of Congress, "contending that the people were less fit Judges and that the Legislatures would be less likely to promote the adoption of the new Government, if they were to be excluded from all share in it" (1:132). On June 13, Pinckney argued that it was necessary to decide how the Senate would be apportioned before deciding whether the origination of money bills should be confined to the House (1:234).

Composition of the Senate. On June 25, Pinckney delivered an extended speech to the convention regarding the composition of the Senate. Pinckney observed that the most singular fact about the United States was the fact that "there are fewer distinctions of fortune & less of rank, than among the inhabitants of any other nation" (1:398). He expected this relative equality would continue into the foreseeable future and therefore thought that the lessons to be drawn from the British constitution, which he believed "to be the best constitution in existence," were limited (1:398). Specifically, Pinckney doubted the propriety of using a peerage "for forming a Legislative balance between the inordinate power of the Executive and the people" (1:399). Instead, the system to be established "must be suited to the habits & genius of the People it is to govern, and must grow out of them" (1:402).

Pinckney believed that men in the United States fell into three classes—professional men, commercial men, and those with landed interests (1:402). From this point forward, his speech is difficult to follow. It seemed, however, to call for reserving local rights to the states (2:404). At the same time, he apparently continued to favor a congressional negative of state laws (1:412), and he may even have introduced such a plan, although it is not included in convention notes (1: 412). It is not at all clear exactly how Pinckney hoped that the Senate would represent the three central interests that he identified.

Representation in the House. On July 6, Pinckney opposed re-examination of the formula whereby the House of Representatives would have one representative for every 40,000 inhabitants. He thought that this measure would be better than state contributions of revenue because it would fluctuate less. He wanted blacks to be counted equally with whites for purposes of representation, but was willing to settle for the three-fifths formula (1:542).

Qualifications of Members. On July 26, Pinckney seconded a motion by Virginia's George Mason that would have required qualifications of landed property for, and the exclusion of individuals having unsettled accounts from, serving in Congress (2:121). He further hoped to extend such qualifications to all three branches of government (2:122). Later in the day, Pinckney said that he had reconsidered the idea of excluding public debtors since it would exclude individuals who had purchased confiscated property or property in the West (2:126).

Pinckney favored a motion raising the citizenship requirements for members of the Senate from four to fourteen years. He thought there would be particular danger of foreign intrigues in this body since it was responsible for managing foreign affairs (2:235). When this was initially rejected, he pushed for a 10-year citizenship requirement (2:239). When some delegates objected that it would not be fair to impose citizenship requirements on those who were already in the country, Pinckney said that current laws varied widely and that the convention was in a situation where it was appropriate to consider "first principles" (2:271).

Pinckney was concerned when a committee failed to report property qualifications for members of Congress and left this issue to the first Congress. He feared that this body might set the qualifications so as either to favor the rich or the poor. His argument then took an interesting turn. Contending that he opposed "an undue aristocratic influence in the Constitution," he said that it was necessary for members of all three branches to possess "competent property to make them independent & respectable" (2:248). As for him, he thought a president should have at least one hundred thousand dollars, and that judges and members of Congress should have at least half this amount (2:248). This would certainly have been a relatively substantial sum in a nation that Pinckney thought was characterized by relative equality.

Eligibility for Other Offices. Pinckney opposed making members of Congress ineligible to other offices, and made at least three arguments against this. He thought it was degrading, inconvenient, and impolitic (2:283); he later argued that it was also contrary to state practice (2:287). Pinckney indicated that he hoped that the Senate might especially "contain the fittest men" and "become a School of Public Ministers, a nursery of Statesmen" (2:283). He was willing to support a clause, eventually adopted, preventing members for accepting offices for which they received pay without first resigning (2:284). Opposing congressional ineligibility to other offices on September 3, Pinckney observed that this eligibility should be like "the policy of the Romans in making the temple of virtue the road to the temple of fame" (2:490). He anticipated that the first Congress would "be composed of the ablest men to be found," and he did not want them excluded from other offices, like the judiciary, that would be formed during this Congress (2:491).

Powers and Limits. Pinckney opposed vesting the power to make war in Congress as a whole. It feared that it would be too slow, that it would meet too infrequently, and that the House of Representatives would be too large for this purpose (2:318). He thought this power would be better vested in the Senate. He did not think that equal state representation would prove deleterious in such circumstances because all states would have a stake in the survival of the nation (2:318).

Pinckney favored congressional regulation of the militia. He had little faith in the state militia as then constituted. He further thought that over reliance on such under-trained troops was evident in the states' "rapid approaches toward anarchy" (2:332).

One of Pinckney's most important contributions to the Constitution may have been the idea of enumerating and limiting congressional powers. On August 20, he submitted a series of proposals for consideration by the Committee of Detail, some provisions of which, while not making it into the original Constitution, later reappeared as provisions within the Bill of Rights. These included the following provisions: each house should be judge of its own privileges and its members should have certain privileges going to and from that body (also see 2:502); the executive and each house of Congress should be able to request the Supreme Court to give its opinions on important matters of law; the writ of habeas corpus should be guaranteed; liberty of the press; a prohibition of troops in time of peace without legislative assent; military subordination to the military; a prohibition against quartering troops in private homes without consent; a prohibition on dual office holding; a prohibition of religious tests; the designation of the United States as one corporate body; authorization for Congress to create a great seal of the United States; a provision that all commissions should be in the name of the United States; and the extension of judicial jurisdiction over controversies between the United States and states and between the United States and state citizens (2:341–42).

On August 23, Pinckney introduced the resolution that provided that no individual holding public office in the United States should be able without congressional approval to accept any emolument, office, or title from foreign states (2:389). Pinckney introduced a resolution on August 28 providing that the writ of habeas corpus should only be suspended on the most urgent occasions, and then for a period not to exceed twelve months (2:438).

On August 29, Pinckney advocated a provision, later adopted, granting Congress power to establish uniform laws on bankruptcies (2:447). He also introduced the motion prohibiting religious oaths as a condition for public office (2:468). On September 14, Pinckney seconded James Madison's motion to grant Congress the power to establish a national university in which no preference would be made on the basis of religious affiliation (2:616).

On September 14, Pinckney opposed a provision limiting a standing army (2:617). On this same day, he advocated a provision designed to provide for freedom of the press (2:617), a provision similar to one later incorporated into the First Amendment. Later in the day, he favored a motion providing for congressional accounting of expenditures "from time to time" rather than annually (2:619).

Other Matters. Pinckney favored having the national capital in a place other than a state capital. However, he thought it would be appropriately located in "a large town or its vicinity" (2:127). He did not think that it was necessary to specify congressional meeting times within the Constitution (2:198). Pinckney seconded a motion to allow Congress to appoint the treasurer (2:314).

On August 29, Pinckney introduced a resolution providing that two-thirds majorities of both houses of Congress would be required for regulating commerce. He identified five distinct interests corresponding to different sections of the country and including fisheries, free grade wheat and flour, tobacco, and rice and indigo (2:449). He argued that these interests "would be a source of oppressive regulations if no check to a bare majority should be provided" (2:449). He also gave insight into his view of human nature by observing, "States pursue their interest with less scruple than individuals" (2:449). Pinckney further observed that allowing Congress to regulate commerce "was a pure concession on the part of the S. States," reasoning that "They did not need the protection of the N. States at present" (2:449). He indicated that he considered the division between the North and South as an even greater division than the five interests he had previously identified (2:450).

Pinckney favored allowing a two-thirds majority of both houses of Congress to override presidential vetoes. He feared that an alternative proposal for a three-fourths vote would put "a dangerous power in the hands of a few senators headed by the President" (2:586).

Presidency

On June 1, Pinckney said that he favored "a vigorous Executive" (1:64). However, he feared that the executive would take up the power of war and peace that the Continental Congress exercised and thought that this "would render the Executive a Monarchy, of the worst kind, to wit an elective one" (1:65). He nonetheless seconded a motion by James Wilson to vest the executive power in a single individual (1:65; also see 1:88). Pinckney opposed a provision granting the president power to exercise unspecified powers that were neither legislative nor judicial in nature, but he reasoned that such powers were already implicit in the power of the executive to carry into effect national laws (1:67).

On June 1, Pinckney supported a seven-year presidential term (1:68). On July 25, when the convention was considering a six-year term, Pinckney proposed that no individual should be able to serve for more than six of any twelve years, thus avoiding the problems that might be created if the Congress had to decide to reelect a sitting president (2:112).

On July 17, Pinckney favored congressional selection of the president. He believed that legislators, being most interested in the laws they had adopted, would "be most attentive to the choice of a fit man to carry them properly into execution" (2:30). By contrast, he thought that popular elections would "be led by a few active & designing men" and that, in such circumstances "the most populous States by combining in favor of the same individual will be able to carry their points" (2:30). On August 24, Pinckney moved to require majority attendance in Congress when the president was being selected (2:403). He later proposed a two-thirds attendance requirement for the Senate when that institution was being considered as the one to determine presidential elections (2:526).

On September 4, Pinckney opposed the electoral college on four grounds. He thought it would effectively give power to the Senate; he questioned whether electors would know the respective candidates; he feared that it would lead to executive re-eligibility, which he opposed; and he thought it would be inappropriate to involve the Senate in this mechanism, since it would have the responsibility of judging cases of presidential impeachment (2:501). Pinckney renewed his opposition to the electoral college on the following day, again raising four arguments that largely tracked his arguments of the previous day (2:511).

On July 20, Pinckney opposed the impeachments of presidents while they were serving in office (2:64). He feared that if the legislature directed such impeachments, they would be held "as a rod over the Executive and by that means effectually destroy his independence" and negate his veto power (2:66; also see 2:551, applying this argument specifically to trials by the U.S. Senate). He further contended that presidential powers "would be so circumscribed as to render impeachments unnecessary" (2:68).

Judiciary

On June 5, after the Committee of the Whole decided to strike the provision providing that the legislature would appoint judges, Pinckney notified the convention that he hoped to restore this power to the entire Congress (1:121). On June 13, however, after first proposing that the national legislature should make such appointments, Pinckney withdrew his motion after Madison argued in favor of appointment by the Senate (1:233). On July 21, Pinckney argued that the Senate was to be preferred to the president in making appointments because "the Executive will possess neither the requisite knowledge of characters, nor confidence of the people for so high a trust" (2:81). On September 7, Pinckney opposed a role for the Senate in confirming any appointments accept for ambassadors, which he did not think the president should appoint (2:539).

Although he had originally favored a Council of Revision, Pinckney indicated on June 6 that he no longer believed that it was proper to put heads of departments in such a council since the president would already have power to call upon them (1:139). As he later expressed this, if the delegates were to have "an able Council," then "it will thwart him" whereas if he had "a weak one," then "he will shelter himself under their sanction" (2:329). Pinckney also indicated that he opposed including judges in such a council (1:139). He later argued that this would "involve them in parties, and give a previous tincture to their opinions" (2:298).

Slavery

On June 11, Pinckney seconded a resolution by Pennsylvania's James Wilson providing that representation in the House of Representatives should be apportioned according to the population of whites and free inhabitants and three-fifths of other persons (1:201). On other occasions, he argued that blacks should count equally for purposes of state representation. On July 12, he argued that counting blacks equally with whites for purposes of representation was just because "The blacks are the labourers, the peasants of the Southern States: they are as productive of pecuniary resources as those of the Northern States. They add equally to the wealth, and considering money as the sinew of war, to the strength of the nation" (1:596).

Pinckney did not view slavery as a moral issue. Characteristic of such a position, on August 8, he indicated that he "considered the fisheries & the Western frontier as more burdensome to the U.S. than the slaves" (2:223).

On August 21, Pinckney said that South Carolina would never accept the Constitution if it prohibited the slave trade, observing, "In every proposed extension of the powers of Congress, that State has expressly & watchfully excepted that of meddling with the importation of Negroes"

(2:364). He held out the prospect, however, that the state might eliminate this trade on its own, as Virginia and Maryland had already done (2:365). The next day, Pinckney went on to argue, "If slavery is wrong, it is justified by the example of all the world" and observed that "In all ages one half of mankind have been slaves" (2:371). He again held out the prospect, however, that South Carolina might abolish the slave trade on its own and indicated that he would personally favor such a move (2:371).

On August 28, Pinckney seconded a motion made by fellow delegate Pierce Butler and soon thereafter retracted. It was designed to require that "fugitive slaves and servants" were "to be delivered up like criminals" (2:443).

Amendment and Ratification

On June 5, the Committee of the Whole was debating a provision providing for an amending process to which the assent of Congress would not be required. Pinckney doubted the "propriety or necessity" of either the provision as a whole, or, as seems more likely, of the exclusion of the legislature (1:121). Later that day, Pinckney favored the ratification of a new constitution by nine or more states (1:123). On August 31, he favored using conventions for this purpose (2:476). He wanted the Committee of Style to prepare an address to the people to accompany the Constitution (2:564).

When George Mason announced his decision not to sign the Constitution on September 17, Pinckney said that this gave "a peculiar solemnity to the present moment." He feared however that "nothing but confusion & contrariety" could result from allowing states to propose amendments, and he thought that "Conventions are serious things, and ought not to be repeated." Like other delegates, Pinckney had concerns about the proposed Constitution. He especially "objected to the contemptible weakness & dependence of the Executive" and to the fact that a majority of Congress had power to control interstate commerce. Fearing "the danger of a general confusion, and an ultimate decision by the Sword," Pinckney decided that adoption of the Constitution was a safer and more desirable option (2:632).

Life after the Convention

Pinckney was elected to, and appears to have had a major influence at, the South Carolina ratifying convention, where he gave the opening speech. In a speech that repeated some of the themes of Franklin's final speech to the convention in Philadelphia, Pinckney observed:

Upon the whole, he could not but join those in opinion who have asserted that this is the best government that has ever yet been offered to the world, and that, instead of being alarmed at its consequences, we should be astonishingly pleased that one so perfect could have been formed from such discordant and unpromising materials. In a system founded upon republican principles, where the powers of government are properly distributed, and each confined to a separate body of magistracy, a greater degree of force and energy will always be found necessary than even in a monarchy. ("Debates in the Legislature" 1788)

Pinckney served four times as a governor, and also served as a U.S. senator, as a state representative, and as a member of the U.S. House of Representatives. Initially a Federalist, Pinckney later supported Democratic-Republican Thomas Jefferson for the presidency but was never trusted by James Madison, who rarely had kind words to say about him. Jefferson rewarded Pinckney by appointing him as the U.S. minister to Spain. Pinckney died on October 29, 1824 after decades of public service, and was buried in the churchyard of St. Philip's. After his original grave in Charlestown, South Carolina was located, a new marker was added on December 6, 1949. Pinckney's Snee Farm is now a national historic site.

Further Reading

Bradford, M. E. 1981. *Founding Fathers: Brief Lives of the Framers of the United States Constitution*. 2nd ed. Lawrence: University Press of Kansas.

"Debates in the Legislature and in Convention of the State of South Carolina, on the Adoption of the Federal Constitution." January 16–19, 1788. Constitution Society. http://www.constitution.org/rc/rat_sc-l.htm. Accessed 7/15/2012.

Farrand, Max, ed. 1966. *The Records of the Federal Convention of 1787*. 4 vols. New Haven, CT: Yale University Press.

Matthews, Marty D. 2004. *Forgotten Founder: The Life and Times of Charles Pinckney*. Columbia: University of South Carolina Press.

Oliar, Dotan. 2009. "The (Constitutional) Convention on IP: A New Reading," *UCLA Law Review* 57 (December): 421–79.

Williams, Frances Leigh. 1978. *A Founding Family: The Pinckneys of South Carolina*. New York: Harcourt Brace Jovanovich.

EDMUND RANDOLPH (1753–1813)
VIRGINIA

Edmund Randolph was born on August 10, 1753 near Williamsburg, Virginia to John Randolph and Ariana Jennings Randolph, members of one of Virginia's most prominent families. Edmund Randolph attended the College of William and Mary and studied in his father's law office before beginning practice at age twenty. Uncle Peyton Randolph, who was a close friend of George Washington, was president of the First Continental Congress. When Edmund Randolph's parents left for England rather than participate in the revolution, Edmund chose to cast his lot with the patriot cause, serving for a time as an aide-de-camp to General Washington, before returning to Virginia having to help his aunt upon the death of his uncle.

Randolph was the youngest delegate at the Virginia State convention of 1776, the same year he was chosen as the state's attorney general and the year he married Elizabeth Nicholas (who was born just a day after him), with whom he would have five children. Elizabeth was the daughter of Robert Carter Nicholas, a devoted member of the Episcopal Church and a role model for Randolph, who appears to have abandoned his early deism for Anglican orthodoxy (Hardwick 2009, 202). In the years following, Randolph served as mayor of Williamsburg, as a rector of the College of William and Mary, as a clerk of the Virginia House of Delegates, and as a member of the Continental Congress. He resigned from this Congress to pursue the practice of law, which was one of the largest in Virginia. Randolph attended the Annapolis Convention and was chosen that same year as governor of Virginia. Randolph was a handsome man who was regarded as a good speaker.

At the Convention

As state governor, Edmund Randolph headed the Virginia delegation at the Constitutional Convention and joined Madison in persuading Washington to attend. As leader of his delegation, Randolph presented the Virginia Plan, usually thought to be the primary brainchild of Virginia's James Madison (one of the difficulties in assessing Randolph's contribution is in attempting to ascertain how much of the Virginia Plan he accepted). Randolph arrived in Philadelphia on May 15, but was one of only three delegates who stayed to the end of the convention and did not sign the document. Although many attributed his action (or inaction) to political ambitions, Randolph at least partially redeemed himself in the eyes of many of the Constitution's supporters when he helped in the effort for constitutional ratification in his home state.

Speech Introducing the Virginia Plan

Randolph prefaced his speech on the Virginia Plan by expressing regret that the task of introducing such a momentous plan should "fall to him, rather than those, who were of longer standing in life and political experience" (Farrand 1966, 1:18) but indicating that his fellow delegates had chosen him for the task. Randolph divided his speech—one of the few that is described in far greater detail in the convention's official journal than in Madison's notes—into four parts. These included: the properties that governments should possess, the defects of the Articles of Confederation, the dangers of the situation at hand, and the remedies. Under the first heading, Randolph argued that governments should be able to secure themselves against foreign invasions and internal dissentions, to secure blessings that states were unable to secure on their own, to protect itself against state encroachment, and secure its authority over state constitutions (1:18).

Randolph did not believe it was fair to impute the problems under the Articles of Confederation to the authors of this government who had to work "in the then infancy of the science, of constitutions, & of confederacies" and prior to such time as many problems had revealed themselves. Randolph identified five varieties of problems, each corresponding to the goals that Randolph had identified governments as pursuing. He believed the Articles lacked inadequate power to protect against foreign invasion, both because their power to wage war was inadequate and because they "could not cause infractions of treaties or of the law of nations, to be punished" (1:19). He argued that the government had shown similar inability to deal with domestic disturbances. The nation was unable to secure the benefits that might come from "a productive impost—counteraction of the commercial regulations of other nations—pushing of commerce ad libitum—&c &c" (1:19). He also observed that the national government was unable to protect itself against state encroachments and that it was not paramount to state constitutions (1:19).

Randolph identified the dangers of "anarchy" and of "the laxity of government every where" (1:19). He believed the remedy should proceed according to "the republican principle" (1:19). He accordingly followed by outlining the fifteen provisions of the Virginia Plan.

These provisions respectively provided for:

- A "correction" and "enlargement" of the Articles so as to accomplish its purposes
- Representation in the legislature on the basis of tax contributions or the number of "free inhabitants"
- A bicameral Congress
- Selection of the first branch by the people of the states for yet to be designated terms, subject to recall
- Selection of the second branch by members of the first from among nominees submitted by state legislatures
- The power of each house to originate acts in all cases "to which the separate States are incompetent, or in which the harmony of the United States may be interrupted by the exercise of individual Legislation" (1:21) and to veto all state laws or call forth the militia against states failing to fulfill their duties
- A national executive chosen by the national legislature for a single term, the length of which was yet to be determined
- A Council of Revision consisting of the executive and select members of the judiciary with the power to veto acts of Congress, subject to majority override
- A national judiciary to consist of a Supreme Court and other courts established by Congress
- The admission of new states
- Guarantees of republican governments for the states
- The continuation of Congress until adoption of the new government
- Oaths binding state officials to support the new government
- A provision for the adoption of future amendments (1:20–22)

Randolph ended his speech asking the delegates not to let slip "the present opportunity of establishing general peace, harmony, happiness and liberty in the U.S." (1:23).

Randolph's introduction of the Virginia Plan undoubtedly shocked many delegates in departing so radically from the existing government under the Articles of Confederation. On the next day, Randolph introduced a resolution more accurately describing the scope of the changes he had proposed (1:30). Randolph also introduced a proposal that the existing congressional system should be proportional "and not according to the present system" (1:31). Asked by South Carolina's Charles Pinckney whether he meant to abolish the state governments, Randolph said "that he meant by these general propositions merely to introduce the particular ones which explained the outlines of the system he had in view" (1:34). Similarly, when asked on May 31 to explain how many members he contemplated would be in the Senate, Randolph observed "that details made no part of the plan, and could not perhaps with propriety have been introduced," but did indicate that he thought that the second branch should be smaller than the first so as "to be exempt from the passionate proceedings to which numerous assemblies are liable" (1:51). He further traced such defects to "the turbulence and follies of democracy" (1:51).

Federalism

Perhaps reflecting a somewhat less nationalistic view of the subject than did Madison, when asked about the Virginia Plan, Randolph "disclaimed any intention to give indefinite powers to the national Legislature, declaring that he was entirely opposed to such inroads on the State jurisdictions, and that he did not think any considerations whatever could ever change his determination" (1:53). Indeed, when Delaware's Gunning Bedford proposed on July 17 that Congress should be able to legislate "in all cases for the general interests of the Union, and also in those to which the States are separately incompetent," Randolph objected that this involved "the power of violating all the laws and constitutions of the States, and of intermeddling with their police" (2:26).

On June 11, Randolph did support a provision for state officials to take an oath to support the national Constitution (1:203). Consistent with his criticisms of the Articles in introducing the Virginia Plan, Randolph indicated later in the convention (July 18) that Congress needed to be able to guarantee states a "republican" form of government (2:47); indeed, he wanted to go further and affirmatively specify that states could form no other kind (2:48).

In a discussion of the Full Faith and Credit Clause on August 29, Randolph indicated that "there was no instance of one nation executing the judgments of the Court of another nation" (2:448). He accordingly proposed a substitution whereby states would recognize the legal acts recorded under the seal of authority of another (2:448). Randolph renewed objections to the Full Faith and Credit Clause on September 3, observing that one of his concerns about the Constitution was that "its definitions of the power of the Government was so loose as to give it opportunities of usurping all the State powers" (2:489).

Comparing Plans

It may well have been a simple act of courtesy, but on June 14, Randolph seconded a proposal by New Jersey's William Paterson postponing a report from the Committee of the Whole so as to give Paterson time to prepare what became known as the New Jersey Plan (1:240). After this plan was considered, some delegates argued that the New Jersey Plan better reflected the sentiments of the people and was thus more likely to be adopted. Randolph responded that "it would be treason to our trust, not to propose what we found necessary" (1:255). He pointed anew to the problems of the existing government, and argued that the two remedies were "coercion" or "real legislation." He believed the former was *"impracticable, expensive,* [and] *cruel to individuals."* He further believed that such a plan tended "to habituate the instruments of it to shed the blood & riot in the spoils of their fellow Citizens, and consequently trained them up for the service of Ambition" (1:256). By contrast, he favored direct control by the national government over individuals. He argued that the Congress under the Articles constituted "a mere diplomatic body" whose members were "always obsequious to the views of the States" (1: 256). He concluded, "A Natl. Govt. alone, properly constituted, will answer the purpose; and he begged it to be considered that the present is the last moment for establishing one" (1:256).

Randolph expressed dismay over the strong language of Delaware's Gunning Bedford suggesting that the small states might seek foreign allies (1:514). Randolph claimed that neither the small states nor the large could exist well without the other, and that such an attempt would "involve the whole in ruin" (1:515).

When the convention reached the Great Compromise involving representation in the two houses of Congress, one of the provisions of this compromise called for restricting the origination of money bills to the House. Although a number of large state supporters including James Madison of Virginia and James Wilson of Pennsylvania questioned the wisdom of this move, Randolph was among those who successfully supported the restoration of this provision for fear that its elimination would endanger the entire compromise (2:230; also see 2:232, 2:234). He believed that the origination of money bills would actually provide the House of Representatives with an advantage (2:263; also see 2:273), and he was concerned about popular opinion. He explained on August 13:

> We had numerous & monstrous difficulties to combat. Surely we ought not to increase them. When the people behold in the Senate, the countenance of an aristocracy; and in the president, the form at least of a little monarch, will not their alarms be sufficiently raised without taking from their immediate representatives, a right which has been so long apportionment to them. (2:278–79)

For the same reason, he thought that the power to declare war should be entrusted to the House rather than the Senate (2:279).

Randolph thought that Congress should have the power to refer some federal appointments to state executives or legislatures (2:405–6).

Congress

House of Representatives. Randolph favored terms of two years rather than three for members of the House of Representatives. He actually preferred annual elections, which he believed the people favored, but he thought that they would be inconvenient for a government the size of the United States (1:360).

Senate. Although Randolph had been somewhat vague about the initial configuration of the U.S. Senate, he favored seven-year terms for senators (1:218), with terms to end so that relatively equal numbers would annually come up for election (1:408). He argued that the "democratic licentiousness of the State Legislatures proved the necessity of a firm Senate" (1:218). He also foresaw this body as guarding against possible combinations of the executive with demagogues in the first branch (1:218). Randolph thought that it would be difficult for an aristocratic Senate, such as Gouverneur Morris of Pennsylvania proposed, to coexist with a democratic House (1:514). When the convention tied in a vote over representation in the Senate, Randolph proposed a temporary adjournment (2:17–18).

Randolph favored executive appointment in the cases of senatorial vacancies. He observed that some state legislatures only met once a year and that, as a smaller body, the Senate could not afford vacancies. He believed that the executive could be trusted with such interim appointments (2:231).

Randolph thought that a 14-year citizenship requirement for senators was too long. Prefacing his remarks with the comment that he "did not know but it might be problematical whether emigrations to this Country were on the whole useful or not," he continued by pointing to promises that the nation had extended to foreigners during the American Revolution and feared that, if these were not kept, immigrants might oppose the new system. He said he could accept no more than a seven-year citizenship requirement (2:237), although he subsequently supported a nine-year requirement (2:239). He favored substituting a four-year for a seven-year citizenship requirement in the House (2:268).

Powers. When the convention discussed whether Congress should have the power to issue paper money, Randolph expressed his "antipathy" to such a power, but he opposed an absolute bar since "he could not foresee all the occasions that might arise" (2:310). When the convention was discussing a provision to prohibit the taxation of incoming slaves, Randolph was among those who favored a compromise. He observed that the convention faced a dilemma: "By agreeing to the clause, it would revolt the Quakers, the Methodists, and many others in the States having no slaves. On the other hand, two States might be lost to the Union" (2:374). Randolph favored a provision specifying that the new government would have the power to fulfill the obligations entered into by the previous Congress (2:376). He also favored a provision providing that all debts entered into under the Articles would remain valid under the new government (2:414).

Randolph wanted to grant Congress the power to provide for uniform arming and training of the militia. He doubted that "the Militia could be brought into the field and made to commit suicide on themselves" and observed that states were currently neglecting the militia and that members of the state legislatures were courting popularity "too much to enforce a proper discipline" (2:387).

Randolph had reservations about allowing each House of Congress to judge the privileges of its members (2:503). On September 14, Randolph seconded Madison's motion that would have allowed Congress to charter corporations (2:615). He also seconded a motion by Virginia's George Mason that would have included an admonition against standing armies in times of peace (2:617).

Other Matters. Randolph opposed allowing states to pay members of Congress. He believed that this would lead to "a dependence . . . that would vitiate the whole System" and "The whole nation has an interest in the attendance & services of its members" and should accordingly pay them (1:372).

Randolph did not favor allowing Congress to decide when to reapportion itself. He observed that "a pretext would never be wanting to postpone alterations, and keep the power in the hands of those possessed of it" (1:561; also see 1:567). Randolph proposed periodic censuses for this purpose (1:571). He observed that "If a fair representation of the people be not secured, the injustice of the Govt. will shake it to its foundations" (1:580). Randolph wanted the formula for counting slaves as three-fifths of a person in representation for the House of Representatives specifically secured in the Constitution:

> He urged strenuously that express security ought to be provided for including slaves in the ratio of Representation. He lamented that such a species of property existed. But as it did exist the holders of it would require some security. (1:594)

Randolph and Madison supported a motion giving members of Congress the power to compel the attendance of absent members. He also favored Madison's idea that the Constitution should require a two-thirds vote to expel members of Congress (2:254). He supported a motion by Gouverneur Morris that would allow any member to call for a roll-call vote (2:255).

Randolph favored the clause preventing members of Congress from being able to accept offices for which the emoluments had been increased during their terms as a way of closing the door on "influence & corruption" (2:290; also see 2:491). He was willing to make an exception for individuals who might be needed to command military forces (2:290). Randolph and Madison favored preventing any new pay raises for Congress from going into effect until the passage of three years (2:430).

Presidency

Apart from the reference to the alliance of the executive and the judiciary in a Council of Revision, the Virginia Plan had been silent as to how many individuals should constitute the executive branch. Randolph came out on June 1 in opposition to a single executive, which he regarded as "the foetus [fetus] of monarchy" (1:66). Opposing Pennsylvania's James Wilson on this point, Randolph believed that an executive composed of three men could just as easily provide for "vigor, dispatch & responsibility" as one (1:66). Randolph elaborated on his arguments the following day. He said that a single executive was adverse to the "temper" of the people, that a plurality could accomplish the same objects, that the people would not place confidence in a single executive, and that a single executive (who would tend to be from the center of the nation) would leave more remote areas of the nation on an unequal footing (1:88).

The Virginia Plan called for Congress to select the president. Randolph opposed a plan introduced by Elbridge Gerry, which would have entrusted presidential selection to state governors, who would have votes in proportion to their state's population. Randolph argued that the small states would not have a chance of selecting one of their own by this procedure. He also feared that governors would not be familiar enough with individuals outside their own states to be able to make good choices. He further feared that state governors would see the president as a rival and that "They will not cherish the great Oak which is to reduce them to paltry shrubs" (1: 176). On July 2, Randolph indicated that he was willing to allow each state to have an equal voice in the selection of the president (1:514).

Randolph had questions about the electoral college (2:500). He apparently preferred legislative selection. He thought that if the new system were to be adopted, the House, rather than the Senate, should make the final selection of candidates if none of them received a majority (2:502; 2:513).

At a time (July 19) when the convention was still contemplating legislative selection of the president, Randolph opposed allowing the president to be eligible for more than one term. He argued, "If he should be re-appointable by the Legislature, he will be no check on it. His revisionary power will be of no avail" (2:55).

Randolph was a strong proponent of executive impeachment. He observed that "Guilt wherever found ought to be punished" (2:67). He further feared that the executive would have "great opportunitys of abusing his power; particularly in time of war when the military force, and in some respects the public money will be in his hands. Should no regular punishment be provided, it will be irregularly inflicted by tumults & insurrections" (2:67). At that point, Randolph was considering the possibility that state judges might serve as a forum for such impeachments or that there might be some forum that would act as a preliminary inquest (2:67).

Randolph proposed a revised variant of the Presentment Clause, allowing for a presidential veto of congressional legislation, that the convention adopted on August 16 (2:305). He opposed allowing the vice president to serve as president of the Senate (2:537). Randolph did not think the president should have the power to pardon treason, observing, "The President may himself be guilty. The Traytors may be his own instruments" (2:616).

Judiciary

On June 13, Randolph and Madison successfully proposed that the juris-diction of the national judiciary "should extend to cases, which respect the collection of the National revenue, impeachments of any national officers, and questions which involve the national peace and harmony" (1:232). On July 18, he indicated that he did not think that state courts could be trusted to enforce national laws (2:46).

On July 18, Randolph said that he favored the appointment of judges by Congress rather than by the executive (2:43). He indicated that the hopes of receiving appointments would be more "diffusive if they de-pended on the Senate, the members of which wd. be diffusively known, than if they depended on a single man who could not be personally known to a very great extent; and consequently that opposition to the System, would be so far weakened" (2:43). On July 21, however, Randolph seemed to have changed his mind.

Randolph opposed a provision that would have permitted the removal of judges by the president on a petition from Congress. He feared that the result would be that of "weakening too much the independence of the Judges" (2:429).

Other Matters

When Benjamin Franklin proposed that the convention should begin to start each day with prayer, Randolph proposed that the convention request a sermon for the Fourth of July as a substitute (1:452).

Randolph served on three committees at the convention—the Original Apportionment of Congress Committee, the Committee of Detail, and the Committee on Interstate Comity and Bankruptcy. Among Randolph's more interesting notes from the Committee of Detail are his notations regarding drafting a constitution. He observed that two considerations needed to be foremost:

1. To insert essential principles only, lest the operations of government should be clogged by rendering those provisions permanent and unalter-able, which ought to be accommodated to times and events, and
2. To use simple and precise language, and general propositions, accord-ing to the example of the (several) constitutions of the several states. (For the construction of a constitution of necessarily differs from that of law). (2:137)

Amendment and Ratification

On June 11, Randolph agreed with fellow Virginian George Mason that the new Constitution would prove to be defective and that it would be better to provide for a process of amending the document than, in Mason's words, "to trust to chance and violence" (1:203). On June 20, Randolph said that it was important to refer the new document to the people for their approval (1:336). He reiterated this idea on July 23. Randolph feared that referring the Constitution to approval to state legislatures would put power into the hands of "local demagogues who will be degraded by it from the importance they now hold" and who would accordingly "spare no efforts to impede that progress in the popular mind which will be necessary to the adoption of the plan" (2:89). He further observed that "some of the States are averse to any change in their Constitution, and will not take the requisite steps, unless expressly called upon to refer to the question to the people" (2:89). Randolph suggested on August 30 that nine states should be sufficient to ratify the new document (2:469). The next day, he suggested that if the Constitution were not in a "final form" that would "permit him to accede to it," then "the State Conventions should be at liberty to propose amendments to be submitted to another General Convention which may reject or incorporate them, as shall be judged proper" (2:479).

The Decision Not to Sign

Randolph sent the first signal that he might not sign the new Constitution on August 29 when he argued that failure to adopt a provision requiring a two-thirds congressional majority for the adoption of navigation acts "would compleat the deformity of the system" (2:452). Without going into details on his view, he explained: "What he had in view was merely to pave the way for a declaration which he might be hereafter obliged to make if an accumulation of obnoxious ingredients should take place, that he could not give his assent to the plan" (2:453).

On September 10, Randolph expressed renewed reservations about the Constitution. He tied them to how the Constitution would be ratified. Randolph said that he had been among those who had been convinced "that radical changes in the system of the Union were necessary" (2:560). Believing that the convention had subsequently departed in significant respects from the "republican" principles of the original Virginia Plan, he said that he favored allowing states to propose amendments to the Constitution, which would be considered by a second convention (2:561). Later in the day, he listed his own specific objections, some of which he appeared to have been expressing for the first time. He disfavored the role of the Senate in sitting as a court of impeachment; he believed that a vote by three-fourths rather than two-thirds of each house should be required to override a presidential veto; he thought there were too few representatives in the House of Representatives; he believed there should be a restriction on a standing army in times of peace; he opposed the Necessary and Proper Clause; he thought there should be further restraints on the power to enact navigation acts; he disfavored the provision related to the taxation of exports; he feared the power of Congress to intervene in state affairs on the petitions of state governors; he believed there needed to be "a more definite boundary between the General & State Legislature—and between the General and State Judiciaries;" he thought the president's power to pardon treason was too broad; and he was concerned about the ability of members of Congress to set their own compensation (2:563–64). Having rhetorically asked whether he was "to promote the establishment of a plan which he verily believed would end in Tyranny," he then equivocated by indicating that "he must keep himself free, in case he should be honored with a Seat in the convention of his State, to act according to the dictates of his judgment" (2:564). He reiterated his call to allow states to either adopt the Constitution or propose amendments, which would then be considered in yet another convention (2:564).

Randolph repeated his concerns on September 15. Expressing the psychological pressures that he must have felt at not joining the majority of his colleagues in signing the document, he nonetheless kept his future options open.

> Mr. Randolph animadverting on the indefinite and dangerous power given by the Constitution to Congress, expressing the pain he felt at differing from the body of the Convention, on the close of the great & awful subject of their labours, and anxiously wishing for some accommodating expedient which would relieve him from his embarrassments, made a motion importing "that amendments to the plan might be offered by the State Conventions, which should be submitted to and finally decided on by another general Convention" Should this proposition be disregarded, it would he said be impossible for him to put his name to the instrument. Whether he should oppose it afterwards he would not then decide but he would not deprive himself of the freedom to do so in his own State, if that course should be prescribed by his final judgment. (2:631)

Randolph reiterated his concerns on September 17, again indicating that his refusal to sign the document at the convention did not mean that "he should oppose the Constitution without doors. He meant only to keep himself free to be governed by his duty as it should be prescribed by his future judgment" (2:645). Urged by fellow members to sign in attestation to the unanimity of the states, Randolph responded that this would be the same as giving his approval: "He repeated that in refusing to sign the Constitution, he took a step which might be the most awful of his life, but it was dictated by his conscience, and it was not possible for him to hesitate, much less, to change" (2:646). He continued to fear that giving the people an all or nothing option, rather than allowing them to propose amendments "would really produce the anarchy & civil convulsions which were apprehended from the refusal of individuals to sign it" (2:646).

Life after the Convention

Although Randolph had refused to sign the Constitution at the convention, Madison continued to woo him, knowing that his support at the state's ratifying convention in Richmond could prove to be essential. As he watched eight other states ratify, Randolph decided that it would be better to lose a limb than "assent to the dissolution of the Union" (Reardon 1974, 139). Defending his moderate Federalist stance against Antifederalist attacks at the Richmond Convention by Patrick Henry, Randolph declared that the new national government would only be able to exercise powers that the Constitution specifically granted to it.

Randolph was part of a committee that drafted a resolution accompanying the state's ratification, which articulated the view that "the powers granted under the Constitution being derived from the people of the United States may be resumed by them whensoever the same shall be perverted to their injury or oppression and . . . every power not granted thereby remains with them and at their will" (quoted by Gutzman 2004, 492). Kevin R. C. Gutzman believes that this statement, rather than Jefferson and Madison, was the source for the doctrine of interposition that they expressed in the Virginia and Kentucky Resolutions of 1798 in opposition to the congressional adoption of the Alien and Sedition Acts, the latter of which they argued violated not only the First Amendment protections of speech and press, but also invaded powers reserved to the states under the Tenth Amendment.

President Washington subsequently named Randolph as the nation's first attorney general where he established many important precedents. As attorney general he successfully argued the government's case in *Chisholm v. Georgia* allowing Georgia to be sued without its consent by out-of-state citizens (1793), only to see this decision overturned by the Eleventh Amendment. Randolph served less successfully as secretary of state to George Washington in part because his moderation was distrusted by both sides, with Thomas Jefferson once calling him "the poorest chameleon I ever saw, having no color of his own and reflecting that nearest him. When he is with me, he is a whig. When with Hamilton he is a tory. When with the president, he is that [which he thinks will please him]" (quoted in Tachau 1986, 16).

After losing Washington's confidence, Randolph returned to Virginia to practice law. Although he was a highly successful practitioner, he faced increasing debts in later life, a period during which he began writing a history of Virginia published long after his death near Millwood, Virginia on September 12, 1813. He was buried in Millwood's Old Chapel Cemetery. The Grand Lodge of Freemasons in Virginia, where Randolph had served as a grand master, built a monument in Millwood to honor Randolph in 1940. Randolph's daughter Lucy married Peter Daniel, who had studied law under her father and became a Supreme Court justice. A son, Peyton, wrote a multivolume *Reports of Virginia Appeals Court*. Randolph was not directly related to the irascible congressman named John Randolph.

Further Reading

Crews, Ed. 2012. "Meet Betsy and Edmund." *Colonial Williamsburg Journal* 34 (Summer): 21–23.

Farrand, Max, ed. 1966. *The Records of the Federal Convention of 1787*. 4 vols. New Haven, CT: Yale University Press.

Gutzman, Kevin R. C. 2004. "Edmund Randolph and Virginia Constitutionalism." *The Review of Politics* 66 (Summer):469–97.

Hardwick, Devin R. 2009. "Anglican Moderation: Religion and the Political Thought of Edmund Randolph." In *The Forgotten Founders on Religion and Public Life*, edited by Daniel L. Dreisbach, Mark David Hall, and Jeffry H. Morrison, 196–219. Notre Dame: University of Notre Dame Press.

Meister, Charles W. 1987. *The Founding Fathers*. Jefferson, NC: McFarland & Company.

Reardon, John J. 1974. *Edmund Randolph: A Biography*. New York: Macmillan.

Tachau, Mary K. Bonsteel. 1986. "George Washington and the Reputation of Edmund Randolph." *Journal of American History* 73 (June): 15–34.

Thomas, Emory M. 1969. "Edmund Randolph, His Own Man." *Virginia Cavalcade* 18: 5–12.

Vile, John R. 2001. "Edmund Randolph." In *Great American Lawyers: An Encyclopedia*, edited by John R. Vile, 2:577–82. Santa Barbara, CA: ABC-CLIO.

GEORGE READ (1733–1798)
DELAWARE

George Read was born in Cecil County, Maryland on September 18, 1733 of Irish immigrant parents who were planters. Read attended the Reverend Francis Alison's Academy in New London, Pennsylvania and read law before being admitted to the bar first in Pennsylvania and then in Delaware where he had moved. He was appointed attorney general for Delaware 10 years after being admitted to the bar. In 1763, he married Gertrude (Gitty) Ross Till (1732–1802), a widow and sister of George Ross, who later signed the Declaration of Independence; Read and his wife had three sons and a daughter who survived to adulthood.

Read served from 1765 to 1780 as a Delaware legislator and from 1774 to 1779 as a representative to the Continental Congress. There he sided with John Dickinson in voting against independence but, unlike Dickinson, Read still chose to sign the Declaration of Independence. One of the state's most powerful politicians during the Revolutionary War period, his opponents sometimes called him "Dionysius, Tyrant of Delaware" (Gillespie and Lienesch 1989, 32). Active in drawing up Delaware's constitution, he served as the state's acting president from 1777 to 1778. A judge of the court of appeal in admiralty under the Articles of Confederation, which he had reluctantly supported, Read attended the Annapolis Convention prior to going to the Constitutional Convention.

At the Convention

Read was present on the opening day of convention business on May 25, but he attended under a restraint, which he himself had helped to author, that did not bind all the delegates. On May 30, he accordingly moved to postpone consideration of congressional regulation since he and other Delaware delegates had been instructed not to yield the state's equal suffrage and might feel compelled to leave the convention if the matter were pursued (Farrand 1966, 1:37). When Madison suggested that this matter might be resolved by sending it to committee, presumably the Committee of the Whole, Read was apparently not completely satisfied (1:37), but he did not leave the convention.

In a letter that Read wrote to John Dickinson on May 21, he indicated that existing plans seemed predicated on giving the smaller states a single representative in the lower house of Congress. He accordingly indicated that "I suspect it to be of importance to the small States that their deputies should keep a strict watch upon the movements and propositions from the larger States, who will probably combine to swallow up the smaller ones by addition, division, or impoverishment" (3:26).

Federalism

After reading the above letter, it is surprising to find that Read's most distinctive contribution to the convention was openly to question the continuing existence of the states. It is, of course, possible that Read thought that eliminating the states would also eliminate any advantages then enjoyed by the larger states. However, one observer has interpreted Read's position as "part of a rhetorical strategy designed to protect the people of his state from political impotence and to secure for them as much influence as could be acquired" (Bradford 1994, 106). Read first advanced his view that states should be diminished, if not abolished, on June 6:

> Too much attachment is betrayed to the State Governmts. We must look beyond their continuance. A national Govt. must soon of necessity swallow all of them up. They will soon be reduced to the mere office of electing the national Senate. He was agst. patching up the old federal System: he hoped the idea wd. be dismissed. It would be like putting new cloth on an old garment. The confederation was founded on temporary principles. It cannot last: it cannot be amended. If we do not establish a good Govt. on new principles, we must either go to ruin, or have the work to do over again. The people at large are wrongly suspected of being averse to a Genl. Govt. The aversion lies among interested men who possess their confidence. (1:137).

Read reiterated this theme on June 11 when the convention was discussing a provision for guaranteeing the territory of each state. He felt that such a provision "abetted the idea of distinct States wch. would be a perpetual source of discord" (1:202). He further observed, "There can be [no] cure for this evil but in doing away [with the] States altogether and uniting them all into [one] great Society" (1:202).

In a discussion of Senate terms on June 26, Read again argued that state lines should, as much as possible, be ignored. Addressing the small states, he said that "it was in their interest that we should become one people as much as possible, that State attachments shd. be extinguished as much as possible, that the Senate shd. be so constituted as to have the feelings of citizens of the whole" (1:424).

Read argued even more forcefully for his views on June 19. He said that "he shd. have no objection to the system if it were truly national, but it has too much of a federal mixture in it" (1:463). He did not believe that the small states had much to fear; indeed, he thought the large states labored under the weakness of trying to govern areas that were too large. By contrast, "Delaware had enjoyed tranquility & he flattered himself wd. continue to do so" (1:463). Again Read argued that the solution was to incorporate all the states into one system:

> If the States remain, the representatives of the large ones will stick together, and carry every thing before them. The Executive also will be chosen under the influence of this partiality, and will betray it in his administration. These jealousies are inseparable from the scheme of leaving the States in Existence. They must be done away. The ungranted lands also which have been assumed by particular States must also be given up. (1:463)

Read indicated that he favored the plan that Alexander Hamilton had introduced and would rather have it than the Virginia Plan.

On August 8, Read opposed long periods of state residence as a condition to holding legislative offices. He observed that "we were now forming a *Natil* Govt. and such a regulation would correspond little with the idea that we were one people" (2:217). On August 18, Read further opposed leaving the appointment of militia officers to the states. He argued that if such a power were to remain with the states, it should be invested in the governors rather than in state legislatures (2:333).

Congress

On June 7, Read proposed that the president should appoint members of the Senate from nominees suggested by state legislatures. He indicated that he feared delegates would be "alarmed" at his proposal (1:151). Instead, it simply failed to receive either a second or other support. On June 24, when other delegates were suggesting terms of from four to seven years, Read proposed that members of the Senate should serve during good behavior, that is, for life (1:409). This would have given members of that body the same independence that members of the federal judiciary enjoy today. When this resolution received little support, Read advocated nine-year terms (1:421). Read appeared to believe that this would give senators greater independence from their states.

On June 13, Read indicated that he favored the provision limiting the origination of money bills to the House of Representations. However, he did not think this should prevent the Senate from amending such bills (1:234). On August 9, Read said that although he did not consider the origination of money bills in the House of Representatives to be important and had previously voted for striking it, he was willing to restore it for those who thought it was an essential element of the compromise relating to state representation within Congress (2:232–33).

On July 9, Read questioned why Delaware had only one representative and Georgia had three (1:561). Alluding on July 10 to the fact that his state and Rhode Island would each only have one representative if the initial House had, as proposed, only 65 members, Read proposed doubling this number. He argued that states with a small number of representatives might sometimes find themselves unrepresented, and he doubted that the people would "place their confidence" in so small a number (1:570). Consistent with his earlier support for the Hamilton plan, Read further observed, "He hoped the objects of the Genl. Govt. would be much more numerous than seemed to be expected by some gentlemen, and that they would become more & more so" (1:570). He further suggested that representation for new western states might be limited by putting a cap on the whole number of representatives (1:570). On July 13, Read said that he suspected some of the larger states were not taking their full share of representatives in order to avoid their share of taxes. He thought that both should be apportioned fairly (1:601).

Consistent with his view, Read argued on July 11 that "the Legislature ought not to be too much shackled" (1:582). He feared that such restraints would act like religious creeds, which embarrassed those who agreed with them and produced dissatisfaction among others (1:582). Consistent with his view, Read supported congressional regulation over state elections, granting Congress not only the power to alter state regulations but also to provide for such regulations in cases where states failed to act on their own (2:242).

One power that Read did not want Congress exercising was the power to issue, or emit, paper money. On August 16, he said that the exercise of such a power "would be as alarming as the mark of the Beast in Revelation" (2:310). Similarly, on September 14, Read successfully introduced the words "or other direct tax" after limits on capitation taxes lest "some liberty might otherwise be taken to saddle the States with a readjustment by this rule, of past Requisitions of Congs" (2:618).

Presidency

On August 7, Read supported an absolute presidential veto of congressional laws, saying "He considered this . . . essential to the Constitution, to the preservation of liberty, & to the public welfare" (1:200). Read also believed that the president, and not Congress, should have the power to appoint the national treasurer. He thought that experience in the states had demonstrated that legislatures were inappropriate institutions for making such a choice and he argued that "The Executive being responsible would make a good choice" (2:315).

On August 24, Read offered a motion to grant the president of the Senate the right to cast the deciding vote in the case of a tie in that body for president. The convention rejected this proposal, apparently without a state-by-state record of the vote (2:403). On September 6, Read opposed a motion by Elbridge Gerry of Massachusetts to send the election to the House of Representatives in the case where the Senate did not reelect a candidate by a majority; he expressed his opposition to indulging individual delegates (2:522). When the convention contemplated allowing the House of Representatives to decide elections in which no presidential candidate obtained a majority, Read feared that states, like his own, with only one member, might end up being unrepresented in the case that a member was sick or absent (2:536).

Judiciary

On August 27, Read opposed vesting jurisdiction in cases of both law and equity, the two central divisions of English law, in the same court (2:428). However, the record does not reveal the basis of his opposition.

Life after the Convention

Read was the only individual who signed the Constitution twice, since fellow delegate John Dickinson, a longtime friend who had left the convention because of illness, had asked him to sign on his behalf. Read worked for ratification of the Constitution on his return to Delaware after which he was selected as one of Delaware's first two senators and aligned himself with the Federalist Party, which embodied the principles of Alexander Hamilton, whom Read had largely supported at the convention. He resigned from this post in order to take the post of chief justice of his state, a position in which he served until his death in 1798. The previous year he published a two-volume *Laws of Delaware*. Read died on September 21, 1798 in New Castle, where he was buried near the Immanuel Episcopal Church.

Further Reading

Bradford, M. E. 1994. *Founding Fathers: Brief Lives of the Framers of the United States Constitution*. 2nd ed. Lawrence, KS: University Press of Kansas.

Farrand, Max, ed. 1966. *The Records of the Federal Convention of 1787*. 4 vols. New Haven, CT: Yale University Press.

Gillespie, Michael Allen, and Michael Lienesch. 1989. *Ratifying the Constitution*. Lawrence: University Press of Kansas.

Read, William T. 1870. *Life and Correspondence of George Read, Signer of the Declaration of Independence*. Philadelphia: J. B. Lippincott & Co.

JOHN RUTLEDGE (1739–1800)
SOUTH CAROLINA

John Rutledge was born in Charleston, South Carolina on September 17, 1739 to Dr. John Rutledge, a physician who had immigrated from Ireland, and his fifteen-year-old wife, Sarah Hext Rutledge, who had inherited a great deal of money. Rutledge's father died in 1740, but a clergyman educated him before he studied law under a local lawyer and then attended the Inns of Court in England, where he was admitted to the bar in 1760, just a year before he was admitted to the practice of law in South Carolina. After his return, Rutledge married Elizabeth Grimke (1741–1792), by whom he would have 10 children, including one who would serve in the U.S. House of Representatives. By his marriage, he also became related to Angelina and Sarah Grimke, who went on in the 1830s to become prominent South Carolina abolitionists.

A tall and proud member of South Carolina's low country planter class, known for his oratorical abilities, which even Patrick Henry had commended, Rutledge was appointed as the state's attorney general when he was only twenty-five. The next year he was elected to the First Continental Congress where, with Samuel Adams, Rutledge became an early advocate for independence. After attending the Second Continental Congress (during which his younger brother, Edward, signed the Declaration of Independence), Rutledge helped write his state constitution, under which he served as the state's first president. He became governor under a new state constitution adopted in 1778 and tried during much of the Revolutionary War, often acting with near-dictatorial powers, to protect his state. He was elected to the Continental Congress in 1782, and became chief judge of South Carolina's Court of Chancery, thus having experience with all three branches of government. Apparently fearful that people were forgetting the importance of the union of states, Rutledge named his seventh child, a son, "States Rutledge" (Barry 1971, 308).

Rutledge has been described as being "well built," as having "reddish brown hair and highly arched nostrils" and as speaking well, but often quite fast (Meister 1987, 271). He arrived in Philadelphia by ship on May 18 and spent his first three weeks staying at the house of Pennsylvania's James Wilson before joining his wife at the Indian Queen when she arrived about three weeks later (Barry 1971, 315). Rutledge was present on the opening day of convention business on May 25 (Washington had reported his arrival on May 17), and he seconded the motion made by Robert Morris nominating George Washington as president of the convention. In so doing he indicated that he hoped, as proved to be the case, that the vote would be unanimous and that "the presence of Genl Washington forbade any observations on the occasion which might otherwise be proper" (Farrand 1966, 1:3).

Perhaps seeking some regional balance, on May 30, the convention selected Nathaniel Gorham of Massachusetts over Rutledge as chair of the Committee of the Whole by a vote of seven to one (1:29). Rutledge's nomination was itself, however, an honor, and Rutledge did his share of work on other committees. He served on the committee formed on July 2 to compromise on representation in Congress, on the committees formed on July 6 and July 9 for ascertaining and revising the initial membership of Congress, and on the committee formed on August 29 on interstate comity and bankruptcy. Most importantly, Rutledge chaired the five-member Committee of Detail, formed on July 24. One of the convention's most important committees, it introduced the idea of enumerated powers and otherwise tilted the document in a more state-friendly direction. Rutledge's service on this committee led "an aged friend" writing on behalf of nullification and secession in 1863 incorrectly to identify Rutledge as "the author of the Constitution" (See Cruger 1863).

Congress

Selection of Members. On June 6, Rutledge seconded a motion by fellow South Carolinian Charles Pinckney providing that the state legislatures, rather than the people, should select members of the first branch of Congress. Rutledge presumably agreed with Pinckney's explanation that states would be more likely to ratify a system in which they had such a part (1:132). On June 21 he offered another reason. Distinguishing "between a mediate & immediate election by the people," he argued that elections by state legislatures would be more "refined" and would result in the selection of "fitter men" (1:359). He doubted that the delegates to the convention would be of the same character if the people, rather than the state legislatures, had selected them.

Representation. On June 11, Rutledge argued that apportionment in the House should "be according to the quotas of contribution" (1:196; also see 1:201 where Rutledge supports the introduction of a motion to this effect). When the convention was about to discuss the powers of Congress, Rutledge proposed postponing this matter until the delegates resolved the more fundamental question of how states would be represented (1:436). On July 5, Rutledge repeated his view that the convention should apportion seats in Congress not simply according to population but also according to property, observing, "Property was certainly the principal object of Society" (1:534).

When the convention settled on sixty-five representatives for the House, including three for New Hampshire, Rutledge proposed reducing its representation to two, but he based his justification both on his view that New Hampshire's population did not entitle her to three and that "it was a poor State" (1:566). Rutledge seemed most concerned about the admission of western states. On July 11 he observed that "The Western States will not be able to contribute in proportion to their numbers, [and] they shd. not therefore be represented in that proportion" (1:582). Rutledge indicated on August 30 that he did not believe that states should be partitioned without their consent, although he did not think that either Virginia or North Carolina would try to hold on to their lands, which then included the states of Tennessee and Kentucky, beyond the mountains (2:462).

On July 16, the decisive day in which the convention finally voted to grant states equal representation in the Senate, as proposed by a committee on which Rutledge had served, he opposed an adjournment "because he could see no chance of a compromise" (2:19). Rutledge explained that the decision to be made was simply whether the large states would agree or not. For his part, he was willing to compromise:

> He conceived that although we could not do what we thought best, in itself, we ought to do something. Had we not better keep the Govt. up a little longer, hoping that another Convention will supply our omissions, than abandon every thing to hazard. Our Constituents will be very little satisfied with us if we take the latter course. (2:19)

In opposing a motion to double the size of the House of Representatives, Rutledge argued that existing state legislatures had too many members, that states would see that their members attended Congress, and, in what is one of the most erroneous predictions of the convention, that he doubted that Congress would need to meet for more than six to eight weeks a year (1:570). On August 7, Rutledge did introduce a motion specifying that Congress should meet at least once a year (2:200).

Rutledge accused those who favored the provision limiting the origination of money bills to the House of Representatives of being inconsistent in advocating this because the House of Lords used it, but not also following the House of Lords in permitting the upper house to amend such bills. Using an expression popular at the time, he believed the people would regard such a concession as "a mere tub to the whale" (2:279), that is, as a diversion. As for Rutledge, if the Constitution were to lodge an exclusive right anywhere, he thought that it should lodge it in the Senate:

> The Senate being more conversant in business, and having more leisure, will digest the bills much better, and as they are to have no effect, till examined & approved by the H. of Reps there can be no possible danger. (2:279)

Length of Terms and Pay. On June 12, Rutledge proposed that terms for members of the U.S. House of Representatives should be for two years (1:214), as the convention eventually decided. On this same day, Rutledge proposed that members of the Senate should receive no salary. Had this measure been adopted, it would have presumably reserved seats only for those wealthy enough to serve without pay (1:219), thus giving the Senate a more aristocratic cast similar to that of the House of Lords in England.

Eligibility for Other Offices. On June 23, Rutledge indicated that he favored keeping Congress "as pure as possible, by shutting the door against appointments of its own members to offices, which was one source of its corruption" (1:386). Recognizing that evasion would be possible, he supported a provision that not only barred sitting members but also those who had served within a year (1:390).

Qualifications. On August 8, Rutledge proposed that members of the House should be required to reside at least seven years in their states, but, indicative of his perception of widely different sectional interests, he seemed more concerned about immigrants from other parts of United States than from abroad. He thus observed that "An emigrant from N. England to S.C. or George would know little of its affairs and could not be supposed to acquire a thorough knowledge in less time" (2:217). When others proposed the possibility of lowering the residency requirement to one year, Rutledge proposed three instead (2:218). When the convention agreed to a seven-year citizenship requirement for members of the House, Rutledge said that he thought that an even longer period should be required of senators, who would exercise greater powers (2:239). He later favored a provision that would apply qualifications to those who had already immigrated as well as to those who would immigrate in the future. He observed that the need for precaution was as great in the former case as in the latter (2:270).

As chair of the Committee of Detail, Rutledge said that his committee had not proposed any qualifications for members of Congress because they could not agree. He observed that there was danger of displeasing the people by making them too high or of rendering qualifications of no effect by setting them too low (2:249). Soon thereafter, however, he proposed that the Constitution should make such qualifications the same as those for members of the state legislatures (2:251), qualifications that would presumably vary from state to state.

Powers. On May 31, Rutledge joined Charles Pinckney in objecting to the provision in the Virginia Plan granting Congress power to legislate in all cases in which the state proved "incompetent." They thought this word was too vague (1:53). Rutledge repeated this opposition on July 16 (2:17). Significantly, the Committee of Detail that Rutledge chaired substituted specific grants of powers for such broad statements.

Rutledge opposed granting Congress power to guarantee states a republican form of government, but only because he thought it to be unnecessary. In his view "Congs. had the authority if they had the means to co-operate with any State in subduing a rebellion. It was & would be involved in the nature of the thing" (2:48).

Rutledge joined Charles Pinckney in opposing congressional control over state elections. The two delegates thought that the states "could & must be relied on in such cases" (2:240). Rutledge proposed an amendment of the Supremacy Clause (more forcefully emphasizing the Constitution) that the convention accepted on August 23 (2:389).

Rutledge did not approve of the requirement, which some fellow southern delegates favored, to require two-thirds majorities in Congress to regulate trade. He thought that fears of abuse were overdrawn and that the convention should make decisions with the future in view: "As we are laying the foundation for a great empire, we ought to take a permanent view of the subject and not look at the present moment only" (2:452). He thought that navigation laws were particularly needed to gain trade with the West Indies and feared that a two-thirds requirement would make this difficult. He proposed the establishment of a committee to consider the assumption of state debts, and believed that relieving states of such debts "would conciliate them to the plan" (2:327).

Powers. Rutledge wanted both to prohibit congressional taxation of exports and the taxation of slave imports (2:306). On August 18, Rutledge introduced a motion to prevent funds appropriated for public creditors from being diverted to other purposes (II2:326).

Rutledge supported a constitutional provision on ex post facto laws. North Carolina's Hugh Williamson had argued that such a provision had worked in his state because it gave judges something to "take hold of," but Rutledge did not address this specific issue (2:376). Rutledge did indicate on August 28 that he favored making the provision for the writ of habeas corpus "inviolable." He did not believe "that a suspension could ever be necessary at the same time through all the States" (2:438). On August 28, Rutledge introduced a motion prohibiting Congress from passing bills of attainder or retrospective laws (2:440). The convention adopted, but later modified, this motion.

Rutledge used his strongest language in opposing the idea of a congressional veto of state legislation; he indicated that this was a make or break issue for him. Believing that human shackles were a matter of interest rather than morality, he felt more strongly about the possibility of shackling the states:

If nothing else, this alone would damn and ought to damn the Constitution. Will any State ever agree to be bound hand & foot in this manner. It is worse than making mere corporations of them whose bye laws would not be subject to this shackle. (2:391)

Other Matters. On August 11, Rutledge joined Virginia's James Madison in proposing to exempt the Senate from publishing its proceedings when it was not acting in its legislative capacity (2:259). On August 24, Rutledge persuasively observed that since the Constitution was entrusting the federal judiciary with jurisdiction over disputes between the states, there would be no need for a special commission, such as had existed under the Articles of Confederation, to deal with such problems (2:401–2). Rutledge unsuccessfully proposed on September 8 that treaties should require the consent of two-thirds of all senators, rather than two-thirds of a quorum (2:549). Rutledge opposed a provision that would have required Congress to vote by joint ballot for the treasurer; he favored allowing this officer to be appointed, as the officer now is, in the same manner as other officers (2:614).

Presidency

On June 1, after exhorting his colleagues, who may have been reserved because of the presence of George Washington, not to be shy about expressing their opinions, Rutledge indicated that he favored a single executive but that he did not want to give this executive the power of war and peace. Rutledge reasoned that a single executive would be preferable because "A single man would feel the greatest responsibility and administer the public affairs best" (1:65). He and Charles Pinckney made a motion to this effect on the following day (1:88).

On June 1 Rutledge suggested that the Senate should have the power to select the president (1:69). On July 19, he was still advocating legislative selection of the president, believing that the Constitution could secure presidential independence with a provision making the president ineligible for reelection (2:57). When the convention was still considering legislative selection of the president on August 24, Rutledge argued that Congress should make such a choice by joint ballot rather than allowing each house to vote individually (2:401). On September 5, even after an electoral college was proposed, Rutledge continued to support a plan whereby a joint ballot of Congress would select the president to a single, seven-year term (2:511). When it was suggested that the Senate should select the president from among the top three candidates, Rutledge supported a measure, which would have granted Congress almost complete discretion, allowing it to choose from among the top thirteen candidates (2:515).

On June 5, Rutledge indicated that he did not think that the president should have the power to appoint judges. He feared that "The people will think we are leaning too much towards Monarchy" (1:119). On September 15, Rutledge joined with Benjamin Franklin to prohibit the president from accepting any emolument from the United States or the states other than his salary (2:616).

Judiciary

In opposing presidential selection of members of the judiciary on June 5, Rutledge did not favor establishing lower federal courts. He believed that state courts would be adequate for hearing cases in the first instance (1:119). Later that day he reiterated that he thought state courts would be adequate to the job and argued that the creation of federal courts was an encroachment on the states that would create "unnecessary obstacles to their adoption of the new system" (1:124).

Rutledge opposed combining members of the judiciary with the president in a Council of Revision. He argued that this was both improper and unnecessary. As to propriety, "The Judges ought never to give their opinion on a law till it comes before them"; as to necessity, the president would have cabinet officers to advise him (2:80).

Rutledge struck a blow for judicial independence on August 27 when he opposed a motion offered by Delaware's John Dickinson that would have allowed the president to remove federal judges on the application of Congress. Rutledge suggested that the fact that federal courts would sometimes have "to judge between the U.S. and particular States" would be "an insuperable objection to the motion" (2:428). However, on September 14, Rutledge introduced a motion to suspend individuals who were impeached from office until they could be tried, a provision that may well have threatened the independence of individuals who were charged but never convicted (2:612).

Slavery

As a representative from a state in the Deep South, Rutledge defended the institution of slavery. When Maryland's Luther Martin objected that a prohibition on the taxation of slave imports encouraged them, posed threats to internal security, and was inconsistent with the ideas of the American Revolution, Rutledge said that there was nothing to fear from slave insurrections and that he was willing to exempt the northern states from helping to quell them (2:364). Rutledge further argued that the issue of slavery was one of economic interest, and that the northern states should consider the advantages they offered:

> Religion & humanity had nothing to do with this question—Interest alone is the governing principle with Nations—The true question at present is whether the Southn. States shall or shall not be parties to the Union. If the Northern States consult their interest, they will not oppose the increase of Slaves which will increase the commodities of which they will become the carriers. (2:364)

Rutledge was vehement in his position that the people of the Carolinas and Georgia would never give up their right to import slaves, even though they were not at the time exercising it (2:373). He was influential near the end of the convention (September 10) in securing a provision preventing a constitutional amendment of the right of southern states to import slaves until 1808 (2:559).

Ratification

Rutledge did not believe it necessary for Congress to approve the new Constitution before it could be sent to state conventions for their approval (2:563). Perhaps anxious to leave, on September 15 Rutledge opposed composing an address to the people to accompany the Constitution. He believed that Congress could compose such an address if it proved necessary and that, in any event, delegates to the convention could explain to their constituents what they had done (2:623).

Attempts to Speed Convention Proceedings

On August 15, Rutledge opposed postponing a motion and "complained much of the tediousness of the proceedings" (2:301). Three days later he proposed that the convention keep more regular hours from 10:00 a.m. to 4:00 p.m. (2:328). Despite his weariness, Rutledge stayed to the end of the convention and signed the Constitution.

Life after the Convention

Rutledge supported the Constitution within his state. Appointed by President Washington as an associate justice of the U.S. Supreme Court, gout prevented him from attending the court in New York but did not stop him from riding the expansive southern circuit. In 1791, Rutledge left the U.S. Supreme Court to become chief justice of the South Carolina Court of Common Pleas, but he was shattered by the death of both his wife and his mother in 1793. At Rutledge's request, Washington appointed him in 1795 to an interim term as chief justice of the U.S. Supreme Court. After Rutledge imprudently spoke out against the Jay Treaty, however, Alexander Hamilton and others who had previously held him in high esteem opposed his nomination, and the Senate rejected his nomination. Broken in spirit and hounded by financial difficulties, Rutledge unsuccessfully attempted to drown himself and battled bouts of insanity until his death on July 18, 1800. Although he had inherited 60 slaves and battled to preserve the institution at the convention, by the time of his death Rutledge had freed all but one of them (Hakim 2003, 182). He is buried in the churchyard of St. Michael's in Charleston. Rutledge's home, which was built in Charleston in 1763, has been restored and converted into an inn.

Further Reading

Barnwell, Robert W., Jr. 1941. "The Dictator." *The Journal of Southern History* 7 (May): 215–24.

Barry, Richard. 1971. *Mr. Rutledge of South Carolina*. Freeport, NY: Books for Libraries Press. Reprint of 1942 original.

Cruger, Lewis. 1863. *Catechism of the Constitution of the United States: A Brief Exposition of the True Elementary Principles of that Great Compact Between Sovereign States*. (n.p.).

Cushman, Clare, ed. 1995. *The Supreme Court Justices, Illustrated Biographies, 1789–1995*. Washington, DC: Congressional Quarterly.

Farrand, Max, ed. 1966. *The Records of the Federal Convention of 1787*. 4 vols. New Haven, CT: Yale University Press.

Hakim, Joy. 2003. *From Colonies to Country*. Vol. 3 of *A History of the United States*. New York: Oxford University Press.

Haw, James. 1997. *John & Edward Rutledge of South Carolina*. Athens, GA: University of Georgia Press.

———. 1998. "John Rutledge: Distinction and Declention." In *Seriatim: The Supreme Court before John Marshal*, edited by Scott Douglas Gerber, 70–96. New York: New York University Press.

McCowan, George S., Jr. 1961. "Chief Justice John Rutledge and the Jay Treaty." *The South Carolina Historical Magazine* 62 (January): 10–23.

Meister, Charles W. 1987. *The Founding Fathers*. Jefferson, NC: McFarland & Co.

Webber, Mabel L. 1930. "Dr. John Rutledge and His Descendants." *The South Carolina Historical and Genealogical Magazine* 31 (January): 7–25.

ROGER SHERMAN (1721–1793)
CONNECTICUT

The second oldest member of the convention (Benjamin Franklin was the oldest), Connecticut's Roger Sherman was one of the rare individuals who signed the Declaration of Independence, the Articles of Confederation, and the U.S. Constitution. He was born on April 9, 1721 in Newton, Massachusetts, to a farm family. He sat under the preaching of, and may have been partly educated by, Samuel Dunbar, a Harvard graduate and student of Cotton Mather who preached at the Congregational Church that Sherman attended in his youth in Stoughton; later in life he sat under the teachings of Jonathan Edwards Jr., whom he strongly supported.

Sherman's father died in 1741, and the son moved in 1743 to New Milford, Connecticut, where he was a cobbler. Appointed two years later as a surveyor, Sherman set up a store with his brother and married Elizabeth Hartwell (1726–1760). They had seven children, four of whom lived to adulthood; after Elizabeth died, Sherman married Rebecca Prescott (1742–1813), a much younger woman by whom he had eight additional children.

Sherman published yearly almanacs from 1750 to 1761. He was admitted to the bar in 1754, served in the Connecticut legislature, became a judge in New Haven and later in the superior court of Connecticut, was a member of the governor's council, served as treasurer of Yale, as mayor of New Haven, and as a delegate to the Continental Congresses. He and Richard Law helped revise all of Connecticut's statutes. At the Second Continental Congress, Sherman served on the five-man committee to write the Declaration of Independence (Thomas Jefferson did most of the writing) as well as on the committee responsible for writing the Articles of Confederation (John Dickinson was the primary author).

At the Convention

Unlike most of the other delegates, Sherman did not follow the contemporary style of wearing a powdered wig to cover his brown hair. Sherman is the subject of one of William Pierce's most fascinating descriptions of fellow delegates at the convention. Referring to him as exhibiting "the oddest shaped character I ever remember to have met with," Pierce continued:

> He is awkward, un-meaning, and unaccountably strange in his manner. But in his train of thinking there is something regular, deep and comprehensive, yet the oddity of his address, the vulgarisms that accompany his public speaking, and that strange New England cant, which runs through his public as well as his private speaking make everything that is connected with him grotesque and laughable;—and yet he deserves infinite praise,— no Man has a better Heart or a clearer Head. If he cannot embellish he can furnish thoughts that are wise and useful. He is an able politician, and extremely artful in accomplishing any particular object;—it is remarked that he seldom fails. (Farrand 1966, 3:88–89).

Despite a physical awkwardness reminiscent of his Puritan roots, Sherman was one of the more influential members of the U.S. Constitutional Convention, often successfully battling James Madison and helping to craft compromises between the large and small states and between the North and the South. He was seated on Wednesday, May 30, a day after Edmund Randolph had shocked many of the delegates by proposing the far-reaching Virginia Plan. On his first day at the convention, Sherman indicated that he thought that Congress needed additional powers, especially over raising money. By James Madison's assessment, however, Sherman seemed not to "be disposed to Make too great inroads on the existing system" in part because he feared that the convention might not attain anything if it sought too much (1:35). A Sherman biographer has identified him as a strong "republican" who favored "a strong legislature and a strong states'-rights position" (Collier 1971, 242). Sherman was one of the major forces at the convention behind the Great Compromise, which balanced the apportionment by population in the U.S. House of Representatives with equal state representation in the Senate.

Federalism

Consistent with his view that the Articles of Confederation required relatively minor alterations, Sherman was a strong proponent of states' rights.

He indicated on June 6 that he thought the objects of the Union could be boiled down to: "1. defence agst. foreign danger. 2. agst. internal disputes & a resort to force. 3. Treaties with foreign nations 4[.] regulating foreign commerce, & drawing revenue from it" (1:133). Sherman accordingly favored leaving states in charge of most matters and limiting the powers of the general government:

> All other matters civil & criminal would be much better in the hands of the States. States may indeed be too small as Rhode Island, & thereby be too subject to faction. Some others were perhaps too large, the powers of Govt not being able to pervade them. He was for giving the General Govt. power to legislate and execute within a defined province. (1:133)

Rufus King summarized Sherman's sentiments in this same speech: "I am agst. a Genl. Govt. and in favor of the independence and confederation of the States, with powers to regulate commerce & draw therefrom a revenue" (1:143).

When the delegates were discussing the possibility of a congressional negative on state laws, Sherman did not initially oppose the measure but suggested that such cases should be clearly "defined" (1:166). Later in the convention, he argued that such a negative would be unnecessary since courts would invalidate laws in opposition to the Constitution (2:27). In a somewhat cleverer argument, he observed that the presence of a negative might make it appear as though laws that were not negated were therefore valid (2:28). Still later in the convention, Sherman observed that the Supremacy Clause made the congressional veto of state laws unnecessary (2:390). He cited the provision granting the courts the power to settle disputes between the states as a reason that the new Constitution did not require an elaborate mechanism, like that under the Articles of Confederation, for settling such disputes (2:401).

When the convention discussed requiring state officials to take an oath of office, Sherman opposed it "as unnecessarily intruding into the State jurisdictions" (1:203). He thought that states should not only determine the pay of members of Congress but that they should also be responsible for providing for it (1:373). Using a biblical analogy, he argued that making members of Congress ineligible for state offices would be setting up a kingdom making war against itself (1:386).

Sherman was willing to defend state actions under the Articles of Confederation as flowing from lack of congressional power rather than from state delinquency (1:349). He observed that "Cong. is not to blame for the faults of the States. Their measures have been right, and the only thing wanting has been, a further power in Congs. to render them effectual" (1:487).

In arguing for equal representation in the Senate, Sherman observed that the measure was not so much "a security for the small States; as for the State Govts. which could not be preserved unless they were represented & had a negative in the Genl. Government" (1:5). Sherman expressed concern that the powers entrusted to the general government needed to be more clearly defined. In proposing an alternative, he sought to provide a guarantee that exercises of congressional powers would not interfere with state police powers (2:25). He apparently was an early proponent of enumerating congressional powers, although convention notes do not contain his original list (2:26).

Sherman was willing to retain the clause granting Congress power to oversee state elections of its members, but he said that "he had himself sufficient confidence in the State Legislatures" (2:241). Sherman favored allowing Congress to tax imports but not exports except for "such articles as ought not to be exported" (2:308). He thought that "the oppression of the uncommercial States was guarded agst. by the power to regulate trade between the States," but he feared that the addition of an export tax "would shipwreck the whole" (2:308).

During the discussion of war powers, Sherman indicated that he believed that Congress should have the power not simply to "declare," but also to "make" war. He apparently believed that the executive function should be largely limited to repelling attack, and that the term "declare" would overly narrow congressional powers (2:318). Sherman's approach to national assumption of state debts was somewhat different. He was willing to "authorize" such assumption, but unwilling to specify that Congress should specifically do so (2:327). He hoped essentially to leave this matter where it was under the Articles of Confederation (2:356).

Sherman seconded a motion by Ellsworth designed to allow states to retain some control over their militia, in part because he did not believe states would be willing to part with such power (2:331). He regarded the state power to call on their militia as a concurrent power, like the power of taxation, that the states should exercise in conjunction with the national government (2:332; also see 2:386). Sherman was dead set against restricting the right of the states to appoint only lower militia officers (2:388). He observed that the provision in the Constitution limiting Congress to appropriating money for the military for no more than two years did not prohibit it from making more frequent reports; at the same time, he indicated that he favored limiting the number of troops that could be kept during times of peace (2:509).

Sherman opposed a provision that would have prohibited states from laying duties of tonnage for clearing harbors or erecting lighthouses. He argued that "The power of the U. States to regulate trade being supreme can controul interferences of the State regulations [when] such interferences happen; so that there is no danger to be apprehended from a concurrent jurisdiction" (2:625).

Sherman thought it possible, however, to distinguish between treason against the United States as a whole and treason against an individual state (2:349). Sherman opposed granting Congress power to tax exports, but it is not clear in context whether he thought that individual states should be able to exercise this power on their own (2:361).

Sherman was a strong advocate of fiscal responsibility and favored taking away the power of states to emit, or issue, paper money. He observed that "If the consent of the Legislature could authorize emissions of it, the friends of paper money would make every exertion to get into the Legislature in order to license it" (2:439). Sherman was willing to allow states to exercise embargo power as necessary "to prevent suffering & injury to their poor" (2:440). He favored allowing Congress to decide when states could tax imports from neighboring states (2:441). He did not favor the motion by Benjamin Franklin allowing Congress to cut canals; he believed that this would have local benefits and that the states should accordingly act in such cases (2:615).

Congress

Representation. Consistent with his view that the convention should make relatively modest changes in the Articles of Confederation, Sherman favored state legislative, rather than popular, election of members of Congress. He expressed doubts about direct democracy: "The people . . . should have as little to do as may be about the Government. They want [lack] information and are constantly liable to be misled" (1:48). By May 31, Sherman was advocating that each state legislature should elect a single member to the U.S. Senate (1:52), and on June 11 (in the solution eventually adopted in the Great Compromise of July 16), he suggested that states might be represented according to population in the House and equally in the Senate. Sherman was among those who argued that the small states could never accept a plan that did not give them equal representation in at least one house (1:201).

When Pennsylvania's James Wilson argued that the Constitution should apportion Congress so as to give equal rights to all, Sherman responded that "the question is not what rights naturally belong to men; but how they may be most equally & effectually guarded in Society" (1:450). Sherman argued that there was no real difference between giving large and small states an equal vote than in giving an equal vote to the rich and the poor (1:450).

Later professing to regard the slave trade as "iniquitous," Sherman felt bound to uphold the Three-fifths Clause as "having been Settled after much difficulty & deliberation" (2:221). It appears, however, that Sherman tried to obscure this representation behind the formula for direct taxes:

> Mr. Sherman. did not regard the admission of the Negroes into the ratio of representation, as liable to such insuperable objections. It was the freemen of the Southn. States who were in fact to be represented according to the taxes paid by them, and the Negroes are only included in the Estimate of the taxes. (2:223)

Expressing disappointment with the slave trade but believing "it best to leave the matter as we find it" lest the introduction of a provision on the subject alienate some of the southern states, Sherman observed that slavery seemed to be dying out in the United States (2:369–70). Somewhat thereafter he observed that "it was better to let the S. States import slaves than to part with them, if they made that a sine qua non [an absolute condition for Union]" (2:374). He added the fascinating observation that he opposed a tax on slave importation "because it implied that they were *property*" (2:374; also see 2:416). Similarly, in opposing the Fugitive Slave Clause, Sherman argued that he "saw no more propriety in the public seizing and surrendering a slave or servant, than a horse" (2:443).

Sherman had an eye for details. He thus introduced the motion modifying the motion for one representative in the House for every 40,000 persons to "not exceeding" this number (2:221).

Sherman argued that granting states equal representation in the Senate would actually increase the vigor of Congress. He observed:

> If they vote by States in the 2d. branch, and each State has an equal vote, there must be always a majority of States as well as a majority of the people on the side of public measures, & the Govt. will have decision and efficacy. If this be not the case in the 2d. branch there may be a majority of the

States agst. public measures, and the difficulty of compelling them to abide
by the public determination, will render the Government feebler than it
has ever yet been. (1:550)

When Congress appointed a committee to come up with the initial
representation in the House of Representatives, Sherman questioned how it
had done so (1:559). He was among those who supported sending the matter
back to a committee with a representative from each of the states present.
He served on this committee (in place of Oliver Ellsworth who was sick at
the time) as well as on a later committee to discuss commercial discrimination and the Committee on Postponed Matters.

Ironically, when the committee formed to reconsider representation in
the House representation proposed raising the initial number of representatives from 56 to 65, Sherman said that he would have preferred a House of
50 members, believing that, the travel such a position required "will make
it difficult to prevail on a sufficient number of fit men to undertake the
service" (1:569). Initially opposing the requirement that Congress should
have to reapportion itself at set times, Sherman observed that he "was agst.
Shackling the Legislature too much. We ought to choose wise & good men,
and then confide in them" (1:578). Later in the day, however, Sherman said
that arguments by Edmund Randolph and George Mason, both of Virginia,
had convinced him that "the *periods* & the *rule* of revising the Representation ought to be fixt by the Constitution" (1:582). When the convention was
discussing a proposal whereby Congress would select the U.S. treasurer,
Sherman opposed a provision for a "joint" ballot in the view that it would
favor the larger states (2:314).

Selection of Members. Sherman clearly believed that states should
choose members of both the House and the Senate. On June 6, Sherman
argued that proposals for popular election would effectively destroy the
states (1:133). On June 7, he supported a motion by Delaware's John Dickinson for allowing state legislatures to choose senators. He thought that this
would give states an interest in supporting the general government and thus
maintain "a due harmony between the two Governments" (1:150). Later that
day, he argued that state legislative selection of senators was more likely to
result in the selection of "fit men" (1:154).

Terms. On June 12, Sherman proposed that members of the House
of Representatives should be elected annually (1:214). On June 21, he
indicated that he still continued to favor annual elections but could accept them biennially. The key was that "the representatives ought to return

home and mix with the people. By remaining at the seat of Govt. they would acquire the habits of the place which might differ from those of their Constituents" (1:362).

Sherman thought a term of seven years was too long for senators but supported a five-year term (1:218). A practical man, Sherman later seconded Hugh Williamson's motion for a six-year Senate term on the basis that such a term would make rotation easier (1:409). Sherman tied his view of term lengths to his view that governments should preserve liberties:

> Govt. is instituted for those who live under it. It ought therefore to be so constituted as not to be dangerous to their liberties. The more permanency it has the worse if it be a bad Govt. Frequent elections are necessary to preserve the good behavior of rulers. They also tend to give permanency to the Government, by preserving that good behavior, because it ensures their re-election. (1:423)

Qualifications. When the convention voted to require each member of the House of Representatives to be a "resident" of the state, Sherman proposed that the term "inhabitant" would be "less liable to misconstruction" (2:216). Sherman did not believe that the United States had assured immigrants that they would enjoy equal privileges with individuals born on the continent, and he therefore saw no problem in allowing states to set requirements as to when such individuals had the right to vote (2:270).

Origination of Money Bills. Prior to the adoption of the Connecticut Compromise, Sherman did not think it would matter whether money bills could originate in one House or the other. He observed that "as both branches must concur, there can be no danger whichever way the Senate be formed." He further opined that "We establish two branches in order to get more wisdom which is particularly needed in the finance business" (1:234). He later considered this provision for House origination of money bills to be vital to the compromise (2:4).

On a related matter, Sherman wanted to tie the congressional power of laying taxes and duties to payment of debts and expenses "incurred for the common defence and general welfare" (2:414). On this matter, he carried only his home state.

Sherman opposed supermajority requirements for navigation acts that delegates from the southern states favored. He argued that the diversity of interests in the nation would provide security against measures directed against individual states. He further observed that the requirement that nine states give approval to key measures under the Articles of Confederation had often proved to be "embarrassing" (2:450).

There is a story indicating that, while serving on the Committee of Style, Gouverneur Morris attempted to change the General Welfare Clause by setting it apart from the power to tax and spend by a semicolon, rather than as previously, by a comma. According to this story, it was Sherman who caught the change and insisted that the comma be re-substituted (Farrand1913, 182–83). Although the story is probably apocryphal and is generally cited to highlight Morris's reputation for sharp dealing, it might just as easily point to Sherman's reputation for attention to detail.

Unicameral or Bicameral? After the convention decided to proceed with the discussion of the Virginia Plan over the New Jersey Plan, Sherman supported a motion by New York's John Lansing, which would simply vest the existing unicameral Congress under the Articles of Confederation with new powers. Sherman observed that "the complaints at present are not that the views of Congs. are unwise or unfaithful, but that that their powers are insufficient for the executive of their views" (1:341). Sherman repeated his view that adding a branch elected by the people would simply lead to mischief:

> If another branch were to be added to Congs. to be chosen by the people, it would serve to embarrass. The people would not much interest themselves in the elections, a few designing men in the large districts would carry their points, and the people would have no more confidence in their new representatives than in Congs. (1:342)

On this occasion, however, Sherman indicated that he could support a bicameral Congress as long as states were given equal representation in one house (1:343). Reflective of his conciliating temper, on June 21 Sherman further accepted the idea of popular election of one house (1:359).

Pay. Perhaps because he had been a cobbler, Sherman had an unusual perspective on Congressional pay. At a time when others feared that Congress might abuse its power by paying too much, Sherman feared that it might pay too little and that "men ever so fit could not serve unless they were at the same time rich" (2:291). He favored fixing a moderate allowance to be paid out of national coffers, perhaps $5 a day, and allowing states to supplement this (2:291).

Other Matters. Sherman believed that members of Congress should be eligible to accept state offices (1:386). Although he sympathized with the objective behind prohibiting members from accepting other federal offices, he did not favor it (1:388). In another context, he indicated that "The Constitution shd. lay as few temptations as possible in the way of those in power" (2:287).

At a time when some delegates wanted to reserve control of the new government to the states that created it, Sherman believed it was important to treat new states equally with those already in the Union. Although he did not think it likely that new states would outnumber existing states in the foreseeable future, he observed, "We are providing for our posterity, for our children & our grand Children, who would be as likely to be citizens of new Western States, as of the old States. On this consideration alone, we ought to make no such discrimination" (1:3; also see 2:454).

Sherman favored setting both the times that Congress should meet and the frequency with which it should do so. He believed that this would help avoid disputes over the subject between the two houses (2:199). He was confident that there would be sufficient business, much of it involving the West, to require annual meetings (2:199).

Sherman had an interesting perspective on roll-call votes in Congress. He feared that they were mischievous since "the reasons governing the voter never appear along with them" (2:255). Sherman joined Elbridge Gerry of Massachusetts in thinking that Congress should not have to publish its proceedings when these related to treaties and military operations (2:260). When the convention was still anticipating allowing Congress to select the president, Sherman opposed a joint ballot on the grounds that this would take from the states the negative they were intended to have through their representation in the Senate (2:401).

Sherman believed that the provision preventing a religious test as a condition to office was unnecessary, "the prevailing liberality being a sufficient security agst. such tests" (2:468). However, he opposed vesting Congress with the power to adopt uniform laws on bankruptcy for fear that they might, as in England, make this offense punishable by death (2:489).

On September 7, Sherman believed that the need for secrecy required that the Senate, rather than both houses of Congress, should ratify treaties (2:538). The next day, Sherman suggested that some agreements should require the approval of the entire legislature (2:548). He also did not think that the Senate should be able to approve treaties with less than a majority of its membership, but thought that a two-thirds majority could prove too "embarrassing" (2:549).

Presidency

Selection. Sherman's initial view of the presidency was that the institution should be "nothing more than an institution for carrying the will of the Legislature into effect" (1:65). He accordingly proposed that the person or persons occupying this position should be appointed by the legislature. He was even willing to allow Congress to decide whether the office would be singular or plural (2:65). Somewhat later, Sherman appeared to lean in favor of a single executive, as long as an Executive Council supported him (1:97). On August 15, Sherman indicated that he opposed both an absolute executive veto and an alliance between the president and the judges:

> Can one man be trusted better than all the others if they all agree? This was neither wise nor safe. He disapproved of Judges meddling in politics and parties. We have gone far enough in forming the negative as it now stands. (2:300)

On September 12, Sherman was among those who favored allowing a two-thirds, rather than a three-fourths, majority of Congress to override a presidential veto. As on previous occasions, he observed that "it was more probable that a single man should mistake or betray this sense [of the people] than the Legislature" (2:585).

Sherman had no more faith in the popular choice of a president than in popular choice of the legislature. He observed that the people "will never be sufficiently informed of characters, and besides will never give a majority of votes to any one man" (2:29). He further anticipated that popular election would privilege the larger states: "They will generally vote for some man in their own State, and the largest State will have the best chance for the appointment" (2:29).

As a member of the Committee on Postponed Matters, Sherman had a role in the development and defense of the electoral college. In defending the institution of the vice president, which emerged as part of this plan, Sherman observed that this office had been created for the person who came in second, largely to keep the president independent of Congress. He did not oppose an alteration requiring that the president, like the vice president, have a majority of electoral votes (2:499). Sherman was not troubled by the vice president's role in presiding over the Senate; indeed, he noted that without such a responsibility, "he would be without employment" (2:537). Sherman favored the electoral college in part because he believed that it gave due powers to both the House and the Senate (2:512–13), and he worked to see that the proposal continued to do so (1:522). He was influential in seeing that when the House of Representatives had to choose among the top candidates for president, it did so with each state having a single vote (2:527).

Other Matters. Sherman favored presidential re-eligibility to office (2:33). He strongly disfavored a motion that would allow the president to serve during good behavior (2:33).

Sherman identified excessive executive independence with "tyranny" (1:68). On June 1, he indicated that he favored a three-year renewable executive term, opposing "the doctrine of rotation as throwing out of office the men best qualified to execute its duties" (1:68). However, consistent with his view of legislative sovereignty, on the next day he further stated that he thought the Congress should have the power to remove the executive "at pleasure" (1:84). Sherman was willing to accept the idea of a conditional, but not an absolute, veto: "we ought to avail ourselves of his [the president's] wisdom in revising the laws, but not permit him to overrule the decided and cool opinions of the Legislature" (1:99).

Sherman wanted to limit the number of individuals the president could appoint, especially in cases of officers in peacetime; Sherman feared that such appointments might become a source of "corruption" in the new government (2:405). Sherman favored limiting the presidential power to grant reprieves and pardons only to such time as the Senate could concur in such measures (2:419). He further wanted it to be clear that the president would command the militia only in cases where it was called into service of the entire nation (2:426). Sherman opposed congressional eligibility to other offices for fear that this would "give too much influence to the Executive" in the use of his appointment power (2:490).

Judiciary

Sherman supported a resolution by South Carolina's John Rutledge to strike the provision from the Virginia Plan providing for inferior federal courts. Sherman, who may also have feared the centralizing tendency of such courts, argued that it was too expensive to constitute federal courts when state courts could be utilized for the same purposes (1:125). Later in the convention, Sherman said he was willing to grant Congress the power to establish lower federal courts "but wished them to make use of the State Tribunals whenever it could be done. with safety to the general interest" (2:46). Sherman proposed on June 13 that Congress should appoint members of the U.S. Supreme Court, but withdrew his motion when Madison suggested that the Constitution should vest this power exclusively in the Senate (1:233). Sherman thought that senators were more likely than the president to spread such appointments throughout the nation (2:41).

Sherman favored a provision that would have allowed the president to remove judges on the application of Congress. He professed to see "no contradiction of impropriety" in such a mechanism, which he believed to be similar to one in Great Britain (2:428). Sherman did not think that it would be appropriate for members of the U.S. Supreme Court to sit in on the impeachment of the president who had appointed them (2:551).

Other Matters

Sherman was among the delegates who favored Franklin's proposal that each day's proceedings at the convention should begin with prayer (1:452), although it seems more likely that he did so "with a devout and fervent belief in the efficacy of prayer" and not largely to engender a spirit of unity among delegates (Boyd 1932, 233). Within Connecticut, Sherman had favored the established religion but was "remarkably tolerant of other Christians" (Hall 2009, 264), including Anglicans.

Sherman did not favor Gerry's and Mason's motion for a bill of rights. He pointed out that existing state declarations of rights would remain in effect, that it was difficult to specify some matters, like trial by jury, and that, in such cases, Congress could be trusted (2:588). Similarly, Sherman did not think it was necessary to provide for freedom of the press under the new Constitution since "The power of Congress does not extend to the Press" (2:618).

Sherman favored the appointment of the secretary of the treasury by separate votes of each house of Congress (2:614).

Ratification

On June 5, Sherman indicated that he did not think it was necessary to ratify the Constitution in popular conventions. He favored following the provisions under the Articles of Confederation for approval by Congress and ratification by state legislatures (1:122). On August 30, Sherman proposed that the new Constitution should not go into effect until ratified by 10 states (2:468–69), but the next day he was openly wondering if it would be proper for it to be ratified by less than a unanimous vote (2:475). By September 10, Sherman was willing to accept ratification by nine states but also wanted the convention to submit the new plan to Congress (2:561).

Sherman initiated the proposal that allowed Congress to propose constitutional amendments for state ratification (2:558). Previously, the delegates had been considering a provision whereby Congress only had authority to propose a convention to propose amendments at the requests of the states. Sherman advocated omitting the specific requirement that three-fourths of the states ratify amendments, leaving future Congresses to decide the specific majority (2:630).

On September 15, Sherman expressed fears that three-fourths of the states might gang up on the minority to either abolish them or strip them of their equal representation in the Senate. He moved that the provision prohibiting a restriction of state importation of slaves for 20 years should be extended "to provide that no State should be affected in its internal police, or deprived of its equality in the Senate" (2:629). He succeeded in getting the latter portion of this proposal incorporated into the Constitution, in part by moving at one point to strike out the amending process altogether (2:630).

Life after the Convention

Sherman returned to Connecticut to advocate the ratification of the Constitution. He served as a member of the first U.S. House of Representatives and was then chosen as a U.S. senator. Initially opposed to adding a bill of rights (he thought it was likely to be both unnecessary and ineffectual), Sherman succeeded in seeing that these guarantees were appended to the end of the Constitution rather than integrated into the text of the document as Virginia's James Madison advocated. Sherman joined a request in the first Congress that resulted in Washington's 1789 Thanksgiving Day Proclamation (Hall 2009, 269). A hearty man with numerous descendants, Sherman died of typhoid fever on July 23, in 1793 and was buried in New Haven's Millwood Cemetery.

Further Reading

Boardman, Roger Sherman. 1938. *Roger Sherman: Signer and Statesman*. Philadelphia: University of Pennsylvania Press.

Boutell, Louis Henry. 1896. *The Life of Roger Sherman*. Chicago: McClurg.

Boyd, Julian. 1932. "Roger Sherman: Portrait of a Cordwainer Statesman." *The New England Quarterly* 5, 221–36.

Collier, Christopher. 1971. *Roger Sherman's Connecticut: Yankee Politics and the American Revolution*. Middleton, CT: Wesleyan University Press.

Farrand, Max. 1913. *The Framing of the Constitution of the United States*. New Haven, CT: Yale University Press.

Farrand, Max, ed. 1966. *The Records of the Federal Convention of 1787*. 4 vols. New Haven, CT: Yale University Press.

Gerber, Scott D. 1996. "Roger Sherman and the Bill of Rights," *Polity* 28 (Summer): 521–40.

Hall, Mark David. 2009. "Roger Sherman: An Old Puritan in a New Nation." In *The Forgotten Founders on Religion and Public Life,* edited by Daniel L. Dreisbach, Mark David Hall, and Jeffrey H. Morrison, 248–77. Notre Dame: University of Notre Dame Press.

Meister, Charles W. 1987. *The Founding Fathers*. Jefferson, NC: McFarland & Company.

Robertson, David Brian. 2005. "Madison's Opponents and Constitutional Design." *The American Political Science Review* 99 (May): 225–43.

Richard Dobbs Spaight (1758–1802)
North Carolina

Richard Dobbs Spaight was born in New Bern, North Carolina on March 25, 1758 to Richard Spaight, an Irish immigrant who had accompanied his uncle, the royal governor Arthur Dobbs, to North Carolina in 1754, and Elizabeth Wilson. Spaight's parents died when he was young, and he was sent first to Ireland and then to the University of Glasgow where he was studying when the Revolutionary War started.

Spaight returned from Scotland to defend his native homeland, to claim a sizeable inheritance, and served in the war as an aide-de-camp to the brigadier general of the North Carolina militia. He was subsequently elected to the North Carolina legislature, to the Congress under the Articles of Confederation, and as speaker of the North Carolina House, where he expressed his opposition to judicial review. In the Continental Congress, Spaight was credited with helping nix Thomas Jefferson's prohibition of slavery in the western territories. Perhaps influenced by the Virginia Plan, Spaight appears largely to have supported those at the convention advocating greater powers for the national government.

At the Convention

Spaight was present for the opening day of business in Philadelphia on May 25, 1787. On May 28, Spaight introduced a motion that would have specified that, while the delegates should not be precluded from revisiting issues when they had cause to do so, they should also be cautioned against revising measures that were "the result of mature discussion" too hastily (Farrand 1966, 1:10).

Congress

On May 30, the convention was debating how to apportion representation in Congress. The Virginia Plan had proposed that this formula be based on "the quotas of contribution, or on the number of free inhabitants"; Spaight seconded a motion by Alexander Hamilton of New York using the latter portion of the formula only (1:35). It seems odd that, as a southerner, Spaight would have supported such a measure.

On May 31, Spaight introduced a motion providing that state legislatures should choose senators directly, rather than, as the Virginia Plan had proposed, by allowing members of the first branch to choose them from nominees submitted by the state legislatures (1:51). The delegates eventually settled on Spaight's method; it remained in effect until the ratification of the Seventeenth Amendment in 1913 vested this choice directly in the voters of each state. On June 12, Spaight further proposed that members of the Senate should serve for seven-year terms (1:218). This proposal came relatively close to the term of six years that the convention eventually adopted.

On June 23, Spaight proposed dividing the question as to whether members of Congress should be ineligible to other offices while they were serving and for one year afterward (1:390). The immediate outcome was approval for the first part of the resolution but not for the second.

On August 11, the convention was discussing a provision that would prohibit one house of Congress from meeting in a city other than the one where both were meeting. Spaight feared that this would permanently establish the capital in New York. He observed that the first Congress would begin there and that "they will never be able to remove; especially if the Presidt. should be [a] Northern Man" (2:261). Pennsylvania's Gouverneur Morris immediately chided that "such a distrust is inconsistent with all Govt." (2:261), indicating that, on this issue at least, Spaight might have been regarded as expressing too regional a perspective.

The next day, however, Spaight wrote a letter to James Iredell, a future Supreme Court justice, indicating that he was in fact taking a national perspective. Noting that he hoped the convention would end between September 1 and 15, Spaight went on to observe:

It is not probable that the United States will in future be so ideal as to risk their happiness upon the unanimity of the whole; and thereby put it in the power of one or two States to defeat the most salutary propositions, and prevent the Union from rising out of that contemptible situation to which it is at present reduced. There is no man of reflection, who has maturely considered what must and will result from the weakness of our present Federal Government, and the tyrannical and unjust proceedings of most of the State governments, if longer persevered in, but must sincerely wish for a strong and efficient National Government. (Hutson 1987, 219)

Somewhat less hopefully, Spaight observed, "We may naturally suppose that all those persons who are possessed of popularity in the different States, and which they made use of, not for the public benefit, but for their private emolument, will oppose any system of this kind" (Hutson 1987, 219).

At a time when some southern delegates were arguing for a provision that would have required a two-thirds majority for Congress to enact any navigation measures, Spaight disagreed. He observed that if northerners tried to monopolize the carrying trade, "The Southern States could . . . save themselves from oppression, by building ships for their own use" (2:451). On September 7, however, Spaight did support a motion providing that no treaty affecting territorial rights should be made without the concurrence of two-thirds of all the members of the Senate (2:543).

Presidency

On July 23, Spaight joined Georgia's William Houstoun in proposing reconsideration of a provision vesting the appointment of presidential electors in state legislatures. Presumably, Spaight shared Houstoun's concern about "the extreme inconveniency & the considerable expense, of drawing together men from all the States for the single purpose of electing the Chief Magistrate" (2:95). On September 5, Spaight and South Carolina's John Rutledge proposed allowing the Senate to choose among the top thirteen, rather than five, candidates for president (2:515); this measure garnered only the votes of North and South Carolina. On the following day, Spaight proposed a seven-year term for the president (2:525). He also proposed that it would be better for the electors to get together and choose the president in cases in which no one got a majority, than to entrust this power to the Senate (2:526). On September 7, Spaight introduced the successful motion granting that the president fill vacancies when the Senate was in recess by granting commissions that would expire at the end of the next Senate term (2:540).

Ratification

At the first North Carolina ratifying convention that met in Hillsborough in July, 1788, Spaight was a major player who argued vigorously on behalf of what the convention had done. He observed, "It was found impossible to improve the old system without changing the very form; for by that system the three great branches of government are blended together" (3:351). He further observed that the delegates thought that "if so great a majority as nine states should adopt it, it would be right to establish it" (3:351). Responding to criticism, Spaight observed:

> I am, for my part, conscious of having had nothing in view but the liberty and happiness of my country; and I believe every member of that Convention was actuated by motives equally sincere and patriotic. (3:352)

Spaight did not attend the second North Carolina ratifying convention, held in Fayetteville, that ratified the Constitution in November, 1789, but he expressed gratitude "that wisdom has at last prevailed in our councils, and enabled the convention to break through that cloud of ignorance and villainy, which has so long obscured our political horizon" (quoted in Watson and Watson 1987, 13).

Life after the Convention

After the Hillsborough Convention, Spaight married a cousin, Mary (Polly) Jones Leech (1765–1810), of Philadelphia, by whom he fathered four children, three of whom lived into adulthood. Although often hounded by ill health, he served as a member of the North Carolina legislature and as the state's governor (the first ever to have been born in the state). He was elected to the U.S. House of Representatives and then to the state Senate. Over time, he switched allegiance from the Federalist to the Democratic-Republican Party. A dispute that arose in this latter body led Spaight to engage in a duel with John Stanly, his Federalist replacement in Congress. After both duelists missed three shots, Stanly's pistol found its target, and Spaight died in New Bern on September 6, 1802 at the age of forty-four and was buried in nearby "Clermont."

Spaight was a trustee for a number of educational institutions, including the University of North Carolina, and he was an advocate for progressive farming. Upon his death, he owned 89 slaves. Spaight's namesake followed him in a number of political offices, and another son served a term in the state House of Commons. A cypress tree behind the Spaight residence at 520 East Front Street in New Bern marks the site where Spaight pledged to General Nathaniel Greene to aid the patriot cause in the Revolutionary War.

Further Reading

Bradford, M. E. 1994. *Founding Fathers: Brief Lives of the Framers of the United States Constitution*. 2nd ed. Lawrence: University Press of Kansas.

Craige, Burton. 1987. *The Federal Convention of 1787: North Carolina in the Great Crisis*. Richmond, VA: Expert Graphics.

Farrand, Max, ed. 1966. *The Records of the Federal Convention of 1787*. 4 vols. New Haven, CT: Yale University Press.

Mitchell, Memory F. 1964. *North Carolina's Signers: Brief Sketches of the Men Who Signed the Declaration of Independence and the Constitution*. Raleigh: Division of Archives and History, North Carolina Department of Cultural Resources.

Treenholme, Louise Irby. 1967. *The Ratification of the Federal Constitution in North Carolina*. New York: AMS Press.

Watson, Alan D., and Gertrude Carraway Watson. 1987. *Richard Dobbs Spaight*. New Bern, NC: Griffin & Tilghman.

Wheeler, John H. 1879. "Richard Dobbs Spaight, of North Carolina." *The Pennsylvania Magazine of History and Biography* 3:426–29.

Caleb Strong (1745–1819)
Massachusetts

Caleb Strong was born on January 9, 1746, to the family of a tanner in Northampton, Massachusetts, at a time when Jonathan Edwards was serving as the parish minister. After earning a degree at Harvard, he studied law with Joseph Hawley and was admitted to the bar. He served on Northampton's Committee of Safety and was a delegate to the Massachusetts constitutional convention. He also served on the Massachusetts Council and as a member of the state senate before being chosen as one of the state's four delegates to the Constitutional Convention.

A biographer says that Strong was tall, "of moderate fullness of person," and had a "long, oval face" (Lodge 1972, 256). Strong did not serve on any committees during the convention, and he was not a frequent speaker, but he did have something to say about the makeup of each of the three branches of the new government. Although he was a man of strong views, Strong demonstrated a winsomeness and moderation of character that explains his many electoral successes.

At the Convention

Congress

Strong began attending the Constitutional Convention on May 28. The first official action he was recorded as taking was on May 31 when the convention was discussing whether the first branch of Congress should be selected by the people. Pierce somewhat ambiguously recorded that Strong "would agree to the principle, provided it would undergo a certain modification, but pointed out nothing" (Farrand 1966, 1:58).

On June 21 Strong seconded a motion by Connecticut's Oliver Ellsworth favoring yearly elections to the U.S. House of Representatives at a time when the convention was considering terms of two or three years (1:361)—at the Massachusetts ratifying convention, Strong later portrayed the two-year term as a compromise between those who favored annual elections and those who wanted a longer term (3:247). On June 12, Strong and Gerry split the Massachusetts delegation by voting against a seven-year term for senators while fellow delegates King and Gorham voted for it (1:219). On July 2, Strong further favored the commitment of the issue of representation to a committee. At that time, however, he indicated that if the two branches "should be established on different principles, contentions would prevail and there would never be a concurrence in necessary measures" (1:515). On July 14, Strong further indicated his support for the Great Compromise that this committee had formulated. He believed that the convention faced either the prospect of accepting this report or ending in failure: "It is agreed on all hands that Congress are nearly at an end. If no Accommodation takes place, the Union itself must soon be dissolved" (2:7).

Strong poured cold water on the idea that the large states could come up on their own with a plan to which the small states would agree. He further argued that the small states had made a concession in agreeing to allow money bills to be introduced in the House of Representatives, and he thought the larger states were also duty-bound to make their own compromise on representation. Strong appeared to reiterate the importance of this provision on August 9 when he seconded a motion by Virginia's Edmund Randolph to postpone consideration of Senate representation until it was decided whether this provision would remain (2:232). Similarly, on August 15, Strong proposed a motion reinstating the provision limiting the origination of money bills to the House of Representatives but allowing the Senate to propose or concur in amendments to the same (2:297).

On August 14, Strong proposed that members of Congress should be granted four dollars a day for their services (2:293). He would, however, have allowed for states to supplement this amount.

Presidency

On July 24, Strong indicated that he did not think that congressional selection of the president would require that the president be limited to a single term. He anticipated that there would be sufficient legislative turnover so that the second election would be based on a different set of men than the first and that executive corruption of the legislature would not be a major concern. He did not believe that the president would be unduly bound to the legislature through gratitude and feared that an electoral college would be too complex. He also feared "that the first characters in the States would not feel sufficient motives to undertake the office of Electors" (2:100).

Judiciary

On July 21, Strong went on record against allying the judiciary with the executive in forming a Council of Revision to invalidate congressional laws. He argued that "the power of making ought to be kept distinct from that of expounding the laws. No maxim was better established. The Judges in exercising the function of expositors might be influenced by the part they had taken, in framing the laws" (2:75).

Life after the Convention

Strong left the convention in August because of an illness in the family but later served in the Massachusetts ratifying convention. In defending the Constitution there, Strong disputed accusations that the proposed Constitution was too ambiguous and defended those who had written it:

I think the whole of it is expressed in the plain, common language of mankind. If any parts are not so explicit as they could be, it cannot be attributed to any design; for I believe a great majority of the men who formed it were sincere and honest men. (3:248)

Strong also explained the reasons for the Connecticut Compromise and for other decisions that the convention had made.

Elected to the U.S. Senate where he served from 1789 to 1796, Strong helped draft the Judiciary Act of 1789 and supported the Federalist Party. He was elected governor in 1800, and was returned to this position in 1812. During the War of 1812, Strong opposed allowing the U.S. government to call out the militia. He supported the Hartford Convention of 1814 and may have actually favored withdrawal from the Union by the New England states. Whereas Democratic-Republicans were seeking westward expansion (James Madison had argued in Federalist No. 10 that a large land area would help republican governments combat the mischiefs of faction), in a letter of February 1815, Strong indicated that he thought that "The territory of the United States is so extensive as to forbid us to indulge the expectation that we shall remain many years united" and that he still had hopes that "We may be happy as neighbors, where a union would be inconvenient" (quoted in Lodge, p. 155).

Strong died in Northampton on November 7, 1819 and was buried in the city's Bridge Street Cemetery. He and his wife Sara Hooker (the daughter of Jonathan Edwards' successor, the Reverend John Hooker), who preceded him in death in 1817, had nine children.

Further Reading

Bradford, M. E. 1994. *Founding Fathers: Brief Lives of the Framers of the United States Constitution.* 2nd ed. Lawrence: University Press of Kansas.

"A Biography of Caleb Strong 1745–1819," From Revolution to Reconstruction. http://www.let/rug.nl/usa/B/strong/strong.htm. Accessed 7/6/2012.

Farrand, Max, ed. 1966. *The Records of the Federal Convention of 1787.* 4 vols. New Haven, CT: Yale University Press.

Lodge, Henry Cabot. 1972. "Caleb Strong." In *Studies in History*, 224–61. Freeport, NY: Books for Libraries Press. Reprint of 1884 original.

GEORGE WASHINGTON (1732–1799)
VIRGINIA

George Washington was born on February 22, 1732 in Westmoreland County, Virginia and began his career in surveying. His father died in Washington's youth, and he inherited property not only from his father but also later from his older half-brother, Lawrence. He further increased his wealth in 1759 when he married Martha Dandridge Custis (1731–1802), a wealthy widow with two daughters to whom he served as stepfather (the couple had no children of their own). With Washington's service first in the French and Indian War and then as commander in chief of America's revolutionary forces, he had a far more continental perspective than many of the delegates.

Washington was a handsome man who grew to be six feet two inches tall and had extraordinary large hands and a vigorous physique; he cut a fine figure riding horses and from early in his career, fellow citizens thought he had a special destiny. He was elected to the Continental Congress in 1774 after having previously served in the Virginia House of Burgesses. With his military record (it also helped that he was from the South at a time when New England states were taking the lead), he was a logical choice for commander in chief, to which position he was unanimously elected by Congress. As his anguished letters demonstrated, he was particularly aware of Congress's difficulties in fulfilling its obligations to his troops. After the war, Washington set an example that will forever be honored in republican governments by renouncing any attempts to crown him as king. He further dissuaded unpaid troops from marching on Congress to demand their rights by force of arms, and returned to his beloved plantation at Mt. Vernon (Schwartz 1983). Sometimes cash poor, Washington was one of the wealthiest men in the nation.

Increasingly pessimistic about the nation's prospects under the Articles of Confederation, Washington's house served as the gathering place for Virginia and Maryland delegates discussing navigation on the Potomac River. This meeting was in turn the launching pad for the Annapolis Convention, which issued the call for the convention in Philadelphia.

At the Convention

In 1787, the fifty-five-year-old Washington had a worldwide reputation that he was reluctant to hazard at a convention for which the prospects were so uncertain. Fellow Virginian James Madison played a particularly active role in convincing him that his presence was necessary to rescue the government, and he reluctantly came, arriving early and spending the following months at the home of Robert Morris, who had proved so helpful in financing the Revolutionary War. Washington attended every day of the convention, after which he returned to Mt. Vernon.

Scholars generally agree that George Washington was the "father of the country" and that his attendance at the Constitutional Convention, his support for the document, and his service for two terms as president were indispensable to the new republic. Addressed as "His Excellency" during the convention, state delegation unanimously elected him as the convention's president on May 25. His only possible rival for the post was the ailing Benjamin Franklin, with whom he had dined shortly after arriving in Philadelphia. With the approval of Franklin, who was unable to attend that day because of illness, fellow Pennsylvanian Robert Morris placed Washington's name in nomination.

In resolutions adopted on the next day of business after Washington was selected as convention president, members agreed on a series of formalities that played to Washington's strengths. Members would not take their seats until he had taken his. Each member who wanted to speak would address the president, and while a delegate spoke, "none shall pass between them, or hold discourse with another, or read a book, pamphlet or paper, printed or manuscript" (Farrand 1966, 1:11). When the convention adjourned at the end of each day, each member was required to stand until Washington had left the room (1:12). The symbolism must have been impressive. John Langdon, a New Hampshire delegate, attempted to convey the scene in a letter to a friend on August 1, 1787:

> Figure to yourself the Great Washington, with a Dignity peculiar to himself, taking the Chair. The Notables are seated, in a Moment and after a short Silence the Business of the day is open'd with great Solemnity and good Order. The Importance of the Business, the Dignified Character of Many, who Compose the Convention, the Eloquence of Some and the Regularity of the whole gives a Ton[e] to the proceedings which is extreamly pleasing. (Hutson 1987, 201)

Washington's role as president is believed to have had a sobering influence on the convention. Georgia's William Pierce reported that on one occasion during the convention when he found that a delegate had dropped notes of the proceedings in the state house, Washington addressed his fellows:

> I am sorry to find that some one Member of this Body, has been so neglectful of the secrets of the Convention as to drop in the State House a copy of their proceedings, which by accident was picked up and delivered to me this Morning. I must entreat Gentlemen to be more careful, least our transactions get into the News Papers, and disturb the public repose by premature speculations. I know not whose Paper it is, but there it is (throwing it down on the table), let him who owns it take it." At the same time he bowed, picked up his Hat, and quitted the room with a dignity so severe that every Person seemed alarmed. (3:86–87)

Pierce reported that he himself was extremely alarmed and was only reassured when he returned to his lodging at the Indian Queen and found his own copy. He also reports that no one ever stepped forward to claim the missing papers.

Although his letters testify that Washington was far more adept at written words than many contemporary politicians, he was a reluctant speaker who gained power more from his actions than from his speeches. He is only recorded as giving two formal speeches during the convention. The first was an acceptance speech, which he delivered after delegates chose him as president of the convention and Robert Morris and John Rutledge escorted him to the raised dais. His speech was undoubtedly longer than Madison's summary, but the summary adequately conveys the quiet dignity that the General was able to project:

> he thanked the Convention for the honor they had conferred on him, reminded them of the novelty of the scene of business in which he was to act, lamented his want of [better qualifications], and claimed the indulgence of the House towards the involuntary errors which his inexperience might occasion. (1:3–4)

Apart from rulings that he had to make in his role as president, he then fell largely silent until the final day of the convention, when he spoke in favor of permitting one representative for every 30,000 residents rather than for every 40,000 (2:644), and when, later in the day, he asked the delegates what they wanted him to do with the convention's journals. Commenting on Washington's intervention in the seemingly trivial matter of the number of individuals each U.S. representative would represent, one author has observed: "The size of the districts was not a major issue. By breaking his silence to endorse a minor change, Washington was signifying to the delegates that no major changes needed to be made" (Brookhiser 1996, 68).

Glenn Phelps, a student of Washington's constitutional philosophy who has attempted to analyze Washington's positions at the convention by drawing from Madison's records of the Virginia delegation's votes, says that Washington pursued two major concerns: first, he consistently supported an energetic executive, and second, with the exception of opposing the power to emit paper money, he consistently favored stronger powers for the national government (1993, 1–3, 4). Phelps further notes, "The Constitution addressed nearly every major concern that he had raised in the previous six or seven years and did so in ways that fit well with his avowed goals" (1993, 116).

Washington's prestige undoubtedly aided in the initial reception that the convention provided to the Virginia Plan. Washington appears to have encouraged fellow delegates to consider not simply what they thought the people would adopt, but what they needed. At the outset of the convention, Washington thus observed:

> It is possible that no plan we suggest will be adopted. Perhaps another dreadful conflict is to be sustained. If, to please the people, we offer what we ourselves disapprove, how can we afterwards defend our work? Let us raise a standard to which the wise and honest can repair; the event is in the hands of God. (Lee 1932, 25)

There is evidence that widespread anticipation that Washington would serve as the nation's first chief executive made delegates more willing to vest this institution in a single individual and give it greater powers than they might otherwise have been willing to entrust to it. South Carolina's Pierce Butler thus observed that members had "cast their eyes towards General Washington as President; and shaped their ideas of the Powers to be given a President, by their opinions of his Virtue" (Quoted in Rhodehamel 1998, 109). In unsuccessfully arguing that the president should not receive a salary, Benjamin Franklin pointed on June 2 to Washington's laudable example when serving as commander in chief of the Revolutionary forces (1:84). Two days later, Franklin observed that "The first man, put at the helm will be a good one. No body knows what sort may come afterwards" (1:103).

Consistent with the rule of secrecy that the convention adopted, Washington's diaries do not give the substance of the events that transpired at the convention, but they show that he engaged in an active social life, where his behind-the-scene interactions with other delegates and comments on their work may very well have been influential. He also used a break in convention proceedings to revisit Valley Forge, where he and his troops had spent such a miserable winter during the Revolutionary War.

Washington is the further source of a number of anecdotes; not all can be verified, but each illumines one or another aspect of his character. Pierce's description of Washington's alleged comments after discovering a copy of the proceedings has been noted above. Gouverneur Morris of Pennsylvania further told how he responded to a bet by New York's Alexander Hamilton that he could not slap the General on the shoulder in a public gathering and won only after receiving considerable mortification by Washington's icy response (3:85). Washington was later alleged to have poured coffee into a saucer and blown over it to explain to Thomas Jefferson why the convention had agreed on a bicameral rather than a unicameral Congress (3:359), with the Senate "cooling" the passions of the House. In discussions about prohibiting a standing army of any more than 3,000 troops, Washington was reputed to have whispered to a fellow delegate that "no foreign enemy should invade the United States at any time, with more than three thousand troops" (Hutson 1987, 229). When Alexander Hamilton was alleged to have opposed Franklin's motion that each day begin with prayer on the basis that the convention should not ask for foreign aid, Washington was reported to have "fixed his eye upon the speaker, with a mixture of *surprise* and *indignation*, while he uttered this impertinent and impious speech, and then looked around to ascertain in what manner it affected others" (3:472). Even the President's chair became the subject of comment, when on the convention's last day, Benjamin Franklin professed to believe that the sun painted on the back slat was rising on a new day.

Some true, some apocryphal, and some a mixture of both, these stories (like Parson Weems's later embellishments of Washington's life, as in his story of Washington chopping down a cherry tree) illustrated the quiet dignity of a man whose very presence could call out the best behavior in those around him. It is perhaps significant that the idea of breaking the convention into a Committee of the Whole presided over by Nathaniel Gorham rather than by Washington was abandoned when debates over the respective merits of the proposals for state representation in the Virginia and New Jersey Plans got serious.

Life after the Convention

After the convention, Washington carefully followed the progress of ratification, maintaining a vigorous correspondence and using his personal influence wherever possible in the Constitution's favor. One sad result of the convention was that the long friendship between Washington and his neighbor George Mason came to an end with the latter's refusal to sign the Constitution. The support of the Constitution by both Washington and Franklin was a major argument that Federalists made in its favor. Washington authorized Madison to signal his support at the Virginia ratifying convention.

Washington remains the only president ever unanimously selected by the electoral college. Although he had mixed feelings about accepting yet another position that might further hazard the reputation he had so assiduously cultivated, he proceeded to his inauguration in triumph, cheered by 20,000 citizens in Philadelphia and greeted by a banner in Trenton, where he had previously fought a battle, that read: "THE DEFENDER OF THE MOTHERS WILL BE THE PROTECTOR OF THE DAUGHTERS" (Brookhiser 1996, 73). He was inaugurated at Federal Hall in New York City on April 30, 1789 where Chancellor Robert Livingston of that state administered his oath. In his inaugural address, Washington thanked God for guiding the steps of the new nation through its recent deliberations:

> Every step by which they [the people] have advanced to the character of an independent nation seems to have been distinguished by some token of providential agency; and in the important revolution just accomplished in the system of their united government the tranquil deliberations and voluntary consent of so many distinct communities from which the event has resulted cannot be compared with the means by which most governments have been established without some return of pious gratitude, along with an humble anticipation of the future blessings which the past seem to presage. (quoted in Hunt 1997, 4–5)

Commending the idea of adding provisions like those being considered for the Bill of Rights, Washington avoided specific recommendations while encouraging general action:

> I assure myself that whilst you carefully avoid every alteration which might endanger the benefits of an united and effective government, or which ought to await the future lessons of experience, a reverence for the characteristic rights of freemen and a regard for the public harmony will

sufficient influence your deliberations on the question how far the former can be impregnably fortified or the latter be safely and advantageously promoted. (Hunt 1997, 6)

As the first president under the new government Washington attempted, with only partial success, to rise above the conflicts that quickly developed in his government between Federalists led by his secretary of the treasury, Alexander Hamilton, and Democratic-Republicans, who were led by his secretary of state, Thomas Jefferson, and by James Madison. Washington acted with the knowledge that almost everything he did in office would be considered to be a precedent. During his first administration, he gave his quiet support to adoption of the Bill of Rights. Washington supported the ambitious programs of his secretary of the treasury, including the establishment of a national bank. Washington helped secure the establishment of the nation's capital, which the nation named after him, established in its current location on the Potomac River down from his own plantation. In his farewell address, Washington renewed his concern about the prevalence of party spirit and recommended a policy of avoiding foreign alliances, a policy that served the nation particularly well in its early years.

One of Washington's most important contributions may have been his decision not to seek reelection after his first two terms. He had actually toyed with the idea of retiring after his first term, but proponents of both emerging parties had persuaded him to stay. His decision to retire after his second term set a precedent that lasted until President Franklin D. Roosevelt and that has subsequently been incorporated into the Twenty-second Amendment.

In Adams's administration, Washington accepted the president's request to take military command of American forces in anticipation of a war with France that, fortunately, did not materialize. Washington died at Mt. Vernon (where he was buried) on December 14, 1799, and was famously eulogized by Virginia's Richard Henry Lee who called him "first in war, first in peace, and first in the hearts of his countrymen." Washington, who had long owned and long regretted the institution of slavery, provided that his slaves would be freed upon his death (Wiencek 2003).

On June 22, 2012, a copy of the Constitution and Bill of Rights that Washington had annotated was sold at Christie's in New York for a record-setting $9,826,500. Washington had made special annotations to the section of the Constitution related to executive powers, affirming his desire conscientiously to execute the duties of this office.

Further Reading

Brookhiser, Richard. 1996. *Founding Father: Rediscovering George Washington*. New York: The Free Press.

Chernow, Ron. 2010. *Washington: A Life*. New York: Penguin Press.

Ellis, Joseph J. 2004. *His Excellency: George Washington*. New York: Vintage Books.

Farrand, Max, ed. 1966. *The Records of the Federal Convention of 1787*. 4 vols. New Haven, CT: Yale University Press.

Holcombe, Arthur N. 1956. "The Role of Washington in the Framing of the Constitution." *Huntington Library Quarterly* 29 (August): 317–34.

Hunt, John Gabriel, ed. 1997. *The Inaugural Addresses of the Presidents*. New York: Gramercy Books.

Hutson, James H., ed. 1987. *Supplement to Max Farrand's The Records of the Federal Convention of 1787*. New Haven, CT: Yale University Press.

Lee, Howard B. 1932. *The Story of the Constitution*. Charlottesville, VA: The Michie Company.

Liebiger, Stuart. 1999. *Founding Friendship: George Washington, James Madison, and the Creation of the American Republic*. Charlottesville: University Press of Virginia.

Morrison, Jeffrey H. 2009. *The Political Philosophy of George Washington*. Baltimore, MD: The Johns Hopkins University Press.

Nordham, George Washington. 1987. *George Washington: President of the Constitutional Convention*. Chicago: Adams Press.

Phelps, Glenn A. 1993. *George Washington and American Constitutionalism*. Lawrence: University Press of Kansas.

Rhodehamel, John. 1998. *The Great Experiment: George Washington and the American Republic*. New Haven, CT: Yale University Press.

Schwartz, Barry. 1987. *George Washington: The Making of an American Symbol*. New York: The Free Press.

———. 1983. "George Washington and the Whig Conception of Heroic Leadership," *American Sociological Review* 48 (February): 18–33.

"Washington's Annotated Constitution Makes $9.8M," *Antique Trader* 56 (July 25, 2012), 20.

Wienek, Henry. 2003. *An Imperfect God: George Washington, His Slaves, and the Creation of America*. New York: Farrar, Straus and Giroux.

Note: Publication of *The Papers of George Washington* began at the University of Virginia Press in 1968. Approximately two-thirds of an anticipated 90 volumes have been published to date, with the project scheduled for completion in 2023.

HUGH WILLIAMSON (1735–1819)
NORTH CAROLINA

Hugh Williamson was born in West Nottingham, Pennsylvania on December 5, in 1735 to merchant parents, John W. Williamson and Mary Davison, who had immigrated to the United States from Ireland. After attending a private academy at New London, Pennsylvania, Williamson attended the College of Philadelphia, today's University of Pennsylvania, where he was a member of the first graduating class. After earning an undergraduate degree he returned for theological study, was licensed to preach as a Presbyterian minister (after studying divinity under Dr. Samuel Finley of Connecticut), and picked up a master's degree in mathematics. Williamson later attended the University of Edinburgh and the University of Utrecht from which he earned a medical degree, and was elected in 1768 to the American Philosophical Society.

A fellow doctor described him as "taller than the general standard" and "well proportioned" but "not fleshy," with gray eyes, an aquiline nose, and a prominent chin (quoted in Sheldon 2010, 248). A critic by the name of Archibald McLean said that Williamson "would have made a pretty good pettifogging attorney" while others described his sometimes florid oratory as "grotesque" and provocative of laughter (quoted in Sheldon 2010, 249–50).

Also interested in astronomy, Williamson published scientific papers on such diverse subjects as the transit of Venus and Mercury, comets (on which he believed there was likely to be life), climate change, electric eels, and serpents. He later became a trustee of the University of Pennsylvania and the University of North Carolina, as well as what became the University of Delaware. A witness to the Boston Tea Party, Williamson traveled to England where he formed a friendship with Benjamin Franklin, with whom he had previously sparred in an anonymous pamphlet; his role in the publication of Governor Hutchinson's incriminating correspondence is still disputed. Perhaps because Williamson had initially sought reconciliation with England, Silas Deane thought that Williamson was a British double agent; this report blocked a military commission when he returned to America. Since Philadelphia fell to the British, Williamson moved to North Carolina where he joined his brother in entrepreneurial activities (including land speculation with William Blount) before serving as the surgeon general of the state's militia. Before being selected to attend the Constitutional Convention, he had served in the North Carolina legislature, in the Congress under the Articles of Confederation where he was active in drafting legislation related to the admission of new western states, and as a delegate to the Annapolis Convention. He had, however, arrived too late to participate in the latter.

At the Convention

Williamson was present on the first day of convention business on May 25 and he stayed to the end. He had the advantage of serving in a delegation that was united, observing in a letter of July 19, "There has not in a single important Question been a Division in our Representation nor so much as one dissenting Voice" (Hutson 1987, 175). Little noticed in many histories of the convention, Williamson was the most outspoken member of the North Carolina delegation. He delivered his views on a wide variety of subjects, but his comments were often briefer than those of better known delegates. Williamson may be best known for introducing the motion that terms of senators would be for six years. Seeds of ideas that he planted appear, sometimes somewhat reconfigured, in a number of provisions that the delegates incorporated into the Constitution, and especially in the electoral college mechanism.

Williamson served on five different committees during the convention. These included the committee designed to reconsider the initial representation in the House of Representatives, established on July 9; the committee on state debts and regulation of the militia created on August 18; the committee on slave trade and navigation formed on August 22; the committee on commercial discrimination formed on August 25; and the Committee on Postponed Matters that was created on August 31. Williamson did not chair any of these bodies.

Congress

Representation. On June 9, Williamson attempted to defend representation in Congress on the basis of population by noting that such methods were used in most of the states for representing counties, and that if appropriate in the latter case then it should also be appropriate for the former (Farrand 1966, 1:180). He returned to this theme on June 28.

He suggested that "if any political truth could be grounded on mathematical demonstration, it was that if the states were equally sovereign now, and parted with equal proportions of sovereignty, that they would remain equally sovereign" (1:445).

Williamson feared that if small states had equal votes with the large ones, the former would attempt to put their burdens on the latter. He thought that this problem might be compounded by the addition of western states (1:446). On July 9, Williamson suggested that the idea of apportioning representatives according to population should not equally apply to the West, where he anticipated that property values would be lower (1:560). On August 29, Williamson argued that the reason for granting existing states equal representation within the Senate would not apply to new states that were admitted into the Union (2:454).

When a committee proposed that the initial House of Representatives should consist of 65 delegates, Williamson observed that the northern states had a majority, and he thought that this posed a danger to the southern states (1:567). Whereas some delegates wanted to leave it to Congress to decide when to redistrict, Williamson thought that the Constitution needed to make it explicit when it should do so (1:579). Williamson favored the three-fifths compromise, which counted slaves as three-fifths of a person, in allocating representation in the U.S. House of Representatives (1:581). He proposed reducing New Hampshire's representation in the House of Representatives from three members to two, arguing that the state, delegates from which had not yet arrived at the convention, might not want to pay the extra direct taxes that would be apportioned on the basis of this representation (1:601) but perhaps also being pleased to think of an expedient that would also reduce northern representation. On September 5, however, Williamson argued that Rhode Island should be given more than one member. He also said that he thought that the initial House of Representatives would be too small if it were confined to 65 members (2:511; also see 2:553). On September 14, Williamson wanted to increase the House by half its size, making sure that the smallest states had at least two members (2:612).

By July 2, Williamson was ready for some compromise on the issue of representation. He thus favored establishing a committee for this purpose, observing "If we do not concede on both sides, our business must soon be at an end" (1:515). When one of the compromises that emerged was to restrict the origination of money bills in the lower house, however, Williamson suggested that the convention had things backwards. He reasoned that the people would more closely watch what the Senate did than they would watch the branch that had "most of the popular confidence" (1:544). On August 9, a day after the convention had struck out the provision regarding the origination of money bills, however, Williamson joined Virginia's Edmund Randolph in asking for a reconsideration of this issue (2:230). He indicated that he thought this was one of the conditions on which North Carolina, and other small states, had agreed to the Great Compromise (2:233; also see 2:263 and 2:287). On August 15 he observed that since some thought the restriction on money bills was critical and others thought it only unimportant, the delegates should prefer the former over the latter (2:297). He further observed that many delegates would be unwilling to strengthen the Senate unless the convention reinstituted the prohibition on money bills.

When Virginia's George Mason objected that granting each state three senators would make that body too numerous, Williamson added that it would be more difficult for distant states to send this number than for those that were nearer (2:94). On this same occasion, he indicated that he supported "per capita," or individual, voting in the Senate, rather than by state delegation.

Pay. On June 22 Williamson argued that states should pay the salaries of their own members of Congress. He feared that new western states would be poor and would have different interests from those in the East, and he did not think that existing states should have to pay the salaries of individuals "who would be employed in thwarting their measures & interests" (1:372). In the discussion of June 28, cited above, Williamson feared that new states in the West would be poor and would be tempted to burden the commerce and consumption of the eastern states (1:446).

Williamson proposed that members of Congress should be compensated "for the devotion of their time to the public Service" (1:427). Its purpose appears to have been to eliminate the term "fixed" so as to provide greater flexibility in the future.

Qualifications. On August 7, Williamson opposed making a freehold a condition for voting, but notes of the convention do not record his reasons (2:201). The next day, he opposed requiring a number of years of residency before an individual could run for Congress, observing, "New residents if elected will be the most zealous to Conform to the will of their constituents, as their conduct will be watched with a more jealous eye" (2:218). After the convention voted to accept a requirement that members of the House of Representatives should be citizens for at least seven years, however, Williamson believed the delegates should establish a similar or longer period for the Senate. He observed that "Bribery & Cabal can be more easily practiced in the choice of the Senate which is to be made by the Legislatures composed of a few men, than in the House of Represents. who will be chosen by the people" (2:239). On August 13, Williamson suggested that nine years of residency, rather than seven, should be required for members of the House. He observed:

> He wished this Country to acquire as fast as possible national habits. Wealthy emigrants do more harm by their luxurious examples, than good, by the money, they bring with them. (2:268)

On August 10, Williamson opposed allowing members of Congress to set the amount of property that individuals should own in order to become members. He feared that if members of a single profession (he cited lawyers) dominated Congress, members of this profession might secure the election of other members (2:250).

Williamson indicated on August 14 that he supported a provision making members of Congress ineligible to other offices. He observed that "He had scarcely seen a single corrupt measure in the Legislature of N- Carolina, which could not be traced up to office hunting" (2:287). On September 3, however, Williamson indicated that he did not think members should be ineligible for vacancies in offices that occurred while they were serving (2:490; also see 2:492).

Powers and Limits. On August 16, Williamson supported prohibiting congressional taxation of exports (2:307), and on August 28, he favored an absolute limit on state taxation of imports (2:441). On August 22, Williamson supported a prohibition on ex post facto clauses. He observed that in his own state, a similar provision had worked because it had given judges something to take hold of (2:376). This suggests that he probably favored the power of judicial review, by which judges invalidate legislation that they believe to be unconstitutional in cases which litigants bring before them. Williamson thought that the congressional veto of state legislation was "unnecessary" (2:391). On August 27, Williamson indicated that he thought the Constitution should grant Congress power to designate presidential successors (2:427).

On August 29, Williamson supported a provision, which southern states favored, to require two-thirds majorities of Congress to enact regulations of commerce. He did not believe the requirement for nine votes had defeated any needed measure under the Articles of Confederation (2:450). Interestingly, Williamson said he favored the measure not because he thought it was actually needed to provide security for southern states, which he believed could build their own ships if commercial regulations grew too heavy, but because he thought it would allay southern fears. Similarly, on August 30, Williamson said that he thought that his state was disposed to give up its western lands, which now include the state of Tennessee, but that he did not think the Constitution should compel it to do so (2:462).

On September 7, at a time when some delegates were arguing that Congress should be able to enact treaties of peace more easily than other kinds of treaties, Williamson indicated that he favored similar majorities for these treaties as with others (2:541; also see 2:543 and 2:549). Williamson was apparently concerned that, without such majorities, the interests of the distant states might be sacrificed to others (2:548). This concern appears to have been important. Williamson went on to propose that the Senate should not be able to enter into treaties without giving its members "previous notice" and "a reasonable time for their attending" (2:550).

Other Matters. On June 25, Williamson proposed the current six-year senatorial term. He offered a very practical reason, namely, that it would be easier to provide "rotation" for such a term than for the term of seven years that had been proposed (1:409). As observed below, Williamson also pressed unsuccessfully for longer presidential terms.

On August 9, Williamson supported a motion by Virginia's Edmund Randolph allowing governors to appoint senators in cases of vacancies. Williamson thought that this was necessary since there would be cases where senators would resign or not accept their selection by the legislatures (2:231).

Presidency

On June 1, Williamson argued that there was little difference between having an executive and a council (presumably the proposed Council of Revision) and having a plural executive of three or more persons (1:7; also see 1:97). On July 24, Williamson indicated that he personally favored a plural executive consisting of three men "taken from three districts into which the States should be divided" (2:100). He thought that the veto power would make it especially problematic to invest powers in an individual from a single section. He also feared that a unitary executive would pave the way for a monarchy:

> Another objection agst. a single Magistrate is that he will be an elective king, and will feel the spirit of one. He will spare no pains to keep himself

in for life, and will then lay a train for the succession of his children. It was pretty certain he thought that we should at some time or other have a King; but he wished no precaution to be omitted that might postpone the event as long as possible. (2:101)

If the convention were to stick with a unitary executive, Williamson thought that he should be ineligible to run again. Under such circumstances, he was willing to allow the president to serve for as long as 10 or 12 years (2:101).

Selection. On June 2, Williamson said that he could see nothing but "trouble and expense" from selecting the president through a series of electors rather than allowing their representatives in Congress to do this (1:81). On July 17, Williamson likened the selection of the president by the people to selection "by lot" (1:32). He reasoned that in time most people would know few leaders outside their own state and that candidates in the largest states would therefore be the only ones elected (2:32). Williamson did not think congressional selection would result in overdependency since the presidential salary would be fixed and presidents would not be eligible to a second term (2:32). When on July 19 the convention tentatively settled on a system of electors, Williamson seconded a motion to keep the president from being eligible for another term. He expressed his lack of confidence in the electors and his fears that "they would be liable to undue influence" (2:58).

Williamson appears to have proposed one aspect of the current electoral college when on July 20 he proposed that after the first elections, each state should have a number of electors equal to its membership in the House of Representatives (2:64); the convention eventually combined this number with the number of U.S. senators. The next day, Williamson proposed that the national government should provide compensation for the presidential electors (2:73).

Williamson advanced the seed of another provision of the electoral college on July 25 when he proposed that each elector should vote for three candidates (they would eventually vote for two), with the hope that only the first candidate would be from their own states (2:113). When the convention was discussing the possibility that the Senate should select the president in cases where none received a majority, Williamson objected that this might give this body too much power and suggested that it should have to choose between the top two candidates (2:501). Williamson was particularly concerned that allowing the Senate too much choice "lays a certain foundation for corruption & aristocracy" (2:512). In a speculation that has been emulated by scores of later observers, he pointed out that, with each state having a single vote, and a simple majority of the Senate being necessary to make such a choice, it is possible that a choice might be made by senators representing no more than one-sixth of the people (2:514). He later supported the provision moving the power to choose presidents in cases where none had a majority of the electoral college from the Senate to the House of Representatives (2:522). He feared that choice by the Senate in such cases would tilt the government in an aristocratic direction (2:524). When the convention decided to allow the House to make this decision, Williamson successfully proposed that it should make such a choice by states, rather than per capita (2:527).

Powers. On June 2 Williamson proposed that the president should be removable by conviction of impeachment for "mal-practice or neglect of duty" (1:88). On June 6 he advocated that a conditional veto, one that two-thirds majorities of Congress could override, was preferable to entrusting an absolute veto in the president and a Council of Revision (1:140). On June 8 he expressed further reservations about any veto system "that might restrain the States from regulating their internal police (1:165). On August 7, Williamson introduced a motion to limit executive vetoes to "legislative acts" (2:196).

On August 15, Williamson proposed that it should take a congressional majority of three-fourths, rather than two-thirds, to override a presidential veto (2:301). At this time, he also advocated vesting the veto solely in the president rather than in the president and members of the judiciary, whom he did not think should have a hand in legislation. However, on September 12, Williamson moved to reconsider the provision requiring three-fourths of Congress to override a presidential veto in favor of the current two-thirds. Observing that he had changed his mind on the subject, he now argued, "The former puts too much in the power of the President" (2:585). Subsequently saying that he was "less afraid of too few than of too many laws," he indicated that he feared the three-fourths requirement would make unnecessary laws too difficult to repeal (2:586).

Length of Term. On July 19, Williamson advocated a six-year presidential term. He argued both that more frequent elections would prove to be too expensive and that if elections were too often repeated, "the best men will not undertake the service and those of an inferior character will be liable to be corrupted" (2:59). In apparent support of an effort to go back to legislative selection of the president rather than selection by electors, Williamson supported a seven-year term on July 24 (2:100). On September

6, Williamson unsuccessfully proposed presidential terms of seven years and six years in place of the four-year term that the convention had by then adopted (2:525).

Vice Presidency

On September 7, Williamson expressed his opposition to the creation of the vice presidency. He observed that "He was introduced only for the sake of a valuable mode of election which required two to be chosen at the same time" (2:537).

Judiciary

On August 24, Williamson indicated that he wanted to postpone, rather than strike, a complicated procedure designed to settle land disputes between states. He suggested that such a provision might be needed "in cases where the Judiciary were interested or too closely connected with the parties" (2:401).

Slavery

On August 22 Williamson, who never personally owned any slaves, probably helped pave the way for a compromise on slavery by observing that his home state permitted duties on slave imports. Williamson did not think his state would join the new government if it were to be prohibited from importing slaves and he thought "it was wrong to force any thing down, not absolutely necessary, and which any State must disagree to" (2:373).

On August 25, Williamson further clarified his views. After Gouverneur Morris of Pennsylvania proposed that the Constitution should limit slave importation to the two Carolinas and Georgia, thus subjecting them to special scrutiny, Williamson objected. Noting that "both in opinion & practice he was, against slavery," he added that he "thought it more in favor of humanity, from a view of all circumstances, to let in S—C & Georgia on those terms, than to exclude them from the Union" (2:415–16).

Other Matters

During the discussion as to whether the convention should begin each day with prayer, Williamson, who with his own theological training might have been capable of doing the job, rather pragmatically observed that the real reason the convention had not made provision for doing so was that "The Convention had no funds" (1:452). When the convention was discussing a provision to bind state officials by oath to support the U.S. Constitution, Williamson proposed that national officers should take a reciprocal oath to support the constitutions of the states (2:87).

On July 26, Williamson favored a provision to bar the national capital from being established in a city with a state capitol, but he feared that putting such a provision within the Constitution would stir opposition in such capitals and might be evaded by a state later moving its capital to the national capital (2:127). He later expressed the fear that the capital would never leave New York City (2:262), a city quite distant from his own state.

Ratification

On July 23, Williamson expressed support for a provision whereby either state legislatures or state conventions could ratify the Constitution. He preferred the latter believing that they were "more likely to be composed of the ablest men in the States" (2:91). On September 10, Williamson indicated that he thought the Constitution should first be sent to Congress for its approval (2:563). When the delegates were preparing to sign the Constitution on September 17, Williamson suggested that perhaps there would be greater unanimity if they should instead sign the accompanying letter. As for him, "he did not think a better plan was to be expected and had no scruples against putting his name to it" (2:645).

Life after the Convention

Williamson left the convention for Congress where he helped get the Constitution reported to the states. Although he missed North Carolina's first ratification convention at Hillsborough because of his congressional service, he attended the next one in Fayetteville and argued for its ratification. In February 1788, Williamson published a speech entitled "Remarks on the New Plan of Government." Acknowledging that the new Constitution was imperfect, he still described it as "more free and more perfect than any form of government that ever has been adopted by any nation" (Sheldon 2010, 266). Opposing those who thought a bill of rights was needed, Williamson argued at one part that "the Liberty of the Press and the laws of Mahomet are equally affected by it" (Sheldon 2010, 267), by which he meant not at all. Noting the perils of the existing government under the Articles of Confederation, Williamson implored that:

> We have a common interest, for we are embarked in the same vessel. At present she is in a sea of troubles, without sails, oars, or pilot; ready to be dashed into pieces by every flaw of wind. You may secure a port, unless you think it better to remain at sea. If there is any man among you that wishes for troubled times and fluctuating measures, that he may live by speculations, and thrive by the calamities of the State; this Government is not for him. (Sheldon 2010, 278)

In 1789, when Williamson was 53, he married Maria Apthorp (1767–1790) of New York. The couple had two sons, but Maria died delivering the second child, and both sons died in early manhood.

Elected to Congress, Williamson retired in 1793. He published a two-volume *History of North Carolina* in 1812. He spent the rest of his life in New York where he was very interested in the construction of the Erie Canal; he died while driving his carriage on May 22, 1819 and was buried in the Apthorp family vault in the graveyard of New York City's Trinity Church in Manhattan, not far from the resting place of Alexander Hamilton. Williamson County in Tennessee is named in Williamson's honor; given the scientific credentials that Williamson shared with Benjamin Franklin, it is fitting that the county's seat is Franklin.

Further Reading

Craige, Burton. 1987. *The Federal Convention of 1787: North Carolina in the Great Crisis.* Richmond, VA: Expert Graphics.

Farrand, Max, ed. 1966. *The Records of the Federal Convention of 1787.* 4 vols. New Haven, CT: Yale University Press.

"Hugh Williamson," Penn Biographies. http://www.archives.upenn.edu/people/1700s/williamson_hugh.html. Accessed 7/12/2012.

Mitchell, Memory F. 1964. *North Carolina's Signers: Brief Sketches of the Men Who Signed the Declaration of Independence and the Constitution.* Raleigh: Division of Archives and History, North Carolina Department of Cultural Resources.

Potts, Louis W. 1987. "Hugh Williamson: The Poor Man's Franklin and the National Domain," *North Carolina Historical Review* 64 (October): 371–93.

Sheldon, George F. 2010. *Hugh Williamson: Physician, Patriot, and Founding Father.* New York: Humanity Books.

Whitney, David C. 1974. *Founders of Freedom in America: Lives of the Men Who Signed the Constitution of the United States and So Helped to Establish the United States of America.* Chicago: J. G. Ferguson Publishing Company.

JAMES WILSON (1742–1798)
PENNSYLVANIA

James Wilson was born to a farm family in Carskerdo, Scotland, near St. Andrews, on September 14, 1742. He received a scholarship to attend the University of St. Andrews (he initially studied theology) before immigrating to Pennsylvania in 1765 after the death of his father. Initially employed as a Latin teacher at the College of Philadelphia, today's University of Pennsylvania, he subsequently studied law under John Dickinson.

Wilson established a legal practice in Reading, and later in Carlisle, Pennsylvania, and later still in Philadelphia. Wilson married Rachel Bird (1749–1786) in 1769 and they had six children. Wilson married Hannah Gray (1774–1808, who later married a widower Dr. Thomas Bartlett) in 1793, after the death of his first wife, but the only child of this second union did not survive. Wilson was so respected as an attorney that he served from 1779 to 1782 as the advocate-general for France in the United States. George Washington paid Wilson to accept his nephew Bushrod Washington, who later became a U.S. Supreme Court justice, as a law student.

Wilson was active in public affairs. He chaired the Carlisle Committee of Correspondence and served as a member of the Pennsylvania provincial convention. In 1768 Wilson published a manuscript entitled "Considerations on the Nature and Extent of the Legislative Authority of the British Parliament." As a delegate to the Continental Congress from 1775 to 1777, Wilson signed the Declaration of Independence (one of six signers of the U.S. Constitution to have done so), and was a strong believer in the doctrine of natural rights.

Wilson was appointed in 1782 as a director of the Bank of North America. Wilson served as a Pennsylvania delegate to the Congress under the Articles of Confederation from 1785 to 1787. Wilson was strongly opposed to the constitution that Pennsylvania had adopted in 1776, believing that it was too democratic in character, and he was involved in a number of partisan battles over this document; militiamen actually fired at a crowd from his house in what has been called the Fort Wilson Riot. Wilson was closely allied with fellow delegate Robert Morris and was a strong supporter of the national bank. Only Gouverneur Morris is recorded as having spoken more frequently at the convention than Wilson.

At the Convention

James Wilson was a distinguished delegate in a Pennsylvania delegation of distinguished delegates. A forty-one-year-old, foreign-born lawyer with heavy spectacles who later became a U.S. Supreme Court justice, Wilson was a strong proponent of popular election of both members of Congress and the presidency. He was a consistent advocate of a single executive and allied on many matters with James Madison. At the convention, Wilson often read speeches for his ailing friend, Benjamin Franklin.

Congress

Powers. Wilson's first recorded comment at the U.S. Constitutional Convention indicated both his belief in democratic accountability and his hope for a stronger government. He thus observed on May 31, in defending the idea of popular election of members of the House of Representatives:

> He was for raising the federal pyramid to a considerable altitude, and for that reason wished to give it as broad a basis as possible. No government could long subsist without the confidence of the people. In a republican Government this confidence was peculiarly essential. He also thought it wrong to increase the weight of the State Legislatures by making them the electors of the national Legislature. (Farrand 1966, 1:9)

Wilson thought that "it will have a most salutary influence on the credit of the U. States to remove the possibility of paper money" (2:310). Although he thought that states had abused the power of taxing exports (2:307), he believed that to deny this power to the general government would be unwisely "to take from the Common Govt. half the regulation of trade" (2:362). Wilson apparently seconded a motion by Madison to allow a two-thirds majority of Congress to enact such taxes in the belief that such a power would be better than none at all (1:363), but generally opposed such supermajorities (2:375). He observed that "if every particular interest was to be secured, *unanimity* ought to be required" (2:451). Wilson opposed the provision limiting congressional power to control slave importation (2:372). He favored a motion by Benjamin Franklin to grant Congress the power to cut canals, believing they could become a source of governmental revenue (2:615). Somewhat naively, Wilson, who had been on of the directors of the National Bank, did not believe that listing a power to establish banks "would excite the prejudices & parties apprehended" (2:616). He believed that the government would have the power to create "mercantile monopolies" as part of its "power to regulate trade" (2:616). He also favored a motion by James Madison and Charles Pinckney granting Congress the power to establish a national university (2:616).

The lawyerly side of Wilson was quite evident in his discussion of ex post facto laws. Apparently believing that such laws were legally invalid on their face, he professed that to insert such a prohibition would be to "proclaim that we are ignorant of the first principles of Legislation, or are constituting a Government which will be so" (2:376). He further observed that such prohibitions had not been effective in state constitutions and that "both sides will agree to the principle & will differ as to its application" (2:376). When Gouverneur Morris proposed that Congress should be able to suspend the writ of habeas corpus in cases of rebellion or invasion, Wilson doubted the necessity for such an exception in the belief that judges would be able to decide whether "to keep in Gaol or admit to Bail" (2:438). Wilson did favor a restriction on state interference in private contracts (2:440). He also seemed to question the propriety of the Fugitive Slave Clause by observing that "This would oblige the Executive of the State to do it, at the public expence" (2:443). On another occasion, in which the convention was considering a measure to grant Congress power to punish offenses against the law of nations, Wilson, again reflecting his background as an attorney, observed, "To pretend to *define* the law of nations which depended on the authority of all the Civilized Nations of the World, would have a look of arrogance, that would make us ridiculous" (2:615).

House of Representatives. In defending popular election of the House of Representatives on June 6, Wilson observed:

> The Govt. ought to possess not only 1st. the *force* but 2ndly, the *mind* or *sense* of the people at large. The Legislature ought to be the most exact

transcript of the whole Society. Representation is made necessary only because it is impossible for the people to act collectively. (1:133)

Wilson went on to argue that he thought that the people "would be rather more attached to the national Govt. than to the State Govts. as being more important in itself, and more flattering to their pride" (1:133). He thought there would be less to fear from large districts, where it would be less possible for wicked men to practice intrigue, than in small ones (1:133). On June 21, Wilson observed that he "considered the election of the 1st. branch by the people not only as the corner Stone, but as the foundation of the fabric: and that the difference between a mediate and immediate election was immense" (1:359). Wilson favored annual election of members of the House of Representatives (1:361). He further opposed setting a fixed salary for its members or in allowing state governments to fix such salaries (1:373).

Consistent with his democratic leanings, Wilson said that he "was agst. abridging the rights of election in any shape" (1:375). This included setting a minimum age of twenty-five for members of the House (1:375). Similarly, Wilson opposed establishing a long residency requirement for members of the House (2:217), favoring three years over seven (2:230–31; also see 2:251) and four over seven (2:268); he similarly supported reducing the requirements for citizenship in the Senate (2:272). As an immigrant, Wilson admitted that he was influenced by his own situation:

> Mr. Wilson said he rose with feelings which were perhaps peculiar; mentioning the circumstances of his not being a native, and the possibility, if the ideas of some gentlemen should be pursued, of his being incapacitated from holding a place under the very Constitution which he had shared in the trust of making. He remarked that an illiberal complexion which the motion would give to the System and the effect which a good system would have in inviting meritorious foreigners among us, and the discouragement & mortification they must feel from the degrading discrimination, now proposed. (2:237)

He observed, "To be appointed to a place may be matter of indifference. To be incapable of being appointed, is a circumstance grating, and mortifying" (2:237). Later in the convention, Wilson observed that foreign monarchs would use residency requirements for office holding to discourage their subjects from emigrating to the United States (2:272). On September 3, Wilson also observed that excluding members of Congress from other political offices "would be odious to those who did not wish for office, but did not wish either to be marked by so degrading a distinction" (2:491).

Wilson further feared that making members of Congress ineligible to accept other offices would have precluded Congress from appointing George Washington as commander in chief (1:376). Wilson favored solving the problem of legislative partiality to its members by taking all appointment powers out of its hands (1:387). Wilson argued that if the Constitution made members of Congress ineligible to other offices, that body would fail to attract individuals with the requisite talents. He observed that "the ambition which aspired to Offices of dignity and trust" were not "ignoble or culpable" (2:288).

Consistent with the direct election of representatives, Wilson believed that states should receive proportional representation in the House of Representatives. He posed rhetorical questions: "Are not the citizens of Pena. equal to those of N. Jersey? does it require 150 of the former to balance 50 of the latter?" (1:180). Observing that "We have been told that each State being sovereign, all are equal," Wilson then responded, "So each man is naturally a sovereign over himself, and all men are therefore naturally equal" (1:180). Acknowledging that "a new partition of the States is desirable," Wilson recognized that this was "evidently & totally impracticable" (1:180). Despite such rhetoric, Wilson expressed an early willingness to accept the Three-fifths Clause, "this being the rule in the Act of Congress agreed to by eleven States, for apportioning quotas of revenue on the States" (1:201). Wilson, however, wanted to make it clear that this concession was purely one of expediency:

> Are they admitted as Citizens? Then why are they not admitted on an equality with White Citizens? Are they admitted as property? then why is not other property admitted into the computation? These were difficulties however which he thought must be overruled by the necessity of compromise. (1:587)

Wilson did, however, seek to cover the implications of this provision by observing that "less umbrage would perhaps be taken agst. an admission of the slaves into the Rule of representation, if it should be so expressed as to make them indirectly only an ingredient in the rule, by saying that they should enter into the rule of taxation: and as representation was to be according to taxation, the end would be equally attained" (1:595).

After William Paterson had offered the New Jersey Plan as an alternative to the Virginia Plan, Wilson summarized the differences between the two plans. He concluded that "with regard to the power of the convention, he conceived himself authorized to *conclude nothing*, but to be at liberty to *propose any thing*" (1:253). He indicated that the nation needed new powers, but that he was among those who were reluctant to grant such powers to the Congress as currently configured, and that, for this and other reasons, he continued to favor the Virginia Plan. He later observed that "He had been 6 years in the 12 since the commencement of the Revolution, a member of Congress and had felt all its weaknesses" (1:343) and observed that states had been given equal representation in the Articles "of necessity not of choice" (1:343).

Wilson argued that it was necessary to keep the provision requiring that Congress publish a record of its proceedings. The people had a right to know what their government was doing. Moreover, if the delegates eliminated a requirement, which the Articles contained, people would be suspicious of the new government (2:260).

Senate. Early in the convention, Wilson indicated that he favored popular election of both branches of Congress (also see 1:69). He proposed that members of the second branch could be chosen from larger districts, which would apparently have further undermined state sovereignty by crossing state lines (1:52; also see 1:151). Wilson strongly opposed state legislative selection of senators. He feared that "The election of the 2d. branch by the Legislatures, will introduce & cherish local interests & local prejudices" (1:406). Wilson continued to present a view of national citizenship:

> The Genl. Govt. is not an assemblage of States, but of individuals for certain political purposes—it is not meant for the States, but for the individuals composing them: the *individuals* therefore not the *States*, ought to be represented in it. (1:406)

Wilson seconded Nathaniel Gorham's motion for a six-year Senate term. Because he envisioned the Senate as dealing with some matters of foreign policy, Wilson thought that its members needed "to be made respectable in the eyes of foreign nations" (1:426). To this end, he also supported the idea of nine-year Senate terms. Later in the convention, Wilson argued that the Constitution should require the consent of both houses of Congress for the ratification of treaties (2:538); he also feared that the requirement for ratification by a two-thirds majority "puts it in the power of a minority to controul the will of a majority" (2:540; also see 2:548–49).

Wilson continued to oppose equal state representation in the Senate. Like Madison, Wilson believed the issue was one of principle. Faced with threats that some of the small states might leave the Union, Wilson said "the question will be shall less than ¼ of the U. States withdraw themselves from the Union, or shall more than ¾ renounce the inherent, indisputable, and unalienable rights of men, in favor of the artificial systems of States. If issue must be joined, it was on this point he would chuse to join it" (1:482). Wilson reiterated that the Constitution was to be for the benefit of "*men*," and not "for the imaginary beings called *States*" (1:483). Governments could do too much or too little, and the problem with the Articles was that it was doing too little. States were valuable, but they should not be sovereign (1:484).

Faced with the argument that a small Senate where states were represented proportionally might leave some states without any representation, Wilson suggested on June 30 that smaller states might be guaranteed one senator (1:488). On July 14, he further supported a motion introduced by Charles Pinckney of South Carolina proposing that states have from one to five representatives in the Senate for a total of 36 (2:5). Wilson feared that a malapportionment in the original Senate would simply grow with time: "A vice in the Representation, like an error in the first concoction, must be followed by disease, convulsions, and finally death itself" (2:10). Moreover, Wilson linked the current infirmities of the Articles of Confederation to such state equality (2:10).

Like Madison, Wilson did not believe that the "concession" offered on behalf of the smaller states by which money bills would originate in the House amounted to anything significant (1:544; also see 2:4). Asked to compromise, Wilson said that he "was not deficient in a conciliating temper, but firmness was sometimes a duty of higher obligation" (1:550). He later opposed the provision for originating money bills by observing that "with regard to the pursestrings, it was to be observed that the purse was to have two strings, one of which was in the hands of the H. of Reps. the other in those of the Senate. Both houses must concur in untying, and of what importance could it be which untied first, which last" (2:275).

Representation of Western States

On a day (July 13) when Gouverneur Morris was expressing reservations about the power that western states would claim if they were represented like those in the East, Wilson declared that since "all men wherever placed have equal rights and are equally entitled to confidence, he viewed without apprehension the period when a few States should contain the superior number of people. The majority of people wherever found ought in all questions to govern the minority" (1:605). Drawing upon a powerful analogy, he argued that jealousy over the growth of the western states would prove no more productive than British jealousy over the growth of the colonies (1:605). Whereas others were arguing about the correlation between the growth of population and the generation of wealth and suggesting that representation should be based partly on the latter, Wilson argued:

> He could not agree that property was the sole or the primary object of Governt. & Society. The cultivation & improvement of the human mind was the most noble object. With respect to this object, as well as to other *personal* rights, numbers were surely the natural & precise measure of Representation. (1:605)

Presidency

Wilson had a major impact on the construction of the U.S. presidency. He proposed on June 2 that the executive branch should consist of a single individual (1:65). He believed that a single magistrate would give "energy[,] dispatch and responsibility to the office" (1:65). He apparently also favored a single executive as being more likely to keep secrets (see King's notes, 1:70). Wilson associated executive powers with "executing the laws, and appointing officers" not appointed by Congress (1:66), and he seconded a motion that James Madison made to this effect (1:67). Wilson understood that the idea of a single executive would remind some delegates of a monarchy, but he observed that many states already had a single governor, and that these governors had not been kingly. Wilson argued that a government headed by a single man would be more tranquil than one in which three individuals fought for control (1:96). Similarly, Wilson observed that an executive council might be more likely "to cover, than prevent malpractices" (1:97). On June 16, Wilson further observed that "In order to controul the Legislative authority, you must divide it. In order to controul the Executive you must unite it" (1:254).

Wilson favored "an absolute negative" by the executive on congressional legislation as an appropriate means of "self-defense," but he was willing to accept Madison's proposal to give this power jointly to the executive and members of the judiciary (1:98; also see 1:104 and 1:138). He believed that the mere threat of such a veto would often be effective and that, if legislators realized that the president had such power, it "would refrain from such laws, as it would be sure to defeat" (1:100). After the convention rejected the idea of an absolute veto, Wilson argued that Congress should have to muster a majority of three-fourths of its members, rather than a mere two-thirds, to override such vetoes (1:301).

Just as he believed the people should select members of Congress, so too, Wilson favored the direct election of the president by the people. Acknowledging that some might think such a proposal to be "chimerical," Wilson believed that experience in New York and Massachusetts had demonstrated that this could be both "a convenient & successful mode" (1:68). Wilson believed that if the people selected both branches of Congress and the president, all would have sufficient independence (1:69). Although he favored direct election, Wilson appears to have been the first at the convention to have proposed a kind of electoral college. He first advanced this idea on June 2 (1:80). On July 17, Wilson was still defending popular election of the presidency, suggesting that the legislature could choose among candidates in the case that none received a majority of the votes (2:30). On another occasion, Wilson suggested that a select number of congressmen, chosen by lot, might select the president (2:103,105). Wilson was on record as stating that the method of choosing the president was "the most difficult of all on which we have had to decide" (2:501). He feared that the initial committee proposal for the electoral college was too aristocratic, in giving the Senate the power to choose the president when no majority was reached. His objections helped shift this responsibility to the House (2:522–23).

Judiciary

Consistent with his view of a strong presidency, Wilson favored executive, rather than legislative, appointment of judges (1:119; also see 2:389), but was willing to accept presidential nomination and senatorial confirmation as a second best alternative (2:41). He also favored the establishment of lower federal courts and thought they would be essential in admiralty cases (1:124–25).

Wilson proposed on July 21 that the Constitution should associate members of the judiciary with the executive in a Council of Revision. He accepted the idea that judges would have power to invalidate legislation, the power known today as judicial review, in the course of examining cases, but he did not think this would be adequate:

> There was weight in this observation; but this power of the Judges did not go far enough. Laws may be unjust, may be unwise, may be dangerous, may be destructive; and yet not be so unconstitutional as to justify the Judges in refusing to give them effect. Let them have a share in the Revisionary power, and they will have an opportunity of taking notice of these characters of a law, and of counteracting, by the weight of their opinions the improper views of the Legislature. (2:73).

In defending a Council of Revision, Wilson argued that "the separation of the departments does not require that they should have separate objects but that they should act separately tho' on the same objects" (2:78). He further argued that "the joint weight of the two departments was necessary to balance the single weight of the Legislature" (2:79). Wilson was still making this argument on August 14. Drawing from the practice of parliamentary sovereignty in Britain, Wilson observed that "after the destruction of the King in Great Britain, a more pure and unmixed tyranny sprang up in the parliament than had been exercised by the monarch." He further insisted that the Council of Revision was an appropriate defensive power against legislative tyranny (2:301). He thought that a council would be a more appropriate body to confirm presidential appointees than would the Senate (2:542).

Wilson strongly opposed a provision allowing the president to remove judges on the application of Congress, observing, "The Judges would be in a bad situation if made to depend on every gust of faction which might prevail in the two branches of our Govt." (2:429).

Federalism

Wilson was clearly less attached to state governments than to the national government that he envisioned, but when Delaware's George Read suggested the possible abolition of the states, Wilson said that "He saw no incompatibility between the national & State Govts. provided the latter were restrained to certain local purposes" (1:137). He further argued that past confederacies had demonstrated a greater tendency by the parts to swallow the whole than vice versa (1:137; also see 1:355). Wilson often had to defend his intentions in regards to the states. On June 7, he responded to John Dickinson by observing:

He did not see the danger of the States being devoured by the Nationl. Govt. On the contrary, he wished to keep them from devouring the national Govt. He was not however for extinguishing these planets as was supposed by Mr. D.—neither did he on the other hand, believe that they would warm or enlighten the Sun. (1:153)

As on previous occasions, he favored election of members of Congress from large districts, which, it would appear, would not necessarily have been restricted to existing state lines (1:153–54).

On June 8, Wilson attempted further to explain his view of the relation between the state and national governments, in defending a congressional negative over state laws:

Federal liberty is to States, what civil liberty, is to private individuals. And States are not more unwilling to purchase it, by the necessary concession of their political sovereignty, than the savage is to purchase Civil liberty by the surrender of the personal sovereignty which he enjoys in a State of nature. (1:166)

In this same speech, Wilson harkened back to the First Continental Congress, observing, "Among the first sentiments expressed . . . was that Virga. is no more. That Massts. is no [more], that Pa. is no more &c. We are now one nation of brethren" (1:166).

On June 19, Wilson again found himself having to explain that he did not favor a national government that "would swallow up the State Govt's as seemed to be wished by some gentlemen" (1:322). He argued that every large government needed subdivisions and that the states might not "only subsist but subsist on friendly terms" (1:322). Citing the Declaration of Independence, Wilson argued that when the colonies declared their independence, they declared their independence "not *Individually* but *Unitedly* and that they were confederated as they were independent, States" (1:324).

Wilson favored the Guarantee Clause as a way of securing the States "agst. dangerous commotions, insurrections and rebellions" (2:47). He was responsible for a rewording of the clause that made it more palatable to fellow delegates (2:49).

Wilson evidenced his nationalism in his support for a congressional veto of state laws. Arguing that this was "the key-stone wanted to compleat the wide arch of Government we are raising," he argued that such a veto would give the national government the necessary means of self-defense. Still anticipating judicial invalidation of unconstitutional legislation, Wilson argued,

"It will be better to prevent the passage of an improper law, than to declare it void when passed" (2:391).

Wilson favored a motion whereby states could not be forced to divide unless a majority in the state wanted to do so (2:456; 2:462). He wanted to leave state claims to western lands as they were under the Articles (2:465).

Other Matters

Wilson was one of the few delegates to express reservations about the efficacy of binding members of the government through oaths. He observed that "he was never fond of oaths, considering them as a left handed security only" (2:87). He explained that "A good Govt. did not need them. and a bad one could not or ought not to be supported" (2:87). He also feared that individuals might feel so bound to an existing government that they would prove unwilling to make necessary changes.

Wilson was one of five delegates to serve on the influential Committee of Detail, which the convention commissioned on July 24, and he later also served on the Committee on Interstate Comity and Bankruptcy formed on August 29. In defending the decision of the first committee not to formulate a uniform suffrage requirement, Wilson observed that the committee had found it difficult to come up with such a uniform rule and that it was important to avoid "unnecessary innovations." He explained: "It would be very hard & disagreeable for the same persons, at the same time, to vote for representatives in the State Legislature and to be excluded from a vote for those in the Natl. Legislature" (2:201).

Wilson is believed to have influenced the provision in the Constitution related to treason. His statements on the subject indicated that he could see both the advantages and disadvantages of allowing both the nation and the states to prosecute treason as well as the provision providing that conviction of treason should require the testimony of two or more witnesses to an overt act (2:348).

Ratification

Less than two weeks into convention deliberations, Wilson was proposing that the new Constitution might go into effect when ratified by a plurality of the states, "with a door open for the accession of the rest" (1:123). Responding on August 30 to suggestions that nine or ten states might ratify the Constitution, he suggested that eight states would be an appropriate number to ratify the Constitution (2:469). Consistent with his belief in democracy, Wilson subsequently supported Madison's unsuccessful motion for ratification by a majority of people in a majority of the states (2:477).

Wilson strongly opposed the idea of allowing Congress to decide whether or not to approve the new Constitution. When such a measure was being considered, he opined that "After spending four or five months in this laborious & arduous task of forming a Government for our Country, we are ourselves at the close throwing insuperable obstacles in the way of its success" (2:562). Wilson was the delegate who proposed ratification of constitutional amendments by three-fourths of the states after losing a similar proposal for ratification by two-thirds (2:558–59).

Life after the Convention

On October 6, 1787, Wilson delivered his "State House Yard Speech" in support of the new document; Wilson's arguments, including arguments as to why he did not think a bill of rights was necessary, were widely reprinted and may have been as important to the ratification of the Constitution as *The Federalist* (Hall 2012, p. 29). Wilson was the only Pennsylvania delegate who attended the Constitutional Convention who was also selected to serve in the state ratifying convention, where he provided distinguished service. Wilson subsequently became the chief author of the new Pennsylvania Constitution, which included a number of features of the new Constitution, including the institution of a bicameral legislature.

Wilson served from 1789 to 1798 as an associate justice of the United States Supreme Court, writing one of the decisions for the majority in *Chisholm v. Georgia* (1793), which the Eleventh Amendment overturned. From 1790–1791 he was the first professor of law to teach at the University of Philadelphia, where he delivered lectures on the new government he had helped to create.

Long involved in speculation in western lands, as well as a variety of other entrepreneurial activities, Wilson's land speculations ultimately bankrupted him. He resettled in New Jersey, and then fled to North Carolina (where he was imprisoned for a time) to avoid his creditors, one of whom was Pierce Butler, who had also attended the Constitutional Convention-with Wilson. He died at the home of fellow justice James Iredell at Edenton, North Carolina on August 21, 1798. Originally buried in North Carolina, his remains were moved to Christ Church in Philadelphia in 1906, in a ceremony attended by several members of the U.S. Supreme Court.

Further Reading

Conrad, Stephen A. 1985. "Polite Foundation: Citizenship and Common Sense in James Wilson's Republican Theory." *The Supreme Court Review, 1984*, ed. Philip B. Kurland, Gerhard Casper, and Dennis J. Hutchinson. Chicago; The University of Chicago Press, 359–88.

———. 1988. "Metaphor and Imagination in James Wilson's Theory of Federal Union," *Law & Social Inquiry* 13 (Winter): 1, 3–70.

Cushman, Clare, ed. 1995. *The Supreme Court Justices: Illustrated Biographies, 1789–1995.* Washington, DC: Congressional Quarterly.

Farrand, Max, ed. 1966. *The Records of the Federal Convention of 1787.* 4 vols. New Haven, CT: Yale University Press.

Ferris, Robert G. 1976. *Signers of the Constitution.* Washington, DC: U.S. Department of the Interior, National Park Service.

Finkelman, Paul. 1988. "The Pennsylvania Delegation and the Peculiar Institution: The Two Faces of the Keystone State," *The Pennsylvania Magazine of History and Biography* 112 (January): 49–71.

Hall, Mark D. 1997. *The Political and Legal Philosophy of James Wilson, 1742–1798.* Columbia: University of Missouri Press.

———. 1998. "James Wilson: Democratic Theorist and Supreme Court Justice." In *Seriatim: The Supreme Court before John Marshall*, edited by Scott Douglas Gerber, 126–54. New York: New York University Press.

———. 2012. "James Wilson." In *America's Forgotten Founders*, 2nd ed., edited by Gary L. Gregg II and Mark David Hall, 25–38. Wilmington, DE: Intercollegiate Studies Institute.

McLaughlin, Andrew C. 1897. "James Wilson in the Philadelphia Convention." *Political Science Quarterly* 12 (March): 1–20.

Seed, Geoffrey. 1978. *James Wilson.* Millwood, New York: KTO Press.

Smith, Charles Page. 1956. *James Wilson: Founding Father, 1742–1798.* Chapel Hill: University of North Carolina Press.

Wills, Garry. 1987. "Interview with a Founding Father." *American Heritage* 38 (May/June): 83–88.

Wilson, James. 2009. *Collected Works of James Wilson*, edited by Kermit L. Hall and Mark David Hall. 2 vols. Indianapolis: Liberty Fund.

GEORGE WYTHE (1726–1806)
VIRGINIA

George Wythe was born in Elizabeth City County, Virginia in 1726 to a planter family. His father died when he was three years old, but his gifted mother helped in his education that was furthered by an apprenticeship to

his uncle Stephen Dewey, who was an attorney. Wythe married Ann Lewis (1726–1748) who died within eight months, and then moved to Williamsburg where he was successively served as acting attorney general, mayor, vestryman, and clerk of the House of Burgesses. Wythe gained such a reputation for integrity that he was sometimes likened to Aristides "the Just" of ancient Greece.

Wythe moved to Williamsburg, where he established a residence with a new wife; he also inherited a plantation from an older brother. In Williamsburg, Wythe served as a mentor to many young lawyers including Thomas Jefferson, St. George Tucker (who went on to become a prominent legal scholar), and later, Henry Clay. An early advocate of independence, Wythe was elected to serve in the Continental Congress where he signed the Declaration of Independence. He later helped revise the laws of Virginia. In 1779, he became the first professor of law in America (and only the second in the English-speaking world, after Britain's William Blackstone) with an appointment to the College of William and Mary. His students there included John Marshall, a cousin of James Madison with the same name who became president of the College of William and Mary and the first Episcopalian bishop in America, James Monroe, Spencer Roane, and others.

At the Convention

A man of average height with an aquiline nose, at the time of the convention Wythe was balding. He was present for the opening day of business at the Constitutional Convention on May 25 and chaired the convention's first Committee, the three-man Rules Committee. There is a general consensus that this committee set forth orderly procedures that furthered debate and deliberation at the convention.

On May 30, Wythe proposed that the convention vote on one of the Randolph resolutions to establish a government of three branches, but South Carolina's Pierce Butler said that it was not yet ready to do so (Farrand 1966, 1:41). On the next day, Wythe agreed with fellow Virginian James Madison in observing "that it would be right to establish general principles before we go into detail, or very shortly Gentlemen would find themselves in confusion, and would be obliged to have recurrence to the point from whence they sat out" (1:60).

By June 10, Wythe was called home by the illness of his second wife Elizabeth, who died shortly after his return. Madison recorded that Wythe had left a proxy vote in favor of establishing a single executive on June 4. Wythe subsequently resigned from the convention (Hutson 1987, 121).

Life after the Convention

Wythe played a major role in the Virginia ratifying convention where he served as president of the Committee of the Whole and supported the new Constitution. Wythe continued in his role as a chancellor of Virginia (a role that often led to conflict with Edmund Pendleton), later moving to Richmond. Sadly, George Wythe Sweeney, a nephew whom Wythe had befriended but who had gotten into debt, poisoned Wythe, who died in 1806 after both forgiving and disinheriting his nephew. Wythe, who had freed several slaves, appears to have died embracing Christianity. His last words reportedly were "Let me die righteous!" (Dill 1979, 81).

Wythe's house on Palace Street in Williamsburg, which he inherited from his father-in-law and where Wythe lived from 1755 to 1791, was restored as part of today's colonial Williamsburg and is open to the public. Both a southwestern Virginia county and a city (Wytheville) are named after him. The law school at the College of William and Mary is named after him and one of his most illustrious students, Chief Justice John Marshall. Wythe was buried at St. John's Church in Richmond, the scene of Patrick Henry's famous "Liberty or Death" speech. He willed his law books to Thomas Jefferson who observed, in an allusion to a great Roman statesman, that:

> No man ever left behind him a character more venerated than George Wythe. His virtue was of the purest tint; his integrity inflexible, and his justice exact; of warm patriotism, and, devoted as he was to liberty, and the natural and equal rights of man, he might truly be called the Cato of his country. (quoted in "George Wythe" n.d.)

Further Reading

Blackburn, Joyce. *George Wythe of Williamsburg*. New York: Harper & Row, 1975.
Brown, Imogene E. *American Aristides: A Biography of George Wythe*. Madison, NJ: Fairleigh Dickinson University Press, 1981.

Dill, Alonzo. 1979. *George Wythe: Teacher of Liberty*. Williamsburg: Virginia Independence Bicentennial Commission.

Farrand, Max, ed. 1966. *The Records of the Federal Convention of 1787*. 4 vols. New Haven, CT: Yale University Press.

Hutson, James H., ed. 1987. *Supplement to Max Farrand's The Records of the Federal Convention of 1787*. New Haven, CT: Yale University Press.

"George Wythe." n.d. The Colonial Williamsburg Official History Site. http://www .history.org/almanack/people/bios/biowythe.cfm. Accessed 7/11/2012.

Lynch, Jack. 2010. "George Wythe Teaches America the Law." *Colonial Williamsburg Journal* (Spring). http://www.history.org/Foundation/journal/Spring10/educ .cfm. Accessed 7/18/2012.

Smith, Robert W. 2003. "George Wythe." In *Great American Judges: An Encyclopedia*, edited by John R. Vile, 2:835–40. Santa Barbara, CA: ABC-CLIO.

Vile, John R. 2001. "George Wythe." In *Great American Lawyers: An Encyclopedia*, edited by John R. Vile, 2:732–739. Santa Barbara, CA: ABC-CLIO.

ROBERT YATES (1738–1801)
NEW YORK

Robert Yates was born in Schenectady, New York on January 27, 1738. After being educated in New York City, he read law under William Livingston, a future New Jersey governor who also attended the Constitutional Convention, and moved to Albany. He successively served as a city alderman, as a member of the Committee of Safety, as a member of the Provincial Congress, and as a justice of the New York State Supreme Court. He sat on the court from 1777 until 1798, serving as chief during his last eight years. In the winter of 1774–1775, Yates had begun drafting a plan of colonial union that had been drawn in part from Benjamin Franklin's Albany Plan of Union and from a proposal that William Smith Jr. had drafted in 1765 (see Hoffer and Hull 1977). Yates married Jannetje Van Ness (ca.1739–1818), and they had six children.

At the Convention

Yates was seated on the opening day of the convention on May 25. Like fellow delegate John Lansing, selected by the state legislature along with Yates through the influence of New York's governor George Clinton, Yates was in constant conflict with Alexander Hamilton, also from New York. Thus, on May 30 Yates and Hamilton split their votes, with Hamilton voting to establish a national government consisting of three branches and

Yates opposing the motion (Farrand 1966, 1:35). On May 31, Yates reports in notes that are a helpful supplement to those taken by James Madison of Virginia and some other delegates—but that were apparently compromised by partisan editing (see Hutson 1987, 412)—that he voted to accept a proposal for a bicameral Congress. He recorded, "As a previous resolution had already been agreed to, to have a supreme legislature, I could not see any objection to its being in two branches" (1:55).

In notes that Yates made on June 9, it appears as though he added to a speech made by Paterson, probably reflecting his own sentiments on the subject. The paragraph in question upholds the equality of votes of states in a confederation and says that, without them, "there is an end to liberty" (1:183). Yates further observed that "As long therefore as state distinctions are held up, this rule must invariably apply; and if a consolidated national government must take place, then state distinctions must cease, or the states must be equalized" (1:183).

The delegates appointed Yates on July 2 to the committee that was responsible for formulating the Great Compromise. Delegates subsequently appointed him to a committee on July 9 to reconsider the original allocation of votes in the U.S. House of Representatives. He and fellow delegate John Lansing left the convention the next day. Luther Martin later reported that Yates and Lansing "had uniformly opposed the system, and, I *believe*, despairing of getting a *proper one* brought forward, or of *rendering any real service*, they returned no more" (3:190).

Report to the Governor

Yates and Lansing offered a similar assessment in a report to New York governor George Clinton. In this report, they focused on two issues—what they believed to be the lack of authority on the part of the convention to propose a new system rather than revising and amending the old one, and their opposition to consolidated government. They suggested that the convention could have fixed the system by granting to the existing government "the monies arising from a general system of revenue," power to regulate commerce, power to enforce treaties, and "other necessary matters of less moment" (3:246). In arguments that Antifederalists frequently repeated, they argued that a consolidated government over a large territory would be likely to lead to oppression and expense. Once they recognized that the convention was pursuing such an object, they indicated that they thought that further attendance "would be fruitless and unavailing" (3:247).

Opposition to Ratification

Yates may have authored letters under the name of "Brutus" in the *New York Journal* in opposition to the new Constitution. He went on to lead the Antifederalist opposition to the new Constitution at the ratifying convention in Poughkeepsie. He seriously underestimated the opposition, which was aided by the momentum of ratifications from other states and by eventual Federalist willingness to report the Constitution with a series of proposed amendments.

Life after the Convention

Yates did later support the Constitution. In a notable charge to a grand jury after ratification of the Constitution, Yates observed:

> The proposed form of government for the Union has at length received the sanction of so many of the States as to make it the supreme law of the land, and it is not therefore any longer a question, whether or not its provisions are such as they ought to be in all their different branches. We, as good citizens, are bound implicitly to obey them, for the united wisdom of America has sanctioned and confirmed the act, and it would be little short of treason against the republic to hesitate in our obedience and respect to the Constitution of the United States of America. Let me therefore exhort you , Gentlemen, not only in your capacity as grand jurors, but in your more durable and equally respectable character as citizens, to preserve inviolate this charter of our national rights and safety, a charter second only in dignity and importance to the Declaration of our Independence. We have escaped, it is true, by the blessing of Divine Providence, from the tyranny of a foreign foe, but let us now be equally watchful in guarding against worse and far more dangerous enemies,—domestic broils and intestine divisions. (quoted in Yates 1838, 334)

Yates twice ran unsuccessfully for state governor. He died on September 9, 1801. At the time, he had little money, but he was proud of his refusal to profit from estates that the government had confiscated from Tories during the Revolutionary War.

Further Reading

Bradford, M. E. 1994. *Founding Fathers: Brief Lives of the Framers of the United States Constitution*, 2nd ed. Lawrence: University Press of Kansas.

Farrand, Max, ed. 1966. *The Records of the Federal Convention of 1787*. 4 vols. New Haven, CT: Yale University Press.

Hoffer, Peter C., and N. E. H. Hull. 1977. "'To Determine on the Future Government': Robert Yates's Plan of Union, 1774–1775." *William and Mary Quarterly*, 3rd Ser., 34 (April): 298–306.

Hutson, James H. 1987. "Riddles of the Federal Constitutional Convention." *William and Mary Quarterly*, 3rd Ser., 44 (July): 411–23.

Hutson, James H., ed. 1987. *Supplement to Max Farrand's The Records of the Federal Convention of 1787*. New Haven, CT: Yale University Press.

Rogow, Arnold A. 1955. "The Federal Convention: Madison and Yates." *American Historical Review* 60 (January): 323–35.

Westbury, Susan. 2001. "Robert Yates and John Lansing Jr.: New York Delegates Abandon the Constitutional Convention." *New York History*: 82 (October): 312–35.

Yates, Robert. 1838. *Secret Proceedings and Debates of the Convention Assembled at Philadelphia, in the Year 1787, for the Purpose of Forming the Constitution of the United States of America*. Cincinnati: Alston Mygatt.

Dictionary of Key Terms

Actual representation. The idea that a legislative body cannot represent individuals (at least not males) who do not help elect its members. The colonists believed that the British Parliament could not represent them unless they actually sent delegates to London.

Advice and consent. The U.S. president appoints judges, ambassadors, and members of the cabinet to office contingent upon such "advice and consent," or approval, by the president.

Agenda setting. Political scientists use this term to explain how some items gain greater prominence and attention in proceedings than others. At the Constitutional Convention of 1787, the Virginia Plan, because it was audacious and because it was introduced first, set the agenda for much of the subsequent discussion. It chiefly served to get delegates to thinking about replacing, rather than merely modifying, the existing Articles of Confederation.

Albany Plan of Union. A plan of continental union, largely proposed and devised by Benjamin Franklin but never implemented, prior to the establishment of the Articles of Confederation.

Alien and Sedition Acts. Laws adopted under the Federalist administration of John Adams, which sought to make the naturalization of new citizens more difficult and to penalize those who spoke out or wrote against governmental officials. Relying chiefly on the Tenth Amendment, the Virginia and Kentucky Resolutions were adopted in opposition to these laws, the second of which is today understood to have violated the protections of freedom of speech and press that are contained within the First Amendment.

"All men are created equal." A phrase from the Declaration of Independence, often falsely attributed to the U.S. Constitution. The latter document does, however, provide in the Fourteenth Amendment (1868) for "equal protection of the laws."

Annapolis Convention. A meeting of delegates from five states that met in Maryland in September 1786 to discuss matters involving commerce and navigation, and ended up issuing a call for the Constitutional Convention.

Antifederalists. The name, largely coined by opponents, for the individuals who opposed initial ratification of the U.S. Constitution. Opposition by Antifederalists led in part to the adoption of the first ten amendments to the Constitution, known as the Bill of Rights.

Appointments and confirmations. Under the Constitution, the president appoints ambassadors, judges, and cabinet members subject to the "advice and consent" of the U.S. Senate. Judges serve "during good behavior," but court decisions generally allow the president to fire other non-judicial appointees, with or without senatorial consent.

Aristocracy. A government by a small group of elites, often determined in part by hereditary. Most delegates to the Constitutional Convention preferred an aristocracy of talent and virtue, whose members would be chosen through election rather than by wealth or hereditary succession.

Articles. The central division of the U.S. Constitution, of which there are seven.

Articles of Confederation. The plan of government largely written by John Dickinson, modified and accepted by the Continental Congress, and ratified by the last state in 1781, that was in effect when the Constitutional Convention was meeting. The Articles vested primary sovereignty in the states, required a vote of nine states on most key measures, relied on a single unicameral Congress with limited powers in which each state had an equal vote, and required unanimous state consent to constitutional amendments.

Bicameral congress. A legislative body, like that of the British Parliament and like that established by the U.S. Constitution, with two different houses, or chambers.

Bill of Rights. The first ten amendments to the Constitution, largely based on earlier state declarations of rights, which are designed to list key limits on government. Originally applicable only to the national government, the Supreme Court has decided that the Fourteenth Amendment (adopted in 1868) has made most of these rights applicable to the states as well.

Cabinet. A group of key heads of executive departments of the national government who are responsible for advising the U.S. president.

Checks and balances. The idea, partly embodied in separation of powers, that various branches of government should serve as checks on abuses by the other branches.

Chief justice of the United States. The individual, primus inter pares (first among equals), who presides over the Supreme Court of the United States. The Constitution requires that the chief justice is also responsible for presiding over impeachments of U.S. presidents in the U.S. Senate.

Civil War. The conflict from 1861 to 1865 between northern and southern states that resulted in significant constitutional changes, including the elimination of slavery (Thirteenth Amendment, 1865) and the guarantee of the rights of citizenship to all persons "born or naturalized in the United States" (Fourteenth Amendment, 1868).

Commander in chief. The first duty the Constitution lists for the president (actually an office) is that of serving as commander in chief of the nation's armed forces. This is meant to uphold the principle of civilian control over the military. The Constitution balances this power by granting Congress the power to "declare war."

Commerce Clause. One of the primary powers of Congress, which is listed in Article I, Section 8 of the Constitution, grants it power to regulate commerce among the states, with the states and foreign countries, and with Indian tribes. Courts have interpreted the clause to allow regulation of the channels of commerce, the instrumentalities of commerce, and of intrastate commerce that affects such commerce.

Committee of Detail. A five-man committee that the Constitutional Convention created on July 24 to prepare a document summarizing agreements that had been reached to this point. The committee, chaired by John Rutledge of South Carolina, is best known for adding an enumeration of congressional powers.

Committee of Style and Arrangement. A committee of five, headed by William Samuel Johnson of Connecticut, which reworked existing compromises into the language that is currently found in the U.S. Constitution.

Committee of the Whole. A parliamentary device, borrowed from Congress and utilized during the opening days of the Constitutional Convention, that allowed the group to debate and make proposals without the necessity of a daily quorum. Nathaniel Gorham of Massachusetts presided over this committee.

Common law. The system of case law, developed from judicial decisions in England, and often applied in America, with variations based on what were believed to be unique circumstances in the colonies.

Confederal government. A government, like that under the Articles of Confederation and later by the Confederate States of America, that divides power between a central and various constituent geographically-based entities, the latter of which maintain primary sovereignty.

Congress. The bicameral body created by the Constitution of 1787 that makes the laws. It is divided into a House of Representatives, in which states are represented according to population, and a Senate, in which each state has two senators.

Connecticut Compromise. The critical compromise, also known as the Great Compromise, by which the Constitutional Convention decided that states would be represented (as the Virginia Plan had suggested) by population in the House of Representatives and (as the New Jersey Plan) had suggested, equally in the Senate.

Constitutional amending process. Formal process by which written constitutions can be altered. The constitution of the Articles of Confederation required congressional proposals to be unanimously ratified by the states. Article V of the U.S. Constitution allows two-thirds majorities of both houses of Congress (or a convention called at the request of two-thirds of the states) to propose amendments and three-fourths of the state legislatures, or of special state conventions, to ratify them. The first Congress decided that amendments would be added to the end of the Constitution (making constitutional history easier to trace) rather than integrated within the text. As of 2012, 27 amendments have been ratified.

Constitutional Convention of 1787. The gathering of 55 men from 12 states that met at the State House (Independence Hall) in Philadelphia from May to September, 1787, to draw up a plan of government to replace that under the Articles of Confederation, which it then sent to state conventions for ratification.

Constitutional conventions. Gatherings, whose member are typically either elected or chosen by state legislatures, that meet to formulate written documents by which a state or nation will be governed. The framers of the U.S. Constitution thought it was important that this body be different from Congress and that its results be ratified by the people in special ratifying conventions called in the states. The term "convention" is sometimes also used (especially in Britain) as a term for a long-standing governmental practice or usage.

Continental Congresses. Beginning in 1774, and again in 1775, representatives of the colonies sent men to formulate policies for what they regarded as English abuses of their liberties. The Second Continental Congress was responsible for issuing the Declaration of Independence in 1776 and for formulating the Articles of Confederation in 1777, which were ratified by the last state in 1781.

Council of Revision. A proposal in the original Virginia Plan, not embodied in the U.S. Constitution, that would have enabled the executive and selected members of the judiciary to review and void federal laws.

Covenants. Contractual agreements, often considered to be sacred. Such covenants, which are particularly important in Protestant theology, provided part of the historical context for the charters that the British king issued to American colonists and to later state and national constitutions.

Declaration of Independence. The document, largely authored by Thomas Jefferson, and adopted by the Second Continental Congress on July 4, 1776, which proclaimed the colonists' independence from Great Britain and detailed the grievances that had led to the separation. The Declaration is most familiar for its declaration that "all men are created equal" and that they are entitled to the unalienable rights of "life, liberty, and the pursuit of happiness."

Delegates. The 55 individuals from 12 states who attended the Constitutional Convention of 1787 were generally referred to as delegates.

Democracy. A form of government based on the consent of the people. Many of the delegates to the Constitutional Convention preferred an indirect, or representative, democracy rather than the direct democracy, which they thought was more appropriate to smaller governments. In Federalist No. 10, James Madison argued for the superiority of representative democracy over direct democracy.

Democratic-Republican Party. One of the first two national political parties organized by Thomas Jefferson and James Madison that stressed democratic accountability and the rights retained by the states.

District of Columbia. The area between Virginia and Maryland that is designated as the nation's capital. Southern states were particularly desirous of having a capital near them. The site was fairly centrally situated between North and South. Its selection was in part a result of a compromise in which southern delegates agreed to the federal assumption of state debts in exchange for selection of this site.

Due process of law. A concept, often traced back to "the law of the land" in the Magna Carta of 1215 and later incorporated in both the Fifth and

Fourteenth Amendments, which prohibits the taking of life, liberty, or property "without due process of law." Although due process is typically understood to involved proper procedures, there are some cases in which courts have given the provision a substantive dimension.

During good behavior. A term, embodied in the U.S. Constitution, which refers to the terms of national judges and justices. They serve until they resign, retire, die, or are impeached by the U.S. House of Representatives and removed from office by a two-thirds vote of the U.S. Senate. Such tenure is designed to promote judicial independence so that they can interpret the Constitution without fear of adverse consequences.

Electoral college. The mechanism adopted by the Constitutional Convention for selecting the U.S. president. States are apportioned electoral votes according to their total numbers of members of the U.S. House of Representatives and the U.S. Senate, which is in turn derived from the Great Compromise.

Enumerated powers. Powers, chiefly found in Article I, Section 8 of the U.S. Constitution, that specifically describe what Congress can do.

Executive branch. The branch of government, headed by the president, designed to execute the laws. The president makes major appointments and serves as commander in chief of the armed forces.

Extradition. The process by which a state or nation turns over a fugitive to another state or nation for prosecution.

Factions. This is a name for parties or interest groups. In arguing for the new government in Federalist No. 10, James Madison argued that a republican government covering a large land area would better be able to control the baneful influences of such factions than would governments over smaller land areas, where one or more such groups were more likely to be able to exercise dominance.

Federal government. This originally referred to a government, like that under the Articles of Confederation, in which power was divided between a national and various constituent entities, the latter of which remained sovereign. Since the writing of the U.S. Constitution (and its support by Federalists), the term refers to a government in which power is more evenly divided between the two sets of governments, both of which are grounded on written constitutions and both of which have the authority to act directly on the people.

Federalist Papers. A series of 85 essays, originally published as newspaper articles and later collected as a book, that argued on behalf of adoption of the U.S. Constitution. It was written under the pen name of Publius, was authored by Alexander Hamilton, James Madison, and John Jay, and is often cited in interpretations of the Constitution.

Federalists. The name used by individuals who supported the adoption of the U.S. Constitution in the ratification debates. The term was later used by members of one of the first two political parties, founded by Alexander Hamilton. It put particular emphasis on the broad powers exercised by the national government.

Founding Fathers. A collective term usually used to refer to those Americans who were most influential either in establishing the original 13 colonies or in establishing the nation. The term is sometimes used to refer to those who signed the Declaration of Independence and those who either attended and/or signed the Constitution of the United States. The term was first used by President Warren G. Harding.

Fourteenth Amendment. The amendment, ratified in 1868, which overturned the *Dred Scott Decision* (1857) and vested citizenship in all persons born or naturalized in the United States and guaranteed them basic rights like equal protection, due process, and uniform privileges and immunities.

Framers. A term generally used to designate those who attended the Constitutional Convention and help establish the plan of government established by the Constitution.

Franchise. This is another term for the right to vote. In 1787, only a single state (New Jersey) permitted women to vote, and some limited voting to those who owned property. Delegates to the Constitutional Convention decided to allow each state to keep existing voting qualifications in place rather than creating a single uniform national standard.

Fugitive Slave Clause. A provision embodied in Article IV of the Constitution, whereby states were obligated to return individuals who had fled their service in a slave state to go to a free state (the Constitution never used the term slave, which many considered to be an embarrassment).

Full Faith and Credit Clause. A provision found within Article IV of the Constitution that requires states to honor legal judgments that have been made in other states.

General Welfare Clause. This is one of the enumerated powers of Congress that enables it to tax and spend on behalf of the general welfare. The U.S. Preamble also refers to "the general welfare."

Great Compromise. The compromise, also known as the Connecticut Compromise, by which the Constitutional Convention decided that states would be represented (as the Virginia Plan had suggested) by population in the House of Representatives and (as the New Jersey Plan) had suggested, equally in the Senate.

Guarantee Clause. A provision in Article IV of the Constitution that vests the national government with the responsibility of guaranteeing to each state a republican (representative) form of government.

Habeas corpus. A writ that individuals can file to force the government to release them or provide adequate cause for retaining them. The Constitution permits Congress to suspend this writ in times of emergency.

Hartford Convention. A meeting of delegates from New England states that met during the end of the War of 1812 in which disunion was discussed but constitutional amendments were ultimately proposed.

Hereditary succession. A name for the practice whereby kingship and other titles are passed from parent to child. The delegates to the Constitutional Convention of 1787 did not create any hereditary offices and prohibited individuals from accepting foreign titles of nobility without congressional permission.

House of Representatives. The lower house of Congress whose members are apportioned to states according to population and serve for two-year renewable terms. The House of Representatives retains the power to originate all money bills. The law currently caps the size of the House at 435 voting members.

Impeachment. The formal process by which members of the U.S. House of Representatives can bring formal charges against the president, judges, and cabinet officials for treason, bribery, or other "high crimes and misdemeanors." A successful impeachment vote results in a trial by the U.S. Senate, which takes a two-thirds vote to convict.

Implied powers. Those powers which, while not specifically enumerated in the Constitution, can be derived from those powers listed there. The chief decision that had recognized the existence of implied powers is that in *McCulloch v. Maryland* (1819), which upheld the constitutionality of the U.S. Bank as a means of fulfilling taxing and spending powers.

Independence Hall. The building, also known as the Pennsylvania State House, where the Declaration of Independence, the Articles of Confederation, and the U.S. Constitution were formulated and signed.

Judicial branch. The name of the branch of Government, headed by the U.S. Supreme Court, which is designed to interpret the laws. Judges and justices are appointed by the U.S. present subject to the "advice and consent of the senate" and serve "during good behavior."

Judicial review. The power not stated but arguably implicit in the Constitution, by which courts can declare that laws that violate the written Constitution are invalid. *Marbury v. Madison* (1803) is the first major U.S. Supreme Court decision that articulated the justification for this doctrine.

July 4, 1776. The day on which Congress adopted the Declaration of Independence as an explanation of its decision two days earlier to declare independence from Great Britain. July 4 is now celebrated as national Independence Day.

Juries. Many of the Founding Fathers considered juries to be essential to republican government. The Bill of Rights provides both for grand juries, which decide whether to indict, or charge, individuals with crime, and for petit juries, which decide on issues of guilt or innocence, and sometimes assign appropriate penalties.

Jurisdiction. This term refers to the cases that courts can legitimately consider. Under the Constitution, the court hears some cases as a result of their subject matter (those, for example, that deal with the U.S. Constitution or federal laws or treaties) and others based on the party to the suit. The U.S. Supreme Court has a limited number of cases that it hears for the first time (cases of original jurisdiction) and a much larger number of cases that it hears on appeal (cases of appellate jurisdiction).

Liberalism. The name given to a political philosophy, often traced to the English philosopher, John Locke, that stressed the primary role of government in protecting the rights of life, liberty and property.

"Life, liberty, and the pursuit of happiness." Three rights that the Declaration of Independence identifies as natural rights to which it claims that all men are entitled. Sometimes falsely attributed to the Constitution, the latter document does provide protection in the Fifth and Fourteenth Amendments against deprivation of "life, liberty, or property" without "due process of law."

Magna Carta. A document that King John of England signed with his nobles in 1215 (and which was subsequently reaffirmed a number of times by subsequent kings) which, like modern constitutions, provided the basis for parliamentary representation and for basic rights.

Legislative branch. The branch of government, embodied in Congress, that is responsible for adopting laws and exercising taxing and spending powers known as "the power of the purse."

Mayflower Compact. An early example of a governmental covenant in which individuals who arrived in New England on a ship called the Mayflower agreed before leaving the ship to rules by which they would govern themselves.

Militia. State citizens who band together in a military force to protect it. Such a force is often distinguished from more professional standing armies.

Mixed government. The form of government, often attributed to Rome and to Great Britain, in which the government is designed so that different classes are reflected in governmental institutions that help check and balance one another.

Mt. Vernon Conference. A meeting held at George Washington's house in May 1786 between delegates from Maryland and Virginia to discuss issues involving navigation on mutual waterways. This meeting led to the call for the Annapolis Convention to discuss such issues in a larger state context.

Natural rights. Rights, specifically to "life, liberty, and the pursuit of happiness," that the Declaration of Independence asserted were "unalienable rights" beyond governmental power because they were endowed by God.

Necessary and Proper Clause. The clause, sometimes nicknamed "the Elastic Clause," at the end of Article I, Section 8, that has been used as the primary basis for establishing that the Constitution authorizes certain implied powers (like that of creating a bank or conducting congressional investigations) that are not specifically enumerated within the constitution.

Negative of state laws. A proposal within the Virginia Plan that would have vested Congress with the power to nullify state laws. Although the proposal was not adopted, it may partly be reflected in the power of the judiciary to void state laws that it considers to be unconstitutional.

New Jersey Plan. An alternative to the Virginia Plan, introduced by William Paterson of New Jersey (after whom it is sometimes named), intended to retain the existing unicameral Congress with increased powers in which states would retain their equal votes under the Articles of Confederation rather than the bicameral Congress that had been proposed in the Virginia Plan.

Northwest Ordinance of 1787. One of the most significant pieces of legislation adopted by the Congress under the Articles of Confederation permitting the admission of new states in the territory and banning slavery in these states.

"No taxation without representation." A principle that the colonists borrowed from the Magna Carta of 1215, which denied the authority of a legislative body to enact taxes on citizens who were not represented in that body.

Parliament. The English parliament is a bicameral body consisting of an elected House of Commons and an hereditary House of Lords. It traces its foundations back to the Magna Carta of 1215. Its claims to exercise sovereignty over the colonies was met with colonial claims of "no taxation without representation."

Parliamentary sovereignty. The view, held by the British but contested by American colonists, that Parliament was supreme and could do anything that was not naturally impossible.

Political parties. These organizations whose members join around common interests and principles to gain and keep public offices are not specifically mentioned in the U.S. Constitution (indeed, many of the delegates thought that parties had a baneful influence) but are protected by the right of peaceable assembly in the First Amendment and were accommodated by a change to the electoral college implemented by the Twelfth Amendment.

Power to declare war. The Constitution vests this power in Congress while simultaneously designating the president as commander in chief of the nation's armed forces.

Preamble. The name given to the opening paragraph of the U.S. Constitution, which delineates the purposes for which it was established.

Presentment Clause. The constitutional provision that provides for all congressional laws to be presented to the president for his approval or veto. The veto is not absolute; two-thirds majorities of both houses of Congress have the power to override a presidential veto.

President. The head of the executive branch of government. The president serves a four-year term (that can be renewed once) and is commander in chief of the armed forces.

President of the Senate. The vice president of the United States serves in this capacity, which gives him power to preside over this body.

Privileges and Immunities Clause. A clause embodied in Article IV of the Constitution, and later in the Fourteenth Amendment, designed to ensure that states treated out-of-state citizens on the same basis that they treated their own.

Privy Council. A group of advisors, similar to an institution in Great Britain, that Virginia's George Mason wanted to advise the president, but which was rejected at the Constitutional Convention.

Ratifying conventions. Meetings, called within each of the 13 original states, by which the new document was ratified. The Founders believed that such meetings embodied popular sovereignty and that they provided firmer popular foundations for the new document than could mere state legislative ratification.

Republican government. A government, like that created in the U.S. Constitution, in which representatives are accountable to the people through a system of elections.

Republicanism. A system of beliefs that stressed representative government directly accountable to the people and that was typically suspicious of centralized power.

Reserved powers. Because the U.S. Constitution divides powers between the national government and the states, the latter retain powers that have not been delegated. These are referenced in the Ninth and Tenth Amendments to the Constitution.

Revolutionary War. The successful revolt (1776–1781) by the 13 North American colonies against Great Britain and the authority of its Parliament to tax them.

Rules Committee. A committee of three men formed at the beginning of the Constitutional Convention and headed by Virginia's George Wythe that developed rules to facilitate discussion and debate at the convention. The most controversial, albeit arguably wise, decision called for the proceedings to be kept secret.

Senate. The name of the upper house of Congress in which each state is equally represented. Its members serve for six-year renewable terms and are responsible for approving presidential appointments and treaties. Originally appointed by state legislatures, senators have since the adoption of the Seventeenth Amendment (1913) been elected, like members of the U.S. House of Representatives, directly by the people.

Separation of powers. A division of government into different branches. The U.S. Constitution embodied this principle by creating separate legislative, executive, and judicial branches designed respectively to make, to execute, and to interpret the laws.

September 17, 1787. The day on which 39 (one by proxy) of 42 delegates who remained at the Constitutional Convention at Independence Hall in Philadelphia, signed the document. Today, September 17 of each year marks the start of Constitution Week.

Shays's Rebellion. A taxpayer revolt that occurred in Massachusetts during the winter of 1786–1787 and that persuaded some states that they needed to send delegates to a convention to formulate a new constitution that could protect states against such further insurrections.

Single executive. Early in the convention, the delegates (undoubtedly with a view toward George Washington) decided on a single executive. The New Jersey Plan, offered later and rejected, called for a plural executive. In modern times the term unitary executive has been used by those who stress the prerogatives of a single executive.

Slave importation. However divided opinion was on the issue of slavery, there was more general agreement on the evils of the slave trade. Most northern delegates wanted to ban it, but delegates from South Carolina and Georgia were able to get support for a provision that would forbid Congress from forbidding the trade until 1808.

Society of the Cincinnati. A group of veterans of the Revolutionary War that was controversial (and sometimes feared) because it originally provided that membership would be hereditary.

Sovereignty. Supreme authority or power. The British believed that the supreme power in government was vested in a sovereign. The Constitution professes to derive such power from "We the People." The people can exercise such sovereignty either through revolution or through the procedures specified in Article V of the Constitution for amending the document.

Stamp Act Congress. A meeting of the states held in 1765 to discuss common responses to the Stamp Act and other British taxes. This became the prototype for the later Continental Congresses.

Standing army. A professional military force, which many framers feared could undermine civil rights and liberties.

State constitutions. While most Americans probably think more readily of the U.S. Constitution, it was actually preceded by the adoption of state constitutions, which in turn were often preceded by colonial charters. Experiences under state constitutions provided examples for delegates to the Constitutional Convention. State constitutions were often preceded by declarations of rights, which also provided a model for the U.S. Bill of Rights (the first ten amendments) that provide protection for civil rights and liberties.

Supremacy Clause. A provision found in Article VI of the U.S. Constitution that provides that federal law is superior to state law in cases of conflict.

Supreme Court of the United States. The court, created by the Constitution, which heads the federal judicial system. It currently consists of nine individuals (even though it is not specified within the Constitution, the number has been steady for more than 100 years) who are appointed by the president with the advice and consent of the Senate.

Three-fifths Clause. A compromise adopted at the Constitutional Convention whereby slaves (not mentioned as such) were counted as three-fifths of a person toward the allocation of state representation within the U.S. House of Representatives.

Treaties. Formal agreements among nations are often designated as treaties. As commander in chief, the U.S. president and the president's designees typically oversee the negotiation of treaties, which then require the approval of a two-thirds majority of the Senate before they go into effect.

Treaty of Paris. The agreement between Great Britain and the United States that officially ended the Revolutionary War. The difficulty of enforcing this treaty was one of the factors that created pressure for a stronger national government.

Unicameral congress. A legislative body, like that under the Articles of Confederation, with a single house, or chamber.

Unitary government. A government, like that of Great Britain, in which the central authority acts directly on individuals and there are no permanent states with their own constitutions that can claim individual sovereignty.

Unwritten constitution. One like that of Great Britain, which is not based on a single document like the U.S. Constitution, but is garnered from practices and understandings that have been established largely through historical practice.

Veto. The U.S. president has the right to nullify acts with which he does not approve. The veto is not, however, absolute as it may be overridden by two-thirds majorities of both houses of Congress.

Vice president. An office, largely created by the electoral college mechanism, whose occupant presides over the U.S. Senate and who succeeds the president in case of death, impeachment and removal, or disability.

Virginia Plan. The plan introduced by Edmund Randolph, but probably most influenced by James Madison, that called for creating a new national government with a bicameral Congress and three branches of government rather than with the unicameral Congress under the existing Articles of Confederation.

Virginia and Kentucky Resolutions. Resolutions secretly authored by James Madison and Thomas Jefferson and adopted in 1798 by the Virginia and Kentucky state legislatures in opposition to the Alien and Sedition Acts. The resolutions introduced the idea that states had the right to "interpose" themselves against the adoption of what they considered to be unconstitutional state legislation.

Virtual representation. The British Parliament asserted that it had the right to tax the colonists because, as Englishmen, they were virtually represented even though they did not elect delegates to this body.

War of 1812. A conflict between the United States and Great Britain that began in 1812 and ended in 1815 and was largely sparked by U.S. grievances over British trade policies and the impressment of American seamen. The climactic American victory at the Battle of New Orleans actually came after a treaty of peace had been signed in Europe.

"We, the people." The opening words of the Preamble of the U.S. Constitution, attributed to Gouverneur Morris of Pennsylvania. Antifederalists argued that the words, designed to emphasize the grounding of the Constitution in popular consent, were presumptuous and would have preferred to understand the new government as a compact among states.

Written constitution. A constitution, like that of the United States, which attempts in a primary document to delineate the primary structures, powers, and limits of the government. Provisions within such a written constitution are not subject to change by ordinary legislative means but require use of a more stringent constitutional amending process.

Questions about the Delegates

Which delegate had served as a chaplain for Connecticut troops during the Revolutionary War? Abraham Baldwin (Georgia).

Which delegate was largely responsible for founding the University of Georgia? Abraham Baldwin (Georgia).

Which delegate was a close friend of Francis Asbury and served for a time as a Methodist lay minister? Richard Bassett (Delaware).

Which delegate lost his job as a federal appellate judge as a result of legislation adopted by Democratic-Republicans after the election of Thomas Jefferson? Richard Bassett (Delaware).

Which delegate had roomed with James Madison when both were students at the College of New Jersey (today's Princeton University)? Gunning Bedford (New Jersey).

Which delegate, addressing representatives of the larger states at the convention, said, "I do not, gentlemen, trust you"? Gunning Bedford (Delaware).

Which delegate's father was the one-time owner of Raleigh Tavern in Williamsburg, Virginia? John Blair, Jr. (Virginia).

Which delegate accompanied George Washington from the Constitutional Convention to Virginia? John Blair, Jr. (Virginia).

Which delegate is buried outside the Bruton Parish Church in Williamsburg? John Blair, Jr. (Virginia).

385

Which delegate later served as president of the convention that wrote the Tennessee constitution? William Blount (North Carolina).

Which delegate was the first and only U.S. senator ever to be impeached? William Blount (North Carolina).

Which delegate suggested that the delegates should solve the issue of state representation by laying out a map of the United States and partitioning it into thirteen equal parts? David Brearly (New Jersey).

Who is the only delegate who signed the Constitution for whom a portrait has not been located? Jacob Broom (Delaware).

Which delegate helped establish the Chesapeake & Delaware Canal and left money to a group formed to educate African American children? Jacob Broom (Delaware).

Which delegates were born abroad? Pierce Butler, who was born in Ireland (South Carolina), William Richardson Davie, who was born in England (North Carolina), Thomas Fitzsimons, who was born in Ireland (Pennsylvania), Alexander Hamilton, who was born in the British West Indies (New York), William McHenry, who was born in Ireland (Maryland), Robert Morris, who was born in England (Pennsylvania), William Paterson, who was born in Ireland (New Jersey), and James Wilson, who was born in Scotland (Pennsylvania).

Who was the only delegate from South Carolina who did not have an education in the law? Pierce Butler (South Carolina).

Which South Carolina delegate later moved to Philadelphia and served as director of the Second Bank of the United States? Pierce Butler (South Carolina).

Which two delegates to the convention were Roman Catholics? Daniel Carroll (Maryland) and Thomas Fitzsimons (Pennsylvania).

Which delegate wrote essays in support of the new Constitution under the name, "A Friend of the Constitution"? Daniel Carroll (Maryland).

Which delegates had signed the Articles of Confederation? Daniel Carroll (Maryland), John Dickinson (Delaware), Elbridge Gerry (Massachusetts), Gouverneur Morris (Pennsylvania), Robert Morris (Pennsylvania), and Roger Sherman (Connecticut).

Which delegates to the Constitutional Convention had previously signed the Declaration of Independence? George Clymer (Pennsylvania), Benjamin Franklin (Pennsylvania), Elbridge Gerry (Massachusetts), Robert Morris (Pennsylvania), George Read (Delaware), Roger Sherman (Connecticut), James Wilson (Pennsylvania), and George Wythe (Virginia).

Which delegate served as a tax collector in the period leading up to the Whiskey Rebellion? George Clymer (Pennsylvania).

Which delegate served as a model soldier to future President Andrew Jackson? William Richardson Davie (North Carolina).

Which delegate helped to found the University of North Carolina? William Richardson Davie (North Carolina).

Who was the youngest delegate to the Constitutional Convention? Jonathan Dayton, who was twenty-six at the time (New Jersey).

Which delegates were present at the battle of Yorktown that ended the Revolutionary War? Jonathan Dayton (New Jersey), Nicholas Gilman (New Hampshire), Alexander Hamilton (New York), James McHenry (Maryland), John Mercer (Maryland), and George Washington (Virginia).

What city in Ohio is named after a convention delegate? Dayton.

Which delegate to the convention had been dubbed the "Penman of the Revolution"? John Dickinson (Delaware).

Which two delegates had absented themselves when the Second Continental Congress had voted for independence? John Dickinson (Delaware) and Robert Morris (Pennsylvania).

Which delegate chaired the Annapolis Convention that had issued the call for the Constitutional Convention? John Dickinson (Delaware).

Which delegate privately upbraided Madison for "pushing things too far" when it came to representation in Congress based on population? John Dickinson (Delaware).

Which delegate likened the national system to the solar system, where states were planets that should be allowed to move freely? John Dickinson (Delaware).

Which delegates later served on the U.S. Supreme Court? John Blair (Virginia), Oliver Ellsworth (Connecticut), William Paterson (New Jersey), John Rutledge (South Carolina), and James Wilson (Pennsylvania).

Which delegate proposed a formulation of the new government, later repeated by James Madison in The Federalist Papers, *as "partly national; partly federal?"* Oliver Ellsworth (Connecticut).

Who wrote essays under "A Landholder" defending the new Constitution? Oliver Ellsworth (Connecticut).

Which delegate's body was later moved from New York to Georgia? William Few (Georgia).

Which delegate had been verbally pilloried before the English Parliament? Benjamin Franklin (Pennsylvania).

Which delegate wrote the most famous autobiography? Benjamin Franklin (Pennsylvania).

Which delegate proposed that the convention should begin each day with prayer? Benjamin Franklin (Pennsylvania).

Which delegate proposed that the president should serve without pay? Benjamin Franklin (Pennsylvania).

Which delegate professed to see a rising sun on the back of the president's chair? Benjamin Franklin (Pennsylvania).

Which delegate was the oldest to attend the convention? Benjamin Franklin (Pennsylvania). He was eighty-one at the time.

Which three delegates who remained at the Constitutional Convention on September 17 refused to add their signatures? Elbridge Gerry (Massachusetts), George Mason (Virginia), and Edmund Randolph (Virginia).

Which delegate to the convention is most associated with the practice of drawing up political districts so that they favor one or another political party? Elbridge Gerry (Massachusetts).

Which two delegates to the convention were later associated with a mission to France that resulted in the XYZ affair? Elbridge Gerry and Charles Cotesworth Pinckney.

Which delegate later served briefly as vice president under James Madison? Elbridge Gerry.

Which two delegates to the Constitution Convention subsequently were selected as U.S. presidents? James Madison and George Washington.

Which delegates to the convention remained lifelong bachelors? Nicholas Gilman (New Hampshire), Daniel of St. Thomas Jenifer (Maryland), and Alexander Martin (North Carolina).

Which New Hampshire delegate paid both for his own expenses and those of his fellow delegate? John Langdon.

Which two delegates from New Hampshire did not arrive until July 23? Nicholas Gilman and John Langdon.

Which delegate chaired the Committee of the Whole in the opening weeks of the convention? Nathaniel Gorham (Massachusetts).

Which delegate became the first secretary of the treasury under George Washington? Alexander Hamilton (New York).

Which delegate helped mediate a disagreement between William Pierce and a business partner so as to avoid a duel? Alexander Hamilton (New York).

Which delegates were killed in duels? Alexander Hamilton (New York) and Richard Dobbs Spaight (North Carolina).

Which delegate gave the longest speech at the Constitutional Convention? Alexander Hamilton (New York).

Which delegate is most associated with the founding of the Federalist Party? Alexander Hamilton (New York).

Which two delegates were responsible for writing most of The Federalist Papers, *defending ratification of the new Constitution?* Alexander Hamilton (New York) and James Madison (Virginia).

Which delegate was present on the opening day of business on May 25 but appears to have left by June 6? William Churchill Houston (New Jersey).

Which delegate authored an address entitled "Whether the Liberty of the Press Ought to Extend so Far as to Justify the Publishing of the Name of a Person, with Strictures on His Conduct, by an Anonymous Author, or with a Fictitious Signature"? William Churchill Houston (New Jersey).

Which delegate turned down an opportunity to contribute to The Federalist Papers? Gouverneur Morris (Pennsylvania).

Which delegate's house has twice been moved since his death? Alexander Hamilton (New York).

Which two delegates who arrived at the convention on time left the earliest? William Churchill Houston (New Jersey), who was gone by June 6, and George Wythe (Virginia), who left by June 10. Both, however, supported ratification of the document.

Which delegate from Georgia had a famous street in Manhattan named after him? William Houstoun.

Which delegate unsuccessfully ran for vice president in 1812 on a ticket with New York governor DeWitt Clinton? Jared Ingersoll (Pennsylvania).

Which delegate turned down an opportunity to run for vice president in 1812? John Langdon (New Hampshire).

Which delegate to the convention died at the eldest age? William Samuel Johnson (Connecticut), who was ninety-two when he died.

Which delegate to the convention was the last to die? James Madison, Jr. (Virginia) in 1836.

Which delegate's wife was the last to die? Elizabeth Schuler Hamilton, the wife of Alexander Hamilton of New York, lived to be ninety-seven and died on November 9, 1854.

Which delegate headed the committee to put the final touches on the Constitution? William Samuel Johnson (Connecticut).

Which delegate to the convention, like his father, was president of King's College (now Columbia University)? William Samuel Johnson (Connecticut).

Which delegate to the convention was twice defeated for vice president and once for president, all on Federalist tickets? Rufus King (Massachusetts).

Which delegate had the honor in his capacity as Senate pro tempore to count the votes that elected George Washington president? John Langdon (New Hampshire).

Which delegate to the convention is probably best known for his mysterious disappearance? John Lansing (New York).

Which delegate willed his French books to James Madison? Daniel of St. Thomas Jenifer (Maryland).

Which delegate spent a year as a child with a Moravian missionary family living with the Mohawk Indians? William Livingston (New Jersey).

Which delegate befriended Alexander Hamilton when he arrived in the colonies from the West Indies? William Livingston (New Jersey).

Which delegate's expanded house is now part of a museum operated by Kean University? William Livingston (New Jersey).

Which delegate took the most extensive notes at the Constitutional Convention? James Madison (Virginia).

Which delegate's house is known as Montpelier? James Madison (Virginia).

Which delegate was influential in disestablishing the Episcopal Church in Virginia? James Madison (Virginia).

Which delegate secretly authored the Virginia Resolution? James Madison (Virginia).

Which delegates published criticisms of the convention suggesting that it had acted in a conspiratorial fashion? Luther Martin (Maryland) and Robert Yates (New York).

Which delegate was the primary author of the Virginia Declaration of Rights? George Mason (Virginia).

Which delegate went from saying he would rather be buried in Philadelphia that return without a new Constitution, to saying that he would sooner have an arm cut off than sign the document? George Mason (Virginia).

Which delegate's opposition to the Constitution resulted in a rift with his neighbor George Washington? George Mason (Virginia).

Which delegate had a famous American fort named after him? James McHenry (Maryland).

Which delegate to the convention had studied law under Thomas Jefferson? John Mercer (Maryland).

Which delegate appears to have died an alcoholic? Thomas Mifflin (Pennsylvania).

Which delegate had been part of the "Conway Cabal" that had sought to replace George Washington as commander of the patriot forces during the American Revolution? Thomas Mifflin (Pennsylvania).

Which delegate to the convention had both a withered arm and an artificial leg? Gouverneur Morris (Pennsylvania).

Which delegate to the convention was recorded as giving the greatest number of speeches? Gouverneur Morris (Pennsylvania).

Which delegate claimed that he accepted the Constitution, like a wife, already knowing of its bad qualities? Gouverneur Morris (Pennsylvania).

Which delegate did not marry until 1809? Gouverneur Morris (Pennsylvania).

Which delegate was known as the "financier of the American Revolution? Robert Morris (Pennsylvania).

Which delegate hosted George Washington during the Constitutional Convention? Robert Morris (Pennsylvania).

Which delegate was born on Christmas Eve? William Paterson (New Jersey).

Which delegate introduced the New Jersey Plan at the Constitutional Convention? William Paterson (New Jersey).

Which delegates freed their slaves? William Livingston (New Jersey), George Washington (Virginia), who did so in his will, and John Rutledge (South Carolina), who freed all but one of his.

Which delegate studied art under Charles Willson Peale? William Pierce (Georgia).

Which delegate is best known for his character sketches of fellow delegates? William Pierce (Georgia).

Which delegate studied under William Blackstone in England? Charles Cotesworth Pinckney (South Carolina).

Which delegate later mounted a campaign against dueling? Charles Cotesworth Pinckney (South Carolina).

Which delegate's epitaph proclaims, "He maintained the principles of the Constitution"? Charles Cotesworth Pinckney (South Carolina).

Which delegate allowed the story to circulate that he was the youngest member of the convention? Charles Pinckney (South Carolina).

Which delegate appears never to have earned the trust of James Madison? Charles Pinckney (South Carolina).

Which delegate to the convention introduced the Virginia Plan? Edmund Randolph (Virginia).

Which delegate, who refused to sign the Constitution at the convention, supported it at his state's ratifying convention? Edmund Randolph (Virginia).

Which delegate was sometimes called "Dionysius, Tyrant of Delaware?" George Read (Delaware).

Which delegate signed the Constitution not only on his own behalf but also on behalf of fellow delegate John Dickinson? George Read (Delaware).

Which delegate signed the Constitution on his birthday? John Rutledge (South Carolina).

Which southern delegate spent his first three weeks in Philadelphia at the home of James Wilson? John Rutledge (South Carolina).

Which delegate, who claimed that slavery had nothing to do with "religion and humanity" but was solely a matter of "interest," was influential in extending the right of states to import slaves for another twenty years? John Rutledge (South Carolina).

Which delegate appears to have had bouts of insanity after being rejected as chief justice of the U.S. Supreme Court? John Rutledge (South Carolina).

Who was the second-oldest member of the Constitutional Convention? Roger Sherman (Connecticut).

Which two delegates had both published almanacs? Benjamin Franklin (Pennsylvania) and Roger Sherman (Connecticut).

Which delegate to the convention is largely responsible for the fact that constitutional amendments are added to the end of the Constitution rather than integrated within the text? Roger Sherman (Connecticut).

Which delegate was attending the University of Glasgow when the Revolutionary War started? Richard Dobbs Spaight (North Carolina).

Which delegate was born in a town where Jonathan Edwards was serving as the pastor? Caleb Strong (Massachusetts).

Which delegate later served as a Massachusetts governor who resisted sending state militia to fight during the War of 1812 and supported the work of the Hartford Convention? Caleb Strong (Massachusetts).

Which delegate served both as president of the convention and as the first president of the new nation? George Washington (Virginia).

Which delegate later appointed Thomas Jefferson as his secretary of state? George Washington (Virginia).

Which delegate was described as "first in war, first in peace, and first in the hearts of his countrymen"? George Washington (Virginia).

Which delegate annotated a copy of the U.S. Constitution that set a sales record for an American book or historical document? George Washington (Virginia).

Which two delegates may have done more to assure ratification of the Constitution by their presence at the Constitutional Convention rather than by what they publicly said there? Benjamin Franklin (Pennsylvania) and George Washington (Virginia).

Which delegate was ordained to preach, had a medical degree, and was deeply interested in astronomy? Hugh Williamson (North Carolina).

Which delegate was a witness to the Boston Tea Party? Hugh Williamson (North Carolina).

Which North Carolina delegate retired to New York? Hugh Williamson.

Which delegate attributed the convention's decision not to hire a chaplain to begin each day's proceedings with prayer on the fact that it had no funds? Hugh Williamson (North Carolina).

Which delegates had been state governors, chancellors, or presidents? John Dickinson (Delaware), Benjamin Franklin (Pennsylvania), John Langdon (New Hampshire), William Livingston (New Jersey), Alexander Martin (North Carolina), Edmund Randolph (Virginia), and John Rutledge (South Carolina).

Which delegate to the convention probably had the greatest single influence on crafting the presidency? James Wilson (Pennsylvania). One might alternatively argue that the thought that George Washington would serve first in this office also would have been quite influential.

Which delegate engaged in land speculation and died bankrupt in North Carolina at the home of Supreme Court justice James Iredell? James Wilson (Pennsylvania).

Which delegate served as the first professor of law in America? George Wythe (Virginia).

Which delegate helped to educate Thomas Jefferson, John Marshall, and James Monroe? George Wythe (Virginia).

Which delegate chaired the Rules Committee at the Constitutional Convention? George Wythe (Virginia).

Which delegate to the convention died after being poisoned by a nephew? George Wythe (Virginia).

Which delegate willed his law books to Thomas Jefferson? George Wythe (Virginia).

Which delegate had once sought to draft a plan of colonial union that borrowed in part from the Albany Plan of Union and from a proposal drafted by William Smith, Jr.? Robert Yates (New York).

Which two New York delegates left the convention early and did not return? John Lansing and Robert Yates.

Which delegate authored Secret Proceedings and Debates of the Convention*?* Robert Yates (New York).

Which state sent the largest number of delegates to the Constitutional Convention? Pennsylvania, which sent seven.

Which state delegation arrived latest to the convention? New Hampshire, whose two delegates did not arrive until late in July, after other delegates had already agreed to the Great Compromise.

Which of the original thirteen states was not represented by any delegates at the Constitutional Convention? Rhode Island.

Which delegates to the Constitutional Convention were medical doctors? James McClurg (Virginia), James McHenry (Maryland), and Hugh Williamson (North Carolina).

Which college produced the highest number of graduates who attended the Constitutional Convention? The College of New Jersey (today's Princeton University).

Appendix

The Constitution for the United States

We the People of the United States, in Order to form a more perfect Union, establish Justice, insure domestic Tranquility, provide for the common defence, promote the general Welfare, and secure the Blessings of Liberty to ourselves and our Posterity, do ordain and establish this Constitution for the United States of America.

Article. I.
Section. 1.
All legislative Powers herein granted shall be vested in a Congress of the United States, which shall consist of a Senate and House of Representatives.
Section. 2.
The House of Representatives shall be composed of Members chosen every second Year by the People of the several States, and the Electors in each State shall have the Qualifications requisite for Electors of the most numerous Branch of the State Legislature.

No Person shall be a Representative who shall not have attained to the Age of twenty five Years, and been seven Years a Citizen of the United States, and who shall not, when elected, be an Inhabitant of that State in which he shall be chosen.

Representatives and direct Taxes shall be apportioned among the several States which may be included within this Union, according to their respective Numbers, which shall be determined by adding to the whole Number of free Persons, including those bound to Service for a Term of Years, and excluding Indians not taxed, three fifths of all other Persons. The actual

Enumeration shall be made within three Years after the first Meeting of the Congress of the United States, and within every subsequent Term of ten Years, in such Manner as they shall by Law direct. The Number of Representatives shall not exceed one for every thirty Thousand, but each State shall have at Least one Representative; and until such enumeration shall be made, the State of New Hampshire shall be entitled to chuse three, Massachusetts eight, Rhode-Island and Providence Plantations one, Connecticut five, New-York six, New Jersey four, Pennsylvania eight, Delaware one, Maryland six, Virginia ten, North Carolina five, South Carolina five, and Georgia three.

When vacancies happen in the Representation from any State, the Executive Authority thereof shall issue Writs of Election to fill such Vacancies.

The House of Representatives shall chuse their Speaker and other Officers; and shall have the sole Power of Impeachment.

Section. 3.

The Senate of the United States shall be composed of two Senators from each State, chosen by the Legislature thereof for six Years; and each Senator shall have one Vote.

Immediately after they shall be assembled in Consequence of the first Election, they shall be divided as equally as may be into three Classes. The Seats of the Senators of the first Class shall be vacated at the Expiration of the second Year, of the second Class at the Expiration of the fourth Year, and of the third Class at the Expiration of the sixth Year, so that one third may be chosen every second Year; and if Vacancies happen by Resignation, or otherwise, during the Recess of the Legislature of any State, the Executive thereof may make temporary Appointments until the next Meeting of the Legislature, which shall then fill such Vacancies.

No Person shall be a Senator who shall not have attained to the Age of thirty Years, and been nine Years a Citizen of the United States, and who shall not, when elected, be an Inhabitant of that State for which he shall be chosen.

The Vice President of the United States shall be President of the Senate, but shall have no Vote, unless they be equally divided.

The Senate shall chuse their other Officers, and also a President pro tempore, in the Absence of the Vice President, or when he shall exercise the Office of President of the United States.

The Senate shall have the sole Power to try all Impeachments. When sitting for that Purpose, they shall be on Oath or Affirmation. When the President of the United States is tried, the Chief Justice shall preside: And no Person shall be convicted without the Concurrence of two thirds of the Members present.

Judgment in Cases of Impeachment shall not extend further than to removal from Office, and disqualification to hold and enjoy any Office of honor, Trust or Profit under the United States: but the Party convicted shall nevertheless be liable and subject to Indictment, Trial, Judgment and Punishment, according to Law.

Section. 4.

The Times, Places and Manner of holding Elections for Senators and Representatives, shall be prescribed in each State by the Legislature thereof; but the Congress may at any time by Law make or alter such Regulations, except as to the Places of chusing Senators.

The Congress shall assemble at least once in every Year, and such Meeting shall be on the first Monday in December, unless they shall by Law appoint a different Day.

Section. 5.

Each House shall be the Judge of the Elections, Returns and Qualifications of its own Members, and a Majority of each shall constitute a Quorum to do Business; but a smaller Number may adjourn from day to day, and may be authorized to compel the Attendance of absent Members, in such Manner, and under such Penalties as each House may provide.

Each House may determine the Rules of its Proceedings, punish its Members for disorderly Behaviour, and, with the Concurrence of two thirds, expel a Member.

Each House shall keep a Journal of its Proceedings, and from time to time publish the same, excepting such Parts as may in their Judgment require Secrecy; and the Yeas and Nays of the Members of either House on any question shall, at the Desire of one fifth of those Present, be entered on the Journal.

Neither House, during the Session of Congress, shall, without the Consent of the other, adjourn for more than three days, nor to any other Place than that in which the two Houses shall be sitting.

Section. 6.

The Senators and Representatives shall receive a Compensation for their Services, to be ascertained by Law, and paid out of the Treasury of the United States. They shall in all Cases, except Treason, Felony and Breach of the Peace, be privileged from Arrest during their Attendance at the Session of their respective Houses, and in going to and returning from the same; and for any Speech or Debate in either House, they shall not be questioned in any other Place.

No Senator or Representative shall, during the Time for which he was elected, be appointed to any civil Office under the Authority of the United States, which shall have been created, or the Emoluments whereof shall have been encreased during such time; and no Person holding any Office under the United States, shall be a Member of either House during his Continuance in Office.

Section. 7.

All Bills for raising Revenue shall originate in the House of Representatives; but the Senate may propose or concur with Amendments as on other Bills.

Every Bill which shall have passed the House of Representatives and the Senate, shall, before it become a Law, be presented to the President of the United States: If he approve he shall sign it, but if not he shall return it, with his Objections to that House in which it shall have originated, who shall enter the Objections at large on their Journal, and proceed to reconsider it. If after such Reconsideration two thirds of that House shall agree to pass the Bill, it shall be sent, together with the Objections, to the other House, by which it shall likewise be reconsidered, and if approved by two thirds of that House, it shall become a Law. But in all such Cases the Votes of both Houses shall be determined by yeas and Nays, and the Names of the Persons voting for and against the Bill shall be entered on the Journal of each House respectively. If any Bill shall not be returned by the President within ten Days (Sundays excepted) after it shall have been presented to him, the Same shall be a Law, in like Manner as if he had signed it, unless the Congress by their Adjournment prevent its Return, in which Case it shall not be a Law.

Every Order, Resolution, or Vote to which the Concurrence of the Senate and House of Representatives may be necessary (except on a question of Adjournment) shall be presented to the President of the United States; and before the Same shall take Effect, shall be approved by him, or being disapproved by him, shall be repassed by two thirds of the Senate and House of Representatives, according to the Rules and Limitations prescribed in the Case of a Bill.

Section. 8.

The Congress shall have Power To lay and collect Taxes, Duties, Imposts and Excises, to pay the Debts and provide for the common Defence and general Welfare of the United States; but all Duties, Imposts and Excises shall be uniform throughout the United States;

To borrow Money on the credit of the United States;

To regulate Commerce with foreign Nations, and among the several States, and with the Indian Tribes;

To establish an uniform Rule of Naturalization, and uniform Laws on the subject of Bankruptcies throughout the United States;

To coin Money, regulate the Value thereof, and of foreign Coin, and fix the Standard of Weights and Measures;

To provide for the Punishment of counterfeiting the Securities and current Coin of the United States;

To establish Post Offices and post Roads;

To promote the Progress of Science and useful Arts, by securing for limited Times to Authors and Inventors the exclusive Right to their respective Writings and Discoveries;

To constitute Tribunals inferior to the supreme Court;

To define and punish Piracies and Felonies committed on the high Seas, and Offences against the Law of Nations;

To declare War, grant Letters of Marque and Reprisal, and make Rules concerning Captures on Land and Water;

To raise and support Armies, but no Appropriation of Money to that Use shall be for a longer Term than two Years;

To provide and maintain a Navy;

To make Rules for the Government and Regulation of the land and naval Forces;

To provide for calling forth the Militia to execute the Laws of the Union, suppress Insurrections and repel Invasions;

To provide for organizing, arming, and disciplining, the Militia, and for governing such Part of them as may be employed in the Service of the United States, reserving to the States respectively, the Appointment of the Officers, and the Authority of training the Militia according to the discipline prescribed by Congress;

To exercise exclusive Legislation in all Cases whatsoever, over such District (not exceeding ten Miles square) as may, by Cession of particular States, and the Acceptance of Congress, become the Seat of the Government of the United States, and to exercise like Authority over all Places purchased by the Consent of the Legislature of the State in which the Same shall be, for the Erection of Forts, Magazines, Arsenals, dock-Yards, and other needful Buildings;—And

To make all Laws which shall be necessary and proper for carrying into Execution the foregoing Powers, and all other Powers vested by this

Constitution in the Government of the United States, or in any Department or Officer thereof.

Section. 9.

The Migration or Importation of such Persons as any of the States now existing shall think proper to admit, shall not be prohibited by the Congress prior to the Year one thousand eight hundred and eight, but a Tax or duty may be imposed on such Importation, not exceeding ten dollars for each Person.

The Privilege of the Writ of Habeas Corpus shall not be suspended, unless when in Cases of Rebellion or Invasion the public Safety may require it.

No Bill of Attainder or ex post facto Law shall be passed.

No Capitation, or other direct, Tax shall be laid, unless in Proportion to the Census or enumeration herein before directed to be taken.

No Tax or Duty shall be laid on Articles exported from any State.

No Preference shall be given by any Regulation of Commerce or Revenue to the Ports of one State over those of another; nor shall Vessels bound to, or from, one State, be obliged to enter, clear, or pay Duties in another.

No Money shall be drawn from the Treasury, but in Consequence of Appropriations made by Law; and a regular Statement and Account of the Receipts and Expenditures of all public Money shall be published from time to time.

No Title of Nobility shall be granted by the United States: And no Person holding any Office of Profit or Trust under them, shall, without the Consent of the Congress, accept of any present, Emolument, Office, or Title, of any kind whatever, from any King, Prince, or foreign State.

Section. 10.

No State shall enter into any Treaty, Alliance, or Confederation; grant Letters of Marque and Reprisal; coin Money; emit Bills of Credit; make any Thing but gold and silver Coin a Tender in Payment of Debts; pass any Bill of Attainder, ex post facto Law, or Law impairing the Obligation of Contracts, or grant any Title of Nobility.

No State shall, without the Consent of the Congress, lay any Imposts or Duties on Imports or Exports, except what may be absolutely necessary for executing it's inspection Laws: and the net Produce of all Duties and Imposts, laid by any State on Imports or Exports, shall be for the Use of the Treasury of the United States; and all such Laws shall be subject to the Revision and Controul of the Congress.

No State shall, without the Consent of Congress, lay any Duty of Tonnage, keep Troops, or Ships of War in time of Peace, enter into any Agreement or Compact with another State, or with a foreign Power, or engage in War, unless actually invaded, or in such imminent Danger as will not admit of delay.

Article. II.
Section. 1.

The executive Power shall be vested in a President of the United States of America. He shall hold his Office during the Term of four Years, and, together with the Vice President, chosen for the same Term, be elected, as follows:

Each State shall appoint, in such Manner as the Legislature thereof may direct, a Number of Electors, equal to the whole Number of Senators and Representatives to which the State may be entitled in the Congress: but no Senator or Representative, or Person holding an Office of Trust or Profit under the United States, shall be appointed an Elector.

The Electors shall meet in their respective States, and vote by Ballot for two Persons, of whom one at least shall not be an Inhabitant of the same State with themselves. And they shall make a List of all the Persons voted for, and of the Number of Votes for each; which List they shall sign and certify, and transmit sealed to the Seat of the Government of the United States, directed to the President of the Senate. The President of the Senate shall, in the Presence of the Senate and House of Representatives, open all the Certificates, and the Votes shall then be counted. The Person having the greatest Number of Votes shall be the President, if such Number be a Majority of the whole Number of Electors appointed; and if there be more than one who have such Majority, and have an equal Number of Votes, then the House of Representatives shall immediately chuse by Ballot one of them for President; and if no Person have a Majority, then from the five highest on the List the said House shall in like Manner chuse the President. But in chusing the President, the Votes shall be taken by States, the Representation from each State having one Vote; A quorum for this purpose shall consist of a Member or Members from two thirds of the States, and a Majority of all the States shall be necessary to a Choice. In every Case, after the Choice of the President, the Person having the greatest Number of Votes of the Electors shall be the Vice President. But if there should remain two or more who have equal Votes, the Senate shall chuse from them by Ballot the Vice President.

The Congress may determine the Time of chusing the Electors, and the Day on which they shall give their Votes; which Day shall be the same throughout the United States.

No Person except a natural born Citizen, or a Citizen of the United States, at the time of the Adoption of this Constitution, shall be eligible to the Office of President; neither shall any Person be eligible to that Office who shall not have attained to the Age of thirty five Years, and been fourteen Years a Resident within the United States.

In Case of the Removal of the President from Office, or of his Death, Resignation, or Inability to discharge the Powers and Duties of the said Office, the Same shall devolve on the Vice President, and the Congress may by Law provide for the Case of Removal, Death, Resignation or Inability, both of the President and Vice President, declaring what Officer shall then act as President, and such Officer shall act accordingly, until the Disability be removed, or a President shall be elected.

The President shall, at stated Times, receive for his Services, a Compensation, which shall neither be increased nor diminished during the Period for which he shall have been elected, and he shall not receive within that Period any other Emolument from the United States, or any of them.

Before he enter on the Execution of his Office, he shall take the following Oath or Affirmation:—"I do solemnly swear (or affirm) that I will faithfully execute the Office of President of the United States, and will to the best of my Ability, preserve, protect and defend the Constitution of the United States."

Section. 2.

The President shall be Commander in Chief of the Army and Navy of the United States, and of the Militia of the several States, when called into the actual Service of the United States; he may require the Opinion, in writing, of the principal Officer in each of the executive Departments, upon any Subject relating to the Duties of their respective Offices, and he shall have Power to grant Reprieves and Pardons for Offences against the United States, except in Cases of Impeachment.

He shall have Power, by and with the Advice and Consent of the Senate, to make Treaties, provided two thirds of the Senators present concur; and he shall nominate, and by and with the Advice and Consent of the Senate, shall appoint Ambassadors, other public Ministers and Consuls, Judges of the supreme Court, and all other Officers of the United States, whose Appointments are not herein otherwise provided for, and which shall be established by Law: but the Congress may by Law vest the Appointment of such inferior Officers, as they think proper, in the President alone, in the Courts of Law, or in the Heads of Departments.

The President shall have Power to fill up all Vacancies that may happen during the Recess of the Senate, by granting Commissions which shall expire at the End of their next Session.

Section. 3.

He shall from time to time give to the Congress Information of the State of the Union, and recommend to their Consideration such Measures as he shall judge necessary and expedient; he may, on extraordinary Occasions, convene both Houses, or either of them, and in Case of Disagreement between them, with Respect to the Time of Adjournment, he may adjourn them to such Time as he shall think proper; he shall receive Ambassadors and other public Ministers; he shall take Care that the Laws be faithfully executed, and shall Commission all the Officers of the United States.

Section. 4.

The President, Vice President and all civil Officers of the United States, shall be removed from Office on Impeachment for, and Conviction of, Treason, Bribery, or other high Crimes and Misdemeanors.

Article. III.

Section. 1.

The judicial Power of the United States shall be vested in one supreme Court, and in such inferior Courts as the Congress may from time to time ordain and establish. The Judges, both of the supreme and inferior Courts, shall hold their Offices during good Behaviour, and shall, at stated Times, receive for their Services a Compensation, which shall not be diminished during their Continuance in Office.

Section. 2.

The judicial Power shall extend to all Cases, in Law and Equity, arising under this Constitution, the Laws of the United States, and Treaties made, or which shall be made, under their Authority;—to all Cases affecting Ambassadors, other public Ministers and Consuls;—to all Cases of admiralty and maritime Jurisdiction;—to Controversies to which the United States shall be a Party;—to Controversies between two or more States;—between a State and Citizens of another State,—between Citizens of different States,—between Citizens of the same State claiming Lands under Grants of different States, and between a State, or the Citizens thereof, and foreign States, Citizens or Subjects.

In all Cases affecting Ambassadors, other public Ministers and Consuls, and those in which a State shall be Party, the supreme Court shall have original Jurisdiction. In all the other Cases before mentioned, the supreme Court shall have appellate Jurisdiction, both as to Law and Fact, with such Exceptions, and under such Regulations as the Congress shall make.

The Trial of all Crimes, except in Cases of Impeachment, shall be by Jury; and such Trial shall be held in the State where the said Crimes shall have been committed; but when not committed within any State, the Trial shall be at such Place or Places as the Congress may by Law have directed.

Section. 3.

Treason against the United States, shall consist only in levying War against them, or in adhering to their Enemies, giving them Aid and Comfort. No Person shall be convicted of Treason unless on the Testimony of two Witnesses to the same overt Act, or on Confession in open Court.

The Congress shall have Power to declare the Punishment of Treason, but no Attainder of Treason shall work Corruption of Blood, or Forfeiture except during the Life of the Person attainted.

Article. IV.

Section. 1.

Full Faith and Credit shall be given in each State to the public Acts, Records, and judicial Proceedings of every other State. And the Congress may by general Laws prescribe the Manner in which such Acts, Records and Proceedings shall be proved, and the Effect thereof.

Section. 2.

The Citizens of each State shall be entitled to all Privileges and Immunities of Citizens in the several States.

A Person charged in any State with Treason, Felony, or other Crime, who shall flee from Justice, and be found in another State, shall on Demand of the executive Authority of the State from which he fled, be delivered up, to be removed to the State having Jurisdiction of the Crime.

No Person held to Service or Labour in one State, under the Laws thereof, escaping into another, shall, in Consequence of any Law or Regulation therein, be discharged from such Service or Labour, but shall be delivered up on Claim of the Party to whom such Service or Labour may be due.

Section. 3.

New States may be admitted by the Congress into this Union; but no new State shall be formed or erected within the Jurisdiction of any other State; nor any State be formed by the Junction of two or more States, or Parts of States, without the Consent of the Legislatures of the States concerned as well as of the Congress.

The Congress shall have Power to dispose of and make all needful Rules and Regulations respecting the Territory or other Property belonging to the United States; and nothing in this Constitution shall be so construed as to Prejudice any Claims of the United States, or of any particular State.

Section. 4.

The United States shall guarantee to every State in this Union a Republican Form of Government, and shall protect each of them against Invasion; and on Application of the Legislature, or of the Executive (when the Legislature cannot be convened), against domestic Violence.

Article. V.

The Congress, whenever two thirds of both Houses shall deem it necessary, shall propose Amendments to this Constitution, or, on the Application of the Legislatures of two thirds of the several States, shall call a Convention for proposing Amendments, which, in either Case, shall be valid to all Intents and Purposes, as Part of this Constitution, when ratified by the Legislatures of three fourths of the several States, or by Conventions in three fourths thereof, as the one or the other Mode of Ratification may be proposed by the Congress; Provided that no Amendment which may be made prior to the Year One thousand eight hundred and eight shall in any Manner affect the first and fourth Clauses in the Ninth Section of the first Article; and that no State, without its Consent, shall be deprived of its equal Suffrage in the Senate.

Article. VI.

All Debts contracted and Engagements entered into, before the Adoption of this Constitution, shall be as valid against the United States under this Constitution, as under the Confederation.

This Constitution, and the Laws of the United States which shall be made in Pursuance thereof; and all Treaties made, or which shall be made, under the Authority of the United States, shall be the supreme Law of the Land; and the Judges in every State shall be bound thereby, any Thing in the Constitution or Laws of any State to the Contrary notwithstanding.

The Senators and Representatives before mentioned, and the Members of the several State Legislatures, and all executive and judicial Officers, both of the United States and of the several States, shall be bound by Oath or Affirmation, to support this Constitution; but no religious Test shall ever be required as a Qualification to any Office or public Trust under the United States.

Article. VII.

The Ratification of the Conventions of nine States, shall be sufficient for the Establishment of this Constitution between the States so ratifying the Same.

The Word, "the," being interlined between the seventh and eighth Lines of the first Page, the Word "Thirty" being partly written on an Erazure in the fifteenth Line of the first Page, The Words "is tried" being interlined between the thirty second and thirty third Lines of the first Page and the Word "the" being interlined between the forty third and forty fourth Lines of the second Page.

Attest William Jackson Secretary

done in Convention by the Unanimous Consent of the States present the Seventeenth Day of September in the Year of our Lord one thousand seven hundred and Eighty seven and of the Independance of the United States of America the Twelfth

In witness whereof We have hereunto subscribed our Names,

Go. Washington

Presidt and deputy from Virginia

Delaware
Geo: Read
Gunning Bedford jun
John Dickinson
Richard Bassett
Jaco: Broom

Maryland
James McHenry
Dan of St Thos. Jenifer
Danl. Carroll

Virginia
John Blair
James Madison Jr.

North Carolina
Wm. Blount
Richd. Dobbs Spaight
Hu Williamson

South Carolina
J. Rutledge
Charles Cotesworth Pinckney
Charles Pinckney
Pierce Butler

Georgia
William Few
Abr Baldwin

New Hampshire
John Langdon
Nicholas Gilman

Massachusetts
Nathaniel Gorham
Rufus King

Connecticut
Wm. Saml. Johnson
Roger Sherman

New York
Alexander Hamilton

New Jersey
Wil: Livingston
David Brearley
Wm. Paterson
Jona: Dayton

Pennsylvania
B Franklin
Thomas Mifflin
Robt. Morris
Geo. Clymer
Thos. FitzSimons
Jared Ingersoll
James Wilson
Gouv Morris

Selected Bibliography

Adair, Douglass, and Marvin Harvey. 1955. "Was Alexander Hamilton a Christian Statesman?" *William and Mary Quarterly*, 3rd Ser., 12 (April): 308–29.

Adams, William Howard. 2003. *Gouverneur Morris: An Independent Life*. New Haven, CT: Yale University Press.

Ahern, Gregory S. 1998. "The Spirit of American Constitutionalism: John Dickinson's *Fabius Letters*." *Humanitas* 11, no. 2. Center for Constitutional Studies. http://www.nhinet.org/ccs/ccs-res.htm. Accessed 4/8/2004.

Andrews, William Given. 2012. *William Samuel Johnson and the Making of the Constitution*. First published 1887. Whitefish, MT: Kessinger Publishing.

Austin, James. 2009. *The Life of Elbridge Gerry*. 2 vols. First published in Boston: Wells and Lilly, 1828–1892. Bedford, MA: Applewood Books.

Bailyn, Bernard, ed. 1993. *The Debate on the Constitution: Federalist and Antifederalist Speeches, Articles, and Letters during the Struggle over Ratification*. 2 vols. New York: The Library of America.

Bakeless, John, and Katherine Little Bakeless. 1969. *Signers of the Declaration*. Boston: Houghton Mifflin.

Banning, Lance. 1983. "James Madison and the Nationalists, 1780–1783." *William and Mary Quarterly*, 3rd Ser., 40 (April): 227–55.

———. 1995. *The Sacred Fire of Liberty: James Madison and the Founding of the American Republic*. Ithaca: Cornell University Press.

Barnwell, Robert W., Jr. 1941. "The Dictator." *The Journal of Southern History* 7 (May): 215–24.

Barry, Richard. 1971. *Mr. Rutledge of South Carolina*. Freeport, NY: Books for Libraries Press. Reprint of 1942 original.

Bassett, Richard. 2010. *The Protest of the Hon. Richard Bassett*. Belmont, CA: Gale. Reprint of 1802 original.

Beard, Charles A. 1949. *An Economic Interpretation of the Constitution of the United States*. New York: Macmillan.

Beeman, Richard. 2009. *Plain, Honest Men: The Making of the American Constitution*. New York: Random House.

Bence, Evelyn. 2008. *James Madison's Montpelier: Home of the Father of the Constitution*. Orange, VA: The Montpelier Association.

Benton, Wilbourne E., ed. 1986. *1787: Drafting the U.S. Constitution*. 2 vols. College Station: Texas A & M University Press.

Berkin, Carol. 2003. *A Brilliant Solution: Investing the American Constitution*. New York: Harcourt.

Bernstein, Richard B., with Kym S. Rice. 1987. *Are We to Be a Nation? The Making of the Constitution*. Cambridge, MA: Harvard University Press.

Bigler, Philip, and Annie Lorsbach. 2009. *Liberty and Learning: The Essential James Madison*. Harrisonburg, VA: The James Madison Center.

Billias, George Athan. 1976. *Elbridge Gerry: Founding Father and Republican Statesman*. New York: McGraw Hill.

———. 1990. "Elbridge Gerry." *Constitution* 2 (Spring–Summer): 68–74.

Blackburn, Joyce. *George Wythe of Williamsburg*. New York: Harper & Row, 1975.

Bloom, Sol. 1937. *The Story of the Constitution*. Washington, DC: United States Constitutional Sesquicentennial Commission. See "Portraits and Sketches of the Signers of the Constitution," 54–64.

Boardman, Roger Sherman. 1938. *Roger Sherman: Signer and Statesman*. Philadelphia: University of Pennsylvania Press.

Boutell, Louis Henry. 1896. *The Life of Roger Sherman*. Chicago: McClurg.

Bouton, Terry. 2007. *Taming Democracy: "The People," the Founders, and the Troubling Ending of the American Revolution*. New York: Oxford University Press.

Bowers, Catherine Drinker. 1966. *Miracle at Philadelphia: The Story of the Constitutional Convention, May to September 1787*. Boston: Little, Brown.

Boyd, Julian. 1932. "Roger Sherman: Portrait of a Cordwainer Statesman." *The New England Quarterly* 5, 221–36.

Bradford, M. E. 1994. *Founding Fathers: Brief Lives of the Framers of the United States Constitution*. 2nd ed. Lawrence: University Press of Kansas.

Bradsher, Greg. 2006. "A Founding Father in Dissent." *Prologue* 38 (Spring): 30–35.

Brands, H. W. 2000. *The First American: The Life and Times of Benjamin Franklin*. New York: Anchor Books.

Broadwater, Jeff. 2012. *James Madison: A Son of Virginia and Founder of the Nation*. Chapel Hill: The University of North Carolina Press.

———. n.d. "William Richardson Davie." North Carolina History Project. http://www.northcarolinahistory.org/commentary/115/entry. Accessed 7/12/2012.

Brookhiser, Richard. 1996. *Founding Father: Rediscovering George Washington*. New York: The Free Press.

———. 1999. *Alexander Hamilton: American*. New York: Free Press.

———. 2003. *Gentleman Revolutionary: Gouverneur Morris, The Rake Who Wrote the Constitution.* New York: Free Press.

———. 2011. *James Madison.* New York: Basic Books.

Brown, Imogene E. *American Aristides: A Biography of George Wythe.* Madison, NJ: Fairleigh Dickinson University Press, 1981.

Brown, Richard D. 1976. "The Founding Fathers of 1776 and 1787: A Collective View." *William and Mary Quarterly*, 3rd Ser., 33 (July): 465–80.

Brown, William Garrott. 1905. "A Continental Congressman: Oliver Ellsworth, 1777–1783." *American Historical Review* 10 (July): 751–81.

Browne, Gary L. 1988. "Federalism in Baltimore." *Maryland Historical Magazine* 83 (Spring): 50–57.

Brush, Edward Hale. 1926. *Rufus King and His Times.* New York: Nicolas L. Brown.

Burnett, Edmund C. 1938. "The Catholic Signers of the Constitution." In *The Constitution of the United States: Addresses in Commemoration of the Sesquicentennial of its Signing 17 September 1787,* edited by Herbert Wright, 40–54. Washington, DC: Catholic University of America.

Burstein, Andrew, and Nancy Isenberg. 2010. *Madison and Jefferson.* New York: Random House.

Butzner, Jane, compiler. 1941. *Constitutional Chaff—Rejected Suggestions of the Constitutional Convention of 1787 with Explanatory Argument.* New York: Columbia University Press.

Calvert, Jane E. 2007. "Liberty without Tumult: Understanding the Politics of John Dickinson." *The Pennsylvania Magazine of History and Biography* 131 (July): 233–62.

———. 2008. *Quaker Constitutionalism and the Political Thought of John Dickinson.* Cambridge: Cambridge University Press.

Campbell, William W. 1909. "Life and Character of Jacob Broom." *Papers of the Historical Society of Delaware.* Vol. 51. Wilmington: The Historical Society of Delaware.

Carr, William G. 1990. *The Oldest Delegate: Franklin in the Constitutional Convention.* Newark: University of Delaware Press.

Carson, Hampton L. 1889. "Biographies of the Members of the Federal Convention." In *History of the Celebration of the One Hundredth Anniversary of the Promulgation of the Constitution of the United States,* edited by Hampton L. Carson, 1: 135–237. Philadelphia: J. P. Lippincott Company.

Casto, William R. 1994. "Oliver Ellsworth's Calvinism: A Biographical Essay on Religion and Political Psychology in the Early Republic." *Journal of Church and State* 36:507–26.

———. 1995. *The Supreme Court in the Early Republic: The Chief Justiceships of John Jay and Oliver Ellsworth.* Columbia: University of South Carolina Press.

Chadwick, Bruce. 2010. *Triumvirate: The Story of the Unlikely Alliance That Saved the Constitution and United the Nation.* Napierville, IL: Sourcebooks.

Charleton, James H., et al. 1986. *Framers of the Constitution*. Washington, DC: National Archives and Records Administration.

Chernow, Ron. 2004. *Alexander Hamilton*. New York: The Penguin Press.

———. 2010. *Washington: A Life*. New York: Penguin Press.

Chidsey, Donald B. 1964. *The Birth of the Constitution: An Informal History*. New York: Crown Publishers.

Clarkson, Paul S., and R. Samuel Jett. 1970. *Luther Martin of Maryland*. Baltimore: Johns Hopkins University Press.

Coghlan, Francis. 1977. "Pierce Butler, 1744–1822, First Senator from South Carolina." *South Carolina Historical Magazine* 78 (April): 104–19.

Colburne, H. Trevor. 1959. "John Dickinson: Historical Revolutionary." *Pennsylvania Magazine of History and Biography* 83 (July): 271–92.

Coleman, Nannie McCormick. 1910. *The Constitution and Its Framers*. Chicago: The Progress Company.

Collier, Christopher. 1971. *Roger Sherman's Connecticut: Yankee Politics and the American Revolution*. Middleton, CT: Wesleyan University Press.

Collier, Christopher, and James Lincoln Collier. 1986. *Decision in Philadelphia: The Constitutional Convention of 1787*. New York: Random House.

Collins, J. J. 2012. *James Madison: The Father of the Constitution (1751–1836)*. CreateSpace Independent Publishing Platform.

Conley, Patrick T., and John P. Kaminski, eds. 1988. *The Constitution and the States: The Role of the Original Thirteen in the Framing and Adoption of the Federal Constitution*. Madison, WI: Madison House.

———. 1992. *The Bill of Rights and the States: The Colonial and Revolutionary Origins of American Liberties*. Madison, WI: Madison House.

Connelly, William F., Jr. 2010. *James Madison Rules America: The Constitutional Origins of Congressional Partisanship*. Lanham, MD: Rowman & Littlefield.

Conniff, James. 1975. "On the Obsolescence of the General Will: Rousseau, Madison, and the Evolution of Republican Political Thought." *Western Political Quarterly* 28 (March): 32–58.

Conrad, Stephen A. 1985. "Polite Foundation: Citizenship and Common Sense in James Wilson's Republican Theory." In *The Supreme Court Review, 1984*, edited by Philip B. Kurland, Gerhard Casper, and Dennis J. Hutchinson, 359–88. Chicago: The University of Chicago Press.

———. 1988. "Metaphor and Imagination in James Wilson's Theory of Federal Union." *Law & Social Inquiry* 13 (Winter): 1, 3–70.

Corwin, Edward S. 1964. "The Progress of Constitutional Theory between the Declaration of Independence and the Meeting of the Philadelphia Convention." In *American Constitutional History: Essays by Edward S. Corwin*, edited by Alpheus T. Mason and Gerald Garvey. New York: Harper and Row.

Coulter, E. Merton. 1987. *Abraham Baldwin: Patriot, Educator, and Founding Father*. Arlington, VA: Vandamere Press.

Craige, Burton. 1987. *The Federal Convention of 1787: North Carolina in the Great Crisis*. Richmond, VA: Expert Graphics.

Crews, Ed. 2012. "Meet Betsy and Edmund." *Colonial Williamsburg Journal* 34 (Summer): 21–23.

Crowl, Philip A. 1941. "Charles Carroll's Plan of Government." *American Historical Review* 46 (April): 588–95.

Curtis, George Ticknor. 1961. *History of the Origin, Formation, and Adoption of the Constitution of the United States with Notices of Its Principal Framers*. 2 vols. New York: Harper and Brothers.

Cushman, Clare, ed. 1995. *The Supreme Court Justices: Illustrated Biographies, 1789–1995*. 2nd ed. Washington, DC: Congressional Quarterly.

Daanen, Jeroen. n.d. "A Biography of John Langdon 1741–1819." American History: From Revolution to Reconstruction. http://www.let.rug.nl/usa/biographies/john-langdon/. Accessed 7/5/2012.

DeRose, Chris. 2011. *Founding Rivals: Madison vs. Monroe, The Bill of Rights, and the Election That Saved a Nation*. Washington, DC: Regnery.

Dickinson, John. 1970. *The Political Writings of John Dickinson, 1764–1776*, edited by Paul Leicester Ford. New York: Da Capo.

Dill, Alonzo. 1979. *George Wythe: Teacher of Liberty*. Williamsburg: Virginia Independence Bicentennial Commission.

Dos Passos, John. 1957. *The Men Who Made the Nation*. Garden City, NY: Doubleday.

Dreisbach, Daniel L., Mark David Hall, and Jeffrey H. Morrison, eds. 2009. *The Forgotten Founders on Religion and Public Life*. Notre Dame, IN: University of Notre Dame Press.

Edling, Max M. 2003. *A Revolution in Favor of Government: Origins of the U.S. Constitution and the Making of the American State*. New York: Oxford University Press.

Ellis, Joseph J. 2004. *His Excellency: George Washington*. New York: Vintage Books.

Ernst, Robert. 1968. *Rufus King: American Federalist*. Chapel Hill: The University of North Carolina Press.

Farrand, Max. 1913. *The Framing of the Constitution of the United States*. New Haven, CT: Yale University Press.

Farrand, Max, ed. 1966. *The Records of the Federal Convention*. 4 vols. New Haven, CT: Yale University Press.

Federici, Michael P. 2012. *The Political Philosophy of Alexander Hamilton*. Baltimore: The Johns Hopkins University Press.

Fehrenbach, T. R. 1968. *Greatness to Spare: The Heroic Sacrifices of the Men Who Signed the Declaration of Independence*. Princeton, NJ: Van Nostrand.

Ferguson, E. James. 1983. "Political Economy, Public Liberty, and the Formation of the Constitution." *William and Mary Quarterly*, 3rd Ser., 40 (July): 389–412.

Ferris, Robert G. 1976. *Signers of the Constitution: Historic Places Commemorating the Signing of the Constitution*. Washington, DC: U.S. Department of the Interior.

Finkelman, Paul. 1988. "The Pennsylvania Delegation and the Peculiar Institution: The Two Faces of the Keystone State." *Pennsylvania Magazine of History and Biography* 112 (January): 49–71.

———. 1996. *Slavery and the Founders: Race and Liberty in the Age of Jefferson*. Armonk, NY: M. E. Sharpe.

Fiske, John. 1888. *The Critical Period of American History, 1783–1789*. Boston: Houghton Mifflin.

Flower, Milton E. 1983. *John Dickinson: Conservative Revolutionary*. Charlottesville: University Press of Virginia.

Ford, Lacy K., Jr. 1994. "Inventing the Concurrent Majority: Madison, Calhoun, and the Problem of Majoritarianism in American Political Thought." *Journal of Southern History* 60 (February): 19–58.

"The Founding Fathers: A Brilliant Gathering of Reason and Creativity." 1987. Special issue of *Life* magazine, *The Constitution* (Fall): 51–58.

Fradin, Dennis B., and Michael McCurdy. 2005. *The Founders: The 39 Stories Behind the U.S. Constitution*. New York: Walker. (Note: this and the entry that follows are for children).

———. 2001. *The Signers: The 56 Stories Behind the Declaration of Independence*. New York: Walker.

Frisch, Morton J. 1999. *Alexander Hamilton and the Political Order: An Interpretation of His Political Thought and Practice*. New York: Free Press.

Ganter, Herbert Lawrence. 1937. "The Machiavellianism of George Mason." *William and Mary Quarterly*, 3rd Ser., 17 (April): 239–64.

Garraty, John A., and Mark C. Carnes, eds. 1999. *American National Biography*. 24 vols. New York: Oxford University Press.

Gaustad, Edwin S. 2006. *Benjamin Franklin*. New York: Oxford University Press.

Geiger, Mary Virginia. 1943. *Daniel Carroll: A Framer of the Constitution*. Washington, D.C.: Catholic University of America.

Gerber, Scott D. 1996. "Roger Sherman and the Bill of Rights." *Polity* 28 (Summer): 521–40.

Gerber, Scott Douglas, ed. 1998. *Seriatim: The Supreme Court before John Marshall*. New York: New York University Press.

Gibson, Alan. 2006. *Interpreting the Founding: Guide to the Enduring Debates over the Origin and Foundations of the American Republic*. Lawrence: University Press of Kansas.

———. 2007. *Understanding the Founding: The Crucial Questions*. Lawrence: University Press of Kansas.

Gillespie, Michael Allen, and Michael Lienesch. 1989. *Ratifying the Constitution*. Lawrence: University Press of Kansas.

Glenn, Thomas Allen, 1803. *William Churchill Houston, 1746–1788*. Norristown, PA: Privately printed.

Goodrich, Charles A. 1856. *Lives of the Signers to the Declaration of Independence*. New York: William Reed & Co.

Green, Charles E. 1976. "Bedford Was Delaware's Strong Voice at the Constitutional Convention." *The Northern Light: A Window For Freemasonry* 7 (April): 14–15.

Green, Harry Clinton, and Mary Wolcott Green. 1997. *Wives of the Signers: The Women Behind the Declaration of Independence*. Aledo, TX: Wallbuilder Press.

Gregg, Gary L., II, and Mark David Hall, eds. 2011. *America's Forgotten Founders*. 2nd ed. Wilmington, DE: Intercollegiate Studies Institute.

Grundfest, Jerry. 1982. *George Clymer: Philadelphia Revolutionary, 1739–1813*. New York: Arno Press.

Gutzman, Kevin R. C. 2004. "Edmund Randolph and Virginia Constitutionalism." *The Review of Politics* 66 (Summer): 469–97.

———. 2012. *James Madison and the Making of America*. New York: St. Martin's Press.

Hall, Mark David. 1997. *The Political and Legal Philosophy of James Wilson, 1742–1798*. Columbia: University of Missouri Press.

Hamilton, Alexander, James Madison, and John Jay. 1961. *The Federalist Papers*, edited by Clinton Rossiter. New York: New American Library.

Haskett, Richard C. 1950. "William Paterson, Attorney General of New Jersey: Public Office and Private Profit in the American Revolution." *William and Mary Quarterly*, 3rd Ser., 7 (January): 26–38.

Haw, James. 1997. *John and Edward Rutledge of South Carolina*. Athens: University of Georgia Press.

———. 1998. "John Rutledge: Distinction and Declention." In *Seriatim: The Supreme Court before John Marshal*, edited by Scott Douglas Gerber, 70–96. New York: New York University Press.

Hendrickson, David D. 2003. *Peace Pact: The Lost World of the American Founding*. Lawrence: University Press of Kansas.

Henri, Florette. 1971. *George Mason of Virginia*. New York: Atheneum.

Henriques, Peter P. 1989. "An Uneven Friendship: The Relationship between George Washington and George Mason." *Virginia Magazine of History and Biography* 97 (April): 185–204.

Hobson, Charles F. 1979. "The Negative on State Laws: James Madison, the Constitution, and the Crisis of Republican Government." *William and Mary Quarterly*, 3rd Ser., 36 (April): 214–35.

Hoffer, Peter Charles. 2011. *When Benjamin Franklin Met the Reverend Whitefield: Enlightenment, Revival, and the Power of the Printed Word*. Baltimore: The Johns Hopkins University Press.

Hoffer, Peter C., and N. E. H. Hull. 1977. "'To Determine on the Future Government': Robert Yates's Plan of Union, 1774–1775." *William and Mary Quarterly*, 3rd Ser., 34 (April) 298–306.

Holcombe, Arthur N. 1956. "The Role of Washington in the Framing of the Constitution," *Huntington Library Quarterly* 29 (August): 317–34.

Howard, Hugh. 2007. *Houses of the Founding Fathers*. New York: Artisan.

Hutson, James H. 1983. "John Dickinson at the Federal Constitutional Convention." *William and Mary Quarterly*, 3rd Ser., 40: 256–82.

———. 1987. "Riddles of the Federal Constitutional Convention." *William and Mary Quarterly*, 3rd Ser., 44 (July): 411–23.

Hutson, James H., ed. 1987. *Supplement to Max Farrand's The Records of the Federal Convention of 1787*. New Haven, CT: Yale University Press.

Isaacson, Walter. 2003. *Benjamin Franklin: An American Life*. New York: Simon & Schuster.

Jensen, Merrill. 1966. *The Articles of Confederation*. Madison: University of Wisconsin Press.

Johnson, Calvin H. 2005. *Righteous Anger at the Wicked States: The Meaning of the Founders' Constitution*. New York: Cambridge University Press.

Johnson, Eldon L. 1987. "The 'Other Jeffersons' and the State University Idea." *Journal of Higher Education* 58 (March–April): 127–50.

Jones, Charles C. 1891. *Biographical Sketches of the Delegates from Georgia to the Continental Congress*. Boston: Houghton, Mifflin and Company.

Judson, L. Carroll. 1970. *The Sages and Heroes of the American Revolution. Including the Signers of the Declaration of Independence. Two Hundred and Forty Three of the Sages and Heroes Are Presented in Due Form and Many Others Are Named Incidentally*. Port Washington, NY: Kennikat Press. (First printing 1851.)

Kauffman, Bill. 2008. *Forgotten Founder, Drunken Prophet: The Life of Luther Martin*. Wilmington, Delaware: ISI Books.

Kernell, Samuel. 2003. *James Madison: The Theory and Practice of Republican Government*. Stanford, CA: Stanford University Press.

Ketcham, Ralph. 1993. *Framed for Posterity: The Enduring Philosophy of the Constitution*. Lawrence: University Press of Kansas.

Kiernan, Denise, and Joseph D'Agnese. 2009. *Signing Their Lives Away: The Fame and Misfortune of the Men Who Signed the Declaration of Independence*. Philadelphia: Quirk Books.

———. 2011. *Signing Their Rights Away: The Fame and Misfortune of the Men Who Signed the United States Constitution*. Philadelphia: Quirk Books.

Kirschke, James J. 2005. *Gouverneur Morris: Author, Statesman, and Man of the World*. New York: Thomas Dunne Books.

Klein, Milton M. 1958. "The Rise of the New York Bar: The Legal Career of William Livingston." *William and Mary Quarterly*, 3rd Ser., 15 (July): 334–58.

———. 1993. *The American Whig: William Livingston of New York*. Rev. ed. New York: Garland Publishing.

Koch, Adrienne. 1950. *Jefferson and Madison: The Great Collaboration*. New York: Oxford University Press.

Kramer, Larry D. 1999. "Madison's Audience." *Harvard Law Review* 112 (January): 611–79.

Kurland, Philip B., and Ralph Lerner. 1987. *The Founders' Constitution*. 5 vols. Chicago: University of Chicago Press.

Labunski, Richard. 2006. *James Madison and the Struggle for a Bill of Rights*. New York: Oxford University Press.

Lee, Howard B. 1932. *The Story of the Constitution*. Charlottesville, VA: The Michie Company.

Leffler, Richard, John P. Kaminski, and Samuel K. Fore. eds. 2012. *William Pierce on the Constitutional Convention and the Constitution*. Dallas, TX: Harlan Crow Library.

Lemay, J. A. Leo. 2006. *The Life of Benjamin Franklin*. Philadelphia: University of Pennsylvania Press, 2006.

Liebiger, Stuart. 1993. "James Madison and Amendments to the Constitution, 1787–1789: 'Parchment Barriers.'" *Journal of Southern History* 59 (August): 441–68.

———. 1999. *Founding Friendship: George Washington, James Madison, and the Creation of the American Republic*. Charlottesville: University Press of Virginia.

Lipscomb, Terry W. I. *The Letters of Pierce Butler, 1790–1794: Nation-Building and Enterprise in the New American Republic*. Columbia: University of South Carolina Press, 2007.

Livingston, William. 1979–. *The Papers of William Livingston*. 5 vols. Trenton: New Jersey Historical Commission.

Lodge, Henry Cabot. 1972. "Caleb Strong." In *Studies in History*, 224–61. Freeport, NY: Books for Libraries Press. Reprint of 1884 original.

Losing, Benson J. 1995. *Lives of the Signers of the Declaration of Independence*. Aledo, TX: WallBuilder Press.

Lutz, Donald S. 1988. *The Origins of American Constitutionalism*. Baton Rouge: Louisiana State University Press.

Lynch, Jack. 2004. "Mirroring the Mind of Mason." *Colonial Williamsburg* 26 (Spring): 52–55.

Lynch, Jack. 2010. "George Wythe Teaches America the Law." *Colonial Williamsburg Journal* (Spring). http://www.history.org/Foundation/journal/Spring10/educ.cfm. Accessed 7/18/2012.

Maier, Pauline. 2010. *Ratification: The People Debate the Constitution, 1787–1788*. New York: Simon & Schuster.

Mason, Ed. 1975. *Signers of the Constitution*. Builders of a Nation Series, Book 2. Columbus, OH: The Dispatch Printing Company.

Mason, George. 1970. *The Papers of George Mason, 1725–1792*, edited by Robert A. Rutland. 3 vols. Chapel Hill: University of North Carolina Press.

Masterson, William H. 1954. *William Blount*. Baton Rouge: Louisiana State University Press.

Matthews, Marty D. 2004. *Forgotten Founder: The Life and Times of Charles Pinckney*. Columbia: University of South Carolina Press.

Matthews, Richard K. 1995. *If Men Were Angels: James Madison and the Heartless Empire of Reason*. Lawrence: University Press of Kansas.

Mayo, Lawrence Shaw. 1970. *John Langdon of New Hampshire*. Port Washington, NY: Kennikat Press.

McCaughey, Elizabeth P. 1980. *From Loyalist to Founding Father: The Political Odyssey of William Samuel Johnson*. New York: Columbia University Press.

McCowan, George S., Jr. 1961. "Chief Justice John Rutledge and the Jay Treaty." *South Carolina Historical Magazine* 62 (January): 10–23.

McCraw, Thomas K. 2012. *The Founders and Finance: How Hamilton, Gallatin, and Other Immigrants Forged a New Economy*. Cambridge, MA: Belknap Press of Harvard University Press.

McDonald, Forrest. 1985. *Novus Ordo Seclorum: The Intellectual Origins of the Constitution*. Lawrence: University Press of Kansas.

McGee, Dorothy Horton. 1968. *Framers of the Constitution*. New York: Dodd, Mead & Company.

McHenry, James. "James McHenry's Speech to Maryland State House of Delegates." Teaching American History.org. http://teachingamericanhistory.org/library/index.asp?document=2326. Accessed 9/9/2012.

McKenney, Janice E. 2013. *Women of the Constitution: Wives of the Signers*. Lanham, MD: Scarecrow Press.

McLaughlin, Andrew C. 1897. "James Wilson in the Philadelphia Convention." *Political Science Quarterly* 12 (March): 1–20.

Meister, Charles W. 1987. *The Founding Fathers*. Jefferson, NC: McFarland & Company.

Melton, Buckner F., Jr. 1998. *The First Impeachment: The Constitution's Framers and the Case of Senator William Blount*. Macon, GA: Mercer University Press.

Meyers, Marvin, ed. 1973. *The Mind of the Founder: Sources of the Political Thought of James Madison*. Indianapolis: Bobbs-Merrill Company, Inc.

Miller, Helen H. 1975. *George Mason: Gentleman Revolutionary*. Chapel Hill: University of North Carolina Press.

Miller, Melanie Randolph. 2008. *An Incautious Man: The Life of Gouverneur Morris*. 2nd ed. Wilmington, DE: Intercollegiate Studies Institute.

Miller, William L. 1992. *The Business of May Next: James Madison and the Founding*. Charlottesville: University Press of Virginia.

Mitchell, Memory F. 1964. *North Carolina's Signers: Brief Sketches of the Men Who Signed the Declaration of Independence and the Constitution*. Raleigh: Division of Archives and History, North Carolina Department of Cultural Resources.

Monroe, John A. 1945. "The Philadelawareans: A Study in the Relations Between Philadelphia and Delaware in the Late Eighteenth Century." *Pennsylvania Magazine of History and Biography* 69 (April): 128–49.

Morgan, Edmund S. 2002. *Benjamin Franklin*. New Haven, CT: Yale University Press.

Morgan, Robert J. 1988. *James Madison and the Constitution and the Bill of Rights*. New York: Greenwood Press.

Morison, S. E. 1929. "Elbridge Gerry, Gentleman-Democrat." *The New England Quarterly* 2 (January): 6–33.

Morris, Gouverneur. 2012. *To Secure the Blessings of Liberty: Selected Writings of Gouverneur Morris*, edited by J. Jackson Barlow. Indianapolis: Liberty Fund.

Morris, Richard B. 1985. *Witnesses at the Creation: Hamilton, Madison, Jay, and the Constitution*. New York: New American Library.

Morrison, Jeffrey H. 2009. *The Political Philosophy of George Washington*. Baltimore, MD: The Johns Hopkins University Press.

Morton, Joseph C. 2006. *Shapers of the Great Debate at the Constitutional Convention of 1787: A Biographical Dictionary*. Westport, CT: Greenwood Press.

Murchison, William. 2012. *The Cost of Liberty: The Life of John Dickinson*. Wilmington, DE: Intercollegiate Studies Institute.

Natelson, Robert G. 2003. "The Constitutional Contributions of John Dickinson." *Pennsylvania State Law Review* 108 (Fall): 415–77.

Nelson, William E. 1987. "Reason and Compromise in the Establishment of the Federal Constitution, 1787–1801." *William and Mary Quarterly*, 3rd ser., 44 (July): 458–84.

Nordham, George Washington. 1987. *George Washington: President of the Constitutional Convention*. Chicago: Adams Press.

"Notes of Major William Pierce on the Federal Convention of 1787." 1898. *American Historical Review* 3 (January): 310–34.

O'Connor, John E. 1986. *William Paterson: Lawyer and Statesman, 1745–1806*. New Brunswick, NJ: Rutgers University Press.

Pangle, Lorraine Smith. 2007. *The Political Philosophy of Benjamin Franklin*. Baltimore: The Johns Hopkins University Press.

Pattison, Robert E. 1900. "The Life and Character of Richard Bassett." *Papers of the Historical Society of Delaware* 29: 3–19.

Pelton, Robert W. 2012. *Men of Destiny: The Signers of Our Declaration of Independence and Our Constitution*. Charleston, SC: Freedom & Liberty Foundation Press.

Penegar, Kenneth Lawing. 2011. *The Political Trial of Benjamin Franklin: A Prelude to the American Revolution*. New York: Algora Publishing.

Peters, William. 1987. *A More Perfect Union*. New York: Crown Publishers.

Phelps, Glenn A. 1993. *George Washington and American Constitutionalism*. Lawrence: University Press of Kansas.

Potts, Louis W. 1987. "Hugh Williamson: The Poor Man's Franklin and the National Domain," *North Carolina Historical Review* 64 (October): 371–93.

Powell, J. H. 1936. "John Dickinson and the Constitution." *Pennsylvania Magazine of History and Biography* 60 (January): 1–14.

Quinn, C. Edward. 1986. *Signers of the Constitution of the United States*. New York: Bronx County Historical Society.

Rakove, Jack N. 1990. *James Madison and the Creation of the American Republic*. Glenville, IL: Scott, Foresman.

Rappleye, Charles. 2010. *Robert Morris: Financier of the American Revolution*. New York: Simon & Schuster.

Read, James H. 1995. "'Our Complicated System': James Madison on Power and Liberty." *Political Theory* 23 (August): 452–74.

Read, William T. 1870. *Life and Correspondence of George Read*. Philadelphia: J. B. Lippincott & Co.

Reardon, John J. 1974. *Edmund Randolph: A Biography*. New York: Macmillan.

Reynolds, William L., II. 1987. "Luther Martin, Maryland and the Constitution." *Maryland Law Review* 47 (Fall): 291–321.

Rhodehamel, John. 1998. *The Great Experiment: George Washington and the American Republic*. New Haven: Yale University Press.

Richards, Robert H. 1901. "The Life and Character of John Dickinson." *Papers of the Historical Society of Delaware*, vol. 30.

Robertson, David Brian. 2005. "Madison's Opponents and Constitutional Design." *The American Political Science Review* 99 (May): 225–43.

———. 2013. *The Original Compromise: What the Constitution's Framers Were Really Thinking*. New York: Oxford University Press.

Robinson, Blackwell P. 1957. *William R. Davie*. Chapel Hill: University of North Carolina Press.

Roche, John P. 1961. "The Founding Fathers: A Reform Caucus in Action," *American Political Science Review* 55 (December): 799–816.

Rogow, Arnold A. 1955. "The Federal Convention: Madison and Yates." *American Historical Review* 60 (January): 323–35.

Rosen, Gary. 1999. *American Compact: James Madison and the Problem of Founding*. Lawrence: University Press of Kansas.

Ross, George E. 1963. *Know the 56 Signers of the Declaration of Independence*. Chicago: Rand McNally.

Rossiter, Clinton. 1964. *Alexander Hamilton and the Constitution*. New York: Harcourt, Brace & World, Inc.

———. 1966. *1787: The Grand Convention*. New York. W. W. Norton.

Rossman, Kenneth R. 1952. *Thomas Mifflin and the Politics of the American Revolution*. Chapel Hill: University of North Carolina Press.

Rutland, Robert A. 1961. *George Mason: Reluctant Statesman*. New York: Rinehart and Winston, Inc.

———. 1981. "George Mason: The Revolutionist as Conservative." In *The American Founding: Politics, Statesmanship, and the Constitution*, edited by Robert A. Rossum and Gary L. McDowell. Port Washington, NY: Kennikat Press.

———. 1987. *James Madison: The Founding Father*. New York: Macmillan Publishing Company.

Rutland, Robert A., ed. 1994. *James Madison and the American Nation, 1751–1836*. New York: Charles Scribner's Sons.

Sanderson, John, Robert Wain, and Henry D. Gilpin. 1823–1827. *Biography of the Signers to the Declaration of Independence*. 9 vols. Philadelphia: R. W. Pomeroy.

Sargent, Mildred Crow. 2004, 2006. *William Few, A Founding Father: A Biographical Perspective in Early American History*. 2 vols. New York: Vantage Press.

Scarinci, Donald. 2005. *David Brearley and the Making of the United States Constitution*. Public Policy Center of New Jersey.

Schwartz, Barry. 1983. "George Washington and the Whig Conception of Heroic Leadership," *American Sociological Review* 48 (February): 18–33.

———. 1987. *George Washington: The Making of an American Symbol*. New York: The Free Press.

Secret Proceedings and Debates of the Convention Assembled at Philadelphia, in the Year 1787, For the Purpose of Forming the Constitution of the United States of America. 1838. Cincinnati: Alston Mygatt.

Sedwick, Theodore, Jr. 1833. *A Memoir of the Life of William Livingston*. New York: J. & J. Harper. Nabu Public Domain reprint.

Seed, Geoffrey. 1978. *James Wilson*. Millwood, New York: KTO Press.

Senese, Donald J., ed. 1989. *George Mason and the Legacy of Constitutional Liberty: An Examination of The Influence of George Mason on the American Bill of Rights*. Fairfax County, VA: Fairfax County Historical Commission.

Sheldon, George F. 2010. *Hugh Williamson: Physician, Patriot, and Founding Father*. New York: Humanity Books.

Sheldon, Garrett Ward. 2001. *The Political Philosophy of James Madison*. Baltimore: Johns Hopkins University Press.

Siemers, David J. 2002. *Ratifying the Republic: Antifederalists and Federalists in Constitutional Time*. Stanford, CA: Stanford University Press.

Sikes, Lewright B. 1979. *The Public Life of Pierce Butler, South Carolina Statesman*. Washington, DC: University Press of America.

Smith, Charles Page. 1956. *James Wilson: Founding Father, 1742–1798*. Chapel Hill: University of North Carolina Press.

Smith, Craig R. 1993. *To Form a More Perfect Union: The Ratification of the Constitution and the Bill of Rights, 1787–1791*. Lanham, MD: University Press of America.

Smith, James Morton, ed. 1995. *The Republic of Letters: The Correspondence Between Thomas Jefferson and James Madison*. 3 vols. New York: W. W. Norton & Company.

Solberg, Winton, ed. 1958. *The Federal Convention and the Formation of the Union of the American States*. Indianapolis, IN: Bobbs-Merrill.

Spencer, Mark G. 2002. "Hume and Madison on Faction." *William and Mary Quarterly*, 3rd Ser., 59 (October): 869–96.

Steiner, Bernard C. 1907. *Life and Correspondence of James McHenry*. Cleveland: Burrows Brothers. Reprinted 2007, Whitefish, MT: Dessington Publishing.

Stiverson, Gregory A. 1988. "Maryland's Antifederalists and the Perfection of the U.S. Constitution." *Maryland Historical Magazine* 83: 18–35.

St. John, Jeffrey. 1987. *Constitutional Journal: A Correspondent's Report from the Convention of 1787*. Ottawa, IL: Jameson Books.

Stewart, David O. 2007. *The Summer of 1787: The Men Who Invented the Constitution*. New York: Simon & Schuster.

Strayer, Joseph Reese, ed. 2002. *The Delegate from New York or Proceedings from the Federal Convention of 1787 from the Notes of John Lansing, Jr*. Clark, NJ: Lawbook Exchange.

Sumner, William Graham. 1891. *The Financier and the Finances of the American Revolution*. 2 vols. New York: Dodd, Mead & Co.

Tachau, Mary K. Bonsteel. 1986. "George Washington and the Reputation of Edmund Randolph." *Journal of American History* 73 (June): 15–34.

Tarter, Brent. 1991. "George Mason and the Conservation of Liberty." *Virginia Magazine of History and Biography* 99 (July): 279–304.

Thomas, Emory M. 1969. "Edmund Randolph, His Own Man." *Virginia Cavalcade* 18: 5–12.

Toth, Michael C. 2011. *Founding Federalist: The Life of Oliver Ellsworth*. Wilmington, DE: Intercollegiate Studies Institute.

Treenholme, Louise Irby. 1967. *The Ratification of the Federal Constitution in North Carolina*. New York: AMS Press.

Tyler, Lyon G. 1911. "The Medical Men of Virginia." *William and Mary College Quarterly Historical Magazine* 19 (January): 145–62.

Ulmer, S. Sidney. 1960. "The Role of Pierce Butler in the Constitutional Convention." *Review of Politics* 72 (January): 361–74.

Vamn Doren, Charles. 1948. *The Great Rehearsal: The Story of the Making and Ratifying of the Constitution of the United States*. New York: Viking Press.

Ver Sterg, Clarence L. 1954. *Robert Morris: Revolutionary Financier with an Analysis of His Early Career*. Philadelphia: University of Pennsylvania Press.

Vile, John R. 2005. *The Constitutional Convention of 1787: A Comprehensive Encyclopedia of America's Founding*. 2 vols. Santa Barbara, CA: ABC-CLIO.

——. 2012. *The Writing and Ratification of the U.S. Constitution: Practical Virtue in Action*. Lanham, MD: Rowman & Littlefield.

——. *Members of "the Wisest Council in the World": An Examination of William Pierce's Character Sketches of Delegates Who Attended the Constitutional Convention of 1787*. Forthcoming.

——. "William Pierce and Political Rhetoric." *Colonial Williamsburg Journal* (Winter 2014; forthcoming).

Vile, John R., ed., 2001. *Great American Lawyers: An Encyclopedia*. 2 vols. Santa Barbara, CA: ABC-CLIO.

——. ed. 2003. *Great American Judges: An Encyclopedia*. 2 vols., Santa Barbara, CA: ABC-CLIO.

Vile, John R., William D. Pederson, and Frank J. Williams, eds. 2008. *James Madison: Philosopher, Founder, and Statesman*. Athens: Ohio University Press.

Waldstreicher, David. 2009. *Slavery's Constitution: From Revolution to Ratification*. New York: Hill and Wang.

Walling, Karl. 2003. "Alexander Hamilton and the Grand Strategy of the American Social Compact." In *The American Founding and the Social Compact*, edited by Ronald J. Pestritto and Thomas G. West, 199–230. Lanham, MD: Lexington Books.

Watson, Alan D., and Gertrude Carraway Watson. 1987. *Richard Dobbs Spaight*. New Bern, NC: Griffin & Tilghman.

Webber, Mabel L. 1930. "Dr. John Rutledge and His Descendants." *South Carolina Historical and Genealogical Magazine* 31 (January): 7–25.

Webking, Robert H. 1988. *The American Revolution and the Politics of Liberty*. Baton Rouge: Louisiana State University Press.

Weiner, Greg. 2012. *Madison's Metronome: The Constitution, Majority Rule, and the Tempo of American Politics*. Lawrence: University Press of Kansas.

Westbury, Susan. 2001. "Robert Yates and John Lansing, Jr.: New York Delegates Abandon the Constitutional Convention." *New York History* 82 (October): 312–35.

Wheeler, John H. 1879. "Richard Dobbs Spaight, of North Carolina." *Pennsylvania Magazine of History and Biography* 3:426–29.

Whitescarver, Keith. 1993. "Creating Citizens for the Republic: Education in Georgia, 1776–1810." *Journal of the Early Republic* 13 (Winter): 455–79.

Whitney, David C. 1974. *Founders of Freedom in America: Lives of the Men Who Signed the Constitution of the United States and So Helped to Establish the United States of America*. Chicago: J. G. Ferguson Publishing.

Wienek, Henry. 2003. *An Imperfect God: George Washington, His Slaves, and the Creation of America*. New York: Farrar, Straus and Giroux.

Williams, Frances Leigh. 1978. *A Founding Family: The Pinckneys of South Carolina*. New York: Harcourt Brace Jovanovich.

Wills, Garry. 1987. "Interview with a Founding Father." *American Heritage* 38 (May/June): 83–88.

Wilson, James. 2009. *Collected Works of James Wilson*. Edited by Kermit L. Hall and Mark David Hall. 2 vols. Indianapolis: Liberty Fund.

Wood, Gordon S. 1969. *The Creation of the American Republic, 1776–1787*. Chapel Hill: University of North Carolina Press.

———. 1987. *The Making of the Constitution*. Waco, TX: Markham Press Fund.

———. 2004. *The Americanization of Benjamin Franklin*. New York: Penguin Press

Wright, Esmond. 1986. *Franklin of Philadelphia*. Cambridge, MA: Belknap Press.

Wright, Robert K., Jr., and Morris J. MacGregor Jr. 1987. *Soldier-Statesmen of the Constitution*. Washington, DC: Center of Military History, U.S. Army.

Yates, Robert. 1838. *Secret Proceedings and Debates of the Convention Assembled at Philadelphia, in the Year 1787, for the Purpose of Forming the Constitution of the United States of America*. Cincinnati: Alston Mygatt.

Young, Eleanor M. 1950. *Forgotten Patriot: Robert Morris*. New York: Macmillan.

Zahniser, Marvin R. 1967. *Charles Cotesworth Pinckney: Founding Father*. Chapel Hill: University of North Carolina Press.

Zuchert, Michael P. 2003. "The Political Science of James Madison." In *History of American Political Thought*, edited by Bryan-Paul Frost and Jeffrey Sikkenga, 149–66. Lanham, MD: Lexington Books.

Zvesper, John. 1984. "The Madisonian Systems." *Western Political Quarterly* 37 (June): 236–56.

Index

Note: Page numbers for the main entry of delegates are in bold.

About the Author

Dr. **John R. Vile** is a professor of political science and dean of the University Honors College at Middle Tennessee State University. A graduate of the College of William and Mary and the University of Virginia, he is the author and editor of numerous books about the U.S. Constitution and related subjects. These include *The Constitutional Convention of 1787* (2 vols.), *A Companion to the United States Constitution and Its Amendments* (5th ed.), *Essential Supreme Court Decisions: Summaries of Leading Cases in U.S. Constitutional Law* (15th ed.), *Encyclopedia of the First Amendment* (coeditor, 2 vols.), *Encyclopedia of the Fourth Amendment* (coeditor, 2 vols.), *Encyclopedia of Constitutional Amendments, Proposed Amendments and Amending Issues, 1789–2010* (2 vols.; 3rd ed.), and *The Writing and Ratification of the U.S. Constitution: Practical Virtue in Action* (2012).